MANAGEMENT

Knowledge   Skills   Understanding

Financial Times Management is a new business created to deliver the knowledge, skills and understanding that will enable students, managers and organisations to achieve their ambitions, whatever their needs, wherever they are.

Financial Times Pitman Publishing, part of Financial Times Management, is the leading publisher of books for practitioners and students in business and finance, bringing cutting-edge thinking and best practice to a global market.

To find out more about Financial Times Management and Financial Times Pitman Publishing, visit our website at:

www.ftmanagement.com

Frank Wood's
A-Level Accounting

Second Edition

Frank Wood BSc (Econ), FCA
and
Alan Sangster BA, MSc, Cert TESOL, CA

FINANCIAL TIMES
PITMAN PUBLISHING

LONDON · HONG KONG · JOHANNESBURG
MELBOURNE · SINGAPORE · WASHINGTON DC

FINANCIAL TIMES MANAGEMENT
128 Long Acre, London WC2E 9AN
Tel: +44 (0)171 447 2000
Fax: +44 (0)171 240 5771
Website: www.ftmanagement.com

A Division of Financial Times Professional Limited

First published in Great Britain in 1994
Second edition published in 1998

British Library Cataloguing in Publication Data
A CIP catalogue record for this book can be obtained from the British Library

ISBN 0 273 63161 6

10 9 8 7 6 5 4 3 2 1

Printed and bound in Great Britain by Clays Ltd, St Ives plc.

The Publishers' policy is to use paper manufactured from sustainable forests.

Contents

Preface

This book caters for students commencing their second year of study for GCE A-Level Accounting for the various examining bodies in the United Kingdom.

It mainly assumes that a certain amount of ground has been covered in the first year, and the assumptions are shown in Chapter 1. Students should check their own previous knowledge against this list to ensure that their first-year studies are complete. Owing to the importance of company accounts this text gives a full coverage, so for that topic alone there may be said to be some degree of revision included here.

The second year is divided mainly into (i) financial accounting, and (ii) cost and management accounting. The depth in which each section is given is that most suitable for A-Level examinations. Professional examinations would need rather more detail for most topics, but the extra detail would not really be of much importance in most cases. A-Level students should not only know how to tackle accounting problems, they should also understand the basic reasoning which underlies accounting and its methods.

A very welcome aspect of A-Level examinations is that examiners want students to see that there are factors other than pure financial considerations which should affect decisions in the world of business and government. In terms of simply getting better marks in examinations students would be well advised to bring environmental factors into their answers, but the fact that these examinations expect an approach which is not blinkered by accounting knowledge should make these examinations more challenging and interesting both for students and teachers.

All the questions in this book are either from GCE A-Level examination papers or have been devised by ourselves. The answers shown at the back of the book are the result of combined work and checking by ourselves, John Whiteside, Peter Beazeley and David Welch. Should any error(s) remain then we must accept full responsibility. The fact that approximately 50 per cent of the answers are shown in the book means that students can attempt a considerable number of questions and be able to check their own work. The remainder of the questions will be useful for other forms of supplementary work.

A time-saving *Teacher's Manual*, including fully displayed answers to all questions with the suffix 'X' in the text, is available free of charge to teachers who recommend this book on their courses.

We wish to acknowledge the permission to use past examination papers granted by the following examining bodies: Associated Examining Board, University of Cambridge Local Examinations Syndicate, Northern Examinations and Assessments Board (Joint Matriculation Board), London Examinations, a division of Edexcel Foundation, for University of London Examinations, University of Oxford Delegacy of Local Examinations, Welsh Joint Education Committee.

We should also like to thank Noel Williams, Chief Examiner, University of Oxford Delegacy of Local Examinations, and G.L. Brownlee, Chief Examiner, University of Cambridge Local Examinations Syndicate, for their assistance in reviewing the content of the first edition of this book.

Frank Wood and Alan Sangster

Note on the Review Questions

With reference to the answers to questions set by the Associated Examining Board, any answers or hints on answers are the sole responsibility of the authors and have not been provided or approved by the Board.

With reference to the answers to questions set by the Northern Examinations and Assessment Board, the solutions given are the responsibility of the authors and may not necessarily constitute the only possible solutions.

Edexcel Foundation, London Examinations (formerly The University of London Examinations and Assessment Council) accepts no responsibility whatsoever for the accuracy or method of working in the answers given.

UODLE (University of Oxford Delegacy of Local Examinations) and University of Cambridge Local Examinations Syndicate material is reproduced by permission of the University of Cambridge Local Examinations Syndicate. The University of Cambridge Local Examinations Syndicate bears no responsibility for the example answers to questions taken from past UODLE or UCLES question papers which are contained in this publication.

Chapter 1

The Scope of This Book

1.1 Introduction

This book has been written specifically for the second year of study for those who are taking GCE Advanced Level examinations in Accounting for the various UK examining bodies.

It is assumed that you have already covered the first year's work. You should check against the list of topics as shown in Section 1.5 to ensure that you have properly covered the work that you should have done in the first year.

1.2 The Syllabuses

The coverage of the syllabuses for the various examining bodies is largely the same. This book attempts to cover as much of each syllabus as makes sense for anyone taking these examinations. The contents of this book are certainly sufficient to give those with the necessary application and intelligence the ability to achieve marks at the highest grade.

1.3 Review Questions

Many of the review questions at the end of each chapter are from the A-Level examinations themselves. Sometimes there will be questions devised by the authors to fill in gaps or to give a more straightforward approach to the topic.

Practice is essential for success in accounting examinations. Simply reading the text of this book, even though you may fully understand it when you are reading it, is not sufficient. Some of the questions in the examinations will be of the essay variety, but the other questions do demand that you have practical work to carry out. There is no doubt that the more practice you can manage to carry out the greater will be the corresponding increase in the grades you can achieve in the examination.

1.4 Quality Newspapers

It would certainly be beneficial for you to read a 'quality' newspaper regularly, such as *The Times*, *The Guardian*, *The Daily Telegraph*, *The Independent*, or the *Financial Times*. Many of the business issues of the day affect accounting in all sorts of ways. At first, some of the articles may seem to be very hard work indeed to assimilate, but as your studies progress you should find the going easier. Such reading may also help you to give your answers that business background which otherwise you might be lacking.

1.5 The First Year's Coverage

During your first year of study you should have covered the following:

- Double entry records, including the journals, to the trial balance
- Trading and profit and loss account and balance sheet
- Accounting for depreciation
- Accounting for bad debts and provisions for doubtful debts
- Capital and revenue expenditure
- Errors and suspense accounts
- Bank reconciliation statements
- Control accounts
- Single entry and incomplete records
- Receipts and payments and income and expenditure accounts
- Manufacturing accounts
- Departmental accounts
- Columnar day books
- Partnership accounts
    - final accounts
    - goodwill adjustments
    - revaluation of assets
- Stock valuation
- Accounting concepts and conventions
- Introduction to accounting theory

All of these topics are fully covered in *Business Accounting 1* by Frank Wood, published by Financial Times Pitman Publishing. You will also find them in most other basic texts for first-year courses.

Chapter 2

Branch Accounts

2.1 Introduction

For the GCE A-Level examinations it is not necessary for you to do the detailed preparation of branch accounts, which can be relatively complicated. It is required however that the general principles of branch accounting should be understood. That is the object of this chapter.

2.2 Accounting Records and Branches

When we look at accounting records to show transactions at the branches of an organisation, we have a choice of two main methods. These are:

(i) The head office keeps all the accounting records, or
(ii) Each branch has its own full accounting system.

It is easier to understand branch accounts if these two main methods are dealt with separately.

2.3 If the Head Office Maintains All the Accounts

The accounts are used for three main purposes:

(i)   To record transactions showing changes in assets, liabilities and capital.
(ii) To ascertain the profitability of each branch.
(iii) In addition, if possible, to check whether anyone at the branches is stealing goods or cash.

This third purpose is very important for firms that have many branches. The people who manage or work in these branches are receiving and paying out large sums of money. In addition they may be handling large amounts of stocks of goods.

   The branch or branches may be a considerable distance away from the head office. This may mean that the manager, or any of his staff, may think that they can steal things without being caught.

2.4 Methods for Checking Stock and Cash

If a firm with only a few branches sells only very expensive cars, it would be easy to check on purchases and sales of the cars. The number of cars sold would not be very great. Checking that cars or money have not been stolen would be easy.

Whether or not firms, such as stores selling many thousands of cheap items, could check the loss of items in such a way would depend on the circumstances. Computer technology, such as that used by Sainsbury's or Marks & Spencer, enables stores to check quite accurately how many of each item have been sold on a particular day. Whether smaller firms would want to go to such expense and bother is a different matter. Sainsbury's and Marks & Spencer's accountants use the information for many other reasons, e.g. for knowing how many of each item are to be delivered from their warehouses to exactly which store each day. The computerised systems cost a lot of money but, in their cases, they are used to save more money than they cost. Other firms may not be able to afford such technology, or be able to put it to such good use.

For these other firms, the accounting answer to this problem is to record all transactions at the branch in terms of selling prices. Then for each accounting period, it should be possible to check whether the closing stock is as it should be.

For a small branch for example, you may be given the following figures:

	£
Stock on hand at 1 January – at selling price	500
January – Goods sent to the branch by the Head Office – at selling price	4,000
January – Sales by the branch – obviously at selling price	3,800

The calculation of the closing stock becomes:

	£
Opening Stock 1 January (selling price)	500
Add Goods sent to the branch (selling price)	4,000
Goods which the branch had available for sale (selling price)	4,500
Less Goods sold (selling price)	3,800
Closing Stock at 31 January should therefore be (selling price)	700

2.5 Allowances for Deficiencies

In every business there will be:

(i) wastage of goods for some reason — goods may be damaged or broken, or they may be kept too long or somehow waste away.
(ii) stealing by customers, especially in the retail business.
(iii) thefts by employees.

No one can be certain how much stock is wasted or stolen during a period. Only experience will enable a firm to make a good estimate of these losses.

2.6 The Double Column System

At regular intervals, obviously at least once a year but usually more frequently, the head office may draft a trading and profit and loss account for each branch. The trading account can be shown with two columns, one in which goods sent to the branch or in stock are shown at cost price, i.e. the normal basis for any business. This column is therefore part of a normal trading account for the branch. The other column will show all trading account items at selling price. This column allows deficiencies in trading to be compared with the normal deficiency allowed for wastages, etc. It is not a part of the double entry recording; it is a memorandum column for control purposes only.

Exhibit 2.1

This is drafted from the following details for a firm which sells goods at a uniform mark-up of 33⅓ per cent on cost price:

	£
Stock 1 Jan 19X8 (at cost)	1,200
Goods sent to the branch during the year (at cost)	6,000
Sales (selling price)	7,428
Stock 31 Dec 19X8 (at cost)	1,500
Expenses	1,000

Allowances for wastage, etc., one per cent of sales.

Branch Trading and Profit and Loss Account for the year ended 31 December 19X8

	At selling price			At selling price	
	£	£		£	£
Stock 1 Jan 19X8	1,600	1,200	Sales	7,428	7,428
Goods from head office	8,000	6,000	Deficiency (difference)	172	
	9,600	7,200			
Less Stock 31 Dec 19X8	2,000	1,500			
	7,600	5,700			
Gross profit c/d		1,728			
	7,600	7,428		7,600	7,428
Expenses		1,000	Gross profit b/d		1,728
Net profit		728			
		1,728			1,728

As the actual deficiency of £172 exceeds the amount expected, i.e. one per cent of £7,428 = £74, an investigation will be made.

This method is suitable where all the sales are for cash, there being no sales on credit.

When sales are also made on credit these are incorporated into a branch trading and profit and loss account as just described in Exhibit 2.1.

2.7 The Integrated System

The integrated system introduces the idea that the gross profit earned can be calculated by reference to profit margins only. A simple example illustrates this point. Assume that a self-employed travelling salesman sells all his goods at cost price plus 25 per cent for profit. At the start of a week he has £4 stock at cost, he buys goods costing £40, he sells goods for £45 (selling price) and he has goods left in stock at the end of the week which had cost him £8. A normal trading account based on this data is shown below.

Trading Account for the week ended ...

	£		£
Opening stock	4	Sales	45
Add Purchases	40		
	44		
Less Closing stock	8		
Cost of goods sold	36		
Gross profit	9		
	45		45

This could, however, also be shown as:

	£
Profit made when opening stock is sold	1
Profit made when purchases are sold	10
Profit made when all goods are sold	11
But he still has left unsold goods (cost £8) on which the profit still has to be realised	2
Therefore profit realised	9

This could be expressed in account form as:

Salesman's Adjustment Account

	£		£
Gross profit	9	Unrealised profit b/f	1
Unrealised profit c/f	2	Goods bought	10
	11		11

The system uses these ideas in that:

- a branch stock account is kept at selling price. Thus any loss of stock will be shown up, so that relevant action can be taken.
- a branch debtors account is kept at selling price to keep a check on debtors.
- because normally stock should be shown at cost, to make sure that the books balance a branch adjustment account is kept. This shows the profit content only connected with stocks held and stocks sent to the branch. As with the salesman, this account is also used to calculate the branch gross profit.

2.8 If Each Branch Maintains Full Accounting Records

This method is rarely used in firms with many branches. It is more common in a firm with just one or two or a few branches, and is particularly relevant if a branch is large enough to warrant employing a separate accounting staff.

A branch cannot operate on its own without resources, and it is the firm that provides these in the first instance. The firm will want to know how much money it has invested in each branch, and from this arises the concept of branch and head office current accounts. The relationship between the branch and the head office is seen as that of a debtor/creditor. The current account shows the branch as a debtor in the head office records, while the head office is shown as a creditor in the branch records.

The current accounts are used for transactions concerned with supplying resources to the branch or in taking back resources. For such transactions full double entry records are needed both in the branch records and in the head office records, i.e. each item will be recorded twice in each set of records. Some transactions will, however, concern the branch only, and these will merely need two entries in the branch records and none in the head office records.

2.9 Items in Transit

There may well be items in transit between the head office and its branches at the close of an accounting period. Let us look at three possibilities:

● A cheque £5,000 sent from the branch in Dundee on 29 June 19X2 to its head office in Bournemouth is received by the head office on 1 July 19X2.
● Goods £8,800 sent by the head office in Bournemouth on 29 June 19X2 arrive at the branch in Dundee on 3 July 19X2.
● Goods £600 returned by the branch in Dundee on 28 June 19X2 arrive at the head office in Bournemouth on 2 July 19X2.

Now each of the accountants, one at the head office and the other at the branch, has closed off his books as at the end of the financial period, which is 30 June 19X2. This means that in that accounting period:

	Item in head office books	Item in branch books	Item in transit
Cheque sent	None	Bank – £5,000	Bank £5,000
Goods sent to branch	Goods sent +£8,800	None	Goods £8,800
Goods returned by branch	None	Returns +£600	Goods £600

Each of the items, £5,000 bank, £8,800 goods and £600 goods, belong to the business when seen as a whole. Yet none of them are shown as assets currently at the end of the period, simply because they are in transit. They are assets owned by the firm, and must therefore be brought into account. In the final accounts at the end of the period the bank figure of £5,000 must be added to the bank balances, whilst the goods sent and being returned need adding to the stock figures.

2.10 Contribution Accounting and Branch Accounts

Previously in your studies, you may have come across the idea of contribution accounting in departmental accounts. A similar idea will now be employed in branch accounts.

The term 'contribution' means the amount remaining after the cost of goods sold, plus all other variable expenses, have been deducted from the sales figure. Let us look first at the calculation of gross and net profits in the traditional fashion in Exhibit 2.2.

Exhibit 2.2

Year 1	Head Office £	Head Office £	Branch A £	Branch A £	Branch B £	Branch B £
Sales		150,000		80,000		120,000
Less Cost of goods sold		90,000		50,000		75,000
Gross profit		60,000		30,000		45,000
Less Expenses:						
Variable	28,000		15,000		18,000	
Fixed (see Note)	20,000	48,000	17,000	32,000	20,000	38,000
Net profit/(loss)		12,000		(2,000)		7,000

Note: Of the total £30,000 paid by Head Office in fixed expenses a sum of £5,000 each has been charged to Branch A and Branch B, leaving £20,000 to be charged against Head Office.

At first sight it appears that it would be better to shut down Branch A, if it continues to trade like this as it has made a net loss of £2,000. Suppose that Branch A was closed down immediately, and that the sales and expenses of both Head Office and Branch B were exactly the same as above in the following year then the next year's results would be as follows:

Year 2	Head Office £	Head Office £	Branch B £	Branch B £
Sales		150,000		120,000
Less Cost of goods sold		90,000		75,000
Gross profit		60,000		45,000
Less Expenses:				
Variable	28,000		18,000	
Fixed (see Note)	25,000	53,000	20,000	38,000
Net profit		7,000		7,000

Note: As Branch A does not exist then the Head Office fixed expenses are now stated as £25,000, as £5,000 can no longer be charged to the non-existent branch.

Let us now compare the overall results for Years 1 and 2.

		Year 1 £	Year 2 £
Net profit:	Head Office	12,000	7,000
	Branch B	7,000	7,000
		19,000	
Less Net loss: Branch A		2,000	
Final overall net profit		17,000	14,000

We shut down Branch A to save money, and yet we have finished being (£17,000 – £14,000) £3,000 worse off in Year 2. Obviously we took the wrong decision. This was caused by a poor accounting method, and our believing in the final recorded net loss figure for Branch A.

A much more preferable, and less misleading way, is to calculate first of all the contributions made by each branch. For Year 1 this would have been as follows:

		Head Office £	Head Office £	Branch A £	Branch A £	Branch B £	Branch B £
Sales			150,000		80,000		120,000
Less	Cost of goods sold	90,000		50,000		75,000	
	Variable expenses	28,000	118,000	15,000	65,000	18,000	93,000
Contributions			32,000		15,000		27,000
Less	Fixed expenses	30,000		12,000*		15,000*	
	Allocated by						
	Head Office	10,000	20,000	5,000	17,000	5,000	20,000
Net profit/(Loss)			12,000		(2,000)		7,000

* These fixed expenses are wholly incurred by the branches themselves.

We can now see that the contribution by Branch A of £15,000 fully covered its own fixed expenses of £12,000, whilst a surplus of £3,000 was left to be able to contribute towards paying some of the fixed overheads of Head Office. It was precisely because this surplus of £3,000 was not available in Year 2 that we finished up being £3,000 worse off in that year.

Of course, if the contribution from Branch A could not even cover its own fixed overheads in the long run, then we would be justified in considering closing down that branch.

You will see the idea of using the contribution as a basis for decisions once again in Chapter 18 in the part concerned with marginal costing.

2.11 Consequences of Closing Down Branches

This will apply similarly to closing down any section of a business. We are using branches as an example.

Let us consider whether or not we would always close down any branch (or part of a business) where the contribution made by the branch is constantly (or nearly always) less than the fixed overheads of the branch itself, ignoring any extra overheads of the head office.

A business has four branches. Its results for the year are:

Branch	Sales	Cost of goods sold	Variable expenses	Contributions	Own fixed expenses	Net profit (loss)
	£	£	£	£	£	£
C	90,000	50,000	10,000	30,000	8,000	22,000
D	100,000	70,000	18,000	12,000	17,000	(5,000)
E	120,000	65,000	20,000	35,000	12,000	23,000
F	90,000	55,000	8,000	27,000	11,000	16,000

At first sight it might appear that we would want to close down Branch D as it has lost £5,000 for the year. Let us examine some of the factors which could possibly make us want to keep the branch open.

1 Perhaps we could move to cheaper premises at Branch D, and save £8,000 a year in so doing. This would put the branch into profit in future.

2 It could possibly be the case that without Branch D the other branches may not be able to function properly. If some specialist tasks were undertaken there for the other branches, without which the other branches could not operate at all, or very inefficiently, then closing down Branch D would obviously not be in the interests of the firm.

3 The closing down of Branch D could affect the morale of the other employees at the other branches, and could force the best people to take up jobs with rival firms.

4 The poor trading conditions could be temporary at Branch D. For instance, the building of a motorway nearby has affected the ability of customers to get to the branch easily, and so trade has been lost. It will resume as normal once the motorway is completed in three months' time.

5 Possible industrial action by employees could well shut down the firm for a long time, and the risk is too high to take.

6 Perhaps thefts by employees have caused the loss of money, which will be rectified as soon as the offenders have been brought to justice.

7 Even if shut down the buildings at the branch cannot be sold or let to anyone else, and we may still have to pay the rent of £10,000 a year for the next 20 years even though trading has finished. This would result in a loss of £10,000 a year compared with the current loss of £5,000 per year.

8 The firm has decided that the social consequences of closing down the branch are so great that we are prepared to lose money at the branch and help the local economy. The maximisation of profits is not the only criterion for judging actions of a commercial organisation. (See also Chapter 13, Social Accounting.)

9 The branch is used in an experimental fashion, and the lessons learned here can be put to very profitable use at the other branches.

10 We believe that the economy is going to recover and that this branch will be back in profit again.

11 The employees have certain guarantees as to pensions, redundancy pay, etc. that would use up a large capital sum which could be put to very profitable use elsewhere, making far more than the £5,000 a year we have lost.

12 We do not want to let our competitors know that we can be vulnerable, as they could then open up in opposition to the other branches as well.

This is far from being a complete list of all the possible reasons why the firm would not want to shut down Branch D. It does show that one has to look beyond the figures of profits and losses, and understand what is going on in the business before taking decisions such as to shut down part or whole of a business.

You should aim to give this view of the whole of the affairs of a business when answering GCE A-Level questions. Answers concerned with ratios or the interpretation and understanding of accounts which simply give all the accounting figures or ratios will get very few marks. Show that you understand that the accounting figures are simply one guide, and what they really mean depends on so many other factors. Use your imagination to visualise what could be happening in a real business.

REVIEW QUESTIONS

Advice:

The questions that are set for GCE A-Level are not very technical questions concerned with branch accounts, which one might expect in professional examinations. Instead they are largely concerned with how well, or badly, a branch has performed. This often includes the question asking your advice as to what action you would recommend to the proprietors of the business, usually whether or not a particular branch should be closed down.

In particular, Sections 2.10 and 2.11 of the text should come in useful for a lot of questions on branch accounts at A-Level. Remember, where it makes sense, to bring in factors 1 to 12 as shown in 2.11. Examiners want to see scripts which realise that the figures only tell part of the story.

Note: Questions with the letter X shown after the question number do NOT have answers shown at the back of the book. Answers to the others are shown on page 366 onwards.

2.1 Bettermake Ltd has been selling household goods as a retailer for several years. On 1 January 19X0 a decision was taken to open retail shops in Bexville and Amstead, two neighbouring towns. The following summarised information is available for the financial year ended 31 December 19X0:

		Bettermake Ltd				
		Head Office Shop £000		Bexville Shop £000		Amstead Shop £000
Sales		150		30		55
Cost of goods sold		60		15		23
Gross profit		90		15		32
Variable expenses	15		12		16	
Fixed expenses	28	43	13	25	10	26
Net profit/(loss)		47		(10)		6

The fixed costs of the two branches consist of the following components:
(i)   Head Office has allocated £6,000 of its own fixed expenses to each branch.
(ii) The remaining fixed expenses are wholly attributable to the branches.

Required:
(a) Explain what is meant by the accounting term 'contribution'.   *(5 marks)*
(b) Identify the contribution made by each branch to the company for the year ended 31 December 19X0.   *(5 marks)*
(c) Prepare a brief report for the Board of Bettermake Ltd providing a financial analysis of the results of the whole business for the year ended 31 December 19X0.   *(7 marks)*
(d) Identify the circumstances in which a retail branch shop should be closed.   *(3 marks)*

(Associated Examining Board GCE A-Level)

2.2X Geotrad Ltd operate as a retail organisation trading at the Head Office in Newcastle and at a branch in Hexham.

The following summarised information was available for the year ended 31 May 19X9.

	Head Office Newcastle £000	Branch Hexham £000
Sales	1,800	300
Cost of goods sold	1,050	190
Variable expenses	300	35
Fixed expenses	150	5

In addition to the branch's own fixed and variable expenses listed above, £90,000 of the Head Office expense costs is to be transferred from Head Office and charged against the branch.

Note: The above summarised year end figures do not include adjustments in respect of the additional information items 1, 3 and 4 below.

Additional information

1

	Head Office £	Branch £
Variable expenses in arrears	4,500	1,900
Fixed expenses in advance	2,800	1,000

2 Stocks of goods held at 31 May 19X9 (excluding goods in transit) were:

	Head Office £	Branch £
Cost price	50,000	8,000
Market price	52,000	8,000

Goods sent to the branch are currently invoiced at cost price.

3 Geotrad pays all its salesmen commission on sales, but only after the relevant year's sales targets have been met.

In the financial year ended 31 May 19X9 the respective sales targets were:

	£
Head Office	1,400,000
Hexham Branch	290,000

Commission is only paid on those sales that exceed the target and at the following rates:

	%
Head Office	2
Hexham Branch	3

The commission is paid in the year following the year of the sale.

4 Goods, which cost £11,000, had been packed ready to send to the branch, but they were still in the Head Office warehouse. No documentation had been received by the branch, but appropriate entries had been made in the Head Office books.

The goods had not been included in the Head Office end-of-year stock taking.

5 The management of Geotrad Ltd have been concerned about the recent poor trading performance of the branch, and they are anticipating a branch loss for the first time. One director suggested that the branch should be closed down if any significant loss is recorded.

Required:

(*a*) For the year ended 31 May 19X9, separate trading and profit and loss accounts for the branch and Head Office. Use columnar form. *(10 marks)*

(*b*) (i) Calculate the contribution made by the branch to the profits of the business as a whole.

(ii) Write a brief report as to whether the branch should be closed. *(9 marks)*

(*c*) (i) State the normally accepted accounting basis for the valuation of the closing stock.

(ii) Determine the value of the closing stock for the whole business as at 31 May 19X9. *(6 marks)*

(Associated Examining Board GCE A-Level)

2.3 Spencer Reddaway had been selling goods as a retailer for some years and he decided to expand by opening two branches.

All goods were invoiced to the branches at cost. He expected the branches to show a gross profit/sales ratio in the region of 25 per cent and at least to make some net profit.

The following information is available for the financial year ended 30 June 19X1, this being the second year of operation for the branches:

	Branch A £	Branch B £
Sales	800,000	1,200,000
Goods from Head Office sent to branch	660,000	1,035,000
Branch variable expenses	70,000	80,000
Branch fixed expenses (wholly attributable to the branches)	60,000	60,000
Goods returned by branch to Head Office	54,000	38,000
Branch stocks:		
Opening	40,000	65,000
Closing	73,000	141,900
(valued at invoiced price)		

Additional information

1 Both branches were run by managers. Managers receive a commission of 1 per cent of net sales, payable three months after the end of an accounting year.

Managers were also responsible for half of all stock losses at their respective branches.

2 Year-end stock taking revealed redundant and damaged stock as follows:

Branch A	Branch B
£3,000	£1,900

The stock values above as at 30 June 19X1 have not been adjusted for these amounts.

3 Reddaway was aware that both branches benefited from some of the facilities provided by the Head Office and he decided that for the year ended 30 June 19X1 he would allocate £190,000 of Head Office expenditure equally between the two branches.

4 Reddaway had received a report from both branch managers that they were experiencing difficulties in collecting debts from a number of trade debtors. Some of these debts had been outstanding for 18 months and despite repeated attempts at collection they had failed. The amount of debts involved were:

	Branch A	Branch B
	£12,000	£18,000

The owner has not yet decided to write these debts off as bad.

Required:

(a) Columnar revenue accounts for **both** of the branches for the year ended 30 June 19X1 clearly showing the gross profit and net profit.

(12 marks)

(b) A report to Reddaway advising him on the profitability of his branches.
Your report should consider whether the branches should continue to operate or not. Use appropriate financial analysis to support your reasoning.

(8 marks)

(c) As Reddaway's accountant advise him as to how to improve the settlement of debts. Your advice should include a consideration of the effect of poor credit control on:
   (i)   the cash flow
   and (ii)   the profitability of the branches. *(5 marks)*

(Associated Examining Board GCE A-Level)

2.4X Central Farm Machines Limited owns a number of depots in various parts of the country. As part of their normal review procedures, the company is currently considering the results of two of its depots for the last completed financial year; the summarised results are as follows:

Trading and profit and loss accounts	Redton £	Blueton £
Sales – 12 Ploughwell Mark II tractors	480,000	480,000
Cost of sales	360,000	420,000
Gross profit	120,000	60,000
Overhead expenses excluding depreciation	(77,200)	(77,200)
Plant and machinery depreciation	(4,000)	(5,600)
Net profit/(loss)	£38,800	£(22,800)

Balance sheets at end of last financial year

	Redton £	Blueton £
Freehold land at cost	30,000	60,000
Plant and machinery:		
At cost *less* depreciation	20,000	44,800
Stock at cost		
Ploughwell Mark II tractors		
4 @ £30,000 each	120,000	
2 @ £35,000 each		70,000
Balance at bank	24,000	19,200
Net capital employed	£194,000	£194,000

Each of the company's depots is responsible for its own purchasing policy, Redton has been able to benefit from the bulk purchase of tractors at especially favourable prices. Both the Redton and Blueton depots occupy sites of similar size and current market value; the plant and machinery of both depots is very similar but bought at different times.

It is company policy to pay a special bonus to the managers of depots making a profit.

Required:

A report addressed to the managing director of Central Farm Machines Limited concerning the comparative results of the Redton and Blueton depots for the last completed financial year.

(25 marks)

Notes:
1 Reports should indicate any additional information required.
2 Reports should include recommendations concerning the payment of the special bonus so far as each branch is concerned.

(Reproduced by permission of the University of Cambridge Local Examinations Syndicate)

2.5 A. Telford, R. Stevenson and J. Napier are in partnership trading as 'Pine Products'. They operate on a branch accounting basis with three branches at Pilingdown, Chambers and Stratnorth. The Chambers branch acts as head office and purchases, stores, and distributes the goods for resale. In addition, the head office provides administrative support for the branches. The following draft trading and profit and loss accounts have been prepared by the partners for the year ended 30 April 19X8:

	Chambers (Head Office) £	£	Stratnorth £	£	Pilingdown £	£
Sales		230,000		120,000		140,000
Cost of sales						
Opening stock	31,000		16,000		19,000	
Goods from head office	–		70,000		102,000	
Goods from Stratnorth	–		–		15,000	
Purchases	371,000		30,000*		–	
Goods to branches	(194,000)		–		–	
Closing stock	(38,000)		(17,500)		(14,000)	
		170,000		98,500		122,000
Gross profit		60,000		21,500		18,000
Less Expenses						
General expenses	10,500		4,500		5,300	
Fixed administrative expenses	6,400†		2,000		4,100	
Variable costs	18,900		8,400		12,200	
		35,800		14,900		21,600
Profit/(Loss)		£24,200		£6,600		£(3,600)

* Included in this figure is £16,500 representing goods sent to Pilingdown.
† £12,500 less amounts charged to branches.

Additional information
1 On 30 April 19X8 Chambers had despatched goods, at cost, to branches as follows:

	£
Stratnorth	12,000
Pilingdown	10,000

These goods were received by the branches on 3 May 19X8.

2 Stratnorth purchased some goods locally and regularly supplied goods to the Pilingdown branch. £1,500 of goods were sent on 29 April 19X8 and had not been received by Pilingdown at the year end date.

3   The following stock losses and gains were computed after the preparation of the draft accounts:

	£
Stratnorth	1,500 loss
Pilingdown	740 gain
Chambers	290 loss

4   The partnership agreement provides for:
   (i)   partners' salaries of:

	£	
A. Telford	4,500	per annum
R. Stevenson	5,000	per annum
J. Napier	3,000	per annum

   (ii) Interest at 8 per cent p.a. on partners' capital account balances which were throughout the year ended 30 April 19X8 as follows:

	£
A. Telford	15,000
R. Stevenson	12,000
J. Napier	18,000

   (iii) Partners to share the balances of profits and losses equally.

5   The partners wish to improve the profitability of Pilingdown and the partnership in general and are considering the following two courses of action:

Option A   Increase the selling space of the Pilingdown branch and also change the type of goods sold there which would have the effect of increasing gross profit at Pilingdown by 50 per cent. The variable costs would increase by £3,400 and there would be increased general expenses of £3,000 at this branch.

Option B   Close the Pilingdown branch and transfer the business to Stratnorth. This would increase the gross profit of Stratnorth by £7,000 and incur redundancy costs of £5,500. In addition, the overall fixed administrative expenses would decrease by £3,000 and Stratnorth's variable costs and general expenses would increase by £700 and £400 respectively.

Required:

(a) Prepare a trading and profit and loss account for the partnership for the year ended 30 April 19X8 that EXCLUDES the options outlined in 5 above. (Separate accounts for the branches are NOT required.)

(9 marks)

(b) Prepare a statement of the appropriation of net profit as calculated in (a) between the partners.

(8 marks)

(c) Prepare a statement which shows the financial impact of each of the options in 5 above and critically evaluate the options.

(6 marks)

(*Associated Examining Board GCE A-Level*)

Chapter 3

Accounting for Hire Purchase and Leasing Transactions

3.1 Nature of Hire Purchase

Hire Purchase is a means of buying assets. Instead of paying at the time of purchase, or shortly afterwards, a hire purchase contract is different. The essential differences are:

(i)   The asset does not belong to the purchaser when it is received from the supplier. Instead it belongs to the supplier providing the hire purchase.
(ii) The purchaser will pay for the item by instalments over a period of time. This may be as long as for two or three years.
(iii) The hire purchase price will be higher than the price would have been if paid immediately, i.e. the cash price. The extra money paid is for interest.
(iv) The asset does not legally belong to the purchaser until two things happen:
   (a) the final instalment is paid, and
   (b) the purchaser agrees to a legal option to buy the asset.

If the purchaser wants to, he could stop paying the instalments. He would then have to give the asset back to the seller. He would not be able to get a refund of instalments already paid.

If the purchaser is unable to continue paying the instalments, the seller could normally repossess the asset. The seller would keep all the instalments already paid.

For GCE A-Level examinations it will not be necessary for you to be able to enter hire purchase transactions in the books of either the purchaser or the seller. This chapter therefore limits itself to an appraisal of the general principles of hire purchase, and its implications for both profitability and liquidity of the organisations concerned.

3.2 Law of Hire Purchase

The Hire Purchase Act 1964 governs all hire purchase transactions.

3.3 Interest Payable on Hire Purchase

When each payment is made on a hire purchase contract, it will consist of the following:

(i) some of the instalment will be paying off part of the amount owing for the cash price of the asset;
(ii) the rest of the instalment will be for the interest that has accrued for the period of time.

The total payment, (i) + (ii), made for each instalment may either be of equal amounts or unequal amounts. The most common type is where equal amounts have to be paid.

3.4 Accounting for Hire Purchase

Accounting treats assets bought on hire purchase as though they immediately belong to the purchaser.

This is because businesses normally buy assets on hire purchase with the intention of paying all the instalments, so that the asset will finally belong to them. As they mean to keep the asset and legally own it on the final payment, accounting enters it as though legal ownership occurred on purchase.

The total purchase price is split into two parts for the accounts:

(i) **Cash price.** This is the amount to be debited to the fixed asset account.
(ii) **Interest.** This is an expense of borrowing money and needs charging to an expense account, i.e. hire purchase interest account.

As interest accrues over time, each period should be charged only with the interest accrued for that period. This is shown in Exhibit 3.1.

Exhibit 3.1

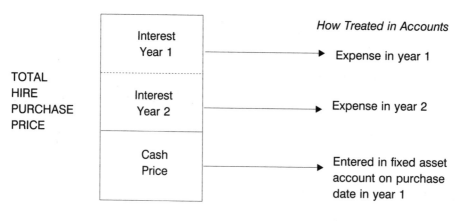

3.5 Depreciation on Assets Bought on Hire Purchase

Depreciation is based on the cash price. The interest does not enter depreciation calculations.

3.6 The Seller's Books: Apportionment of Profits

There are many ways of drawing up the final accounts of a business that sells goods on hire purchase. The method used should be the one most suitable for the business for the calculation of profits.

The total profit for the seller of goods on hire purchase breaks down as follows:

	£
Profit on item sold: Cash price *less* cost	xxx
Profit made because of interest charged	xxx
	xxx

Take as an example a firm which has bought a machine for £2,100. It would sell it for a cash price of £3,000. The hire purchase price is £3,618, payable by three annual instalments of £1,206 on the last day of each year. Remembering that less interest is earned each year because less is owed by the purchaser after each instalment is paid, the total profit which will be made is:

		£	£
Profit on sale of machine: Cash price		3,000	
Cost		2,100	900
Profit earned by charging interest:	19X3	300	
	19X4	209	
	19X5	109	618
Total profit over 3 years			1,518

3.7 Apportionment of Profit on Sale

There are two main methods of dealing with the problem of how to split the £900 profit on sale of the machine shown in Section 3.6.

(i) It is considered profit in the period in which it was first sold to the purchaser. In this case the £900 would all be shown as profit for 19X3.
(ii) The profit is divided among the three years in the ratio of cash received from instalments.

3.8 Reasons for Buying on Hire Purchases

It would not be logical for someone who had £3,000 available to buy the machine described in Section 3.6 to purchase it on hire purchase terms for £3,618, unless they could have earned more than £618 from the alternative use of the £3,000.

This means that if, for example, you could have earned £750 elsewhere in the three years by not paying out all the £3,000 immediately, but simply paying the hire purchase instalments, then you would be £132 better off at the end of the three years:

	£
Earned elsewhere	750
Paid in interest	618
Better off by	132

The usual reason for buying on hire purchase is simply that a firm does not have the money available to buy the item outright for the cash price. The hire purchase company is therefore helping the firm to finance its needs.

Normally, if a firm can borrow money from a bank by means of an overdraft, then this would be much cheaper. This is because bank overdraft rates of interest are usually far less than the rates of interest charged by the hire purchase company.

Banks, however, are likely to take far fewer chances than hire purchase companies. This means that very often the firm cannot get an overdraft for a long enough period to finance the purchase of fixed assets. As a consequence of the higher risks involved, a hire purchase company will naturally charge higher rates of interest to compensate for that risk.

3.9 Hire Purchase and Liquidity

If a firm buys on hire purchase, instead of purchasing outright, then this will help its liquidity in the short term. Let us look at the liquid position of firm A which is buying the £3,000 machine on hire purchase, compared with firm B which buys for cash immediately. Assume that both had the same liquid assets before the purchase:

	Before (both) £	After Purchase (A)	(B)
Current assets	4,000	4,000	1,000
Current liabilities	1,000	1,000	1,000
Current ratio	4:1	4:1	1:1

In the short term, therefore, liquidity will be affected immediately. Of course, during the next three years firm A will have to pay for the machine and so liquidity will then compare with that of B, if the hire purchase interest is ignored.

3.10 Hire Purchase and Profitability

Buying assets on hire purchase will naturally affect profitability, as the interest charge is an expense against profits. If the firm could have purchased the assets from within its own resources quite easily then that would normally have been the best course.

The question that should be asked is 'will the firm be better off financially if we buy this asset on hire purchase, rather than not buy it at all or pay for it outright?'. If the answer is 'yes', hire purchase should be used.

3.11 Accounting for Leases

What the financial world has seen in recent years is a very large increase in the leasing of assets instead of purchasing them.

Leases can appropriately be classified into *finance leases* and *operating leases*. The distinction between a finance lease and an operating lease will usually be evident from the substance of the contract between the lessor and the lessee. A *finance lease* usually involves repayment to a lessor by a lessee of the full cost of the asset together with a return on the finance provided by the lessor. As such, a lease of this type is normally non-cancellable or cancellable only under certain conditions, and the lessee enjoys all the risks and rewards associated with the ownership of an asset, other than the legal title.

An *operating lease* involves the lessee paying a rental for the hire of an asset for a period of time which is normally substantially less than its useful economic life. The lessor retains the risks and rewards of ownership of an asset in an operating lease and normally assumes responsibility for repairs, maintenance and insurance.

Briefly, a *finance lease* should be accounted for by the lessee as if it were a purchase of property rights in an asset with simultaneous recognition of the obligation to make future payments, in the same way that a hire purchase is normally accounted for. Under an *operating lease*, only the rental will be taken into account by a lessee. The substance of a transaction rather than its legal form should govern the accounting treatment.

In other words, in accounts show:

Operating leases
  Charge rentals in the profit and loss account
Finance leases
  Charge finance interest in the profit and loss account
  Charge depreciation on the asset in the profit and loss account
  In the balance sheet:
    show capital value of the asset
    show depreciation written off the asset
    show amount still owing in respect of the asset

A finance lease or hire purchase of a machine would therefore mean that given:

(i)   cost price of the machine if we had bought it, would have been £21,600
(ii) depreciation of the machine to date of the balance sheet would be £7,200
(iii) after adjusting for interest not yet accrued we would still have to pay £8,400 in respect of the machine

then the balance sheet would appear:

Balance Sheet as at ...

	£	£		£
Machinery at cost	21,600		Amount owing on hire purchase/lease	8,400
less depreciation	7,200	14,400		

This portrays economic reality, but it does not portray the legal aspects. The machinery does not belong to us, yet it is shown as an asset belonging to us. As the machinery does not belong to us, the depreciation does not attach to us, although it is shown as such in our books.

This therefore is a prime example of 'substance over form' being used in accounting. Basically it is that accounting should portray the economic reality of a transaction rather than simply the legal reality. Bear this in mind when you get asked a question about 'substance over form'.

Leasing first became popular because there were various tax advantages which were available to firms that leased assets instead of buying them outright. Many of these tax advantages have now been reduced.

The other reason for the popularity of leasing was that it allowed 'off-balance-sheet-financing'. This happens where a business has the use of a fixed asset, but neither the fixed asset nor the amount owing on it appears in the balance sheet. As you will see later in this book, this makes it appear that the company is performing rather better than it is in fact, as a higher percentage return on capital employed will be calculated.

To help remedy such distortions in accounts and to bring about uniformity, SSAP 21 was introduced. This is where the rules for dividing leases into operating leases and finance leases originated.

REVIEW QUESTIONS

Advice:

You are not supposed to know the technicalities of drawing up hire purchase accounts in the books of the seller or of the purchaser. You are, however, supposed to know the basic principles underlying hire purchase accounts.

The questions to be asked will probably be part of a much bigger question, or may be in the form of essay type questions.

Watch out for questions on:

● reasons for buying on hire purchase – see Section 3.8
● how hire purchase affects liquidity – see Section 3.9
● a concepts question on 'substance over form' – see Section 3.11, such a question being difficult to answer without a concrete example like this
● what the differences are between operating leases and finance leases – see Section 3.11 – this is important because of the growth of leasing
● a good example of 'off-balance-sheet-financing' – see Section 3.11.

The author expects that the contents of this chapter will start to figure much more prominently in A-Level examinations in the future.

Note: Questions with the letter X shown after the question number do NOT have answers shown at the back of the book. Answers to the others are shown on page 366 onwards.

3.1 Describe the circumstances under which a firm might buy fixed assets on hire purchase instead of paying for them immediately.

3.2X One of the concepts of accounting is that of 'substance over form'. With particular reference to hire purchase, how do the balance sheet entries bear out the basic principles underlying the concept?

3.3 Give an example as to how the purchase of a machine on hire purchase will affect the liquidity of a firm compared with a firm which buys fixed assets by immediate payment.

3.4X How can the Return on Capital Employed be affected by 'off-balance-sheet-financing'?

Chapter 4

The Issue of Shares and Debentures

*Note: Anyone who has not read Chapter 41 on limited companies in **Frank Wood's Business Accounting 1, Seventh Edition** would be well advised to do so before attempting this chapter.*

4.1 The Issue of Shares

In the case of public companies a new issue of shares can be very costly indeed, and the number of shares issued must be sufficient to make the cost worthwhile. However, for simplicity, so that the principles are not obscured by the difficulties of grappling with large amounts, the numbers of shares shown as issued in the illustrations that follow will be quite small.

Shares can be issued being payable (*a*) immediately on application, or (*b*) by instalments. The first instances will be of shares being paid for immediately. Issues of shares may take place on the following terms connected with the price of the shares:

(*a*) Shares issued at par. This would mean that a share of £1 nominal value would be issued for £1 each.
(*b*) Shares issued at a premium. In this case a share of £1 nominal value would be issued for more than £1 each, say for £3 each.
(*c*) At one time, shares could be issued at a discount. Thus, shares each of £5 nominal value might have been issued for £3 each. However, this is no longer permitted, having been expressly forbidden in the 1980 Companies Act.

4.2 Share Premiums and Discounts

This will all seem rather strange at first. How can a £1 share, which states that value on the face of it, be issued for £3 each, and who would be foolish enough to buy it? On the other hand, surely there would have been a queue of people waiting to buy a £5 share for £3 each. The reasons for this apparently strange state of affairs stem from the Companies Act requirement that the Share Capital Accounts always show shares at their nominal value, irrespective of how much the shares are worth or how much they are issued for. To illustrate this, the progress of two firms can be looked at, firm A and firm B. Both firms started in business on 1 January 19X1 and issued 1,000 ordinary shares each of £4 nominal value at par. Ignoring any issue expenses, the balance sheets on that date would appear:

Firms A Ltd and B Ltd

Balance Sheet as at 1 January 19X1

	£
Bank	4,000
Capital	4,000

Five years later, on 31 December 19X5, the balance sheets show that the companies have fared quite differently. It is to be assumed here, for purposes of illustration, that the balance sheet values and any other interpretation of values happen to be identical.

£4,000 capital is needed by A Ltd, and this is to be met by issuing more ordinary shares. Suppose that another 1,000 ordinary shares of £4 nominal value each are issued at par. Column (a) shows the balance sheet before the issue, and column (b) shows the balance sheet after the issue has taken place.

A Ltd Balance Sheets (Solution 1) as at 31 December 19X5

	(a) £	(b) £
Fixed and current assets (other than bank)	9,000	9,000
Bank	1,000	5,000
	10,000	14,000
Financed by		
Ordinary share capital	4,000	8,000
Profit and loss (undistributed profits)	6,000	6,000
	10,000	14,000

Now the effect of what has happened can be appreciated. Before the new issue there were 1,000 shares. As there were £10,000 of assets and no liabilities, then each share was worth £10. After the issue there are 2,000 shares and £14,000 of assets, so that now each share is worth £7. This would be extremely disconcerting to the original shareholders who see the value of each of their shares fall immediately by £3.

On the other hand, the new shareholder who has just bought shares for £4 each sees them rise immediately to be worth £7 each. Only in one specific case would this be just, and that is where each original shareholder buys an equivalent number of new shares. Otherwise this obviously cannot be the correct solution. What is required is a price which is equitable as far as the interests of the old shareholders are concerned, and yet will attract sufficient applications to provide the capital required. As in this case the balance sheet value and the real value are the same, the answer is that each old share was worth £10 and therefore each new share should be issued for £10 each. The balance sheets will now appear:

A Ltd Balance Sheets (Solution 2) as at 31 December 19X5

	(a) £	(b) £
Fixed and current assets (other than bank)	9,000	9,000
Bank	1,000	11,000
	10,000	20,000
Financed by		
Ordinary share capital (at nominal value)	4,000	8,000
Share premium (see note below)		6,000
Profit and loss	6,000	6,000
	10,000	20,000

Thus in (a) above 1,000 shares own between them £10,000 of assets = £10 each, while in (b) 2,000 shares are shown as owning £20,000 of assets = £10 each. Both the old and new shareholders are therefore satisfied with the bargain that has been made.

Note: The **share premium** shown on the capital side of the balance sheet is needed, ignoring for a moment the legal requirements to be complied with in company balance sheets, simply because the balance sheet would not balance without it. If shares are stated at nominal value, but issued at another price, the actual amount received increases the bank balance, but the share capital shown is increased by a different figure. The share premium therefore represents the excess of the cash received over the nominal value of the shares issued.

The other, B Ltd, has not fared so well. It has, in fact, lost money. The accumulated losses are reflected in a debit balance on the profit and loss account as shown in the following balance sheet (c). It can be seen that there are £3,000 of assets to represent the shareholders' stake in the firm of 1,000 shares, i.e. each share is worth £3 each. If more capital was needed 1,000 more shares could be issued. From the action taken in the previous case it will now be obvious that each new share of £4 nominal value will be issued for its real value of £3 each. The balance sheets will appear:

B Ltd Balance Sheets (correct solution) as at 31 December 19X5

	(c)	(d)
Fixed and current assets (other than bank)	2,000	2,000
Bank	1,000	4,000
Discounts on shares (*see below*)	1,000	
Profit and loss – debit balance (accumulated losses)	1,000	1,000
	4,000	8,000
Ordinary share capital	4,000	8,000

Once again, as the share capital is shown at nominal value, but the shares issued at a different figure, the difference being **discounts on shares** must be shown in order that the balance sheet may balance. It is, of course, not actually an asset, it is merely a balancing figure needed because the entries already made for an increase in the ordinary share capital and the increase in the bank balance have been at different figures. The figure for discounts on shares therefore rectifies the double-entry 'error'.

Although shares cannot now be issued at a discount, there will very occasionally still be items in company balance sheets for discounts on shares issued before 1980. Although not listed as an item in the balance sheet formats per the 1985 Companies Act, a separate heading will have to be inserted to accommodate the item.

For the purpose of making the foregoing explanations easier it was assumed that balance sheet values and other values were the same. This is very rarely true for all the assets, and in fact there is more than one other 'value'. A balance sheet is a historical view of the past based on records made according to the firm's interpretation and use of accounting concepts and conventions. When shares are being issued it is not the historical view of the past that is important, but the view of the future. Therefore the actual premiums and discounts on shares being issued is not merely a matter of balance sheet values, but on the issuing company's view of the future and its estimate of how the investing public will react to the price at which the shares are being offered.

It is to be noted that there are no restrictions on issuing shares at par or at a premium. The actual double entry accounts can now be seen.

4.3 Shares Payable in Full on Application

The issue of shares in illustrations 1, 2, and 3 which follow are based on the balance sheets that have just been considered.

1 Shares issued at par

1,000 ordinary shares with a nominal value of £4 each are to be issued. Applications, together with the necessary money, are received for exactly 1,000 shares. The shares are then allotted to the applicants.

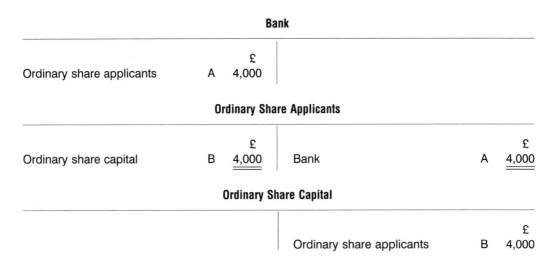

Bank

		£				
Ordinary share applicants	A	4,000				

Ordinary Share Applicants

		£				£
Ordinary share capital	B	4,000	Bank	A	4,000

Ordinary Share Capital

				£
	Ordinary share applicants	B	4,000

It may appear that the ordinary share applicants account is unnecessary, and that the only entries needed are a debit in the bank account and a credit in the ordinary share capital account. However, applicants do not always become shareholders; this is shown later. The applicant must make an offer for the shares being issued, accompanied by the necessary money, this is the application. After the applications have been vetted the allotments of shares are made by the company. This represents the acceptance of the offer by the company and it is at this point that the applicant becomes a shareholder. Therefore A represents the offer by the applicant, while B is the acceptance by the company. No entry must therefore be made in the share capital account until B happens, for it is not until that point that the share capital is in fact in existence. The share applicants account is therefore an intermediary account pending allotments being made.

2 Shares issued at a premium

1,000 ordinary shares with a nominal value of £4 each are to be issued for £10 each (*see* A Ltd previously). Thus a premium of £6 per share has been charged. Applications and the money are received for exactly 1,000 shares.

Bank

	£	
Balance b/fwd	1,000	
Ordinary share applicants	10,000	

Ordinary Share Applicants

		£			£
Ordinary share capital	A	4,000	Bank		10,000
Share premium	B	6,000			
		10,000			10,000

Share Premium

				£
		Ordinary share applicants	B	6,000

Ordinary Share Capital (A. Ltd)

			£
	Balance b/fwd		4,000
	Ordinary share applicants	A	4,000

Note: A is shown as £4,000 because the share capital is shown at nominal value and not as total issued value. B, the £6,000 share premium, must therefore be credited to a share premium account to preserve double entry balancing.

3 Shares issued at a discount (prior to 1980)

1,000 ordinary shares with a nominal value of £4 each are to be issued for £3 each (*see* B Ltd previously). Thus a discount of £1 per share is being allowed. Applications and the money are received for exactly 1,000 shares.

Bank

	£	
Balance b/fwd	1,000	
Ordinary share applicants	3,000	

Ordinary Share Applicants

	£		£
Ordinary share capital	4,000	Bank	3,000
		Discounts on shares	1,000
	4,000		4,000

Ordinary Share Capital

		£
	Balance b/fwd	4,000
	Ordinary share capital	4,000

Discounts on Shares

	£	
Ordinary share applications	1,000	

4 Oversubscription and undersubscription for shares

When a public company invites investors to apply for its shares it is obviously very rare indeed if in fact applications for shares equal exactly the number of shares to be issued. Where more shares are applied for than are available for issue, then the issue is said to be **oversubscribed**. Where fewer shares are applied for than are available for issue, then the issue has been **undersubscribed**.

With a brand-new company a minimum amount is fixed as being necessary to carry on any further with the running of the company. If the applications are less than the minimum stated, then the application monies must be returned to the senders. This does not apply to an established company. If therefore 1,000 shares of £1 each are available for issue, but only 875 shares are applied for, then only 875 will be issued, assuming that this is above the fixed minimum figure. The accounting entries will be in respect of 875 shares, no entries being needed for the 125 shares not applied for, as this part does not represent a transaction.

The opposite of this is where the shares are oversubscribed. In this case some sort of rationing is applied so that the issue is restricted to the shares available for issue. The process of selecting who will get how many shares depends on the policy of the firm. Some firms favour large shareholders because this leads to lower administrative costs. Why the costs will be lower will be obvious if the cost of calling a meeting of two companies each with 20,000 shares is considered. H Ltd has 20 shareholders with an average holding of 1,000 shares each. J Ltd has 1,000 shareholders with an average holding of 20 shares each. They all have to be notified by post and given various documents including a set of the final accounts. The cost of printing and sending these is less for H Ltd with 20 shareholders than for J Ltd with 1,000 shareholders. This is only one example of the costs involved, but it will also apply with equal force to many items connected with the shares. Conversely, the directors may prefer to have more shareholders with smaller holdings, one reason being that it decreases the amount of voting power in any one individual's hands. The actual process of rationing the shares is then a simple matter once a policy has been agreed. It may consist of scaling down applications, of drawing lots or some other chance selection, but it will eventually bring the number of shares to be issued down to the number of shares available. Excess application monies will then be refunded by the company.

An issue of shares where 1,000 ordinary shares of £1 nominal value each are to be issued at par payable in full, but 1,550 shares are applied for, will appear as follows:

Bank

	£		£
Ordinary share applicants	1,550	Ordinary share applicants (refunds)	550

Ordinary Share Applicants

	£		£
Bank	550	Bank	1,550
Ordinary share capital	1,000		
	1,550		1,550

Ordinary Share Capital

			£
		Ordinary share applicants	1,000

4.4 Issue of Shares Payable by Instalments

The shares considered so far have all been issued as paid in full on application. Conversely, many issues are made which require payment by instalments. These are probably more common with public companies than with private companies. It should be noted that a public company is now not allowed to allot a share unless there has been paid on it a sum equal to at least one-quarter of its nominal value plus the whole of any premium.

The various stages, after the initial invitation has been made to the public to buy shares by means of advertisements (if it is a public company), etc., are as follows:

A   Applications are received together with the application monies.

B   The applications are vetted and the shares allotted, letters of allotment being sent out.

C   The excess application monies from wholly unsuccessful, or where the application monies received exceed both the application and allotment monies required, and partly unsuccessful applicants, are returned to them. Usually, if a person has been partly unsuccessful, his excess application monies are held by the company and will reduce the amount needed to be paid by him on allotment.

D   Allotment monies are received.

E   The next instalment, known as the first call, is requested.

F   The monies are received from the first call.

G   The next instalment, known as the second call, is requested.

H   The monies are received from the second call.

This carries on until the full number of calls has been made, although there is not usually a large number of calls to be made in an issue.

The reasons for the payments by instalments becomes obvious if it is realised that a company will not necessarily require the immediate use of all the money to be raised by the issue. Suppose a new company is to be formed, it is to buy land, erect a factory, equip it with machinery and then go into production. This might take two years altogether. If the total sum needed was £1,000,000, the allocation of this money could be:

	£
Cost of land, payable within 1 month	300,000
Cost of buildings, payable in 12 months' time	200,000
Cost of machinery, payable in 18 months' time	200,000
Working capital required in 24 months' time	300,000
	1,000,000

The issue may therefore well be on the following terms:

	Per Cent
Application money per share, payable immediately	10
Allotment money per share, payable within 1 month	20
First call, money payable in 12 months' time	20
Second call, money payable in 18 months' time	20
Third call, money payable in 24 months' time	30
	100

The entries made in the share capital account should equal the amount of money requested to that point in time. However, instead of one share applicants account, this is usually split into several accounts to represent the different instalments. For this purpose application and allotment are usually joined together in one account, the application and allotment account, as this cuts out the need for transfers where excess application monies are held over and set off against allotment monies needed. When allotment is made, and not until then, an entry of £300,000 (10 per cent + 20 per cent) would be made in the share capital account. On the first call an entry of £200,000 would be made in the share capital account, likewise £200,000 on the second call and £300,000 on the third call. The share capital account will therefore contain not the monies received, but the amount of money requested. Exhibit 4.1 now shows an instance of a share issue.

Exhibit 4.1

A company is issuing 1,000 7 per cent preference shares of £1 each, payable 10 per cent on application, 20 per cent on allotment, 40 per cent on the first call and 30 per cent on the second and final call. Applications are received for 1,550 shares. A refund of the money is made in respect of 50 shares, while for the remaining 1,500 applied for, an allotment is to be made on the basis of 2 shares for every 3 applied for (assume that this will not involve any fractions of shares). The excess application monies are set off against the allotment monies asked for. The remaining requested instalments are all paid in full. The letters by the side of each entry refer to the various stages outlined earlier.

Bank

		£			£
Application and allotment:			Application refund	C	5
Application monies	A	155			
Allotment monies					
(£1,000 × 20% less excess					
application monies £50)	B	150			
First call	F	400			
Second call	H	300			

Application and Allotment

		£				£
Bank – refund of application monies	C	5	Bank		A	155
Preference share capital	B	300	Bank		B	150
		305				305

First Call

		£				£
Preference share capital	E	400	Bank		F	400

Second and Final Call

		£				£
Preference share capital	G	300	Bank		H	300

7 per cent Preference Share Capital – Nominal Part

	£			£
		Application and allotment	B	300
		First call	E	400
Balance c/d	1,000	Second call	G	300
	1,000			1,000
		Balance b/d		1,000

If more than one type of share is being issued at the same time, e.g. preference shares and ordinary shares, then separate share capital accounts and separate application and allotment accounts and call accounts should be opened.

The privatisation of British Telecom and the water industries were both examples of (i) oversubscription and (ii) payment by instalments.

4.5 Forfeited Shares

Sometimes a shareholder fails to pay the calls requested from him. The Articles of Association of the company will probably provide that the shareholder will have his shares forfeited, provided that certain safeguards for his protection are fully observed. In this case the shares will be cancelled, and the instalments already paid by the shareholder will be lost to him.

After the forfeiture, the company may reissue the shares, unless there is a provision in the Articles of Association to prevent it. There are certain conditions as to the prices at which the shares can be reissued. These are that the amount received on reissue plus the amount received from the original shareholder should at least equal (*a*) the called-up value where the shares are not fully called up, or (*b*) the nominal value where the full amount has been called up. Any premium previously paid is disregarded in determining the minimum reissue price.

Exhibit 4.2

Take the same information as that contained in Exhibit 4.1, but instead of all the calls being paid, Allen, the holder of 100 shares, fails to pay the first and second calls. He had already paid the application and allotment monies on the required dates. The directors conform to the provisions of the Articles of Association and (A) Allen is forced to suffer the forfeiture of his shares. (B) The amount still outstanding from Allen will be written off. (C) The directors then reissue the shares at 75 per cent of nominal value to J. Dougan. (D) Dougan pays for the shares.

First Call

		£				£
Preference share capital		400	Bank			360
		___	Forfeited shares	(B)		40
		400				400

Second Call

		£				£
Preference share capital		300	Bank			270
		___	Forfeited shares	(B)		30
		300				300

7 per cent Preference Share Capital

		£			£
Forfeited shares	(A)	100	Application and allotment		300
Balance c/d		900	First call		400
			Second call		300
		1,000			1,000
			Balance b/d		900
Balance c/d		1,000	J. Dougan	(C)	100
		1,000			1,000
			Balance b/d		1,000

Forfeited Shares

		£			£
First call	(B)	40	Preference share capital	(A)	100
Second call	(B)	30			
Balance c/d		30			
		100			100
J. Dougan (see following note)		25	Balance c/d		30
Balance c/d		5			
		30			30

Bank

	£			
First call (£900 × 40%)	360			
Second call				
(£900 × 30%)	270			
J. Dougan (D)	75			

J. Dougan

	£			£
Preference share capital	100	Bank (D)		75
		Forfeited shares (discount on		
		reissue) *see* following note		25
	100			100

Note: The transfer of £25 from forfeited shares account to J. Dougan's account is needed because the reissue was entered in the preference share capital account and Dougan's account at nominal value, i.e. following standard practice of a share capital account being concerned with nominal values, but Dougan was not to pay the full nominal price. Therefore the transfer of £25 is needed to close his account.

The balance of £5 on the forfeited shares account can be seen to be: Cash received from original shareholder on application and allotment £30 + from Dougan £75 = £105. This is £5 over the nominal value so that the £5 appears as a credit balance. This is usually stated to be either transferred to a profit on reissue of forfeited shares account, but it really cannot be thought that this is followed in practice for small amounts. More normally it would be transferred to the credit of a share premium account.

4.6 Calls in Advance and in Arrear and the Balance Sheet

At the balance sheet date some shareholders will not have paid all the calls made, these are collectively known as **calls in arrear**. On the other hand, some shareholders may have paid amounts in respect of calls not made by the balance sheet date. These are **calls in advance**.

Calls in arrear, i.e. **Called up share capital not paid** is to be shown in the balance sheet in one of the positions shown in the format per the 1985 Companies Act. There is no specified place for calls in advance, so this will be inserted in the balance sheet as an extra heading.

4.7 Bonus Shares

These are shares issued to existing shareholders free of charge. An alternative name is scrip issue.

If the articles give the power, and the requisite legal formalities are observed, the following may be applied in the issuing of bonus shares:

1 The balance of the profit and loss appropriation account.
2 Any other revenue reserve.
3 Any capital reserve, e.g. share premium.

This thus comprises all of the reserves.

There is an argument that this should never be needed, as can be illustrated by taking a somewhat exaggerated example, shown in Exhibit 4.3.

Exhibit 4.3

A company, Better Price Ltd, started business 50 years ago with 1,000 ordinary shares of £1 each and £1,000 in the bank. The company has constantly had to retain a proportion of its profits to finance its operations, thus diverting them from being used for cash dividend purposes. Such a policy has conserved working capital.

The firm's balance sheet as at 31 December 19X7 is shown as:

Better Price Ltd

Balance Sheet as at 31 December 19X7
(before bonus shares are issued)

	£
Fixed assets	5,000
Current assets *less* Current liabilities	5,000
	10,000
Share capital	1,000
Reserves (including profit and loss account balance)	9,000
	10,000

If in fact an annual profit of £1,500 was now being made, this being 15 per cent on assets employed, and £1,000 could be paid annually as cash dividends, then the dividend declared each year would be 100 per cent, i.e. a dividend of £1,000 on shares of £1,000 nominal value. It is obvious that the dividends and the share capital have got out of step with one another. Employees and trade unions may well become quite belligerent, as owing to the lack of accounting knowledge, or even misuse of it, it might be believed that the firm was making unduly excessive profits. Customers, especially if they are members of the general public, may also be deluded into thinking that they are being charged excessive prices, or, even though this could be demonstrated not to be true because of the prices charged by competitors, they may well still have the feeling that they are somehow being duped.

In point of fact, an efficient firm in this particular industry or trade may well be only reasonably rewarded for the risks it has taken by making a profit of 15 per cent on assets employed. The figure of 100 per cent for the dividend is due to the very misleading convention in accounting in the UK of calculating dividends in relationship to the nominal amount of the share capital.

If it is considered, in fact, that £7,000 of the reserves could not be used for dividend purposes, due to the fact that the net assets should remain at £8,000, made up of fixed assets £5,000 and working capital £3,000, then besides the £1,000 share capital which cannot be returned to the shareholders there are also £7,000 reserves which rationally cannot be returned to them. Instead of this £7,000 being called reserves, it might as well be called capital, as it is needed by the business on a permanent basis.

To remedy this position, as well as some other needs less obvious, bonus shares were envisaged. The reserves are made non-returnable to the shareholders by being converted into share capital. Each holder of one ordinary share of £1 each will receive seven bonus shares (in the shape of seven ordinary shares) of £1 each. The balance sheet, if the bonus shares had been issued immediately, would then appear:

Better Price Ltd

Balance Sheet as at 31 December 19X7
(after bonus shares are issued)

	£
Fixed assets	5,000
Current assets *less* Current liabilities	5,000
	10,000
Share capital (£1,000 + £7,000)	8,000
Reserves (£9,000 − £7,000)	2,000
	10,000

When the dividends of £1,000 per annum are declared in the future, they will amount to:

$$\frac{£1,000}{£8,000} \times \frac{100}{1} = 12.5 \text{ per cent.}$$

This will cause less disturbance in the minds of employees, trade unions, and customers.

Of course the issue of bonus shares may be seen by any of the interested parties to be some form of diabolical liberty. To give seven shares of £1 each free for one previously owned may be seen as a travesty of social justice. In point of fact the shareholders have not gained at all. Before the bonus issue there were 1,000 shares that owned between them £10,000 of net assets. Therefore, assuming just for this purpose that the book 'value' is the same as any other 'value', each share was worth £10. After the bonus issue each previous holder now has eight shares for every one share he held before. If he had owned one share only, he now owns eight shares. He is therefore the owner of $\frac{8}{8,000}$ part of the firm, i.e. a one thousandth part. The 'value' of the net assets are £10,000, so that he owns £10 of them, so his shares are worth £10. This is exactly the same 'value' as that applying before the bonus issue was made.

It would be useful in addition, to refer to other matters for comparison. Anyone who had owned a £1 share 50 years ago, then worth £1, would now have (if he was still living after such a long time) eight shares worth £8. A new house of a certain type 50 years ago might have cost £x, it may now cost £8x, the cost of a bottle of beer may now be y times greater than it was 50 years ago, a packet of cigarettes may be z times more and so on. Of course, the firm has brought a lot of trouble on itself by waiting so many years to capitalise reserves. It should have been done by several stages over the years.

This is all a very simplified, and in many ways an exaggerated version. There is, however, no doubt that misunderstanding of accounting and financial matters has caused a great deal of unnecessary friction in the past and will probably still do so in the future. Yet another very common misunderstanding is that the assumption the reader was asked to accept, namely that the balance sheet values equalled 'real values', is often one taken by the reader of a balance sheet. Thus a profit of £10,000 when the net assets book values are £20,000 may appear to be excessive, yet in fact a more realistic value of the assets may be saleable value, in this case the value may be £100,000.

The accounting entries necessary are to debit the reserve accounts utilised, and to credit a bonus account. The shares are then issued and the entry required to record this is to credit the share capital account and to debit the bonus account. The journal entries would be:

The Journal

	Dr	Cr
	£	£
Reserve account(s) (show each account separately)	7,000	
Bonus account		7,000
Transfer of an amount equal to the bonus payable in fully-paid shares		
Bonus account	7,000	
Share capital account		7,000
Allotment and issue of 7,000 shares of £1 each, in satisfaction of the bonus declared		

4.8 Rights Issue

A company can also increase its share capital by making a **rights issue**. This is the issue of shares to existing shareholders at a price lower than the ruling market price of the shares.

The price at which the shares of a very profitable company are quoted on the Stock Exchange is usually higher than the nominal value of the shares. For instance, the market price of the shares of a company might be quoted at £2.50 while the nominal value per share is only £1.00. If the company has 8,000 shares of £1 each and declares a rights issue of one for every eight held at a price of £1.50 per share, it is obvious that it will be cheaper for the existing shareholders to buy the rights issue at this price instead of buying the same shares in the open market for £2.50 per share. Assume that all the rights issue was taken up, then the number of shares taken up will be 1,000 (i.e. 8,000 ÷ 8), and the amount paid for them will be £1,500. The journal entries will be:

The Journal

	Dr	Cr
	£	£
Cash	1,500	
Share capital		1,000
Share premium		500
Rights issue of 1 for every 8 shares held at a price of £1.50, nominal value being £1.00		

It is to be noted that because the nominal value of each share is £1.00 while £1.50 was paid, the extra 50p constitutes a share premium to the company.

Notice also that the market value of the shares will be reduced or 'diluted' by the rights issue, as was the case for bonus shares. Before the rights issue there were 8,000 shares at a price of £2.50, giving a market capitalisation of £20,000. After the issue there are 9,000 shares and the assets have increased by £1,500. The market value may therefore reduce to £2.39 [(20,000 + 1,500)/9,000], although the precise market price at the end of the issue will have been influenced by the information given surrounding the sale about the future prospects of the company and may not be exactly the amount calculated.

4.9 The Issue of Debentures

The entries for the issue of debentures are similar to those for shares. It would, however, certainly not be the normal modern practice to issue debentures at a premium. If the word 'debentures' appears instead of 'share capital', then the entries in the accounts would be identical.

4.10 Shares of No Par Value

It can be seen that the idea of a fixed par value for a share can be very misleading. For anyone who has not studied accounting, it may well come as a shock to find that a share with a par value of £1 might in fact be issued for £5. If the share is dealt in on the Stock Exchange a potential investor might find a £1 share selling at £10 or even £20, or equally well it may sell for only 10p.

Another disadvantage of a par value is that it can give people entirely the wrong impression of the activities of a business. If a par value is kept to, and the dividend based on that, then with a certain degree of inflation the dividend figure can look excessive. Many trade union leaders would howl with disapproval if a dividend of 100 per cent were declared by a company. But is this so excessive? Exhibit 4.4 gives a rather different picture.

Exhibit 4.4

Allen bought a share 40 years ago for £1. At the time he was satisfied with a return of 5 per cent on his money. With a 5 per cent dividend he could buy a certain amount of goods which will be called x. Forty years later to buy that same amount of goods, x, he would need, say, 20 times as much money. Previously 5p would have bought x, now it would take £1. To keep his dividend at the same level of purchasing power he would need a dividend now of 100 per cent, as compared with the 5 per cent he was receiving 40 years ago.

In the United States of America, Canada and Belgium as well as other countries, no par value is attached to shares being issued. A share is issued at whatever price is suitable at the time, and the money received is credited to a share capital account.

4.11 Gearing

This topic appears very frequently in GCE A-Level examinations, and quite rightly so, for it is an important part of understanding about accounts and the risks under which firms operate. It must be stressed that there is more than one way of calculating gearing ratios, so you must spell out in your examination paper which method you have used.

The most widely used method is as follows:

$$\frac{\text{Long-term loans} + \text{preference shares}}{\text{Total shareholders' funds} + \text{long-term loans}} \times \frac{100}{1}$$

Long-term loans include debentures. Total shareholders' funds include preference shares and ordinary shares and all the reserves.

Let us look at the calculation of the gearing of two companies, A Ltd and B Ltd. Both have already been trading for five years.

Year 5: Items per balance sheet	A Ltd	B Ltd
	£	£
10% Debentures	10,000	100,000
10% Preference shares	20,000	50,000
Ordinary shares	100,000	20,000
Reserves	70,000	30,000
	200,000	200,000

Gearing ratios:

A Ltd
$$\frac{10,000 + 20,000}{10,000 + 20,000 + 100,000 + 70,000} \times \frac{100}{1} = 15\% \text{ (low gearing)}$$

B Ltd
$$\frac{100,000 + 50,000}{100,000 + 50,000 + 20,000 + 30,000} \times \frac{100}{1} = 75\% \text{ (high gearing)}$$

Now let us look at how dividends are affected, given the same level of profits made before payment of debenture interest and preference dividends. All the profits made in these years are to be distributed.

A Ltd: Low gearing

		Year 6	Year 7	Year 8	Year 9
		£	£	£	£
Profits before deducting the following:		20,000	15,000	30,000	40,000
Debenture interest	1,000				
Preference dividend	2,000	3,000	3,000	3,000	3,000
Profits left for ordinary dividend		17,000	12,000	27,000	37,000
Rate of ordinary dividend		17%	12%	27%	37%

B Ltd: High gearing

		Year 6	Year 7	Year 8	Year 9
		£	£	£	£
Profits before deducting the following:		20,000	15,000	30,000	40,000
Debenture interest	10,000				
Preference dividend	5,000	15,000	15,000	15,000	15,000
Profits left for ordinary dividend		5,000	–	15,000	25,000
Rate of ordinary dividend		25%	–	75%	125%

A company with a high percentage of gearing ratio is said to be *high geared*, whereas one with a low percentage of gearing is said to be *low geared*. As you can see from the above example, the proportionate effect gearing has upon ordinary shareholders is far greater in a high-geared company, ranging from 0 to 125 per cent dividend for B Ltd, whilst the range of ordinary dividends for A Ltd varied far less and lay between 17 and 37 per cent.

A high rate of debt (i.e. long-term loans and preference shares) means that in bad times very little might be left over for ordinary shareholders after payment of interest on the debt items and also preference dividends. In good times, however, the ordinary shareholders will enjoy a far higher return than in a low-geared company.

This means that people investing in ordinary shares in a high geared company are taking a far greater risk with their money than if they had invested instead in a low-geared company. It would have only required a drop of profits of £5,000 in year 6 for B Ltd to find that there would be no ordinary dividends at all for both years 6 and 7. Such a drop in year 6 for A Ltd would still have allowed a dividend of 12 per cent for both of years 6 and 7. Investors therefore who are prepared to risk their money in the hope of large dividends would have chosen B Ltd, whilst those who wanted to cut down on their risk and be more certain about receiving dividends would choose A Ltd.

4.12 Changing the Gearing of a Company

The management might decide that for various reasons it would like to change the gearing of the company. It can do this as follows:

To *reduce gearing*	To *increase gearing*
1 By issuing new ordinary shares	1 By issuing debentures
2 By redeeming debentures	2 By buying-back ordinary shares in issue
3 By retaining profits	3 By issuing new preference shares

Such changes will be influenced by what kinds of investors the company wishes to attract. A highly geared company will attract risk-taking buyers of ordinary shares, whilst a low-geared company will be more attractive to potential ordinary shareholders who wish to minimise risk.

4.13 The Investor: Choosing between Shares and Debentures

The choice of an investor will always be related to the amount of acceptable risk. We can list the possible investments under the headings of risk.

Lowest risk:
Debenture holders have their interest paid to them whether or not profits are made. This contrasts with shares, both preference and ordinary, where there have to be profits available for distribution as dividends.

In addition, should there be insufficient cash funds available to pay debenture dividends, many debentures give their holders the right to sell off some or all of the assets of the company, and to recoup the amount of their debentures before anyone else has a claim. Such an investment does not have as much security as, say, government stocks, but it certainly ranks above the shares of that same company.

Medium risk:
Preference shares have their dividends paid after the debenture interest has been paid, but before the ordinary shareholders. They still are dependent upon profits being available for distribution. If they are of the cumulative variety then any shortfall can be carried forward to future years and paid before any ordinary dividends are taken.

Highest risk:
Ordinary shares. They must give way to both debenture holders and to preference shares for interest and dividends. However, should the remaining profits for distribution be very high then they may get a very high return on their money.

REVIEW QUESTIONS

Advice:

Questions involving the issue of shares are usually not very difficult, and you can achieve a high percentage of the marks quite easily.

Remember that the share capital accounts are concerned with the (called-up part) nominal value of the shares.

A 'rights issue' is entered exactly the same as an ordinary issue of shares. The only difference is that the rights issue is pitched at a somewhat lower price than would be asked from people who were to become shareholders for the first time.

You should master Section 4.11 (Gearing). There are a lot of questions which include something on gearing.

Remember that a bonus issue of shares means changing equivalent amounts from being reserves into being share capital.

4.1 A limited company has a nominal capital of £120,000 divided into 120,000 ordinary shares of £1 each. The whole of the capital was issued at par on the following terms:

	Per share
Payable on application	£0.125
Payable on allotment	£0.25
First call	£0.25
Second call	£0.375

Applications were received for 160,000 shares and it was decided to allot the shares on the basis of three for every four for which applications had been made. The balance of application monies were applied to the allotment, no cash being refunded. The balance of allotment monies were paid by the members.

The calls were made and paid in full by the members, with the exception of a member who failed to pay the first and second calls on the 800 shares allotted to him. A resolution was passed by the directors that he should forfeit the shares. The forfeited shares were later issued to D. Regan at £0.90 each.

Show the ledger accounts recording all the above transactions, and the relevant extracts from a balance sheet after all the transactions have been completed.

4.2X Badger Ltd has an authorised capital of £100,000 divided into 20,000 ordinary shares of £5 each. The whole of the shares were issued at par, payments being made as follows:

	£
Payable on application	0.5
Payable on allotment	1.5
First call	2.0
Second call	1.0

Applications were received for 32,600 shares. It was decided to refund application monies on 2,600 shares and to allot the shares on the basis of two for every three applied for. The excess application monies sent by the successful applicants is not to be refunded but is to be held and so reduce the amount payable on allotment.

The calls were made and paid in full with the exception of one member holding 100 shares who paid neither the first nor the second call and another member who did not pay the second call on 20 shares. After requisite action by the directors the shares were forfeited. They were later reissued to B. Mills at a price of £4 per share.

You are to draft the ledger accounts to record the transactions.

4.3 The balance sheet of De Vere Carter plc included the following information at 31 May 19X2:

	£
Issued share capital:	
Ordinary shares of £1 each, fully paid	240,000
10% Preference shares of £1 each, fully paid	90,000
Reserves:	
Share premium account	65,000
Capital redemption reserve	40,000
Revaluation reserve	120,000
Profit and loss account	56,000

On 1 June 19X2, the company is planning to increase its ordinary share capital in the following ways:

(i) An issue of bonus shares to existing members, with one bonus share being issued for every three ordinary shares held. The directors wished to retain the maximum flexibility regarding future dividend payments, so an appropriate choice of reserves was to be made for the purpose of the bonus issue.

(ii) A rights issue, whereby existing shareholders (both of ordinary and preference shares) may subscribe for five ordinary shares at £1.90 each for every three shares of either class held (excluding bonus shares). £1 is payable on application (by 30 June 19X2), and 90p on allotment (by 31 July 19X2).

(iii) A public issue of 100,000 ordinary shares to be made at £2.50 each, with £1.10 payable on application (by 30 June 19X2) and the balance on allotment (by July 19X2). Existing shareholders are to be given priority, as their applications will be accepted before those of the general public.

Applications were received as follows:

1 90% of the rights issue was taken up, and paid for by the due dates.

2 Existing shareholders applied for, and were allotted, 60,000 of the share issue. Other applications totalled 90,000 shares, and these were scaled down on a pro-rata basis, with excess application money being refunded on 10 July 19X2. All application and allotment monies were paid by the due date, with the exception of £3,000 allotment money due from existing shareholders.

(a) Show the company's application and allotment account, and ordinary share capital account for the period 1 June 19X2 to 31 July 19X2.

(12 marks)

(b) Calculate the final number of shares held by a shareholder with an initial holding of 900 ordinary shares, who applied for the rights issue and 500 shares in the new share issue.

(3 marks)

(c) Explain two advantages and two disadvantages to a company of raising funds by a share issue, and suggest three alternative ways of raising funds that the company could have considered.

(10 marks)

(University of London: GCE A-Level)

4.4X Aggressive Marketing plc., whose entire equity is made up of 100,000 25 pence shares, is in need of finance for planned expansion. It has therefore duly registered the required prospectus and attracted applications for 250,000 shares at a premium of 10 pence. Applicants have paid 20 pence on application, the balance (which includes the premium) being due on notification of allotment. The existing shareholders have only approved a further issue of 200,000 shares so the directors have resolved to allot the new issue to applicants as follows:

(i)   Applicants for 5,000 shares are to be refused as their individual applications are for insufficient shares to justify the administration costs involved. Their application monies are to be returned to them.

(ii) Applicants for 15,000 shares are to be allotted shares in accordance with their applications.

(iii) Other applicants will be allotted the remaining shares in proportion to their individual applications but, rather than refunding application monies, these are to be retained by the company on account of the balance due on allotment.

   It has also been resolved that existing shareholders should have the advantage of a rights issue of 50,000 shares at nominal value. The terms of the issue are that 25 pence is to be paid on application. No shareholder has an odd number of shares. After formal notification to those qualified, application monies for 40,000 shares have been received. The only asset the company has is cash.

Required:

(i)   Application and allotment, share capital and share premium accounts to reflect the above transactions.

(16 marks)

(ii) A calculation of the worth of one share owned by an investor who has subscribed for his rights and paid the monies due from him.

(7 marks)

(iii) The company's balance sheet at the completion of the above transactions.   *(5 marks)*

(Welsh Joint Education Committee: GCE A-Level)

4.5 Channel Ltd, a manufacturer of confectionery, is considering expanding its production to commence exporting into Europe. To achieve this the company will need to invest £3,000,000 in fixed assets and an additional £2,000,000 is required to fund an increase in working capital.

It is company policy to depreciate fixed assets at the rate of 15 per cent per annum on cost. Two alternative methods of financing the necessary investment are being considered.

Alternative 1
To issue 5,000,000 of its 50p ordinary shares at £1 per share. The directors expect the annual dividend payable to ordinary shareholders to remain at 20 per cent.

Alternative 2
To purchase the fixed assets on credit. The terms of the credit agreement provide for four annual instalments of £1,000,000 commencing at the end of the first year. Assume that interest accrues evenly over the period of the loan. To finance the working capital requirement, the company will be able to negotiate a bank overdraft facility for two years. The overdraft is expected to average £1,500,000 in the first year and £500,000 in the second year. The bank will charge interest at the rate of 20% per annum on the overdraft.

Required:

(a) The entries which would appear in the revenue accounts at the end of the first year for both alternatives, showing clearly the section of the revenue accounts which would be affected.

(5 marks)

(b) The relevant extracts from the balance sheet at the end of the first year for both alternatives.

(6 marks)

(c) Discuss the financial implications of both proposals for an existing shareholder in Channel Ltd.

(6 marks)

(Associated Examining Board: GCE A-Level)

4.6X
(a) The two companies A. Brown Ltd and C. Dawes Ltd have the following capital structures:

	AB	CD
	£000	£000
Ordinary £1 shares fully paid	2,000	800
Preference shares (14%)	1,100	500
Debentures (12%)	900	2,700

Debenture interest is an allowable expense against corporation tax, which for 19X9 and 19X0 stands at 45 per cent. For both companies, the return on total capital employed during 19X9 was 25 per cent and during 19X0 it was 10 per cent. All profits remaining after the payment of debenture interest, corporation tax, and preference dividend are paid to holders of the ordinary shares.

Calculate the percentage return on the ordinary shares for each company for 19X9 and 19X0.

(18 marks)

(b) Use your answer to (a) above to illustrate:
   (i) the value of incorporating some gearing into a company's capital structure, and
   (ii) the factors which may limit the proportion of debt capital to equity within a company's capital structure.
   Be careful to define your terms. *(7 marks)*

(University of London: GCE A-Level)

4.7 The directors of Shapers plc are considering an expansion of the company's operations which it is estimated will require a further £5,000,000 to be invested in the company.

The following information has been extracted from the latest published balance sheet of the company:

	£
Ordinary shares of 25p each, fully paid	2,600,000
8% Preference shares of £1.00 each, fully paid	1,400,000
Share premium account	200,000
Revaluation reserve	400,000
General reserve	500,000
Retained earnings	800,000
6% Loan stock 19X4/X5	1,000,000

The current price of the company's ordinary shares is 60p whilst that of the preference shares is par.

The directors are now considering how to raise the additional capital and have asked the company's financial adviser to report on the advantages and disadvantages of each of the following in meeting the company's projected capital needs:

A rights issue of ordinary shares at par
A rights issue of ordinary shares at a premium of 20p per share
A bonus issue of ordinary shares
An issue of 8% preference shares of £1.00 each at par
An issue of 6% Loan stock at par.

Required:

As the company's financial adviser, prepare a report to the directors on their proposals. *(25 marks)*

(Reproduced by permission of the University of Cambridge Local Examinations Syndicate)

4.8X The chief accountant of Corchester Ltd had prepared the following balance sheet as at 1 July 19X4.

	£000	£000
Fixed assets		
Freehold property		100
Other fixed assets		480
		580
Current assets (including bank)	440	
Less current liabilities	200	
		240
		820
Financed by		
Issued and paid up share capital:		
400,000 ordinary shares of £1 each		400
150,000 8% redeemable preference shares of £1 each		150
		550
Reserves		
Capital redemption reserve	100	
Share premium account	50	
General reserve	45	
Profit and loss account	75	
		270
		820

The directors had decided to carry out the following transactions during July and August 19X4:

(1) 8 July: A rights issue of one ordinary share for every four held was made at £1.20 per share. All shareholders took up their rights.

(2) 1 August: A bonus issue was made of one ordinary share for every ten held, based on the revised ordinary share capital. That was carried out by utilising equal amounts from the revenue reserves.

(3) 5 August: 40,000 preference shares were redeemed at a premium of 5p per share. This was achieved out of profits with the exception of the premium which was covered by the share premium account.

(4) 15 August: The freehold property was revalued at £130,000.

(5) 19 August: Fixed assets costing £10,000 were purchased on credit.

Required:

(a) A balance sheet as at 19 August 19X4 after the completion of all transactions
     indicated above   *(20 marks)*

(b) Describe the features of
     (i) a rights issue of shares   *(5 marks)*
     (ii) a bonus issue of shares   *(5 marks)*

(c) Explain the differences between capital and revenue reserves.   *(5 marks)*

(Associated Examining Board: GCE A-Level)

Chapter 5

Companies Purchasing and Redeeming Their Own Shares and Debentures

5.1 Redemption and Purchase of Shares

The words 'purchasing' and 'redeeming' may appear to be exactly the same as far as this chapter is concerned. To all intents and purposes they are the same, for both involve an outflow of cash by the company to get back its own shares and then cancel them. However, from a rather more legal and precise point of view, 'redeeming' means the buying back of shares which were originally issued as being 'redeemable' in that the company stated when they were issued that they would be, or could be, redeemed (i.e. bought back by the company). The terms of the 'redemption' (buying back) would be stated at the time when the shares were issued. However, when shares are issued and are not stated to be 'redeemable' then, when they are bought back by the company it is then said to be the 'purchase' of its shares by the company, usually in the open market.

Until 1981 a company in the United Kingdom could not in normal circumstances 'purchase' its own shares. In addition, 'redemption' was limited to one type of share, **redeemable preference shares**. This had not been the case in the United States and Europe for many years where companies had, with certain restrictions, been allowed to buy back their own shares. The basic reason why this was not allowed in the UK was the fear that the interests of creditors could be adversely affected if the company used its available cash to buy its own shares, thus leaving less to satisfy the claims of the creditors. The possibilities of abuse with preference shares was considered to be less than with ordinary shares, thus it was possible to have redeemable preference shares.

Now, subject to certain conditions, a company can buy back any of its own shares whether or not they are stated to be redeemable:

1 The company must be authorised to do so by its own articles of association.
2 After buying back the shares there must still be left some shares which cannot be bought back.
3 They have to be fully paid up by the shareholder before they can be bought back.
4 The company must, after the purchase of its own shares, have at least two shareholders remaining.
5 For private companies there are extra concessions but these are outside the scope of the GCE A-Level syllabuses, and so will not be dealt with here.

In addition, public limited companies have a limit placed on them as to the amount of shares they can buy back. The amount paid should not be greater than the total of:

(i) Money received from the proceeds of a new issue of shares, and

(ii) The amount available as distributable profits, i.e. reserves and the balance of the profit and loss account which could legally be paid out as cash dividends.

5.2 Advantages of Purchase and Redemption of Shares

Certainly there are quite a few possible advantages of a company being able to buy back its own shares. These are strongest in the case of private companies. For public companies the main advantage is that those with surplus cash resources could find it useful to be able to return some of this surplus cash back to its shareholders by buying back some of its own shares, rather than have pressure put on them to use such cash in uneconomic ways.

For private companies the main possible advantages would appear to be overcoming snags which occur when a shareholder cannot sell his shares on the 'open market', i.e. a stock exchange. This means that:

(a) It will help shareholders who have difficulties in selling their shares to another individual to be able to realise their value when needed, for any reason.

(b) People will be more willing to buy shares from private companies. The fear of not being able to dispose of them, previously led to finance being relatively difficult for private companies to obtain from people outside the original main proprietors of the company.

(c) In many 'family' companies cash is needed to pay for taxes on the death of the shareholder.

(d) Shareholders with grievances against the company can be bought out, thus contributing to the more efficient management of the company.

(e) Family-owned companies will be helped in their desire to keep control of the company when a family shareholder with a large number of shares dies or retires.

(f) Similar to public companies, as described above, the company could return unwanted cash resources back to its shareholders.

(g) For both private companies, and for public companies whose shares are not listed on a stock exchange, it may help boost share schemes for employees, as the employees would know that they could fairly easily dispose of the shares instead of being stuck with them.

5.3 Accounting Entries

Whether shares are redeemed (i.e. shares originally described as redeemable) or purchased (shares not originally described as redeemable) does not affect the debit and credit entries except for one thing. This is that the word 'redeemable' will appear in the title of the accounts dealing with redeemable shares.

When shares are redeemed (or purchased), the accounting entries needed will depend on how the financing of the redemption has been arranged. As shares redeemed at a premium can involve further complications, we will first of all look at shares redeemed at par. Note that shares can only be redeemed or purchased when they are fully paid.

To get the reader used to journal entries, and then seeing the effect on the face of the balance sheet, journal style entries will be shown first, followed by the balances for the balance sheet.

1 Shares redeemed at par

(i) Where redemption is fully covered by an issue of new shares

In this case it is simply a matter of recording the issue of the new shares, and the reduction of the old share capital account with the old shares redeemed.

Exhibit 5.1

£2,000 preference shares are redeemed/purchased at par, a new issue of £2,000 ordinary shares at par being made for the purpose.

		Dr £	Cr £
(A1)	Bank	2,000	
(A2)	Ordinary share applicants		2,000
	Cash received from applicants		
(B1)	Ordinary share applicants	2,000	
(B2)	Ordinary share capital		2,000
	Ordinary shares allotted		
(C1)	Preference share capital	2,000	
(C2)	Preference share purchase*		2,000
	Shares to be redeemed/purchased		
(D1)	Preference share purchase*	2,000	
(D2)	Bank		2,000
	Payment made to redeem/purchase shares		

*Note: In all the examples which follow, the shares being purchased/redeemed are preference shares. In fact they could be any type of share, ordinary, preference, preferred ordinary, etc. The shares to be redeemed/purchased are transferred to a preference share purchase account. In fact if they were being redeemed it would be a preference share redemption account. It will make it easier to follow if the answers are standardised.

	Balances Before £	Effect Dr £		Effect Cr £	Balances After £
Net assets (except bank)	7,500				7,500
Bank	2,500	(A1) 2,000	(D2) 2,000		2,500
	10,000				10,000
Ordinary share capital	5,000		(B2)	2,000	7,000
Ordinary share applicants	–	(B1) 2,000	(A2)	2,000	–
Preference share capital	2,000	(C1) 2,000			–
Preference share purchase	–	(D1) 2,000	(C2)	2,000	–
	7,000*				7,000*
Profit and loss	3,000				3,000
	10,000				10,000

*Note: total 'capitals' remain the same.

(ii) Where no new shares are issued, but redemption takes place

There has always been a worry that a company might pay out all of its available money to shareholders if the business was seen to be in difficulties, leaving nothing to pay the creditors. If there was no restriction a company could, if it saw that it was going to go out of business:

(a) Pay off most of its share capital back to the shareholders.

(b) Pay out dividends to the shareholders from profits and reserves which were still able to be used for dividend purposes.

This could then mean that the shareholders got all the cash available, leaving nothing to pay the creditors when the company went into liquidation.

To stop this happening, the Companies Act 1985 includes a regulation which states that when redemption takes place which is not covered by a new issue of shares, then an amount equal to the nominal value of shares redeemed is to be transferred from distributable profits to a capital redemption reserve. As this is a capital reserve it cannot be used for the payment of cash dividends.

Exhibit 5.2

£2,000 preference shares redeemed/purchased at par, with no new issue of shares to provide funds for the purpose. Therefore an amount equal to the nominal value of the shares redeemed *must* be transferred from the profit and loss appropriation account to the credit of a capital redemption reserve. (Note: This requires use of the section in the profit and loss account called the profit and loss appropriation account which shows how the net profits are to be appropriated, i.e. how the profits are to be used.)

		Dr £	Cr £
(A1)	Preference share capital	2,000	
(A2)	Preference share purchase		2,000
	Shares to be redeemed/purchased		
(B1)	Preference share purchase	2,000	
(B2)	Bank		2,000
	Cash paid as purchase/redemption		
(C1)	Profit and loss appropriation	2,000	
(C2)	Capital redemption reserve		2,000
	Transfer per Companies Act 1985, Section 45		

	Balances Before £		Effect Dr £			Effect Cr £	Balances After £
Net assets (except bank)	7,500						7,500
Bank	2,500				(B2)	2,000	500
	10,000						8,000
Ordinary share capital	5,000						5,000
Preference share capital	2,000	(A1)	2,000				–
Preference share purchase	–	(B1)	2,000		(A2)	2,000	–
Capital redemption reserve	–				(C2)	2,000	2,000
	7,000*						7,000*
Profit and loss	3,000	(C1)	2,000				1,000
	10,000						8,000

*Note: Total 'capitals' (share capital + non-distributable reserves) remain the same at £7,000.

(iii) Where some new shares are issued, but not enough to cover redemption in full

In this case it is only the deficiency that needs transferring to a capital redemption reserve.

Exhibit 5.3

£2,000 preference shares redeemed/purchased at par, being £1,200 from issue of ordinary shares at par and partly by using appropriation account balance.

		Dr £	Cr £
(A1)	Bank	1,200	
(A2)	Ordinary share applicants		1,200
	Cash received from applicants		
(B1)	Ordinary share applicants	1,200	
(B2)	Ordinary share capital		1,200
	Ordinary shares allotted		
(C1)	Profit and loss appropriation	800	
(C2)	Capital redemption reserve		800
	Part of redemption/purchase not covered by new issue, to comply with Companies Act 1985, section 45		
(D1)	Preference share capital	2,000	
(D2)	Preference share purchase		2,000
	Shares being redeemed/purchased		
(E1)	Preference share purchase	2,000	
(E2)	Bank		2,000
	Payment made for redemption/purchase		

	Balances Before £	Effect Dr £			Effect Cr £	Balances After £
Net assets (except bank)	7,500					7,500
Bank	2,500	(A1)	1,200	(E2)	2,000	1,700
	10,000					9,200
Ordinary share capital	5,000			(B2)	1,200	6,200
Ordinary share applicants	–	(B1)	1,200	(A2)	1,200	–
Preference share capital	2,000	(D1)	2,000			–
Preference share purchase	–	(E1)	2,000	(D2)	2,000	–
Capital redemption reserve	–			(C2)	800	800
	7,000*					7,000*
Profit and loss	3,000	(C1)	800			2,200
	10,000					9,200

Note: Total 'capitals' remain the same.

2 Shares redeemed at a premium

(i) Where the shares redeemed were not originally issued at a premium

In respect of the nominal value of the shares being redeemed you should follow the rules already laid down for shares redeemed at par.

In respect of the premium payable, in addition to what you have already done in respect of the nominal value, an amount equal to the share premium has to be transferred from the profit and loss appropriation account balance to the credit of a capital redemption reserve account. This is required by the Companies Act 1985, even if the redemption is financed by the issue of new shares at a premium.

Exhibit 5.4

£2,000 preference shares which were originally issued at par are redeemed/purchased at a premium of 20 per cent. There is no new issue of shares for the purpose. In this example the ordinary shares had been originally issued at a premium, thus the reason for the share premium account being in existence. However, it is *not* the ordinary shares which are being redeemed and therefore the share premium *cannot* be used for the premium on redemption/purchase of the preference shares.

		Dr £	Cr £
(A1)	Preference share capital	2,000	
(A2)	Preference share purchase		2,000
	Shares being redeemed/purchased		
(B1)	Profit and loss appropriation	400	
(B2)	Preference share purchase		400
	Premium on purchase/redemption of shares *not* previously issued at premium		
(C1)	Profit and loss appropriation	2,000	
(C2)	Capital redemption reserve		2,000
	Transfer because shares redeemed/purchased out of distributable profits		
(D1)	Preference share purchase	2,400	
(D2)	Bank		2,400
	Payment on purchase/redemption		

	Balances Before	Effect				Balances After
	£		Dr £		Cr £	£
Net assets (except bank)	7,500					7,500
Bank	2,500			(D2)	2,400	100
	10,000					7,600
Ordinary share capital	4,500					4,500
Preference share capital	2,000	(A1)	2,000			–
Preference share purchase	–	(D1)	2,400	(A2)	2,000	–
				(B2)	400	
Capital redemption reserve	–			(C2)	2,000	2,000
Share premium	500					500
	7,000*					7,000*
		(C1)	2,000			
Profit and loss	3,000	(B1)	400			600
	10,000					7,600

Notice: Total 'capitals' remain the same.

(ii) Where the shares redeemed were originally issued at a premium

If no new shares are being issued for the purposes of redemption, then you must follow the instructions in (*i*) above.

However, if, in addition to the shares originally being issued at a premium, a new issue of shares is being made for the purpose of redemption, then, and only then, an amount calculated as follows can reduce the balance on an existing share premium account. This is shown as (E) in Exhibit 5.5

Exhibit 5.5

Share Premium Account

		£
Credit balance before new issue	(A)	xxx
Add Premium on new issue	(B)	xxx
Balance after new issue	(C)	xxx
Amount that *may* be transferred	(E)	
is lesser of:		
Premiums that were received when it first issued the shares now being redeemed/purchased (D)	xxx	
or		
Balance after new issue (C) above	xxx	
Transfer to share purchase/redemption	(E)	xxx
New balance for balance sheet (could be nil)		xxx

Where the amount being deducted (E) is *less* than the premium paid on the *current* redemption or purchase, then an amount equivalent to the difference must be transferred from the debit of the appropriation account to the credit of the capital redemption reserve account.

Exhibit 5.6

£2,000 preference shares originally issued at premium of 20 per cent are now being purchased/redeemed at a premium of 25 per cent. The position can be shown in three different companies if for the purpose of purchase/redemption:

Company 1 issues 2,400 ordinary £1 shares at par
Company 2 issues 2,000 ordinary £1 shares at 20 per cent premium
Company 3 issues 1,600 ordinary £1 shares at 50 per cent premium.

Share Premium Account

		Company 1	Company 2	Company 3
		£	£	£
Balance before new issue	(A)	150 [1]	400	400
Premium on new issue			400	800 (B)
Balance after new issue	(C)	150	800	1,200
Amount transferable to share purchase/ redemption is therefore lower of (C) or original premium on issue (£400)		150 [2]	400 [2]	400 [2]
New balance for balance sheet		–	400	800

[1] In Company 1 it is assumed that of the original £400 premium the sum of £250 had been used up to issue bonus shares (see Chapter 8 later).

[2] As these figures are less than the premium of £500 *now* being paid, the differences (Company 1 £350: Companies 2 and 3 £100 each) must be transferred from the debit of the profit and loss account to the credit of the preference share/purchase redemption account.

Journal Entries:	Company 1		Company 2		Company 3	
	Dr	Cr	Dr	Cr	Dr	Cr
	£	£	£	£	£	£
(A1) Bank	2,400		2,400		2,400	
(A2) Ordinary share applicants		2,400		2,400		2,400
Cash received from applicants						
(B1) Ordinary share applicants	2,400		2,400		2,400	
(B2) Ordinary share capital		2,400		2,000		1,600
(B3) Share premium		–		400		800
Ordinary shares allotted						
(C1) Preference share capital	2,000		2,000		2,000	
(C2) Preference share purchase		2,000		2,000		2,000
Shares being redeemed/purchased						
(D1) Share premium account	150		400		400	
(D2) Preference share purchase		150		400		400
Amount of share premium						
account used for redemption/purchase						
(E1) Profit and loss appropriation	350		100		100	
(E2) Preference share purchase		350		100		100
Excess of premium payable over						
amount of share premium						
account usable for the purpose						
(F1) Preference share purchase	2,500		2,500		2,500	
(F2) Bank		2,500		2,500		2,500
Amount paid on redemption/purchase						

The following balance sheets for the three companies are given *before* the purchase/redemption. The balance sheets are then shown *after* purchase/redemption.

Balance Sheets (*before* redemption/purchase)

	Company 1	Company 2	Company 3
	£	£	£
Net assets (except bank)	7,500	7,500	7,500
Bank	2,500	2,500	2,500
	10,000	10,000	10,000
Ordinary share capital	4,850	4,600	4,600
Preference share capital	2,000	2,000	2,000
Share premium	150	400	400
	7,000	7,000	7,000
Profit and loss account	3,000	3,000	3,000
	10,000	10,000	10,000

	Company 1	Company 2	Company 3
	£	£	£
Net assets (except bank)	7,500	7,500	7,500
Bank	2,400	2,400	2,400
	9,900	9,900	9,900
Ordinary share capital	7,250	6,600	6,200
Share premium	–	400	800
	7,250	7,000	7,000
Profit and loss account	2,650	2,900	2,900
	9,900	9,900	9,900

5.4   Redemption of Debentures

Unless they are stated to be irredeemable, debentures are redeemed according to the terms of the issue. The necessary funds to finance the redemption may be from:

(*a*) An issue of shares or debentures for the purpose.
(*b*) The liquid resources of the company.

Resembling the redemption of redeemable preference shares, when the redemption is financed as in (*a*), no transfer of profits from the profit and loss appropriation account to a reserve account is needed. However, when financed as in (*b*) an amount equal to the nominal value redeemed may be transferred from the debit of the profit and loss appropriation account to the credit of a reserve account.
   Redemption may be effected:

1   By annual drawings out of profits.
2   By purchase in the open market when the price is favourable, i.e. less than the price which will have to be paid if the company waited until the last date by which redemption has to be carried out.
3   In a lump sum to be provided by the accumulation of a sinking fund, however this is outside the scope of most A-Level examinations.

   The first two methods can now be examined in more detail.

Regular annual drawings out of profits

(a) Redeemed at a premium

In this case the source of the bank funds with which the premium is paid should be taken to be (*a*) share premium account, or if this does not exist, or the premium is in excess of the balance on the account, then any part not covered by a share premium account is deemed to come from (*b*) the profit and loss appropriation account. Exhibit 5.7 shows the effect on a balance sheet where there is no share premium account, while Exhibit 5.8 illustrates the case when a share premium account is in existence.

Exhibit 5.7

Starting with the *before* balance sheet, £400 of the debentures are redeemed at a premium of 20 per cent.

Balance Sheets

	Before £	+ or – £	After £
Other assets	12,900		12,900
Bank	3,400	–480 (A)	2,920
	16,300		15,820
Share capital	10,000		10,000
Debenture redemption reserve	–	+400 (B)	400
Debentures	2,000	–400 (A)	1,600
Profit and loss	4,300	–400 (B)	
		–80 (A)	3,820
	16,300		15,820

Exhibit 5.8

Starting with the *before* balance sheet, £400 of the debentures are redeemed at a premium of 20 per cent.

Balance Sheets

	Before £	+ or – £	After £
Other assets	13,500		13,500
Bank	3,400	–480 (A)	2,920
	16,900		16,420
Share capital	10,000		10,000
Share premium	600	–80 (A)	520
Debenture redemption reserve	–	+400 (B)	400
Debentures	2,000	–400 (A)	1,600
Profit and loss	4,300	–400 (B)	3,900
	16,900		16,420

In both Exhibits 5.7 and 5.8 the debenture redemption reserve account is built up each year by the nominal value of the debentures redeemed each year. When the whole issue of debentures has been redeemed, then the balance on the debenture redemption reserve account should be transferred to the credit of a general reserve account. It is, after all, an accumulation of undistributed profits.

(b) Redeemed by purchase in the open market

A sum equal to the cash actually paid on redemption should be transferred from the debit of the profit and loss appropriation account to the credit of the debenture redemption reserve account. The sum actually paid will of course have been credited to the cash book and debited to the debentures account.

Any discount (or profit) on purchase will be transferred to a reserve account. Any premium (or loss) on purchase will be deemed to come out of such a reserve account, or if no such account exists or it is insufficient, then it will be deemed to come out of the share premium account. Failing the existence of these accounts any loss must come out of the profit and loss appropriation account. It may seem that purchase would not be opportune if the debentures had to be redeemed at a premium. However, it would still be opportune if the premium paid was not as high as the premium to be paid if the final date for redemption was awaited.

5.5 Cancellation of Shares or Debentures Purchased/Redeemed

All shares or debentures purchased/redeemed must be cancelled immediately.

REVIEW QUESTIONS

Advice:

The redemption (or purchase) of a company's own shares or debentures is usually a part of a much larger question. You will notice questions which touch upon this topic at various places in this book besides the ones shown at the end of this chapter.

5.1 Given the same commencing balance sheet, now shown. Exercises 5.1(i) to 5.1(v) inclusive are based on it.

RSV Ltd

Balance Sheet

	£
Net assets (except bank)	20,000
Bank	13,000
	33,000
Preference share capital	5,000
Ordinary share capital	15,000
Share premium	2,000
	22,000
Profit and loss	11,000
	33,000

Note that each of Questions 5.1(i) to (v) are independent of each other. They are not cumulative.

(i) RSV Ltd redeems £5,000 preference shares at par, a new issue of £5,000 ordinary shares at par being made for the purpose. Show the balance sheet after completion of these transactions.

(ii) RSV Ltd redeems £5,000 preference shares at par, with no new issue of shares to provide funds. Show the balance sheet after completing the transaction.

(iii) RSV Ltd redeems £5,000 preference shares at par. To help finance this an issue of £1,500 ordinary shares at par is effected. Show the balance sheet after these transactions have been completed.

(iv) RSV Ltd redeems £5,000 preference shares at a premium of 25 per cent. There is no new issue of shares for the purpose. In this question the share premium account is taken as being from the issue of ordinary shares some years ago. Show the balance sheet after these transactions have been completed.

(v) RSV Ltd redeems £5,000 preference shares at a premium of 40 per cent. There is an issue of £7,000 ordinary shares at par for the purpose. The preference shares had originally been issued at a premium of 30 per cent. Show the balance sheet after these transactions have been completed.

5.2X Questions 5.2X(i) to 5.2X(v) are based on the same commencing balance sheet, as follows:

BAR Ltd
Balance Sheet

	£
Net assets (except bank)	31,000
Bank	16,000
	47,000
Preference share capital	8,000
Ordinary share capital	20,000
Share premium	4,000
	32,000
Profit and loss	15,000
	47,000

Note that Questions 5.2X(i) to (v) are independent of each other. They are not cumulative.

(i) BAR Ltd purchases £10,000 of its own ordinary share capital at par. To help finance this £7,000 preference shares are issued at par. Show the balance sheet after the transactions have been completed.

(ii) BAR Ltd purchases £12,000 of its own ordinary shares at a premium of 20 per cent. No new issue of shares is made for the purpose. It is assumed that the share premium account is in respect of the issue of preference shares some years before. Show the balance sheet after the transactions have been completed.

(iii) BAR Ltd purchases all the preference share capital at par. These shares were not originally redeemable preference shares. There is no new issue of shares to provide funds. Show the closing balance sheet when the transaction has been completed.

(iv) BAR Ltd purchases £12,000 of its own ordinary shares at par, a new issue of £12,000 preference shares at par being made for the purpose. Show the balance sheet after completing these transactions.

(v) BAR Ltd purchases £6,000 of its own ordinary shares at a premium of 50 per cent; they had originally been issued at a premium of 20 per cent. There is an issue of £10,000 preference shares at par for the purpose. Show the amended balance sheet.

5.3 The directors of Racoon plc wish to reduce the company's gearing. The following is an extract from its balance sheet as at 31 May 19X9:

Authorised Share Capital
    25 million ordinary shares of £1 each.
    10 million 6% redeemable preference shares of £1 each, 19X2/19X7
Issued Share Capital
    20 million ordinary shares of £1 each
    10 million 6% redeemable preference shares of £1 each, 19X2/19X7

In addition, the company had debentures totalling £10 million outstanding at 31 May 19X9, which were due for repayment in 19X8.

    The ordinary shares are being traded on the stock market at £2.25 each, the preference shares are traded at £0.90 each, and the debentures at 5% less than par (nominal) value.

(a) Explain in detail three ways in which Racoon plc can reduce its gearing level, and explain *why* the company might wish to reduce its reliance on 'fixed percentage funding'.

    (9 marks)

(b) Set out the journal entries which would be required if the company decided to redeem *half* of its debentures by buying them on the stock market at the current price. A debenture redemption reserve is to be created.
    (6 marks)

(University of London: GCE A-Level)

5.4X The accounts of Richmal plc included the following balances on 31 December 19X2:

	£	£
Issued share capital:		
2m ordinary shares of 25p each, fully paid		500,000
300,000 12% redeemable preference shares of		
£1 each, fully paid		300,000
		800,000
Share premium	20,000	
Retained earnings	243,000	
		263,000
		1,063,000

In January 19X3, the company made a bonus issue of 300,000 ordinary shares of 25p each, by utilising part of the balance of retained earnings. It also redeemed 100,000 redeemable preference shares at a premium of 10p each. When issued, the redeemable preference shares had been sold at £1.06 each.

(a) Prepare the appropriate ledger accounts (excluding the bank account) necessary to record the above transactions.
    (12 marks)

(b) Show the shareholders' funds section of the balance sheet immediately after the bonus issue of ordinary shares and the redemption of preference shares.
    (5 marks)

(c) Explain why a company might choose to issue *redeemable* preference shares.   *(4 marks)*

(d) State the circumstances, where a *capital redemption reserve* is created, and explain why such a reserve is needed.
    (4 marks)

(University of London: GCE A-Level)

Chapter 6

Limited Companies Taking Over Other Businesses

6.1 Introduction

Limited companies will often take over other businesses which are in existence as going concerns. The purchase considerations may either be in cash, by giving the company's shares to the owners, by giving the company's debentures, or by any combination of these three factors.

It must not be thought that because the assets bought are shown in the selling firm's books at that firm's value that the purchasing company must record the assets taken over in its own books at the same value. The values shown in the purchasing company's books are those values at which the company is buying the assets, such values being frequently quite different from those shown in the selling firm's books. As an instance of this, the selling firm may have bought premises many years ago for £1,000 but they may now be worth £5,000. The company buying the premises will obviously have to pay £5,000 and it is therefore this value that is recorded in the buying company's books. Alternatively, the value at which it is recorded in the buying company's books may be less than that shown in the selling firm's books. Where the total purchase consideration exceeds the total value of the identifiable assets then such excess is the goodwill, and will need entering in a goodwill account in the purchasing company's books. Should the total purchase consideration be less than the values of the identifiable assets, then the difference would be entered in a capital reserve account.

Before the accounting entries necessary to record the purchase of a going business are looked at, it must be pointed out that such recording of the transactions is the simple end of the whole affair. The negotiations that take place before agreement is reached, and the various strategies undertaken by the various parties is a study in itself. The accounting entries are in effect the 'tip of the iceberg', i.e. that part of the whole affair which is seen by the eventual reader of the accounts.

6.2 Taking Over a Sole Trader's Business

It is easier to start with the takeover of the simplest sort of business unit, that of a sole trader. Some of the balance sheets shown will deliberately be simplified so that the principles involved are not hidden behind a mass of complicated calculations.

Exhibit 6.1

Earl Ltd is to buy the business of M. Kearney. The purchase consideration is to be £6,000 cash, the company placing the following values on the assets taken over – Machinery £3,000, Stock £1,000. The goodwill must therefore be £2,000, because the total price of £6,000 exceeds the values of Machinery £3,000 and Stock £1,000 by the sum of £2,000. The company's balance sheets will be shown immediately before and immediately after the takeover.

M. Kearney

Balance Sheet

	£
Machinery	1,700
Stock	1,300
	3,000
Capital	3,000

Earl Ltd

Balance Sheet(s)

	Before £	+ or – £	After £
Goodwill		+2,000	2,000
Machinery	11,000	+3,000	14,000
Stock	5,000	+1,000	6,000
Bank	9,000	–6,000	3,000
	25,000		25,000
Share capital	20,000		20,000
Profit and loss	5,000		5,000
	25,000		25,000

Exhibit 6.2

Suppose the purchase had been made instead by issuing 7,000 shares of £1 each at par to Kearney. The goodwill would then be £7,000 – assets taken over £4,000 = £3,000. The balance sheets of Earl Ltd would be:

Earl Ltd

Balance Sheets

	Before £	+ or – £	After £
Goodwill		+3,000	3,000
Machinery	11,000	+3,000	14,000
Stock	5,000	+1,000	6,000
Bank	9,000		9,000
	25,000		32,000
Share capital	20,000	+7,000	27,000
Profit and loss	5,000		5,000
	25,000		32,000

Exhibit 6.3

If the purchase had been made by issuing 5,000 shares of £1 each at a premium of 50 per cent, then the total consideration would have been worth £7,500, which, if the assets of £4,000 are deducted leaves goodwill of £3,500. The balance sheets would then be:

Earl Ltd

Balance Sheets

	Before £	+ or – £	After £
Goodwill		+3,500	3,500
Machinery	11,000	+3,000	14,000
Stocks	5,000	+1,000	6,000
Bank	9,000		9,000
	25,000		32,500
Share capital	20,000	+5,000	25,000
Share premium		+2,500	2,500
Profit and loss	5,000		5,000
	25,000		32,500

Exhibit 6.4

Now, if the purchase had been made by the issue of 1,000 shares of £1 each at a premium of 40 per cent, £3,000 worth of 7 per cent debentures at par and £4,000 in cash, then the total purchase consideration would be shares valued at £1,400, debentures valued at £3,000 and cash £4,000, making in all £8,400. The assets are valued at £4,000, the goodwill must be £4,400. The balance sheets would appear:

Earl Ltd

Balance Sheets

	Before £	+ or – £	After £
Goodwill		+4,400	4,400
Machinery	11,000	+3,000	14,000
Stocks	5,000	+1,000	6,000
Bank	9,000	–4,000	5,000
	25,000		29,400
Share capital	20,000	+1,000	21,000
Share premium		+400	400
Profit and loss	5,000		5,000
Debentures		+3,000	3,000
	25,000		29,400

In each of Exhibits 6.1 to 6.4 it has been assumed that all transactions were started and completed within a few moments. The fact is that an intermediary account would be created but then closed almost immediately when the purchase consideration was handed over. Taking Exhibit 6.3 as an example, there will be a credit in the share capital account and in the share premium account, and debits in the goodwill, machinery and stock accounts. Nevertheless, shares cannot be issued to goodwill, machinery or stocks. They have in fact, been issued to M. Kearney. This means that there should have been an account for M. Kearney, but that the balance on it was cancelled on the passing of the purchase consideration. The actual accounts in the books of Earl Ltd for Exhibit 6.3 were as follows:

Share Premium

	£		£
		M. Kearney	2,500

Share Capital

	£		£
Balance c/d	25,000	Balance b/d	20,000
		M. Kearney	5,000
	25,000		25,000
		Balance b/d	25,000

Profit and Loss

			£
		Balance b/d	5,000

Goodwill

	£		
M. Kearney	3,500		

Machinery

	£		£
Balance b/d	11,000		
M. Kearney	3,000	Balance c/d	14,000
	14,000		14,000
Balance b/d	14,000		

Stock

	£		£
Balance b/d	5,000		
M. Kearney	1,000	Balance c/d	6,000
	6,000		6,000
Balance b/d	6,000		

(In fact the £1,000 would probably be entered in the purchases account. It does, however, obviously increase the actual amount of stock.)

Bank

	£	
Balance b/fwd	9,000	

M. Kearney

	£		£
Consideration passing:		Assets taken over	
Share capital	5,000	Goodwill	3,500
Share premium	2,500	Machinery	3,000
		Stock	1,000
	7,500		7,500

Some accountants would have preferred to use a business purchase account instead of a personal account such as that of M. Kearney.

Sometimes the company taking over the business of a sole trader not only pays a certain amount for the assets but also assumes responsibility for paying the creditors in addition. Take the case of a sole trader with assets valued at Premises £5,000 and Stock £4,000. To gain control of these assets the company is to pay the sole trader £11,000 in cash, and in addition the company will pay off creditors £1,000. This means that the goodwill is £3,000, calculated as follows:

	£	£
Paid by the company to gain control of the sole trader's assets:		
Cash to the sole trader		11,000
Cash to the sole trader's creditors		1,000
		12,000
The company receives assets	£	
Premises	5,000	
Stock	4,000	
		9,000
Excess paid for goodwill		3,000

6.3 Partnership Business Taken Over by a Limited Company

The entries are basically the same as those for a sole trader. However, the main difference is the distribution of the purchase consideration. In the case of a sole trader he gets all of it. In a partnership it has to be divided between the partners.

This means that in a partnership a realisation account will have to be drawn up to calculate the profit or loss on sale of the partnership business. The profit or loss on sale will then be shared between the partners in their profit/loss sharing ratios.

The double entry needed in the partnership books is:

(A)	Transfer assets being disposed of to realisation account:
	Dr Realisation
	Cr Assets (various)
(B)	Enter purchase price:
	Dr Limited company (Purchaser)
	Cr Realisation
(C)	If profit on sale:
	Dr Realisation
	Cr Partners' capitals (profit-sharing ratio)
(D)	If loss on sale:
	Dr Partners capitals (profit-sharing ratio)
	Cr Realisation
(E)	Receipt purchase price:
	Dr Cash
	Dr Shares (if any) in limited company
	Dr Debentures (if any) in limited company
	Cr Limited company (purchaser)
(F)	Final settlement with partners
	Dr Partners' capital and current accounts
	Cr Cash
	Cr Shares (if any) in limited company
	Cr Debentures (if any) in limited company

Entries for these are illustrated in Exhibit 6.5.

Exhibit 6.5

Kay and Lee were in partnership, sharing profits and losses in the ratio 2:1 respectively. The following was their balance sheet as at 31 December 19X4.

Kay and Lee

Balance Sheet as at 31 December 19X4

		£	£
Fixed assets:			
Buildings			30,000
Motor vehicles			15,000
			45,000
Current assets			
Stock		8,000	
Debtors		6,000	
Bank		1,000	15,000
			60,000
Capitals:	Kay	32,000	
	Lee	16,000	48,000
Current accounts:	Kay	3,000	
	Lee	4,000	7,000
Current liabilities			
Creditors			5,000
			60,000

On 1 January 19X5 Cayley Ltd is to take over the assets, other than bank. The purchase price is £80,000, payable by £60,000 in £1 shares in Cayley Ltd at par, plus £20,000 cash. Kay and Lee will pay off their own creditors. Shares are to be divided between the partners on the basis of their profit-sharing ratios.

First, we will see the closing entries in the accounts of Kay and Lee. The only asset account shown will be that of the bank account. The creditors accounts are also not shown. The letters in brackets refer to the description of the double entry given above.

Books of Kay and Lee.

Realisation

	£		£
Assets taken over:		Cayley Ltd (B)	80,000
Buildings (A)	30,000		
Motor vehicles (A)	15,000		
Stock (A)	8,000		
Debtors (A)	6,000		
Profit on realisation:			
Kay ⅔ (C)	14,000		
Lee ⅓ (C)	7,000 21,000		
	80,000		80,000

Cayley Ltd

	£		£
Realisation: sale price (B)	80,000	Bank (E)	20,000
		Shares in Cayley Ltd (E)	60,000
	80,000		80,000

Shares in Cayley Ltd

	£		£
Cayley Ltd (E)	60,000	Capitals: Kay (F)	40,000
		Lee (F)	20,000
	60,000		60,000

Capitals

	Kay £	Lee £		Kay £	Lee £
Shares in Cayley (F)	40,000	20,000	Balances b/f	32,000	16,000
Bank (F)	6,000	3,000	Profit on realisation (C)	14,000	7,000
	46,000	23,000		46,000	23,000

Current Accounts

	Kay £	Lee £		Kay £	Lee £
Bank (F)	3,000	4,000	Balances b/f	3,000	4,000

Bank

	£		£
Bank b/f	1,000	Creditors	5,000
Cayley Ltd (E)	20,000	Capitals: Kay	6,000
		Lee	3,000
		Current Accounts: Kay	3,000
		Lee	4,000
	21,000		21,000

Note: It would have been possible to transfer the balances of the current accounts to the capital accounts before settlement.

Assuming that Cayley Ltd values the buildings at £41,000 and stock at £7,000 its balance sheet at 1 January 19X5 would appear as (B) under. The items shown under (A) were the balances before the takeover.

Balance Sheets

	(A)*Before* £	+ £	− £	(B)*After* £
Goodwill				11,000
Buildings	50,000	41,000		91,000
Motor vehicles	25,000	15,000		40,000
Stock	28,000	7,000		35,000
Debtors	17,000	6,000		23,000
Bank	30,000		20,000	10,000
	150,000	69,000	20,000	210,000
Share capital (£1 shares)	100,000	60,000		160,000
Profit and loss	40,000			40,000
Creditors	10,000			10,000
	150,000	60,000		210,000

6.4 The Takeover of a Limited Company by another Limited Company

One company may take over another company by one of two methods:

1   By buying all the assets of the other company, the purchase consideration being by cash, shares, or debentures. The selling company may afterwards be wound up: either the liquidators may distribute the purchasing company's shares and debentures between the shareholders of the selling company, or else the shares and debentures of the buying company may be sold and the cash distributed instead.

2   By giving its own shares and debentures in exchange for the shares and debentures of the selling company's share and debenture holders. Exhibit 6.6 is an illustration of each of these methods.

Exhibit 6.6

The following are the balance sheets of three companies as on the same date.

Balance Sheets

	R Ltd £	S Ltd £	T Ltd £
Buildings	13,000	–	1,000
Machinery	4,000	2,000	1,000
Stock	3,000	1,000	2,000
Debtors	2,000	1,000	3,000
Bank	1,000	2,000	3,000
	23,000	6,000	10,000
Share capital (£1 shares)	18,000	3,000	5,000
Profit and loss	2,000	1,000	4,000
Current liabilities	3,000	2,000	1,000
	23,000	6,000	10,000

- R takes over S by exchanging with the shareholders of S two shares in R at a premium of 10 per cent for every share they hold in S.

- R takes over T by buying all the assets of T, the purchase consideration being 12,000 £1 shares in R at a premium of 10 per cent, and R will pay off T's creditors. R values T's assets at Buildings £2,000, Machinery £600, Stock £1,400, Debtors £2,500, and the Bank is £3,000, a total of £9,500.

- R's deal with the shareholders of S means that R now has complete control of S Ltd, so that S Ltd becomes what is known as a subsidiary undertaking of R Ltd, and will be shown as an investment in R's balance sheet.

- On the other hand, the deal with T has resulted in the ownership of the assets resting with R. These must therefore be added to R's assets in its own balance sheet. As R has given 12,000 £1 shares at a premium of 10 per cent plus taking over the responsibility for creditors £1,000, the total purchase consideration for the assets taken over is £12,000 + £1,200 (10 per cent of £12,000) + £1,000 = £14,200. Identifiable assets as already stated are valued at £9,500, therefore the goodwill is £14,200 – £9,500 = £4,700.

The distinction between the acquisition of the two going concerns can be seen to be a rather fine one. With S the shares are taken over, the possession of these in turn giving rise to the ownership of the assets. In the books of R this is regarded as an investment. With T the actual assets and liabilities are taken over so that the assets now directly belong to R. In the books of R this is therefore regarded as the acquisition of additional assets and liabilities and not as an investment (using the meaning of 'investment' which is used in the balance sheets of companies). The balance sheet of R Ltd therefore becomes:

R Ltd

Balance Sheet

	Before £		+ or – £		After £
Goodwill		+(T)	4,700		4,700
Buildings	13,000	+(T)	2,000		15,000
Machinery	4,000	+(T)	600		4,600
Investment in S at cost		+	6,600		6,600
Stock	3,000	+(T)	1,400		4,400
Debtors	2,000	+(T)	2,500		4,500
Bank	1,000	+(T)	3,000		4,000
	23,000				43,800
Share capital	18,000	+(S)	6,000		
		+(T)	12,000	=	36,000
Share premium		+(S)	600		
		+(T)	1,200	=	1,800
Profit and loss	2,000				2,000
Current liabilities	3,000	+(T)	1,000		4,000
	23,000				43,800

No entry is necessary in the books of S Ltd, as it is merely the identity of the shareholders that has changed. This would be duly recorded in the register of members, but this is not really an integral part of the double entry accounting system.

If, however, T Ltd is now liquidated, then a realisation account must be drawn up and the distribution of the shares (or cash if the shares are sold) to the shareholders of T Ltd must be shown. Such accounts would appear as follows:

Books of T Ltd

Realisation

	£		£
Book values of assets disposed of:		R Ltd: Total purchase consideration	14,200
Buildings	1,000		
Machinery	1,000		
Stock	2,000		
Debtors	3,000		
Bank	3,000		
Profit on realisation transferred			
to sundry shareholders	4,200		
	14,200		14,200

Share Capital

	£		£
Sundry shareholders	5,000	Balance b/fwd	5,000

Profit and Loss

	£		£
Sundry shareholders	4,000	Balance b/fwd	4,000

Creditors

	£		£
R Ltd – taken over	1,000	Balance b/fwd	1,000

R Ltd

	£		£
Realisation:		Creditors	1,000
Total consideration	14,200	Sundry shareholders: 12,000 £1 shares received at premium of 10 per cent	13,200
	14,200		14,200

Sundry Shareholders

	£		£
R Ltd; 12,000 £1 shares at premium of 10 per cent	13,200	Share capital	5,000
		Profit and loss	4,000
		Profit on realisation	4,200
	13,200		13,200

It can be seen that the items possessed by the sundry shareholders have been transferred to an account in their name. These are (i) the share capital which obviously belongs to them, (ii) the credit balance on the profit and loss account built up by withholding cash dividends from the shareholders, and (iii) the profit on realisation which they, as owners of the business, are entitled to take. As there were 5,000 shares in T Ltd, and 12,000 shares have been given by R Ltd, then each holder of 5 shares in T Ltd will now be given 12 shares in R Ltd to complete the liquidation of the company.

6.5 The Exchange of Debentures

Sometimes the debentures in the company taking over are to be given in exchange for the debentures of the company being taken over. This may be straightforward on the basis of £100 debentures in company A in exchange for £100 debentures in company B. However, a problem can arise when the exchange is in terms of one of both sets of debentures being at a discount or at a premium. The need for such an exchange may be twofold:

(a) To persuade the debenture holders in company B to give up their debentures some form of inducement may be needed, such as letting them have A's debentures at a discount even though they may well be worth the par value.

(b) There may be a difference in the debenture interest rates. For instance, a person with a £100 7 per cent debenture would not normally gladly part with it in exchange for a £100 6 per cent debenture in another company. The first debenture gives him £7 a year interest, the second one only £6 per year. Thus the debenture in the second company may be issued at a discount to redeem the debenture in the first company at a premium. The amount of interest is only one factor; there are also others such as the certainty of the debenture holder regaining his money if the firm had to close down. The precise terms of the exchange cannot be based merely on arithmetical calculations of interest rates, but it is one of the measures taken when negotiating the exchange of debentures.

Exhibit 6.7

1 D Ltd is to give the necessary debentures at a discount of 10 per cent necessary to redeem £9,000 debentures in J Ltd at a premium of 5 per cent. The problem here is to find exactly what amount of debentures must be given by D Ltd.

Answer:

$$\text{Total nominal value of debentures to be redeemed (exchanged)} \times \frac{\text{Redeemable value of each £100 debenture of J Ltd}}{\text{Issue value of each £100 debenture of D Ltd}}$$

$$= \text{Total nominal value of D Ltd to be issued}$$

$$= £9,000 \times \frac{105}{90} = £10,500$$

Thus, to satisfy the agreement, debentures of D Ltd of a total nominal value of £10,500 are issued at a discount of 10 per cent to the debenture holders of J Ltd.

2 H Ltd is to give the necessary debentures at par to redeem £5,000 debentures in M Ltd at a premium of 4 per cent.

$$£5,000 \times \frac{104}{100} = \text{Debentures of £5,200 nominal value are given by H Ltd at par.}$$

REVIEW QUESTIONS

Advice:

Questions on the take-over of other businesses are frequently asked.

6.1 Duke Ltd is considering taking over immediately the business of M. McCarthy a sole trader. McCarthy's balance sheet is as follows:

Balance Sheet

	£
Fixtures	10,000
Motor van	4,000
Stock	3,000
Debtors	2,000
	19,000
Capital	19,000

The balance sheet of Duke Ltd is as follows:

Balance Sheet

	£
Machinery	15,000
Fixtures	21,000
Motor vehicles	6,000
Stock	13,000
Bank	25,000
	80,000
Share capital	50,000
Profit and loss	30,000
	80,000

Duke Ltd places the following values on the assets being taken over: Fixtures £7,000, Motor vehicles £3,500, Stock £1,000 and Debtors £1,500.

McCarthy says that he is willing to be taken over under any one of the following three alternatives:

(i) For £22,000 cash.
(ii) For 20,000 shares in Duke Ltd of £1 each at a premium of 20 per cent.
(iii) For 5,000 shares in Duke Ltd of £1 each at a premium of 20 per cent, and £17,000 of 8 per cent debentures at par.

Show the balance sheet of Duke Ltd as it would appear, after takeover, for each of the possible methods of takeover.

6.2 The balance sheet of Elton Presley, a manufacturer, stood as follows at 31 December 19X1:

	£
Capital	38,000
Plant and machinery (net book value)	26,000
Fixtures and fittings (net book value)	4,600
Stock	9,000
Debtors	6,200
Bank	1,200
	47,000
Less Trade creditors	9,000
	38,000

On 1 January 19X2, the business became a limited company called Nashville Limited. It had an authorised share capital of £70,000 divided into 60,000 ordinary shares of £1 each and 10,000 11 per cent preference shares of £1 each.

Nashville Limited took over the assets and liabilities of Elton Presley at the following agreed valuations.

	Agreed Valuation £	
Plant and machinery	17,000	
Fixtures and fittings	5,000	
Trade creditors	8,800	(less £1,200 which was paid out of Presley's bank account)

All other assets were taken over at book value.

The purchase price of the business, £41,000, was settled by the issue of:

£6,000 8% Debentures 20X1/20X6 at par;
£10,000 11 per cent preference shares of £1 each, issued at par and credited as fully paid; £20,000 ordinary shares at a premium of 25 per cent over par value, to be credited as fully paid.

(a) Prepare the journal entries, including narrations, to close the books of Elton Presley.

(10 marks)

(b) Prepare the balance sheet of Nashville Limited at 1 January 19X2. (9 marks)

(c) Explain your accounting treatment of the difference between the price paid for Elton Presley's business, and the net assets of that business. Suggest how this difference might be accounted for in a year's time, when the company has built up revenue reserves. (6 marks)

(University of London: GCE A-Level)

6.3X The directors of two limited companies, Sparrow Ltd and Owl Ltd, own all the shares in these companies. They have decided to amalgamate their companies. The new company, Kestrel Ltd, will follow the valuation policies of Sparrow Ltd. It has been decided to issue sufficient £2 Ordinary shares at £2.50 each in Kestrel Ltd to equal the total adjusted net assets in Sparrow Ltd and Owl Ltd. The balance sheets of Sparrow Ltd and Owl Ltd at the date of amalgamation are shown below.

Balance Sheet of Sparrow Ltd at 30 April 19X9

	£ Cost	£ Depreciation	£ Net
Fixed assets			
Premises	750,000	50,000	700,000
Plant and machinery	320,000	140,000	180,000
Office equipment	65,000	13,000	52,000
	1,135,000	203,000	932,000
Current assets			
Stock: Raw materials	62,500		
Finished goods	31,400		
		93,900	
Debtors	76,000		
Less provision for bad debts	2,280		
		73,720	
Bank		21,330	
		188,950	
Current liabilities			
Creditors		51,200	
			137,750
			1,069,750
Share capital			
600,000 £1 Ordinary shares			600,000
Reserves			
Share premium		150,000	
General reserve		250,000	
Profit and loss		69,750	
			469,750
			1,069,750

Notes:
(*a*) Sparrow Ltd values its stock on a FIFO basis.
(*b*) Its provision for bad debts is maintained at 3 per cent of debtors.
(*c*) It depreciates its buildings at 2 per cent p.a. on cost, its plant and machinery by 25 per cent p.a. on cost, and its office equipment by 10 per cent p.a. on cost. It considers that motor vehicles should be depreciated using the reducing balance method at 40 per cent p.a.

Balance Sheet of Owl Ltd at 30 April 19X9

	£	£	£
Fixed assets	Cost	Depreciation	Net
Premises	230,000	NIL	230,000
Motor vehicles	160,000	96,000	64,000
Office equipment	35,000	21,000	14,000
	425,000	117,000	308,000
Current assets			
Stock of finished goods		33,200	
Debtors (net)		48,510	
Bank		18,690	
		100,400	
Current liabilities			
Creditors	24,500		
Accruals	800		
		25,300	
			75,100
			383,100
Long-term liability			
12% Bank loan 19X1			120,000
			263,100
Share capital			
100,000 £1 Ordinary shares			200,000
Reserves			
General reserve		50,000	
Profit and loss		13,100	
			63,100
			263,100

Notes:
(*a*) Stock is valued on the LIFO basis. If the FIFO basis had been used there would be a difference of £2,300 at a time of rising prices.
(*b*) Owl maintains its provision for bad debts at 1 per cent of debtors.
(*c*) Owl has never charged depreciation on its buildings, which are now 5 years old and cost £150,000 originally. For the purposes of the amalgamation, Owl's land has been revalued at £105,000. Owl depreciates its office equipment by 40 per cent p.a. on cost. This equipment is now eighteen months old. Motor vehicles have been depreciated by 20 per cent p.a. on cost for the three years they have been owned by Owl.

It has been decided that Kestrel Ltd should repay Owl's bank loan on 1 May from the proceeds of an issue at par on the same date of £150,000 of 10 per cent debentures 19X4–X7, which will also provide funds for expansion.

Required:

A   A revaluation account for Owl Ltd. All workings should be clearly shown.   *(13 marks)*

B   A calculation of the number of shares in Kestrel Ltd which the directors of Sparrow Ltd and Owl Ltd respectively will be entitled to.   *(5 marks)*

C   A balance sheet of Kestrel Ltd as at 1 May 19X9, assuming that all the debentures have been issued.   *(14 marks)*

D   A discussion of the possible advantages and disadvantages that Sparrow Ltd and Owl Ltd might obtain by amalgamating to form Kestrel Ltd.   *(8 marks)*

(Total marks 40)

(University of Oxford Delegacy of Local Examinations: GCE A-Level)

6.4   At the close of business on 31 December 19X9, the partners of Combine and Company had the following balances on their capital and current accounts:

Capital accounts	£
Arthur	13,000
Barbara	12,000
Carl	10,000

Current accounts	£
Arthur	6,000
Barbara	5,000
Carl	2,000 (Debit)

At 31 December 19X9, the goodwill of the partnership was agreed at £38,000, but the goodwill account in the partnership's books had stood at a valuation of £2,000 for many years. Arthur, Barbara and Carl shared partnership profits and losses in the ratio 5:3:2 respectively.

On 1 January 19X0, the partners decided to convert their partnership into a limited company, Unity Limited, and the following decisions were taken.

1   That the company should have an issued and fully paid up share capital of 60,000 ordinary shares of £1 each, to be issued amongst the partners in *equal* proportions.
2   That Arthur should acquire a vehicle owned by the partnership at a valuation of £1,500, which was £600 less than its book value. All other assets and liabilities will be transferred to the company.
3   Any balances remaining on partners' current accounts after the above decisions have been implemented should be transferred to partners' capital accounts. The balances on the capital accounts should then be settled by the partners paying in cash to or drawing out cash from the partnership bank account.

Assume that sufficient cash is available for this purpose.

(a)   Show the entries in the partners' capital and current accounts required to close off the partnership books.   *(8 marks)*

(b)   Show the opening balance sheet of Unity Limited as at 1 January 19X0.   *(3 marks)*

(c)   Advise Unity Limited regarding the permissible ways in which the asset of goodwill might be treated in the company balance sheet at 31 December 19X0.   *(4 marks)*

(University of London: GCE A-Level)

6.5X Penny and Victor are in partnership, sharing profits and losses in the ratio 3 : 2. On 31 May 19X0 the balance sheet of the partnership was as follows:

Fixed assets	£	£	£
Freehold land and buildings			52,000
Machinery			60,000
Fixtures			9,000
Motor vehicles			22,000
Computers			13,000
			156,000
Current assets			
Stock		9,000	
Debtors		12,000	
Bank and cash		3,000	
		24,000	
Current liabilities			
Creditors	7,000		
Loan from Connie	4,000		
		11,000	
			13,000
			169,000
Capital accounts			
Penny		102,000	
Victor		67,000	
			169,000

On 1 June 19X0, the partnership was dissolved, and a Company, PVC Limited was formed to take over the business. The following values were agreed:

	£
Goodwill	20,000
Freehold land and buildings	70,000
Machinery	40,000
Fixtures	6,000
Motor vehicles (*see* note 1)	7,000
Computers	12,000
Stock	9,000
Debtors	10,000
Bank and cash	3,000
Creditors	7,000
Loan from Connie (*see* note 2)	4,000

Notes:
1 Penny acquired one of the vehicles, which had a book value of £11,000, for her private use at an agreed valuation of £10,000.
2 Connie's loan was not taken over by the new company. Instead, the debt to Connie was settled by an issue of shares:

The authorised capital of the company was in the form of ordinary shares of £1 each, and they were issued at a premium of 70p each. The shares were allocated as follows:
(i) To Connie: the exact number of shares necessary for her to own $\frac{1}{40}$th of the new company.
(ii) To the partners: in the same proportion as the closing balances on their capital accounts.

3   No current accounts are maintained.

Required:

(a) The capital accounts of Penny and Victor, showing the entries required to close off the books of the partnership. *(12 marks)*

(b) The balance sheet of PVC Limited on 1 June 19X0. *(4 marks)*

(c) A breakdown of the shareholdings of Penny, Victor and Connie. *(4 marks)*

(d) An explanation of the permissible treatments of goodwill in the limited company's accounts, according to standard accounting practice. *(5 marks)*

(University of London: GCE A-Level)

6.6 Magnum Limited was incorporated on 1 January 19X0 with an authorised capital of £150,000 divided into ordinary shares of £0.50 each to acquire immediately the entire share capital of Micro Limited and the business of John and Mary Jones, a partnership.

The summarised balance sheets as at 31 December 19X9 of Micro Limited and John and Mary Jones are as follows:

	Micro Limited £	*John and Mary Jones* £
Freehold land and buildings	30,000	50,000
Plant and machinery	20,000	35,000
Stock in trade	18,000	9,000
Debtors	7,000	11,000
Balance at bank	5,000	3,000
	£80,000	£108,000
Ordinary shares of £1 each, issued fully paid	50,000	–
Capital accounts: John Jones	–	56,000
Mary Jones	–	40,000
Retained earnings	24,000	–
Creditors	6,000	12,000
	£80,000	£108,000

● A very recent purchase of shares in Micro Limited valued the shares at £1.40 each; it has been agreed that the sale of the share capital to Magnum Limited should be based on that share value.

● John and Mary Jones share profits and losses in the ratio 3:2 respectively.

● All the assets and liabilities, with the exception of the balance at bank, of John and Mary Jones are being acquired by Magnum Limited. The agreed purchase price of the partnership business is £110,000 to be satisfied by the issue of fully paid shares in Magnum Limited. For the purposes of the business purchase, the following revaluations have been agreed for assets of the partnership:

	£
Freehold land and buildings revalued at	60,000
Plant and machinery revalued at	29,000
Stock in trade revalued at	7,000

● The partnership balance at bank is to be taken over by John Jones.

- The Magnum Limited £0.50 ordinary shares are valued at £0.80 each.
- Following the sale of the partnership business, John and Mary Jones shared the resultant assets between themselves on an equitable basis.

Required:

(a) The balance sheet of Magnum Limited, in as much detail as possible, immediately after the completion of the transactions with Micro Limited and John and Mary Jones.   *(11 marks)*

(b) A statement showing the distribution of partnership assets between John and Mary Jones following the sale of their business.   *(10 marks)*

(c) Two distinct reasons why balance sheets may not be good indicators of the value of businesses.   *(4 marks)*

(Reproduced by permission of the University of Cambridge Local Examinations Syndicate)

6.7 Mater and Pater each own a small business and they agree to merge their respective businesses into a company, Family Limited, with effect from 1 October 19X0. It was agreed that the issued share capital of Family Limited should be 1000 shares of £1 each held equally between Mater and Pater, and on 1 October 19X0 they each paid £500 into a newly-opened company bank account.

Except for paying company formation expenses of £200, the company bank account was not used and Mater and Pater continued trading much as before except for using the company's name on all their stationery and letterheads. The accounting reference date for the company is fixed at 31 March. At 31 March 19X1, after preparing the profit and loss accounts of the separate businesses, the three trial balances appeared as follows:

	Mater Dr £	Mater Cr £	Pater Dr £	Pater Cr £	Family Limited Dr £	Family Limited Cr £
Share capital						1,000
Capital, 1 April 19X0		80,000				
Capital, 1 July 19X0				50,000		
Net profit, 12 months		18,000				
Net profit, 9 months				9,900		
Current assets	67,400		40,600		800	
Current liabilities		33,500		12,100		
Fixed assets, cost and depreciation						
1 April 19X0	90,000	27,000				
1 July 19X0			60,000	30,000		
Depreciation to 31 March 19X1						
12 months		9,000				
9 months				4,500		
Paid to Family Limited	500		500			
Formation expenses					200	
Drawings £800 per month	9,600					
£600 per month			5,400			
	167,500	167,500	106,500	106,500	1,000	1,000

Mater and Pater agree that:

1 All assets and liabilities are to be taken over by the Company on 1 October 19X0 at book values;

2   Goodwill is to be valued as follows: Mater £8,000, Pater £4,000. It is to be written-off in four equal annual instalments on the accounting reference date;

3   Any necessary apportionments are to be made on a strict time basis;

4   Directors' salaries are to be paid with effect from 1 October 19X0 at the following annual rates: Mater £12,000, Pater £9,000;

5   The balance due to Mater and Pater at 1 October 19X0 following the sale of their businesses are to be treated as loans to the company.

Required:

(a) A calculation at 30 September 19X0 of the net assets of the business of Mater and that of Pater.   *(7 marks)*

(b) A profit and loss account for the Company, Family Limited, for the six months ended 31 March 19X1.   *(6 marks)*

(c) The balance sheet of Family Limited at 31 March 19X1.   *(12 marks)*

(Reproduced by permission of the University of Cambridge Local Examinations Syndicate)

Chapter 7

Provisions, Reserves and Liabilities

7.1 Provisions

A **provision** is an amount written off or retained by way of providing for depreciation, renewals or diminution in value of assets; or retained by way of providing for any known liability of which the amount cannot be determined with 'substantial' accuracy. This therefore covers such items as **provisions for depreciation**. A **liability** is an amount owing which can be determined with substantial accuracy.

Sometimes, therefore, the difference between a provision and a liability hinges around what is meant by 'substantial' accuracy. Rent owing at the end of a financial year would normally be known with precision, this would obviously be a liability. Legal charges for a court case which has been heard, but for which the lawyers have not yet submitted their bill, would be a provision.

7.2 Revenue Reserves

A **revenue reserve** is where an amount has been voluntarily transferred from the profit and loss appropriation account by debiting it, thus reducing the amount of profits left available for cash dividend purposes, and crediting a named **reserve account**. The reserve may be for some particular purpose, such as a **foreign exchange reserve account** created just in case the firm should ever meet a situation where it would suffer loss because of devaluation of a foreign currency, or it could be a **general reserve account**.

Such transfers are, in fact, an indication to the shareholders that it would be unwise at that particular time to pay out all the available profits as dividends. The resources represented by part of the profits should more wisely and profitably be kept in the firm, at least for the time being. Revenue reserves can be called upon in future years to help swell the profits shown in the profit and loss appropriation account as being available for dividend purposes. This is effected quite simply by debiting the particular reserve account and crediting the profit and loss appropriation account in that future year.

7.3 General Reserves

A **general reserve** may be needed because of the effect of inflation. If in the year 19X3 a firm needs a working capital of £4,000, the volume of trade remains the same for the next three years but the price level increases by 25 per cent, then the working capital requirements will now be £5,000. If all the profits are distributed, the firm will still only have £4,000 working capital which cannot possibly finance the same volume of trade as it did in 19X3. Transferring annual amounts of profits to a general reserve instead of paying them out as dividends is one way to help overcome this problem. On the other hand it may just be the convention of conservatism asserting itself, with a philosophy of 'it's better to be safe than sorry', in this case to restrict dividends because the funds they would withdraw from the business may be needed in a moment of crisis. This is sometimes overdone, with the result that the firm has excessive amounts of liquid funds being inefficiently used, whereas if they were paid out to the shareholders, who after all are the owners, then the shareholders could put the funds to better use themselves.

Under normal circumstances the remaining balance carried forward on the profit and loss account is treated as a revenue reserve.

7.4 Capital Reserves

A **capital reserve** is normally quite different from a revenue reserve. It is a reserve which is *not* available for transfer to the profit and loss appropriation account to swell the profits shown as available for cash dividend purposes. Most capital reserves can never be utilised for cash dividend purposes; notice the use of the word 'cash', as you have seen in Chapter 4 that bonus shares may be issued as a 'non-cash' dividend.

The ways that capital reserves are created must therefore be looked at.

Capital reserves created in accordance with the Companies Acts

The Companies Acts state that the following are capital reserves and can never be utilised for the declaration of dividends payable in cash:

(a) capital redemption reserve – *see* Chapter 5.
(b) share premium account – *see* Chapter 4.
(c) revaluation reserve – where an asset has been revalued then an increase is shown by a debit in the requisite asset account and a credit in the Revaluation Account. The recording of a reduction in value is shown by a credit in the asset account and a debit in the Revaluation Account.

Capital reserves created by case law

There have been quite a few law cases to establish exactly whether an item would be a distributable profit or not and therefore available for cash dividend purposes. The difference determines whether an item should be transferred to a capital reserve account as not being distributable, or else to a revenue reserve account if it is distributable. These cases will have to be studied at the more advanced stages of accounting, and so will not be dealt with here.

7.5 Nature of Reserves

In Sections 7.2, 7.3, and 7.4 we have looked at how revenue reserves and capital reserves have been created. We must now get rid of a misconception, common among students and some businessmen alike, that reserves mean that somewhere there is an investment held in cash, or shares, or similar, which could be used to pay for whatever was needed by the company.

The creation of a reserve has come about by a debit entry and a credit entry in the books. A general reserve, for instance, has been created by debiting the appropriation account and crediting a general reserve account. It did not involve, at the same time, putting some money into a special bank account.

A company can therefore have quite large amounts of reserves and yet have a very large bank overdraft. Obviously if (say) £200,000 had been appropriated as a general reserve then that amount could not in that year have been paid out as a dividend. Labelling that amount as transferred to a general reserve account is a way of saying that we do not want to pay that amount out as dividends in that year. Therefore the bank overdraft will be £200,000 less than it would have been if the reserve had not been made, and it had instead been paid out as a dividend. This is not the same as saying that a specific investment or banking was made when the reserve was first made.

7.6 Calculation of Profits Available for Payments of Dividends in Cash

Only the 'realised profits' and 'realised losses' come into the calculations of how much can be paid (distributed) as cash dividends, the word 'cash' including payments by cheque. The Companies Acts define realised profits and losses as 'those profits and losses which are treated as realised in the accounts, in accordance with principles generally accepted with respect to the determination of realised profits and losses for accounting purposes at the time when those accounts are prepared'.

This means that what the accounting profession, at the time the accounts are prepared, accept as 'realised profits and losses' is exactly what the law will also accept as correct. In accounting, the realisation concept recognises profit or loss at the point when a contract is made in the market to buy or sell assets. The realisation concept should have been part of your earlier studies.

You have already been told that the law says that capital reserves can never be utilised in the calculation of the amount out of which dividends can be paid in cash. However, reserves which are not capital reserves can be brought into the calculations.

The reserves which are revenue reserves (i.e. they are not capital reserves) have been voluntarily transferred to reserve accounts named for each specific reserve, or else they are in the balance on the profit and loss account after appropriations. They have not been so appropriated because of the need to do it by law. Should the company at any future time, in its wisdom, decide to transfer any or all of them back to the credit of the profit and loss account, and then pay cash dividends out of the then total amount in the profit and loss account, there is nothing in law that says that this cannot be done.

Whether it would be wise from a financial point of view is another matter, and we cannot be too specific about it; it all depends on the circumstances. Let us also be aware that a reserve does not equal cash available for dividend purposes. Let us look at two companies, which, for whatever reason, wish to pay as large a dividend as possible. Their reserves and cash and bank balances are as follows:

	Company A £	Company B £
General reserve	50,000	20,000
Foreign exchange reserve	–	10,000
Asset replacement reserve	70,000	–
Inflation protection reserve	–	5,000
Balance on profit and loss account	30,000	25,000
Cash and bank balances	60,000	90,000

You can see that company A has a total of £50,000 + £70,000 + £30,000 = £150,000, which would be the total of profits available for dividend purposes. In theory it could pay out a dividend of £150,000 in cash. Would it do so?

Immediately you can see that company A only has £60,000 cash and bank balances. It would need another £90,000 from somewhere to be able to pay a dividend of £150,000. It is more than doubtful whether the bank, or anyone else, under normal circumstances would lend the company £90,000 for this reason. It is possible that there are extreme circumstances, which demand extreme answers.

For A-Level examinations you are often called upon to use your imagination and some knowledge of what happens in the real business world, in order to come up with answers which are rational enough but cannot be found within the pages of a textbook. Try to visualise when company A may in fact decide to pay a dividend of £150,000 given the above facts about the reserves and the cash and bank balances.

Here are some possibilities:

● an unwelcome takeover bidder has appeared. The company is advised that if it pays the maximum dividend possible, the takeover bid will be averted.

● a new system of taxation will mean that dividends will suffer tax at the rate of 98 per cent (a number of wealthy taxpayers did pay at this rate in the 1970s!). Payment of dividends before the new tax year will only suffer tax at 40 per cent. Most of the shareholders are wealthy people. The answer – pay out as big a dividend as possible now.

The £90,000 needed might possibly be raised by the issue of shares or debentures, or by selling off some unwanted fixed assets.

Under normal circumstances, it is likely that a much smaller dividend would be paid. If it was desired to pay a dividend of £50,000, then £20,000 could be transferred to the credit of the profit and loss account which, added to the existing balance of £30,000, would give profits available of £50,000. The company would decide how much to transfer from the other revenue reserves to make up this amount.

Company B has a total of £20,000 + £10,000 + £5,000 + £25,000 = £60,000 available for distribution as dividends. It has £90,000 cash and bank balances and, under normal circumstances, it could pay such a dividend. Whether it would do so would depend on the circumstances and needs of the company.

We must remember that the cash and bank balances are needed, not just for dividend purposes, but for all sorts of other necessary expenditures. We have to see the company as a whole, and to understand all of its needs, before we can say whether or not it would make sense to pay a particular rate of dividend.

7.7 Allowable Reductions of Capital Reserves

We have already seen that capital reserves cannot be used for the purpose of increasing profits available for *cash* dividend purposes. Within the confines of the GCE A-Level syllabuses, what they can be used for now follows. Beware, there are other uses, but these include topics which are not covered in your examinations and are, therefore, beyond the scope of this textbook.

Capital redemption reserve (for creation, *see* Chapter 5)

To be applied in paying up unissued shares of the company as fully-paid shares. These are commonly called 'bonus shares', and are dealt with in Chapter 4.

Share premium account (for creation, *see* Chapter 4)

(*a*) The same provision referring to bonus shares as exists with the capital redemption reserve.
(*b*) Writing off preliminary expenses.
(*c*) Writing off expenses and commission paid on the issue of shares or debentures.
(*d*) In writing off discounts on shares or debentures issued (for creation of these accounts, *see* Chapter 4).
(*e*) Providing any premium payable on redemption or purchases of shares or debentures.

Revaluation reserve

Where the directors are of the opinion that any amount standing to the credit of the revaluation reserve is no longer necessary then the reserve must be reduced accordingly. An instance of this would be where an increase in the value of an asset had been credited to the revaluation account, and there had subsequently been a fall in the value of that asset.

Reserves created by case law

These can be used in the issue of bonus shares or in the paying up of partly paid shares.

REVIEW QUESTIONS

Advice:

You can expect quite a lot of questions which have some bearing on this chapter. These are mainly:

(i)   to what uses you can put the reserves
(ii) the differences between capital and revenue reserves
(iii) an issue of bonus shares and the use of reserves thereby
(iv) to calculate exactly what dividends can be paid by cash from the balances of reserves and the profit and loss account
(v)   the use of the revaluation reserve

   Which kinds of reserves can be brought into the calculation of the maximum amount which could be paid out as *cash* dividends? This asks you to distinguish between *revenue* reserves which can be used for cash dividend purposes, whilst *capital* reserves cannot. On the other hand, capital reserves can be used in the calculations of how many (free) bonus shares can be issued to shareholders.

Examples:

(i)   A question which asks you to transfer a capital reserve back to the credit side of the profit and loss appropriation account. This cannot be allowed as it means in effect that it would swell the amount of profits available for distribution as cash dividends.
(ii) A question which asks you to revalue the property and to show the increase in the value on the credit side of the profit and loss appropriation account. This should be credited to a capital reserve account instead.

7.1 The following constitutes the share capital and reserves of Seeds Ltd and Plant Ltd:

		Seeds Ltd £	Plant Ltd £
Share capital:	£1 ordinary	200,000	300,000
	£1 Preference 10%	50,000	80,000
Share premium account		35,000	24,000
Asset revaluation reserve		10,000	–
General reserve		40,000	70,000
Foreign exchange reserve		5,000	–
Fixed assets replacement reserve		–	20,000
Profit and loss account before dividends		45,000	63,000

The companies have the following dividend policies:

Seeds Ltd: to retain a balance of £25,000 on the profit and loss account and to pay a preference dividend and the highest possible dividend on ordinary shares. All the relevant reserves can be called on for this purpose.

Plant Ltd: the same policy as Seeds Ltd, except that £40,000 is to be left in the general reserve account.

Required:

Showing your workings, calculate the percentage dividends which can be paid on ordinary shares for each company in keeping with the policies laid down.

7.2X The directors of Dennis plc are to meet shortly to consider the amount of dividend which they should pay to the shareholders of the company. The draft audited balance sheet shows the following reserves:

	£
Share premium account	60,000
Capital redemption reserve	100,000
Asset revaluation reserve	200,000
General reserve	50,000
Profit and loss account	100,000

The asset revaluation reserve arose during the year when a building was revalued from £300,000 to £500,000.

(*a*) State, with reasons, the extent to which each of the five reserves can be used for the payment of dividends. (*5 marks*)

(*b*) Calculate the maximum *percentage* dividend which could be paid, assuming that the issued share capital at the balance sheet date consisted of 2 million ordinary shares of 25p each. (*5 marks*)

(*c*) The company intends to replace its buildings in four years' time, at an anticipated cost of £1,500,000. It proposes to create an asset replacement reserve to ensure that sufficient cash is available to purchase the new buildings at the appropriate time. Comment on this proposal. (*5 marks*)

(*University of London: GCE A-Level*)

7.3 Grimble Limited's trial balance at 31 December 19X0 includes the following credit balances.

	£
Net profit for the year (before taxation and dividends)	265,500
Retained profits brought forward	188,300
9% Preference share capital (fully paid)	56,000
Ordinary share capital (fully paid)	280,000
Capital redemption reserve	147,000
7% Debentures	95,000

The directors make the following decisions which affect the draft accounts.

1 Taxation of £60,000 is to be provided for on the profits.
2 Capital redemption reserves are to be used for an issue of bonus shares in the ratio of one bonus share for every two shares held.
3 Whilst the first half-year's debenture interest and interim preference dividend had been paid and included within the draft accounts, the remaining amounts are still to be provided for.
4 Fixed assets are to be revalued upwards by £20,000.
5 No interim dividend on the ordinary shares has been paid, but a final dividend of 20p per share is proposed. No final dividend is to be paid on the bonus shares issued.

Required:

(a) The profit and loss appropriation account for the year ended 31 December 19X0. *(8 marks)*

(b) A revised extract from the company's trial balance after the five decisions have been incorporated within the accounts, showing all outstanding balances which can be calculated from the information available. *(7 marks)*

(*University of London: GCE A-Level*)

7.4X After the trading and profit and loss accounts had been drawn up for Lemon Limited for the year ended 31 May 19X9, the following balances remained in the accounts:

	Dr £	Cr £
Ordinary share capital (£1 shares)		170,000
10% redeemable £1 preference shares		50,000
Debtors and creditors	96,800	65,302
Goodwill	20,000	
Fixed assets	187,600	
Stock	34,080	
Bank balance	94,200	
Profit and loss account		117,378
Share premium account		30,000
	432,680	432,680

After the trial balance was extracted, the directors decided to:

1 convert the existing £1 ordinary shares into shares with a nominal value of 50p;
2 redeem the 10% redeemable £1 preference shares at a premium of 5% (the shares had been issued originally at a premium of 10%);
3 issue bonus shares by utilising the value remaining in the share premium account after allowing for the premium payable on the redemption of the preference shares;
4 write off the goodwill;
5 propose a dividend of 10p per share on all ordinary shares of 50p each, including those issued by way of bonus.

Required:

(a) Show the ordinary share capital account, the share premium account and the ordinary dividend account as they would appear after the above decisions were implemented. *(9 marks)*

(b) Prepare the (unpublished) balance sheet as at 31 May 19X9, after the implementation of all the directors' decisions and assuming no other transactions. *(10 marks)*

(c) Give two reasons why a company might wish to issue *bonus* shares to its existing shareholders. *(6 marks)*

(*University of London: GCE A-Level*)

7.5 Expansion plc is to issue shares to the public at the same time as a rights issue is made to its existing members. Bonus shares will also be issued.

The company's most recent balance sheet provides the following information:

	£
Paid up share capital	
100,000 preference shares at £1	100,000
500,000 ordinary shares at 50p	250,000
Reserves	
Share premium account	100,000
Capital redemption reserve	75,000
Revaluation reserve	100,000
General reserve	200,000
Asset replacement reserve	50,000
Profit and loss account	75,000
	£950,000

Authority to increase the company's capital has been obtained.

An extraordinary meeting of members has resolved the following:

(i) One bonus share is to be issued for each five ordinary shares held.
(ii) Both preference and ordinary shareholders will be allowed to subscribe for ten ordinary shares for every ten shares (excluding bonus shares) of either class held: 10p per share is payable on application and 80p on allotment.
(iii) Additional shares may be applied for both by existing shareholders and the public. Applications from existing shareholders are to be accepted in full before any allotments are made to the public: 25p per share is payable on application and £1.50 on allotment.

When the application lists closed it was found that:

(i) The rights issue was entirely taken up and no shareholder at the time held less than 10 shares. No shareholders held any fraction of 5 shares.
(ii) Existing shareholders applied for and were allotted 50,000 shares.
(iii) Members of the public sent in application monies for a further 75,000 shares, of which only 50,000 were allotted. The directors allotted two shares for every three applied for. No fractional adjustments were required.

Required:

(a) An extract from the company's balance sheet showing the shares and reserves after the allotments have taken place but before amounts due on allotment have been paid. *(10 marks)*

(b) A statement of the entries to be included in the bank account. *(4 marks)*

(c) An explanation of why shares are sometimes issued at a premium. *(4 marks)*
(*Welsh Joint Education Committee: GCE A-Level*)

7.6X The financial information below was extracted from the balance sheets of two companies as at 30 June 19X0.

	Postgate plc £000	Coalux plc £000
Authorised share capital		
£1 Ordinary shares	500	400
11% £1 Preference shares	250	–
Called up share capital		
£1 Ordinary shares, fully paid	350	400
11% £1 Preference shares fully paid	250	–
Reserves		
Share premium	150	200
Other capital reserves	250	100
Retained earnings	350	300
Loan capital		
9% Debenture stock (2008)	200	–
10% Debenture stock (2006)	–	50
Current liabilities	140	190

Additional information:

1   Both companies revalued their freehold land and buildings with effect from 1 July 19X0. The revaluations were as follows:

	Balance Sheet Value as at 30 June 19X0 £000	Balance Sheet Revaluation £000
Postgate plc	300	500
Coalux plc	150	200

2   The board of directors of Postgate plc had already approved a bonus issue of shares earlier in the year. The bonus issue is to be effected on 1 July 19X0 on the following terms:

One bonus share for every ordinary share currently held.

The issue is to be funded, one half from the capital reserves and one half from the retained earnings.

3   Coalux had approved a rights issue on the following terms:

One new ordinary share for every two ordinary shares currently held.

The issue price was fixed at £1.50 per share. The issue was fully subscribed and the funds received on 1 July 19X0.

Required:

(a)   For each of the companies explain the significance of the items **1** to **3** above on the financing of the company subsequent to 1 July 19X0.   *(8 marks)*

(b)   When a limited company is considering the raising of further capital, briefly identify the relative merits of:

   (i)   Ordinary shares
   (ii)   Debenture stock

   as sources of capital.   *(8 marks)*

(c) Explain what is meant by 'gearing', a term frequently used in the analysis of limited companies' balance sheets. *(4 marks)*

(d) Calculate a gearing factor for each of the companies, Postgate plc and Coalux plc, as at 2 July 19X0. *(5 marks)*

(Associated Examining Board: GCE A-Level)

7.7 The summarised draft balance sheet as at 30 April 19X0 of T. Torrents Limited is as follows:

	Cost	Aggregate Depreciation	
	£	£	£
Fixed assets			
Freehold land and buildings	60,000	4,000	56,000
Plant and machinery	47,000	14,100	32,900
Motor vehicles	16,000	9,600	6,400
	123,000	27,700	95,300
Current assets			
Stock		29,000	
Trade debtors and amounts prepaid		14,000	
Balance at bank		7,000	
		50,000	
Amounts falling due within one year			
Trade creditors and accrued charges		9,800	
			40,200
			135,500
Amounts falling due after more than one year			
8% Debenture stock			40,000
			£95,500
Represented by capital and reserves			
Ordinary shares of £1 each fully paid			60,000
Share premium account			10,000
Retained earnings			25,500
			£95,500

It has now been discovered that effect has not yet been given in the company's accounts for the year ended 30 April 19X0 to the following matters:

(i) On 1 May 19X9, the company sold machine KM623 for £5,000; this machine had been bought on 1 May 19X6 for £12,000. The company received goods valued at £5,000 in settlement for the machine. It is company policy for all plant and machinery to be depreciated at 12½ per cent per annum on cost.

(ii) On 30 April 19X0, the company purchased £6,000 of its 8 per cent Debenture stock for £5,200. The relevant cheque was not presented for payment until 4 May 19X0 and has been omitted from the company's cash book.

(iii) A provision for doubtful debts of 2½ per cent of debts outstanding at 30 April 19X0 is to be created; amounts prepaid at 30 April 19X0 amounted to £400.

(iv) The freehold land and buildings has been revalued at 30 April 19X0 at £70,000; it is proposed to give effect to this revaluation in the accounts.

(v) It has been discovered that a piece of equipment belonging to a customer and held by the company for repair was inadvertently added to the company's stock valuation at 30 April 19X0; the item was valued at £2,000.

(vi) The company made a bonus (scrip) issue of one ordinary share of £1 each for every twelve held on 31 December 19X9.

(vii) A final dividend for the year ended 30 April 19X0 on the ordinary share capital of 10p per share is being proposed.

Required:

(a) A corrected balance sheet as at 30 April 19X0 of T. Torrents Limited. *(22 marks)*

(b) Explain the reason for the creation of a share premium account. *(3 marks)*

(Reproduced by permission of the University of Cambridge Local Examinations Syndicate)

Chapter 8

Accounting Standards

8.1 Introduction

Let us assume that you have received a copy of the published final accounts of a company. You want to be sure that you can rely on the methods chosen by the business to calculate its profits and balance sheet values. Without this assurance you would not be able to have any faith at all in the figures, and could not sensibly take any decision concerning your relationship with the company.

Prior to the 1970s, there were very wide variations in the methods used in accounting. There was a general outcry in the national press against the failure of the accounting profession to lay down consistent principles for businesses to follow. This led to the accountancy bodies setting up an organisation to issue statements which would bring about more uniform methods in accounting.

You must appreciate that accounting is used in every kind of business and organisation. It can cover things as different as breweries, churches, mines, oilwells, betting shops, banks, cinemas, circuses, funeral undertakers, farms, waste disposal, deep-sea diving, airlines, estate agents and so on. Now to have very strict and detailed rules covering every aspect of accounting which all these types of organisations have to adhere to would be impossible. In addition, accounting deals with large multinational organisations and your local shop. The very diversity of type of business, and also of size, means that general principles can be laid down, but in detail what would make sense in one company would be absolutely stupid to apply in another company. Thus there has to be some flexibility within the rules laid down, although the general trend is to aim for more uniformity.

8.2 Accounting Standards Board

The organisation originally set up in 1970 by the accountancy bodies to issue details of more uniform methods called them 'Statements of Standard Accounting Practice', abbreviated as SSAPs. When the Accounting Standards Board (ASB) took over in 1990, a total of 25 SSAPs had been issued. Over the years since each of the SSAPs was issued, some had been revised, and some had been scrapped altogether. As part of the changeover in 1990, the accounting standards issued by the ASB are called Financial Reporting Standards (FRSs). The pre-ASB SSAPs remain in force until they are either scrapped or replaced by new FRSs. The ASB is more independent of the accounting bodies than its predecessor and issues its FRSs without formal approval from any other body. However, prior to the release of any new accounting standard, the ASB first releases an Exposure Draft, or FRED, invites comment upon it, and then adjusts the FRED appropriately before releasing it as an FRS.

While there is no general law compelling observation of the standards, accounting standards have had statutory recognition since the Companies Act 1989 was issued. As a result, apart from entities exempted from certain standards or sections within standards – SSAPs 13 (Research and development) and 25 (Segmental reporting), and FRS 1 (Cash flow statements), for example, all contain exemption clauses based on company size – accounting standards must be complied with when preparing financial statements intended to present a true and fair view. The Companies Acts state that failure to comply with the requirements of an accounting standard must be explained in the financial statements.

The main method of ensuring compliance with the standards has always been through the professional bodies own disciplinary procedures on their members. The ASB, however, set up a Review Panel that has power to prosecute companies under civil law where their financial statements contain a major breach of the standards.

8.3 International Accounting Standards

The Accounting Standards Board deals with the United Kingdom. Besides this there is an international organisation concerned with accounting standards. The International Accounting Standards Committee (IASC) was established in 1973. Representatives from each of the founder members, which includes the UK, sit on the committee as well as co-opted members from other countries.

The need for an IASC has been said to be mainly due to:

(a) The considerable growth in international investment. This means that it is desirable to have similar methods the world over so that investment decisions are more compatible.
(b) The growth in multinational firms. These firms have to produce accounts covering a large number of countries. Standardisation between countries makes the accounting work that much easier, and reduces costs.
(c) As quite a few countries now have their own standard setting bodies, it is desirable that their efforts should be harmonised.
(d) Poorer countries, which cannot afford to have standard setting bodies of their own, can adopt the international standards instead of setting their own.

In the United Kingdom the SSAPs and FRSs have precedence over International Accounting Standards. In fact most of the provisions of International Accounting Standards are incorporated in existing SSAPs, or FRSs. Each FRS indicates the level of compliance with the relevant IAS.

8.4 GCE A-Levels and Accounting Standards

The examination syllabuses, and the questions set, do not require you to have anything like a full knowledge of all the accounting standards. In fact, such a knowledge would fill a book of many hundreds of pages. Nevertheless, although some of the A-Level syllabuses may appear to have very little interest in accounting standards, they are included in the syllabuses and questions about them do appear in the A-Level examinations.

In this book we will deal with the accounting standards that appear in at least one A-Level syllabus. In fact, so important are accounting standards that, even though it is not specifically mentioned each time, the accounts shown to you in this book do conform with the accounting standards.

8.5 SSAP 2: Disclosure of Accounting Policies (issued 1971)

This standard, issued in 1971, does not set out to give a basic theoretical framework of accounting. It accepts the view that there may well be more than one accounting method which could be adopted in many cases, as the circumstances of different organisations will vary. Such varying practices may well be suitable in particular cases, but the users of accounting statements should be made aware of which practice has been used in each case.

SSAP 2 requires disclosure when the generally accepted accounting concepts are not complied with. The ones specifically mentioned as being generally applied are *accruals, consistency, going concern,* and *prudence.* SSAP 2 does not mention other concepts and conventions, although it accepts that there are concepts other than the four mentioned. This has been confirmed since SSAP 2 was first issued, a number of other concepts having been formally introduced by the Companies Acts and other accounting standards: the Companies Act 1985 introduced the concept of 'separate determination' – each item included in the financial statements must be evaluated separately before being included in the total for its class. FRS 2: *Accounting for subsidiary undertakings* introduced the 'control' concept, and FRS 5: *Reporting the substance of transactions* introduced the 'substance over form' concept.

Accounting bases are the methods for applying the fundamental accounting concepts to financial transactions and items in financial statements. In particular, they must be used for:

● determining the periods in which revenue and costs should be recognised in the profit and loss account;
● determining the amounts at which material items should be shown in the balance sheet.

Instances where accounting bases are important concerning the above, and the main bases available, are:
● stock and work-in-progress (bases available include FIFO, LIFO, and AVCO);
● depreciation of fixed assets (bases available include straight line method, reducing balance method, depletion unit method, and revaluation method).

Accounting policies are the accounting bases judged by management to be the most appropriate. There should be a note attached to the accounts explaining the policies chosen. Five examples are given to illustrate where judgements may easily vary:

1   methods of depreciating fixed assets;
2   the valuation of stocks and of work-in-progress;
3   capitalisation of development expenditure;
4   the recognition of profit on long-term contracts;
5   hire purchase or instalment transactions.

8.6 SSAP 4: Accounting for Government Grants (revised 1990)

Many different types of grant are, or have been obtainable from government departments. Where these relate to revenue expenditure, e.g. subsidies on wages, they should be credited to revenue in the period when the revenue expenditure is incurred. The principle is that the grants should be recognised in the profit and loss account so as to match with the expenditure to which they are intended to contribute.

Where there are grants relating to capital expenditure, then SSAP 4 states that they should be credited to revenue *over the expected useful economic life of the asset.* This may be achieved by treating the amount of the grant as a deferred income, a portion of which is credited to the profit and loss account annually, over the life of the asset, on a basis consistent with depreciation. The amount of the deferred credit should, if material, be shown separately. It should not be shown as part of shareholders' funds.

The same effect as treating the grant as deferred income would be achieved by crediting the grant to the fixed asset account and depreciating only the net balance of the cost of the asset over its lifetime (depreciation is thus reduced by the grant). However, although this method is acceptable in principle, it is considered to be illegal under the Companies Act 1985, para. 17 of Schedule 4, which requires the balance sheet value of a fixed asset to be its purchase price or production cost.

8.7 SSAP 9: Stocks and Long-term Contracts (revised 1988)

Due to the many varying kinds of businesses and conditions in companies, there simply cannot be one system of valuation for stocks and work in progress. All that the standard can do is to narrow down the different methods that could be used.

Stocks should be stated at the total of the lower of cost and net realisable value of the separate items of stock or of groups of similar items. Profit should not, except in the case of long-term contracts, be recognised in advance, but immediate account should be made for anticipated losses.

In the balance sheet (or in the notes), stocks should be sub-classified so as to indicate the amounts held in each of the main categories in the standard balance sheet formats (as adapted where appropriate) of the Companies Act 1985. (These categories are *raw materials and consumables, work in progress, finished goods and goods for resale,* and *payments on account.*)

Net realisable value consists of the expected selling price less any expenses necessary to sell the product. This may be below cost because of obsolescence, deterioration and similar factors. SSAP 9 also defines 'cost' and certainly in the case of a manufacturing business it will also include overhead expenses, so that prime cost could not be used. Cost is defined in SSAP 9 in relation to the different categories of stocks and work in progress as being:

> *that expenditure which has been incurred in the normal course of business in bringing the product or service to its present location and condition. This expenditure should include, in addition to cost of purchase [as defined later] such costs of conversion [as defined later] as are appropriate to that location and condition.*

Cost of purchase comprises purchase price including import duties, transport and handling costs and any other directly attributable costs, less trade discounts, rebates and subsidies.

Cost of conversion comprises:

(a) costs which are specifically attributable to units of production, i.e. direct labour, direct expenses and subcontracted work;

(b) production overheads (as defined later);

(c) other overheads, if any, attributable in the particular circumstances of the business to bringing the product or service to its present location and condition.)

Production overheads based on the normal level of activity, taking one year with another, should all be included including fixed production overheads. Obviously, neither selling nor general administration costs should be included in cost.

(Notice that abnormal costs should not be included, as they would not have the effect of increasing stock valuation.)

(The LIFO and base stock methods should not be used, as they do not provide an up-to-date valuation. Although LIFO is not accepted by the SSAP, the Companies Act 1985 accepts its use.)

The Standard does accept that replacement cost may, in certain circumstances, be acceptable and therefore the lower of replacement cost or net realisation value may be used since, again, this is in accord with the Companies Act 1985.

Long-term contract work

It is not proposed to discuss it here. Chapter 23 covers this aspect of SSAP 9 in greater detail.

8.8 SSAP 12: Accounting for Depreciation (revised 1987)

This SSAP applies to all fixed assets, except for:

1   Investment properties, dealt with in SSAP 19.
2   Goodwill, dealt with in SSAP 22.
3   Development cost, dealt with in SSAP 13.
4   Investments.

First of all some terms are defined:

- **Depreciation:** 'is the measure of wearing out, consumption or other reduction in the useful economic life of a fixed asset whether arising from use, effluxion of time or obsolescence through technological or market changes'.
- **Useful economic life:** 'of an asset is the period over which the present owner will derive economic benefits from its use'.
- **Residual value:** 'is the realisable value of the asset at the end of its economic life, based on prices prevailing at the date of acquisition or revaluation, where this has taken place. Realisation costs should be deducted in arriving at residual values'.
- **Recoverable amount:** 'is the greater of the net realisable value of an asset (at the date of the balance sheet) and where appropriate, the amount recoverable from its further use'.

Depreciation should be provided in respect of all fixed assets which have a finite useful economic life. It should be provided by allocating the cost less net realisable value over the periods expected to benefit from the use of the asset being depreciated. No depreciation method is prescribed, but the method selected should be that which produces the most appropriate allocation of depreciation to each period in relation to the benefit being received in that period through use of the asset. The depreciation should be calculated on the value as shown on the balance sheet and not on any other figure. It *must* be charged against the profit and loss account, and *not* against reserves.

Useful economic lives should be reviewed on a regular basis, normally at least every five years. Where the amended asset life would materially distort future results if treated normally, it should be treated as an exceptional item as defined by FRS 3: *Reporting financial performance* and included under the same statutory format heading as the ongoing depreciation charge.

The depreciation method may only be changed when to do so will result in an improvement in the true and fair view. A change in method does not constitute a change in accounting policy. When the method is changed, the net book value should be depreciated over the remaining useful economic life of the asset, commencing with the period when the change occurred. Where a change of method occurs, the effect, if material, should be shown as a note attached to the financial statements.

Asset revaluation

Asset revaluation is recommended and if a policy of revaluation is adopted, the valuations should be kept up to date. Any permanent reduction should be written off immediately, the remainder being written off over the asset's remaining useful economic life. Such adjustments are via the profit and loss account.

Depreciation should be charged irrespective of when the asset was revalued. An increased value arising from a revaluation does not mean that depreciation should not be charged. The new value is the one on which future depreciation should be based. Depreciation charged before revaluation should not be credited back to profit and loss.

According to paragraph 21 of FRS 3: *Reporting financial performance*, the profit or loss on the disposal of an asset should be accounted for in the profit and loss account of the period in which the disposal occurs as the difference between the net sale proceeds and the net carrying amount, whether carried at historical cost (less any provisions made) or at a valuation.

Land and buildings

Freehold land

As this normally lasts forever there is no need to depreciate, except in cases of reduction of value by such factors as land erosion, extraction of minerals, dumping of toxic waste, etc.

Buildings

These should be depreciated, except that if the amount is not material and life is expected to be very long then there will be no need to charge depreciation. If estimated residual value equals or is more than net value depreciation can be ignored.

Notes to accounts

The following should be disclosed:

1   Method of depreciation used.
2   Economic life or depreciation rate in use.
3   Total depreciation for period.
4   Depreciable assets – gross amount and accumulated depreciation.

8.9 SSAP 13: Accounting for Research and Development (revised 1989)

SSAP 13 divides research and development expenditure under three headings, except for the location or exploitation of oil, gas or mineral deposits, or where all expenditure will be reimbursed by a third party. The three headings are:

(a) **pure (or basic) research:** experimental or theoretical work undertaken primarily to acquire new scientific or technical knowledge for its own sake rather than directed towards any specific aim or application;

(b) **applied research:** original or critical investigation undertaken in order to gain new scientific or technical knowledge and directed towards a specific practical aim or objective;

(c) **development:** use of scientific or technical knowledge in order to produce new or substantially improved materials, devices, products or services, to install new processes or systems prior to the commencement of commercial production or commercial applications, or to improve substantially those already produced or installed.

Expenditure incurred on pure and applied research can be regarded as part of a continuing operation required to maintain a company's business and its competitive position. In general, one particular period rather than another will not be expected to benefit and therefore it is appropriate that these costs should be written off as they are incurred.

The development of new and improved products is, however, distinguishable from pure and applied research. Expenditure on such development is normally undertaken with a reasonable expectation of specific commercial success and of future benefits arising from the work, either from increased revenue and related profits or from reduced costs. However, development expenditure should be written-off in the year of expenditure, except in the following circumstances when it may be deferred to future periods:

1   there is a clearly defined project; and
2   the related expenditure is separately identifiable; and
3   the outcome of such a project has been assessed with reasonable certainty as to:
    (a) its technical feasibility; and
    (b) its ultimate commercial viability considered in the light of factors such as:
        (i)   likely market conditions (including competing products);
        (ii) public opinion;
        (iii) consumer and environmental legislation;
4   furthermore, a project will be of value only if:
    (a) the aggregate of the deferred development cost and any further development costs to be incurred on the same project together with related production, selling and administration costs is reasonably expected to be exceeded by related future revenues; and
    (b) adequate resources exist, or are reasonably expected to be available, to enable the project to be completed and to provide any consequential increases in working capital.

The elements of uncertainty inherent in the considerations set out in points 1 to 4 are considerable. There will be a need for different persons having differing levels of judgement to be involved in assessing the technical, commercial and financial viability of the project. Combinations of the possible different assessments which they might validly make can produce widely differing assessments of the existence and amounts of future benefits.

If these uncertainties are viewed in the context of the concept of prudence, the future benefits of most development projects would be too uncertain to justify carrying the expenditure forward. Nevertheless, in certain industries it is considered that there are numbers of major development projects that satisfy the stringent criteria set out above.

The Standard says that if the criteria are satisfied then expenditure may be deferred to the extent that its recovery can reasonably be regarded as assured. It is also required that where this policy is adopted, all projects meeting the criteria should be included.

If development costs are deferred, they should be amortised over the period of sale or use of the product.

At each accounting date the unamortised balance of development expenditure should be examined project by project to ensure that it still fulfils the criteria. Where any doubt exists as to the continuation of those circumstances the balance should be written-off.

Fixed assets may be acquired or constructed in order to provide facilities for research and/or development activities. The use of such fixed assets will usually extend over a number of accounting periods and accordingly they should be capitalised and written off over their usual life.

The Standard requires that accounting policy on research and development expenditure should be stated and explained. The total amount of research and development expenditure charged in the profit and loss account should be disclosed, analysed between the current year's expenditure and amounts amortised from deferred expenditure. Movement on deferred expenditure and the amount carried forward at the beginning and end of the period should be disclosed. Deferred development expenditure should be disclosed under intangible fixed assets in the balance sheet.

8.10 SSAP 17: Accounting for Post Balance Sheet Events (issued 1980)

Quite often there will be events occurring after a balance sheet date which will provide evidence of the value of assets, or of the amounts of liabilities, as at the balance sheet date. Obviously any event up to the balance sheet date will have affected the balance sheet. Once the board of directors have formally approved the financial statements it is very difficult to alter them. However, there is the period between these dates during which events may throw some light upon the valuation of assets or amounts of liabilities. SSAP 17 directs its attention to such events during this period.

SSAP 17 brings in two new terms – 'adjusting events' and 'non-adjusting events'.

Adjusting events

These are events which provide additional evidence relating to conditions existing at the balance sheet date. They require changes in amounts to be included in financial statements. Examples of adjusting events are:

(a) **Fixed assets.** The subsequent determination of the purchase price or of the proceeds of sale of assets purchased or sold before the year end.
(b) **Property.** A valuation which provides evidence of a permanent diminution in value.
(c) **Investments.** The receipt of a copy of the financial statements or other information in respect of an unlisted company which provides evidence of a permanent diminution in the value of a long-term investment.

(d) **Stocks and work in progress.**
  (i) The receipt of proceeds of sales after the balance sheet date or other evidence concerning the net realisable value of stocks.
  (ii) The receipt of evidence that the previous estimate of accrued profit on a long-term contract was materially inaccurate.
(e) **Debtors.** The renegotiation of amounts owing by debtors, or the insolvency of a debtor.
(f) **Dividends receivable.** The declaration of dividends by subsidiaries and associated companies relating to periods prior to the balance sheet date of the holding company.
(g) **Taxation.** The receipt of information regarding rates of taxation.
(h) **Claims.** Amounts received or receivable in respect of insurance claims which were in the course of negotiation at the balance sheet date.
(i) **Discoveries.** The discovery of errors or frauds which show that the financial statements were incorrect.

Non-adjusting events

These are events which arise after the balance sheet date and concern conditions which did not exist at that time. Consequently they do not result in changes in amounts in financial statements. They may, however, be of such materiality that their disclosure is required by way of notes to ensure that financial statements are not misleading. Examples of non-adjusting events which may require disclosure are:

(a) **Mergers** and acquisitions.
(b) **Reconstructions** and proposed reconstructions.
(c) **Issues** of shares and debentures.
(d) **Purchases and sales of fixed assets** and investments.
(e) **Loss of fixed assets** or stocks as a result of a catastrophe such as fire or flood.
(f) **Opening new trading activities** or extending existing trading activities.
(g) **Closing a significant part of the trading activities** if this was not anticipated at the year end.
(h) **Decline in the value** of property and investments held as fixed assets, if it can be demonstrated that the decline occurred after the year end.
(i) **Changes in rates of foreign exchange.**
(j) **Government action,** such as nationalisation.
(k) **Strikes** and other labour disputes.
(l) **Augmentation of pension benefits.**

8.11 SSAP 18: Accounting for Contingencies (issued 1980)

The definition given in SSAP 18 is that a contingency is:

> *a condition which exists at the balance sheet date, where the outcome will be confirmed only on the occurrence or non-occurrence of one or more uncertain future events. A contingent gain or loss is a gain or loss dependent on a contingency.*

The overriding concern is the concept of prudence. Quite simply, if one is in doubt then contingent losses must be taken into account but contingent gains are left out. If there is a material contingent loss then it should be accrued if it can be estimated with reasonable accuracy. Otherwise it should be disclosed by way of notes to the financial statements.

8.12 SSAP 22: Accounting for Goodwill (revised 1989)

A brief summary of SSAP 22 is as follows:

1   No amount should be attributed to non-purchased goodwill in the balance sheet of companies or groups.
2   Where goodwill is purchased, the account should be the difference between the fair value of the consideration given (the price paid) and the aggregate of the fair value of the net assets acquired.
3   The amount attributed to purchased goodwill should not include any value for intangible items. The amount paid for these should be included under the heading for intangible assets in the balance sheet.
4   Purchased goodwill should not remain on the balance sheet as a permanent item. It may either be:
    (a) written-off immediately on acquisition against reserves; or
    (b) amortised by charges against the profit and loss on ordinary activities over its useful economic life.
5   Where the fair value of the assets acquired exceeds the fair value of the consideration given (negative goodwill), the excess should be credited directly to reserves.
6   It should not be revalued but, if there is a permanent diminution in its value, it should be written-down immediately through the profit and loss account to its estimated recoverable amount.

Note: In the chapters dealing with consolidated financial statements, a figure for goodwill will often be calculated. It must be borne in mind that this is subject to the contents of SSAP 22 just as much as for a company simply buying the business of a sole trader or partnership.

8.13 FRS 1: Cash Flow Statements (revised 1996)

This was the first financial reporting standard issued following the setting-up of the Accounting Standards Board. It is covered in Chapter 43 of the seventh edition of *Frank Wood's Business Accounting 1*.

8.14 FRS 2: Accounting for Subsidiary Undertakings (issued 1992)

This financial reporting standard is dealt with exclusively in Chapters 11 to 12.

8.15 FRS 3: Reporting Financial Performance (amended 1993)

This is dealt with in Chapter 9.

8.16 FRS 4: Capital Instruments (issued 1993)

This is dealt with in Chapter 10, *see* Section 10.11.

8.17 FRS 5: Reporting the Substance of Transactions (issued 1994)

This standard lays down stricter rules on the 'substance over form' concept, to help stamp out dubious practices designed to make balance sheets look more healthy than they in fact are.

REVIEW QUESTIONS

Advice:

You are not supposed to know everything about the Accounting Standards and the Financial Reporting Standards. This chapter has covered the essential ones for your examinations.

Questions are mainly related to see whether or not you can observe the standards. For example, a distinction has to be made as to what can be charged in the profit and loss account, or credited to it, when calculating net profit for the period. This brings out the point that some things have to be shown in the profit and loss appropriation account which is drawn up *after* the net profit for the period has been calculated, and under no circumstances can they be shown in the main profit and loss account itself.

If the rules were not adhered to then you could not in any way compare this year's net profit with that of last year or any other previous period. Most shareholders and would-be investors place a very high reliance on the net profit figure; therefore it must contain only those things that can properly be charged or credited.

Examples:

(i)   A question which suggests that depreciation should be charged to the appropriation account instead of to the main profit and loss account. This would affect net profit calculations and cannot be allowed.

(ii) It might be suggested that depreciation should not be charged at all for the year on a fixed asset or group of fixed assets. This normally conflicts with SSAP 12 and cannot be allowed.

(iii) Another suggestion may be to carry forward the closing stock at a higher figure than the lower of cost or net realisable value. Normally this cannot be allowed. You are not asked to have knowledge of the extreme cases where this could be otherwise.

(iv) Examiners sometimes try to see if you realise that SSAP 22: *Accounting for Goodwill*, does not allow companies to open accounts for goodwill *unless* they have purchased it. The usual ploy is for the examiner to suggest in a question that because the company has developed such a good reputation over the years the company balance sheet should show a figure for goodwill even though it has not been purchased. This is simply *not* allowed per SSAP 22.

8.1   Queries plc directors have asked you for your advice on items concerning their published accounts. Give your replies in brief form.

(*a*)   Toxic waste has been dumped on some of the freehold land we own. We believe that land should not be depreciated; therefore we cannot charge anything against profits for depreciation.

(*b*)   A fire occurred in the warehouse three days after the financial year end and destroyed £100,000 of goods.

(*c*)   At the year end a law case concerning one of our products is in court. It looks likely that we will have damages estimated almost certainly at £10 million awarded against us.

(*d*)   They estimate goodwill as being worth £50 million, and would like to show it as an asset on the balance sheet.

(*e*)   Another business has been taken over. Assets worth £100 million have been bought for £80 million. We wish to credit £20 million profit to profit and loss.

(f) Some stock of rare metals has shown a large appreciation because of world shortages. We would like to show that stock at its market price in the accounts.

(g) In the directors' opinion it is pointless showing the figure for earnings per share (EPS) as no shareholder has been known to ask for it.

(h) Shareholders prefer the old type funds flow statement (working capital) rather than the cash flow statement. They want to publish the working capital type of statement.

8.2X Ponders Ltd has had a directors' board meeting to which you were invited. During the course of it you were asked the following questions:

(a) Some of our stock is valued at a very low figure as it is currently unusable, and is of no value to anyone else. However, we think there is a possibility of a world shortage of this material in ten years' time. Can we therefore show it at a higher value to reflect this?

(b) We have depreciated land at the same rate as buildings. Need we have done this?

(c) We want to revalue buildings upwards to show the current values. However, we would like to keep depreciation based on the old cost figures, as otherwise our profits will be depressed. Can we do this and keep within the law?

(d) We spend 10 per cent of expenditure on research and development. This amounted to £5 million in the last year. £1 million of this was for land and buildings for use and £4 million on pure and applied research. We can never forecast whether our products will be successful, ours is an industry of chance and luck. Do we have to charge all of the £5 million as expenses against profits?

(e) Can we charge goodwill purchased against profits of this year, or do we have to carry it forward as an asset?

What is your advice to the directors?

8.3 Henry Tompkins who has a little accounting knowledge has just completed the draft final accounts of his company for the year ended 31 May 19X2. The profit, before taxation, of £40,000 is in line with forecast, a matter of much satisfaction for Henry Tompkins particularly during a period of recession.

However, in preparing the accounts it appears that Henry Tompkins made the following decisions:

(i) Depreciation on all fixed assets, other than freehold property, has been provided at half the normal annual rate to allow for the reduced level of activity in the business, the relevant charge in the accounts being £4,000.

(ii) No depreciation has been provided on the freehold property since a recent surveyor's report commented favourably on the standard of maintenance and indicated that overall the property had increased in value.

Note: In the previous year depreciation of freehold property amounted to £8,000.

(iii) A transfer of £18,000 was made from the share premium account to the profit and loss account. This transfer has resulted in the net profit being increased.

(iv) Loan stock interest paid of £15,000 (gross of tax) was included with dividends on the company's ordinary shares as an appropriation of profits. In the opinion of Henry Tompkins, loan stock and ordinary shares are both part of the long-term capital of the company.

Required:

A reasoned comment on the justification for each of Henry Tompkins' decisions.

Note: If any adjustments to the profit, before taxation, of £40,000 are considered necessary, answers should include a detailed statement of the corrected profit, before taxation, for the year ended 31 May 19X2. *(25 marks)*

(Reproduced by permission of the University of Cambridge Local Examinations Syndicate)

8.4X The managing director of Ahlan plc was rather concerned that the provisional final accounts for the company's year ended 31 May 19X0 showed only a very small profit of £50,000.

Recently he had read an article on 'Creative Accounting' and as a consequence of the contents of this document he made the following proposals to the company accountant in order to improve the reported profit:

1   Transfer from general reserve a sum of £800,000 and add it to this year's profit. The managing director reasoned that reserves were there to be drawn upon when times were bad.
2   Revalue the company's freehold land and buildings (current valuation £10m; valued on 1 January 19X0) in anticipation of future rising inflation. The managing director anticipated that the land and buildings would be worth £15m in 5 years' time. The increase in the valuation could be credited to the profit and loss account since the anticipation of this profit could help to smooth out the profit trend.
3   A large stock of raw material (cost £250,000) was redundant. The market value was only £20,000. The loss on stock had already been written off the current year's profit. The managing director argued that it would not be inconvenient to carry the stock for a further year and retain its value at cost. This would show a higher profit.
4   Of the overheads entered in the profit and loss account £150,000 had not yet been paid. If they were temporarily removed from the profit and loss account, the net profit would be higher and the managing director was sure that the creditors would not mind waiting two or three months.

Required:

As the company accountant prepare a report to the managing director of Ahlan plc. Your report should carefully consider **each** of the proposals bearing in mind generally accepted accounting concepts and principles.

(23 marks)

(Associated Examining Board: GCE A-Level)

8.5   A trainee accounting clerk was presented with the following information for three different firms.

1

BDK Ltd
Balance Sheet Extract as at 1 January 19X1

	At cost £	Aggregate depreciation £	Net £
Fixed assets	150,000	(51,000)	99,000

Depreciation has been charged on a straight line basis at 10 per cent per annum on cost. The company charges a full year's depreciation on all fixed assets owned at the end of the accounting year.

During the year ended 31 December 19X1 additional fixed assets were bought for £110,000 on 1 May 19X1. There were no other purchases or sales of fixed assets.

After drawing up the final accounts for 19X1 the company accountant decided to change the basis of calculating depreciation on fixed assets to the reducing balance method. The rate is to be 20% per annum.

2   Paula Rowe Ltd, a retailer, reported the following information for the accounting year ended 31 March 19X1:

	£
Gross profit	50,000
Less Expenses	40,000
Net profit	10,000

The company had agreed and paid for an advertising campaign on 1 April 19X0 at a total cost of £15,000. The campaign commenced on that date and is to continue at a uniform rate until 31 March 19X2.

3   Rendell Stott Ltd, a wholesaler, provided the following information for the accounting year ended 30 April 19X2.

	£		£
Gross profit	80,000	Carriage onwards	3,400
Rent and rates	2,000	Other selling expenses	2,500
Heating and lighting	1,050	Depreciation of fixed assets	8,000
Wages and salaries	19,000	Discounts allowed	1,700
Bad debts written off	20,000	Bank interest	2,500
Advertising	1,500	Insurance	1,400
Motor vehicle expenses	4,600	Postage and stationery	900

Note: Over the last five years bad debts written off had averaged £3,000 per annum.

Required:

(a) Explain what is meant by the:
    (i)   going concern concept;
    (ii)   consistency concept;
    (iii) accruals concept;
    (iv)   materiality concept.   *(10 marks)*

(b) In each of the following identify which of the above accounting concepts should be applied and why:
    (i)   BDK Ltd's treatment of depreciation.
    (ii)   Paula Rowe Ltd's treatment of advertising.
    (iii) Rendell Stott Ltd's treatment of bad debts.   *(8 marks)*

(c) (i)   Calculate the effect on profit for the year ended 31 December 19X1 caused by a change in depreciation in BDK Ltd.
    (ii   Calculate a revised profit for Paula Rowe Ltd for the year ended 31 March 19X1.
    (iii) Draft an appropriately **summarised** profit and loss account for Rendell Stott Ltd for the year ended 30 April 19X2.   *(7 marks)*

(Associated Examining Board GCE A-Level)

8.6X Patrick and Bernard own, in equal shares, the capital of Pompadour Limited, a private manufacturing company formed just over one year ago. The first draft accounts have been prepared as follows:

Balance Sheet – 30 April 19X1

	£000s	£000s		£000s
Plant, equipment at cost	950		Ordinary share capital –	
Less Depreciation	285	665	£1 shares	500
Stock of finished units		240		
Debtors		230	Trade Creditors	535
Profit and loss account		165	Bank overdraft	265
		1,300		1,300

Profit and loss account – year ended 30 April 19X1

	£000s	£000s
Sales (50,000 units at £20 each)		1,000
Less Direct materials	290	
Direct labour	550	
Cost of 70,000 units	840	
Less Stock of 20,000 units	240	
	600	
Depreciation of plant and equipment	285	
Factory overheads	90	
Administration and selling expenses	140	
Research and development expenses	30	
Advertising	20	1,165
Loss for the year		165

You ascertain that:

1 Research and development expenditure is mainly salaries and the cost of materials used in technical experiments and then thrown away.

2 Advertising (£20,000 above) represents a non-returnable deposit to an advertising agency for a campaign to begin later in 19X1.

3 Depreciation has been provided using the reducing balance method (at a rate of 30 per cent) so as to substantially reduce the book value of plant and equipment. The plant and equipment has an estimated useful life of five years with no scrap value.

4 The company has no stocks of raw materials or work in progress.

Patrick and Bernard are surprised at the poor results shown in the above draft accounts. They tell you that sales in the first year were higher than expected and that production at 70,000 units is in line with productive capacity and expected future demand.

To improve the financial figures they propose that the following policies be adopted:

1 Depreciation is to be provided using the straight-line method.

2 A suitable proportion of depreciation and factory overheads is to be included in valuing the stock of finished goods.

3 Advertising and research and development expenditure is to be carried forward and charged next year when the benefits of the expenditure is expected to be seen.

4 The expected profits from an order for 5000 units at £25 each received on 2 May 19X1 should be included in the accounts because the hard work to obtain the order was done in April 19X1.

5 Self-created goodwill of £25,000 should be included in the accounts at 30 April 19X1.

6 Cheques totalling £40,000 and received from debtors in May 19X1 and relating to sales made before 30 April 19X1 should be deducted from the bank overdraft and debtors at 30 April 19X1 so as to improve the current ratio.

Required:

(a) Calculate the effect of the various suggestions made on the accounts by redrafting the profit and loss account and balance sheet in accordance with the proposals made above.   *(15 marks)*

(b) Discuss the principles involved in each suggestion saying whether or not each should be adopted.   *(10 marks)*

(Reproduced by permission of the University of Cambridge Local Examinations Syndicate)

8.7X The practice of accounting is firmly based upon the application of the following concepts:

(1) going concern
(2) accruals
(3) consistency
(4) prudence
(5) materiality

Required:

State clearly your understanding of **each** of these concepts and illustrate the manner in which **each** concept influences the accounts of a business.   *(5 × 6 marks)*

(Associated Examining Board: GCE A-Level)

8.8X "Bad accounting drives out good, and that was what was happening from the mid-1980s on."
            Professor Sir David Tweedie, Chairman of the Accounting Standards Board

With reference to any four areas covered by Statements of Standard Accounting Practice (SSAPs) or Financial Reporting Standards (FRSs), explain why you think that the standards help or hinder "good accounting".   *(20 marks)*

(University of London Examinations and Assessment Council: GCE A-Level)

8.9X The directors of Noggs Limited have valued their stocks at £450,000 at 31 December 19X5. Some of the stock items have been drawn to the attention of the company's auditors:

(i) Two categories of stocks, Nimms and Quibs, have been valued at £23,000. The auditors ascertain that the valuation was based on what the directors considered was the lower of cost and net realisable value, calculated as follows:

	Cost of Raw Materials	Attributable Production Overheads Incurred	Attributable Distribution Overheads to be Incurred	Expected Selling Price
	£	£	£	£
Nimms	16,000	2,000	2,400	17,000
Quibs	4,000	1,000	2,000	8,000
	20,000	3,000	4,400	25,000

Cost	23,000	
Net Realisable Value		29,400

(ii) A raw material, Opprobrium, was bought at several different prices during the year, and the closing stock was valued on a Last In First Out (LIFO) basis. The stock has previously been valued on a First In First Out (FIFO) basis. Stock is valued on a periodic basis. Details of the stock are:

19X5	Received (tonnes)	Cost per tonne £	Issued (tonnes)
Jan	500	35	200
Mar	300	45	500
Jun	600	65	400
Nov	800	90	100

There were no stocks of Opprobrium on 1 January 19X5.

(a) Recalculate the value of Noggs Limited's closing stock at 31 December on the basis of generally accepted accounting principles. *(10 marks)*

(b) Explain the accounting concept which underlies the requirement to value stock at the lower of cost and net realisable value. *(5 marks)*

(University of London Examinations and Assessment Council: GCE A-Level)

Chapter 9

The Published Final Accounts of Limited Companies: Profit and Loss Accounts

9.1 Introduction

When a company draws up its own final accounts, purely for internal use by directors and the management, then it can draft them in any way which is considered most suitable. Drawing up a trading and profit and loss account and balance sheet for the firm's own use is not necessarily the same as drawing up such accounts for examination purposes. If a firm wishes to charge something in the trading account which perhaps in theory ought to be shown in the profit and loss account, then there is nothing to prevent the firm from so doing. On the other hand, the examinee's answers must be based on accounting theory and not on the practice of any particular firm.

When it comes to publication, i.e. when the final accounts are sent to the shareholder or to the Registrar of Companies, then the Companies Acts lay down the information that *must* be shown, and also *how* it should be shown. Prior to 1981, provided the necessary information was shown it was completely up to the company exactly *how* it did so. The provisions of the 1981 Act brought the United Kingdom into line with the Fourth Directive of the EC, and the freedom previously available to companies on how to show the information was removed. There are, however, some advantages to be gained from such standardisation.

9.2 Layout of Accounts

The Companies Acts do, nevertheless, give companies the choice of two alternative formats (layouts) for balance sheets, and four alternative formats for profit and loss accounts. As the reader for this chapter will most probably be studying this for the first time, it would be inappropriate to give all the details of all the formats. In this book, therefore, the reader will be shown an internal profit and loss account which can easily be adapted to cover publication requirements under the Acts, along with a balance sheet.

All companies, even the very smallest, have to produce accounts for shareholders giving the full details required by the Acts. 'Small' and 'medium-sized' companies can, however, file summarised accounts with the Registrar of Companies, but they must still prepare full accounts for their shareholders. In addition, listed companies may send their shareholders summary financial statements in place of the full version, unless a shareholder specifically requests a full version. These points will be examined later.

(At the time of writing, a 'small' company is one for which two of the following are true: turnover does not exceed £2.8 million; the balance sheet total does not exceed £1.4m; the average number of employees does not exceed 50. For 'medium-sized' companies, the equivalent limits are £11.2 million, £5.6 million, and 250 employees.)

Of the four formats which could be used, the format that will be used for the published profit and loss account in this book is Format 1. It is in a vertical style, which is much more modern and also more likely to gain extra marks from examiners and, in addition, it is much more like common UK practice before 1981. The other Formats, not shown in this book, are Format 2 (vertical style) and Formats 3 and 4 (horizontal style).

9.3 Format 1

The Companies Acts show Format 1 as in Exhibit 9.1.

Exhibit 9.1

Profit and loss account formats

Format 1

1 Turnover
2 Cost of sales
3 Gross profit or loss
4 Distribution costs
5 Administrative expenses
6 Other operating income
7 Income from shares in group undertakings
8 Income from participating interests
9 Income from other fixed asset investments
10 Other interest receivable and similar income
11 Amounts written off investments
12 Interest payable and similar charges
13 Tax on profit or loss on ordinary activities
14 Profit or loss on ordinary activities after taxation
15 Extraordinary income
16 Extraordinary charges
17 Extraordinary profit or loss
18 Tax on extraordinary profit or loss
19 Other taxes not shown under the above items
20 Profit or loss for the financial year

This is simply a list and it does not show where subtotals should be placed. The important point is that the items 1 to 20 have to be displayed in that order. If some items do not exist for the company in a given year, then those headings will be omitted from the published profit and loss account. Thus, if the company has no investments, items 7, 8, 9, 10, and 11 will not exist, and item 6 will be followed by item 12 in that company's published profit and loss account. The category reference numbers on the left-hand side of items do not have to be shown in the published accounts.

9.4 Accounts for Internal Use

Exhibit 9.2 shows a trading and profit and loss account drawn up for internal use by a company.

Exhibit 9.2 (accounts for internal use)

Block plc

Trading and Profit and Loss Account for the year ended 31 December 19X6

	£000	£000	£000
Turnover			800
Less Cost of sales:			
Stock 1 January 19X6		100	
Add Purchases		525	
		625	
Less Stock 31 December 19X6		125	
			500
Gross profit			300
Distribution costs:			
Salaries and wages	30		
Motor vehicle costs: Distribution	20		
General distribution expenses	5		
Depreciation: Motors	3		
Machinery	2	60	
Administrative expenses			
Salaries and wages	25		
Motor vehicle costs: Administration	2		
General administration expenses	7		
Auditors' remuneration	2		
Depreciation: Motors	3		
Machinery	1	40	
			100
			200
Other operating income			30
			230
Income from shares in group undertakings		20	
Income from participating interests		10	
Income from shares from non-related companies		5	
Other interest receivable		15	
			50
			280
Amounts written off investments		4	
Interest payable:			
Loans repayable within five years	10		
Loans repayable in ten years' time	6		
		16	
			20
Profit on ordinary activities before taxation			260
Tax on profit on ordinary activities			95
Profit on ordinary activities after taxation			165
Retained profits brought forward from last year			60
			225
Transfer to general reserve		40	
Proposed ordinary dividend		100	
			140
Retained profits carried forward to next year			85

There are no statutory rules concerning how financial statements are drawn up for internal use. However, if the internal accounts were drawn up in a completely different fashion to those needed for publication, then there would be quite a lot of work needed in order to reassemble the figures into a profit and loss account for publication. In Exhibit 9.2 the internal accounts have been drawn up in a style which makes it much easier to get the figures for the published profit and loss account. Examination questions on this topic may ask for both (a) internal and (b) published accounts and it therefore makes it simpler for students if the internal and published accounts follow a similar order of display.

9.5 Accounts for Publication

Note that there are no items in Exhibit 9.2 that would appear under items 15 to 19 in Companies Act Format 1.

Exhibit 9.3 (Accounts for publication)

Block plc

Profit and Loss Account for the year ended 31 December 19X6

	£000	£000
1 Turnover		800
2 Cost of sales		500
3 Gross profit		300
4 Distribution costs	60	
5 Administrative expenses	40	
		100
		200
6 Other operating income		30
		230
7 Income from shares in group undertakings	20	
8 Income from participating interests	10	
9 Income from other fixed asset investments	5	
10 Other interest receivable	15	
		50
		280
11 Amount written off investments	4	
12 Interest payable and similar charges	16	
		20
Profit on ordinary activities before taxation		260
13 Tax on profit on ordinary activities		95
14 Profit on ordinary activities after taxation		165
Retained profits from last year		60
		225
Transfer to general reserve	40	
Proposed ordinary dividend	100	
		140
Retained profits carried to next year		85

Exhibit 9.3 redrafts Exhibit 9.2 into a form suitable for publication according to Format 1, showing only the minimum information that the Companies Acts force us to disclose. These are known as the accounts for publication. The category reference numbers to the left-hand side of Exhibit 9.3 are for the benefit of the reader of this book – they *do not* have to be included.

It would be legally possible for the internal accounts, as shown in Exhibit 9.2 to be published just as they are, because all the items are shown in the correct order. This would not have been possible if the internal accounts were drafted in a completely different order. However, the Companies Act does not force companies to publish full accounts, as a company's competitors may thereby be given information which would lead to them being placed in a better competitive position against the company. The law therefore states the minimum information which must be disclosed. A company can show more than the minimum should it so wish.

Notice also that instead of all the detail regarding cost of sales (2) Distribution costs (4), Administrative expenses (5) shown in the internal set of accounts only the final totals have to be shown.

For the GCE A-Level examinations you do not need a detailed knowledge of all the provisions regarding published accounts. In this book you will find a coverage which, for safety's sake, slightly exceeds what the author thinks you need to know.

9.6 FRS 3: Reporting Financial Performance

Accounting is not a static subject. Changes occur over the years as they are seen to be necessary, and also get general agreement as to their usefulness. Since the advent of SSAPs and FRSs the number of changes that practitioners and students have had to learn has increased at a very fast rate. A prime example of this is the introduction of FRS 3, which necessitates changes to the formats of profit and loss accounts when certain events have occurred.

This Standard superseded SSAP 6: *Extraordinary items and prior year adjustments*, amended SSAP 3: *Earnings per share*, and also made changes as a consequence to various other accounting standards.

Suppose that you are considering the affairs of a business over the years. The business has not changed significantly, there have been no acquisitions, no discontinued operations, no fundamental reorganisation or restructuring of the business, nor have there been any extraordinary items affecting the accounts. In these circumstances, when comparing the accounts over the years, you are comparing like with like, subject to the problem of the effect of inflation or deflation.

On the other hand, suppose that some of the things mentioned have occurred. When trying to see what the future might hold for the company, simply basing your opinions on what has happened in the past can be very confusing.

To help you to distinguish the past and the future, and to give you some idea as to what changes have occurred, FRS 3 requires that the following are highlighted in the profit and loss account if they are material in amount:

(a) *What the results of continuing operations are, including the results of acquisitions.* Obviously acquisitions affect future results, and are therefore included in continuing operations.

(b) *What the results have been of discontinued operations.* This should help distinguish the past from the future.

(c) *The profits or losses on the sale or termination of an operation, the costs of fundamental reorganisation or restructuring, and the profits and losses on the disposal of fixed assets.* The profits and losses concerning these matters are not going to happen again, and so this also helps us distinguish the past from the future.

We can see how FRS 3 requires (a), (b) and (c) to be shown on the face of the profit and loss account in Exhibit 9.4. Not only is the turnover split to show the figures relevant to continuing operations, acquisitions and discontinued operations, the operating profit is split in a similar fashion. In addition any profit or loss on the disposal of the discontinued operations would also be shown. Exhibit 9.4 is restricted to the first 6 categories of Format 1 as this is the part of the statement affected by these FRS 3 requirements. Once again, it uses Block plc for the example.

Exhibit 9.4

Block plc

Profit and Loss Account for the year ended 31 December 19X6 (extract)

			£000	£000
1	Turnover			
	Continuing operations		520	
	Acquisitions		110	
			630	
	Discontinued operations		170	
				800
2	Cost of sales			500
3	Gross profit			300
4	Distribution costs		60	
5	Administrative expenses		40	
				100
	Operating profit			
	Continuing operations		160	
	Acquisitions		60	
		(a)	220	
	Discontinued operations (loss)	(b)	(20)	
				200
	Profit on disposal of discontinued operations	(c)		10
				210
6	Other operating income			20
	Profit or loss on ordinary activities before interest			230

The items marked (*a*), (*b*) and (*c*) can be described as *exceptional* items. They are material in amount, they fall within the ordinary activities of the firm, and need to be shown so that the accounts will give a 'true and fair view'.

They are exceptional in that they are not the ordinary daily occurrence, but remember that they fall within the ordinary activities of the company. FRS 3 requires that three categories of exceptional items be shown separately on the face of the profit and loss account after operating profit and before interest, and included under the appropriate heading of continued or discontinued operations:

● profits or losses on the sale or termination of an operation;
● costs of a fundamental reorganisation or restructuring having a material effect on the nature and focus of the reporting entity's operations;
● profits or losses on the disposal of fixed assets.

Other exceptional items should be credited or charged in arriving at the profit or loss on ordinary activities by inclusion under the heading to which they relate. As they are exceptional (remember they are of material amounts) they should not be hidden from the reader of the accounts. The amount of each exceptional item should be disclosed in a note, or on the face of the profit and loss account, if necessary in order to give a true and fair view.

Other Statements and Notes Required by FRS 3

1 Statement of Total Recognised Gains and Losses

The *statement of total recognised gains and losses* is one of two new primary statements introduced by FRS 3. It shows the extent to which shareholders' funds have increased or decreased from all the various gains and losses recognised in the period, and enables users to consider all recognised gains and losses of a reporting entity in assessing its overall performance; an example of what would be included in the statement would be unrealised gains on fixed asset revaluations. Exhibit 9.5 presents an example of the statement using the data from Block plc. (*Note*: only the profit figure can be found in the profit and loss account. The others have been inserted to demonstrate what the statement looks like. Also, as with all these statements, including the profit and loss account, comparative figures would also be shown.)

Exhibit 9.5

Block plc

Statement of Total Recognised Gains and Losses

	19X6
	£000
Profit for the financial year	165
Unrealised surplus on revaluation of properties	12
Unrealised (loss)/gain on trade investment	(8)
	169
Currency translation differences on foreign currency investments	(5)
Total recognised gains and losses relating to the year	164
Prior period adjustment	(19)
Total gains and losses recognised since last annual report	145

2 Note of Historical Cost Profits and Losses

Where assets have been revalued, which obviously affects depreciation, it may have a material effect upon the results shown in the accounts using the revalued figures. If this is the case, FRS 3 requires that there should also be shown as a note what the profit and loss account would have been if the account had been shown using historical (i.e. not revalued) figures. The note should also show how the reported profit on ordinary activities (using accounts with revalued assets) can be reconciled with that calculated using historical figures, and should also show the retained profit figure for the financial year reported on the historical cost basis. The note should be presented immediately following the profit and loss account or the statement of total recognised gains and losses. An example of the note is presented in Exhibit 9.6. (*Note*: as with the statement of total recognised gains and losses, only the profit figure can be identified in the profit and loss account. Also, comparative figures should be shown.)

Exhibit 9.6

Block plc

Note of Historical Cost Profits and Losses

	19X6
	£000
Reported profit on ordinary activities before taxation	260
Realisation of property revaluation gains of previous years	12
Difference between a historical cost depreciation charge and the	
actual depreciation charge of the year calculated on the revalued amount	1
Historical cost profit on ordinary activities before taxation	273
Historical cost profit for the year retained after taxation, minority interests,	
extraordinary items and dividends (273 − 95 − 100)	78

3 Reconciliation of Movements in Shareholders' Funds

The profit and loss account and the statement of total recognised gains and losses reflect the performance of a reporting entity in a period, but there are other changes that can occur in shareholders' funds that these two statements do not disclose, and which can be important in understanding the change in the financial position of the entity – for example, a new share issue or goodwill written-off. For this reason, FRS 3 also gave the *reconciliation of movements in shareholders' funds* the status of a primary statement, its purpose being to highlight these other changes in the financial position. When shown as a primary statement (there is an option to show it as a note), the reconciliation should be shown separately from the statement of total recognised gains and losses. Exhibit 9.7 presents an example of the statement. (*Note*: the figures can be found in the other statements except for the new share capital, the goodwill written off and the opening shareholders' funds amounts. As before, comparative figures should also be presented.)

Exhibit 9.7

Block plc

Reconciliation of Movements in Shareholders' Funds

	19X6
	£000
Profit for the financial year	165
Dividends	(100)
	65
Other recognised gains and losses relating to the year (net)	(1)
New share capital subscribed	20
Goodwill written off	(25)
Net addition to shareholders' funds	59
Opening shareholders' funds (originally £321,000 before deducting	
prior period adjustment of £19,000)	302
Closing shareholders' funds	361

FRS 3 and Extraordinary Items

You have just seen that in FRS 3 some of the exceptional items have to be highlighted on the face of the profit and loss account, whilst others can be put under appropriate headings with notes giving details being attached to the accounts.

In Exhibit 9.3 all of these exceptional items will have been dealt with by the time that item 14, *profit or loss on ordinary activities after taxation*, has been reached. Extraordinary items, as per Format 1, would be shown after that as items 15, 16, 17, and 18.

Before FRS 3, the distinction between what was an exceptional item and what was an extraordinary item was not as well defined as it could have been. This led to directors of companies sometimes manipulating the figures for their own ends whilst keeping within the necessary legal boundaries.

They did this because the profit per item 14 was a very well-used figure for assessing how well, or otherwise, a company was being managed. It was a vital part of calculating the earnings per share (EPS) which is a main indicator to many people of the company's performance. If a favourable item could be called an 'exceptional item' it would increase the size of the profit per 14. On the other hand, should an item be unfavourable, and therefore lower the figure of profit per 14, then perhaps it could be (and it often was) called an 'extraordinary item' instead. In this way the profit per 14 could be shown at a higher figure than was really justified. Such actions could affect the stock exchange values of the company's shares.

FRS 3 is more strict about what is, or is not, an extraordinary item, and thus to be shown after item 14 in the profit and loss account. Extraordinary items should be:

(a) material items possessing a high degree of abnormality which arise from events or transactions that fall outside the ordinary activities of the business, and
(b) are not expected to recur, and
(c) do not include exceptional items, and
(d) do not include items relating to a prior period merely because they relate to a prior period.

Extraordinary items fall *outside* the 'ordinary' activities of a company, whereas exceptional items fall *within* them. 'Ordinary activities' are any activities undertaken by a reporting entity as part of its business and such related activities in which the reporting entity engages in furtherance of, incidental to or arising from these activities. Ordinary activities include the effects on the reporting entity of any event in the various environments in which it operates. It is little wonder that the ASB did not believe that anything could ever be described as an extraordinary item after the introduction of FRS 3.

FRS 3 and Prior Period Adjustments

A prior period adjustment is a material adjustment applicable to prior periods arising from changes in accounting policies or from the correction of fundamental errors. They do not include normal recurring adjustments or corrections of accounting estimates made in prior periods.

They are accounted for by restating the comparative figures for the preceding period in the primary statements and notes and adjusting the opening balance of reserves for the cumulative effect. The cumulative effect of the adjustments should also be noted at the foot of the *statement of total recognised gains and losses* of the current period (*see*

Exhibit 9.5). The effect of prior period adjustments on the results for the preceding period should be disclosed where practicable.

FRS 3 and Comparative Figures

Comparative figures should be shown for all items in the primary statements and the notes to the statements required by FRS 3. The comparative figures in respect of the profit and loss account should include in the continuing category only the results of those operations included in the current period's continuing operations.

REVIEW QUESTIONS

Advice:

It is important for you to know that the published profit and loss account of a company must show certain items in a given order.

The contents of FRS 3 are likely to attract quite a lot of questions in future. In particular the new definition of extraordinary items per FRS 3 will undoubtedly see quite a crop of questions. Some will come in the form of the directors of a company wanting to class something as extraordinary, and therefore shown after item 14, *Profit or loss on ordinary activities after taxation*.

9.1 From the following selected balances of Rogers plc as at 31 December 19X2 draw up (i) a trading and profit and loss account for internal use, and (ii) a profit and loss account for publication.

	£
Profit and loss account as at 31 December 19X1	15,300
Stock 1 January 19X2	57,500
Purchases	164,000
Sales	288,000
Returns inwards	11,500
Returns outwards	2,000
Carriage inwards	1,300
Wages and salaries (*see* note (*b*))	8,400
Rent and rates (*see* note (*c*))	6,250
General distribution expenses	4,860
General administrative expenses	3,320
Discounts allowed	3,940
Bad debts	570
Debenture interest	2,400
Motor expenses (*see* note (*d*))	7,200
Interest received on bank deposit	770
Income from shares in related companies (gross)	660
Motor vehicles at cost: Administrative	14,000
Distribution	26,000
Equipment at cost: Administrative	5,500
Distribution	3,500
Royalties receivable	1,800

Notes:
(*a*) Stock at 31 December 19X2 £64,000.
(*b*) Wages and salaries are to be apportioned: Distribution costs one-third, Administrative expenses two-thirds.

(c) Rent and rates are to be apportioned: Distribution costs 60 per cent, Administrative expenses 40 per cent.
(d) Apportion Motor expenses equally between Distribution costs and Administrative expenses.
(e) Depreciate Motor vehicles 25 per cent and Equipment 20 per cent on cost.
(f) Accrue auditors' remuneration of £500.
(g) Accrue corporation tax for the year on ordinary activity profits £30,700.
(h) A sum of £8,000 is to be transferred to general reserve.
(i) An ordinary dividend of £30,000 is to be proposed.

9.2 You are given the following selected balances of Federal plc as at 31 December 19X4. From them draw up (i) a trading and profit and loss account for the year ended 31 December 19X4 for internal use and (ii) a profit and loss account for publication.

	£
Stock 1 January 19X4	64,500
Sales	849,000
Purchases	510,600
Carriage inwards	4,900
Returns inwards	5,800
Returns outwards	3,300
Discounts allowed	5,780
Discounts received	6,800
Wages (putting goods into saleable condition)	11,350
Salaries and wages: Sales and distribution staff	29,110
Salaries and wages: Administrative staff	20,920
Motor expenses (see note (c))	15,600
Rent and rates (see note (d))	25,000
Investments in related companies (market value £66,000)	80,000
Income from shares in related companies	3,500
General distribution expenses	8,220
General administrative expenses	2,190
Bad debts	840
Interest from government securities	1,600
Haulage costs: Distribution	2,070
Debenture interest payable	3,800
Profit and loss account: 31 December 19X3	37,470
Motor vehicles at cost: Distribution and sales	75,000
Administrative	35,000
Plant and machinery at cost: Distribution and sales	80,000
Administrative	50,000
Production	15,000
Directors' remuneration	5,000

Notes:
(a) The production department puts goods bought into a saleable condition.
(b) Stock at 31 December 19X4 £82,800.
(c) Apportion Motor expenses: Distribution two-thirds, Administrative one-third.
(d) Apportion Rent and rates: Distribution 80 per cent, Administrative 20 per cent.
(e) Write £14,000 off the value of investments in related companies.
(f) Depreciate Motor vehicles 20 per cent on cost, Plant and machinery 10 per cent on cost.
(g) Accrue auditors' remuneration £2,000.
(h) Accrue corporation tax on ordinary activity profits £74,000.

(*i*)   A sum of £20,000 is to be transferred to debenture redemption reserve.

(*j*)   An ordinary dividend of £50,000 is to be proposed.

9.3X The following selected balances are from the books of Falconer plc as on 31 August 19X4. From them draw up (i) a trading and profit and loss account, for internal use, for the year ended 31 August 19X4, also (ii) a profit and loss account for publication for the year.

	£
Purchases	540,500
Sales	815,920
Returns inwards	15,380
Returns outwards	24,620
Carriage inwards	5,100
Wages – productive	6,370
Discounts allowed	5,890
Discounts received	7,940
Stock 31 August 19X3	128,750
Wages and salaries: Sales and distribution	19,480
Wages and salaries: Administrative	24,800
Motor expenses: Sales and distribution	8,970
Motor expenses: Administrative	16,220
General distribution expenses	4,780
General administrative expenses	5,110
Rent and rates (*see* note (*c*))	9,600
Directors' remuneration	12,400
Profit and loss account: 31 August 19X3	18,270
Advertising costs	8,380
Bad debts	1,020
Hire of plant and machinery (*see* note (*b*))	8,920
Motor vehicles at cost: Sales and distribution	28,000
Administrative	36,000
Plant and machinery: Distribution	17,500
Debenture interest payable	4,800
Income from shares in group companies	12,800
Income from shares in related companies	10,500
Preference dividend paid	15,000
Profit on disposal of investments	6,600
Tax on profit on disposal of investments	1,920

Notes:

(*a*)   Stock at 31 August 19X4 £144,510.

(*b*)   The hire of plant and machinery is to be apportioned: Productive £5,200, Administrative £3,720.

(*c*)   Rent and rates to be apportioned: Distribution two-thirds, Administrative one-third.

(*d*)   Motors are to be depreciated at 25 per cent on cost, Plant and machinery to be depreciated at 20 per cent on cost.

(*e*)   Auditors' remuneration of £1,700 to be accrued.

(*f*)   Corporation tax on profit from ordinary activities for the year is estimated at £59,300.

(*g*)   Transfer £25,000 to general reserve.

(*h*)   Ordinary dividend of £60,000 is proposed.

9.4X From the following balance of Danielle plc you are to draw up (i) a trading and profit and loss account for the year ended 31 December 19X6, for internal use, and (ii) a profit and loss account for publication:

	£
Plant and machinery, at cost (*see* note (*c*))	275,000
Bank interest receivable	1,850
Discounts allowed	5,040
Discounts received	3,890
Hire of motor vehicles: Sales and distribution	9,470
Hire of motor vehicles: Administrative	5,710
Licence fees receivable	5,100
General distribution expenses	11,300
General administrative expenses	15,800
Wages and salaries: Sales and distribution	134,690
Administrative	89,720
Directors' remuneration	42,000
Motor expenses (*see* note (*e*))	18,600
Stock 31 December 19X5	220,500
Sales	880,000
Purchases	405,600
Returns outwards	15,800
Returns inwards	19,550
Profit and loss account as at 31 December 19X5	29,370

Notes:
(*a*) Stock at 31 December 19X6 £210,840.
(*b*) Accrue auditor's remuneration £3,000.
(*c*) Of the Plant and machinery, £150,000 is distributive in nature, whilst £125,000 is for administration.
(*d*) Depreciate plant and machinery 20 per cent on cost.
(*e*) Of the Motor expenses two-thirds is for Sales and distribution and one-third for Administration.
(*f*) Corporation tax on ordinary profits is estimated at £28,350.
(*g*) Proposed ordinary dividend is £50,000.
(*h*) A sum of £15,000 is to be transferred to general reserve.

9.5 The draft accounts of Wilkinson Ltd for the year ended 31 December 19X0 showed a gross profit of £97,000, and a net profit on ordinary activities after taxation of £25,000. Certain errors, listed below, had been made in arriving at these figures.

1 Taxation of £20,000 had been deducted, but no adjustment had been made for the fact that the previous year's provision of £18,000 had proved to be an overestimate when compared to the actual tax liability in that year of £16,000.
2 A building, which was bought on 1 January 19X8 on a fifty year lease at a cost of £80,000, had been revalued on 1 January 19X0 at £100,800. Amortisation in the draft accounts had been calculated at £1,600 for the year.
3 Goods returned to suppliers, totalling £4,025 (including Value Added Tax at 15%), had been added to the sales figure instead of being deducted from the purchases.
4 Value Added Tax (VAT) had been included in the sales figure as shown in the draft trading account. VAT is charged at 15% on all sales, and the amount of sales shown in the draft trading account, including the returns noted in paragraph 3 above, was £199,525.
There was a difference on the draft balance sheet, which was shown in a suspense account.

Required:

(*a*) A detailed summary of the effect of items 1 to 4 above on the draft gross profit and draft net profit on ordinary activities before taxation. *(16 marks)*

(*b*) A reconstruction of the suspense account showing any entries which may have been made in the account as a result of items 1 to 4. *(4 marks)*

(*University of London: GCE A-Level*)

9.6X The accountants of Jarndyce plc, a shoe manufacturer, are considering how they should treat the following items in the profit and loss account of the company for the year ended 31 May 19X1.

(i)   A loss of £200,000 caused by the seizure of company assets during a revolution in Gondwanaland.

(ii) £150,000 redundancy money paid to the former employees of a subsidiary which is continuing to trade.

(iii) £100,000 written off as a bad debt. The average total of debtors during the year was £140,000.

(iv) £50,000 error relating to an undervaluation of the opening stock.

(v)   £70,000 loss on the closure of the company's printing division.

Revenue reserves at 1 June 19X0 total £620,000 and profit for the year ended 31 May 19X1 was £465,000 before any adjustments which might be required by (i)–(v) above.

The accountants have some knowledge of extraordinary items, exceptional items and prior year adjustments, but are unsure if these terms are relevant to any of the above items.

Prepare:

(*a*) the amended profit and loss account for the year ended 31 May 19X1, in as much detail as is possible from the information given *(12 marks)*

(*b*) a statement of the changes in the company's revenue reserves during the year. *(3 marks)*

(*University of London: GCE A-Level*)

Chapter 10

The Published Final Accounts of Limited Companies: Balance Sheets

10.1 Balance Sheet Formats

The Companies Acts set out two formats for the balance sheet, one vertical and one horizontal. The method chosen for this book is that of Format 1 because this most resembles previous UK practice. As it is the vertical style format it will also be looked upon with favour by examiners.

Format 1 is shown as Exhibit 10.1. Monetary figures have been included to illustrate it more clearly.

Exhibit 10.1

Balance Sheet – Format 1

			£	£000s £	£
A		CALLED UP SHARE CAPITAL NOT PAID*			10
B		FIXED ASSETS			
I		Intangible assets			
	1	Development costs	20		
	2	Concessions, patents, licences, trade marks and similar rights and assets	30		
	3	Goodwill	80		
	4	Payments on account	5	135	
II		Tangible assets			
	1	Land and buildings	300		
	2	Plant and machinery	500		
	3	Fixtures, fittings, tools and equipment	60		
	4	Payments on account and assets in course of construction	20	880	
III		Investments			
	1	Shares in group undertakings	15		
	2	Loans to group undertakings	10		
	3	Participating interests	20		
	4	Loans to undertakings in which the company has a participating interest	5		
	5	Other investments other than loans	30		
	6	Other loans	16		
	7	Own shares	4	100	1,115

C CURRENT ASSETS
I Stocks

1	Raw materials and consumables	60	
2	Work in progress	15	
3	Finished goods and goods for resale	120	
4	Payments on account	5	200

II Debtors

1	Trade debtors	200	
2	Amounts owed by group undertakings	20	
3	Amounts owed by undertakings in which company has participating interest	10	
4	Other debtors	4	
5	Called up share capital not paid*	–	
6	Prepayments and accrued income**	–	234

III Investments

1	Shares in group undertakings	40	
2	Own shares	5	
3	Other investments	30	
			75

IV Cash at bank and in hand

	26
	535

D PREPAYMENTS AND ACCRUED INCOME**

	15
	550

E CREDITORS: AMOUNTS FALLING DUE WITHIN ONE YEAR

1	Debenture loans	5	
2	Bank loans and overdrafts	10	
3	Payments received on account	20	
4	Trade creditors	50	
5	Bills of exchange payable	2	
6	Amounts owed to group undertakings	15	
7	Amounts owed to undertakings in which company has participating interest	6	
8	Other creditors including taxation and social security	54	
9	Accruals and deferred income***	–	162

F	NET CURRENT ASSETS (LIABILITIES)	388
G	TOTAL ASSETS LESS CURRENT LIABILITIES	1,513

H CREDITORS: AMOUNTS FALLING DUE AFTER MORE
THAN ONE YEAR

1	Debenture loans	20	
2	Bank loans and overdrafts	15	
3	Payments received on account	5	
4	Trade creditors	25	
5	Bills of exchange payable	4	
6	Amounts owed to group undertakings	10	
7	Amounts owed to undertakings in which company has participating interest	5	
8	Other creditors including taxation and social security	32	
9	Accruals and deferred income***	–	116

I PROVISIONS FOR LIABILITIES AND CHARGES

1	Pensions and similar obligations	20		
2	Taxation, including deferred taxation	40		
3	Other provisions	4	64	

J ACCRUALS AND DEFERRED INCOME***			20	200
				1,313

K CAPITAL AND RESERVES

I	Called up share capital			1,000
II	Share premium account			100
III	Revaluation reserve			20
IV	Other reserves:			
	1 Capital redemption reserve	40		
	2 Reserve for own shares	10		
	3 Reserves provided for by the articles of association	20		
	4 Other reserves	13		83
V	Profit and loss account			110
				1,313

(*)(**)(***)These items may be shown in any of the positions indicated.

It should be noted that various items can be shown in alternative places, i.e.

- **Called up share capital not paid**, either in position A or position CII 5.
- **Prepayments and accrued income**, either CII 6 or as D.
- **Accruals and deferred income**, either E9 or H9, or in total as J.

Items preceded by letters or Roman numerals must be disclosed on the face of the balance sheet, e.g. B Fixed Assets, K II Share Premium Account, whereas those shown with Arabic numerals (you may call them ordinary numbers, 1, 2, 3, 4, etc) may be combined where they are not material or the combination facilitates assessment of the company's affairs. Where they are combined the details of each item should be shown in the notes accompanying the accounts. The actual letters, roman numerals or arabic numbers do *not* have to be shown on the face of the published balance sheets.

10.2 Published Balance Sheets and GCE A-Level Examinations

You will not be expected to remember the full detail for such a balance sheet. This is simply outside the demands of your syllabus. If you can remember the main structure then that will be sufficient.

What you should remember are the main headings and these can be shown as follows:

	£	£	£
FIXED ASSETS			
Intangible assets		xxx	
Tangible assets		xxx	
Investments (long-term)		<u>xxx</u>	xxxx
CURRENT ASSETS			
Stock	xxx		
Debtors	xxx		
Investments (short-term)	<u>xxx</u>	xxxx	
Cash at bank and in hand		<u>xxx</u>	
		xxxx	
CREDITORS: AMOUNTS FALLING DUE WITHIN ONE YEAR (*less*)		<u>xxx</u>	
NET CURRENT ASSETS			<u>xxxx</u>
TOTAL ASSETS *LESS* CURRENT LIABILITIES			xxxx
CREDITORS: AMOUNTS FALLING DUE AFTER MORE THAN ONE YEAR (*less*)			<u>xxx</u>
			xxxx
CAPITAL AND RESERVES			
Called up share capital			xxxx
Share premium account			xxx
Revaluation reserve			xxx
Other reserves			xxx
			<u>xxx</u>
Profit and loss account			xxxx

If you can remember these headings you can then place the individual items under them.

10.3 Further Details for Format 1

The following also apply to the balance sheet in Format 1.

BI Intangible assets. These are assets not having a 'physical' existence as compared with tangible assets which do have a physical existence. For instance you can see and touch the tangible assets of land and buildings, plant and machinery, etc. whereas goodwill does not exist in a physical sense.

For each of the items under fixed assets, whether they are intangible assets, tangible assets or investments, the notes accompanying the accounts must give full details of (i) cost, at beginning and end of financial year, (ii) effect on that item of acquisitions, disposals, revaluations etc. during the year, and (iii) full details of depreciation, i.e. accumulated depreciation at start of year, depreciation for year, effect of disposals on depreciation in the year and any other adjustments.

All fixed assets, including property and goodwill must be depreciated over the period of the useful economic life of each asset. Costs of research must not be treated as an asset, and development costs may be capitalised only in special cases. Any hire-purchase owing must not be deducted from the assets concerned. Only goodwill which has been purchased can be shown as an asset, internally generated goodwill must not be capitalised. (This does not refer to goodwill in consolidated accounts, *see* Chapter 12.)

Where an asset is revalued, normally this will be fixed assets being shown at market value instead of cost, any difference on revaluation must be debited or credited to a revaluation reserve, *see* KIII in the Format.

Investments shown as CIII will be in respect of those not held for the long term.

Two items which could previously be shown as assets, (i) preliminary expenses, these are the legal expenses, etc. in forming the company, and (ii) expenses of and commission on any issue of shares or debentures, must not now be shown as assets. They can be written off against any share premium account balance; alternatively they should be written off to profit and loss account.

Full details of each class of share capital, and of authorised capital, will be shown in notes accompanying the balance sheet.

10.4 Choice of Formats

The Act leaves the choice of a particular format for the balance sheet and the profit and loss account to the directors. Once adopted the choice must be adhered to in subsequent years except in the case that there are special reasons for the change. If a change is made then full reasons for the change must be stated in the notes attached to the accounts.

10.5 Fundamental Accounting Principles

The Companies Acts set out the accounting principles (or 'valuation rules' as they are called in the Fourth Directive of the EC) to be followed when preparing company financial statements.

The following principles are stated in the Acts. (They are covered in fuller detail in chapter 10 of *Business Accounting 1*, 7th Edition.)

(a) A company is presumed to be a going concern.
(b) Accounting policies must be applied consistently from year to year.
(c) The prudence concept must be followed.
(d) The accruals concept must be observed.
(e) Each component item of assets and liabilities must be valued separately. As an instance of this, if a company has five different types of stock, each type must be valued separately at the lower of cost and net realisable value, rather than be valued on an aggregate basis.
(f) Amounts in respect of items representing assets or income may *not* be set off against items representing liabilities or expenditure. Thus an amount owing on a hire-purchase contract cannot now be deducted from the value of the asset in the balance sheet, although this was often done before 1981.

10.6 Reporting Requirements for Small and Medium-sized Companies

Small and medium-sized companies do not have to file a full set of final accounts with the Registrar of Companies. They could, if they wished, send a full set of final accounts, but what they *have* to file is a minimum of 'modified accounts'. They would still have to send a full set to their own shareholders, the 'modified accounts' refer only to those filed with the Registrar.

You are not expected to know the full details of this part of the legislation.

10.7 True and Fair View

When the accounts of a company are published no one, neither the directors nor the auditors, ever state that 'the accounts are correct'. This is because in preparing company accounts many subjective estimates and judgements affect the figures. The valuation of stock, or the estimates of depreciation cannot be said to be correct, just as it is impossible to say that the provision for bad debts is correct. Only time will tell whether these estimates and judgements will turn out to be correct.

The expression that is used is that in the opinion of the directors the accounts give a *true and fair view*. The auditors in their report after examining the books and accounts must also say whether they agree that the accounts give a true and fair view. If not, the auditors will qualify their report in some way.

It is interesting that, contrary to what most of the public think, auditors do not guarantee to discover any fraud that may have occurred. That is not what the audit is for. Following such immense financial scandals as the Maxwell affair, the BCCI bank, Polly Peck and Barlow Clowes there has been pressure exerted upon the accounting profession to reconsider its position regarding the discovery of fraud when auditing the accounts of a company.

10.8 Bills of Exchange

A detailed knowledge of this topic is not needed by A-Level students. You do need to know the basic ideas underlying bills of exchange, and so it is introduced here as they are part of the format of published company balance sheets.

When goods are supplied to someone on credit, or services performed for him, then that person becomes a **debtor**. The creditor firm would normally wait for payment by the debtor. Until payment is made the money owing is of no use to the creditor firm as it is not being used in any way. This can be remedied by factoring the debtors, which involves passing the debts over to a finance firm. They will pay an agreed amount for the legal rights to the debts.

Another possibility is that of obtaining a bank overdraft, with the debtors accepted as part of the security on which the overdraft has been granted.

Yet another way that can give the creditor effective use of the money owing to him is for him to draw a bill of exchange on the debtor. This means that a document is drawn up requiring the debtor to pay the amount owing to the creditor, or to anyone nominated by him at any time, on or by a particular date. He sends this document to the debtor who, if he agrees to it, is said to 'accept' it by writing on the document that he will comply with it and appends his signature. The debtor then returns the bill of exchange to the creditor. This document is then legal proof of the debt. The debtor is not then able to contest the validity of the debt but only for any irregularity in the bill of exchange itself.

The creditor can now act in one of three ways:

1   He can negotiate the bill to another person in payment of a debt. That person may also renegotiate it to someone else. The person who possesses the bill at maturity, i.e. the date for payment of the bill, will present it to the debtor for payment.
2   He may 'discount' it with a bank. 'Discount' here means that the bank will take the bill of exchange and treat it in the same manner as money deposited in the bank account. The bank will hold the bill until maturity when it will present it to the debtor for payment. The bank will make a charge to the creditor for this service known as a discounting charge.

3   The third way open to the creditor is for him to hold the bill until maturity when he will present it to the debtor for payment. In this case, apart from having a document which is legal proof of the debt and could therefore save legal costs if a dispute arose, no benefit has been gained from having a bill of exchange. However, action 1 or 2 could have been taken if the need had arisen.

10.9 Bills Receivable as Contingent Liabilities

The fact that bills had been discounted, but had not reached maturity by the balance sheet date, could give an entirely false impression of the financial position of the business unless a note to this effect is made on the balance sheet. That such a note is necessary can be illustrated by reference to the following balance sheets.

Balance Sheet as at 31 December 19X7

		(a)		(b)
	£	£	£	£
Fixed assets		3,500		3,500
Current assets:				
Stock	1,000		1,000	
Debtors	1,200		1,200	
Bills receivable	1,800		–	
Bank	500		2,300	
	4,500		4,500	
Less Current liabilities	3,000		3,000	
Working capital		1,500		1,500
		5,000		5,000
		£		£
Financed by:				
Capital		5,000		5,000

Balance Sheet (a) shows the position if £1,800 of bills receivable were still in hand. Balance Sheet (b) shows the position if the bills had been discounted, ignoring discounting charges. To an outsider, Balance Sheet (b) seems to show a much stronger liquid position with £2,300 in the bank. However, should the bills be dishonoured on maturity the bank balance would slump to £500. The appearance of Balance Sheet (b) is therefore deceptive unless a note is added, e.g. *Note:* There is a contingent liability of £1,800 on bills discounted at the balance sheet date. This note enables the outsider to view the bank balance in its proper perspective of depending on the non-dishonour of the bills discounted.

10.10 Bills of Exchange and the Balance Sheet

Besides Bills of Exchange to be received there are also bills of exchange in which we have agreed to pay a creditor at a future date. To distinguish between them:

● Bills Receivable: These are bills for debts owing to us which people are going to pay us in the future.
● Bills Payable: These are bills for debts which are owed to other people, and which we are going to have to pay in the future.

Bills receivable are assets, as they are money owing to us, and will therefore be shown as debit balances in the books and trial balance. They will be shown under current assets in the balance sheet.

Bills payable, being money owing by us are liabilities, and are credit balances. Whether they will be shown under item E5 (see Exhibit 10.1) or under H5 will depend on whether we have agreed to pay the amount within the next twelve months, or at a later date.

10.11 FRS 4: Capital Instruments

If a company can make short-term debt (i.e. payable within the next twelve months) look as though it does not have to be paid off within that period, but instead it looks as though the company has several years in which to pay it, then the balance sheet shows what appears to be a much healthier liquid position. Investors may then be fooled into investing in a company which appears to have no short-term problems of shortage of cash funds, only to see the company quickly fall into such problems.

FRS 4 is aimed at preventing devices which could mislead an investor or shareholder. A-Level students do not need to know all the technical details, which include such methods as certain types of debentures, convertible debt and auction market preferred stock. The main provisions of FRS 4 are as follows:

- Liabilities should *not* be shown as being amounts which fall due after one year if in fact a strict interpretation of their contractual maturity means that they are amounts falling due within one year.
- Shareholders' funds must be analysed between equity and non-equity interests.

REVIEW QUESTIONS

Advice:

You are not expected to know all the very detailed requirements concerning company balance sheets. It would be as well, however, if you can remember the basic outline of a company balance sheet as shown in Section 10.2.

10.1 The following balances remained in the books of Owen Ltd on 31 December 19X1, *after* the profit and loss account and appropriation account had been drawn up. You are to draft the balance sheet as at 31 December 19X1 in accordance with the Companies Act.

	Dr £	Cr £
Ordinary share capital: £1 shares		50,000
Preference share capital: 50p shares		25,000
Calls account (ordinary shares)	150	
Development costs	3,070	
Goodwill	21,000	
Land and buildings – at cost	48,000	
Plant and machinery – at cost	12,500	
Provision for depreciation: Buildings		16,000
Provision for depreciation: Plant and machinery		5,400
Shares in undertakings in which the company has a participating interest	35,750	
Stock: Raw materials	3,470	
Stock: Finished goods	18,590	

Debtors: Trade	17,400	
Amounts owed by undertakings in which company has participating interest	3,000	
Prepayments	1,250	
Debentures (*see* note 1)		10,000
Bank overdraft (repayable within 6 months)		4,370
Creditors: Trade (payable within 1 year)		12,410
Bills payable (*see* note 2)		3,600
Share premium		20,000
Capital redemption reserve		5,000
General reserve		4,000
Profit and loss account		8,400
	164,180	164,180

Notes:

1 Of the debentures £6,000 is repayable in 3 months' time, while the other £4,000 is repayable in 5 years' time.

2 Of the bills payable, £1,600 is in respect of a bill to be paid in 4 months' time and £2,000 for a bill payable in 18 months' time.

3 The depreciation charged for the year was: Buildings £4,000, Plant and machinery £1,800.

10.2 After the profit and loss appropriation account has been prepared for the year ended 30 September 19X4, the following balances remain in the books of Belle Works plc. You are to draw up a balance sheet in accordance with the Companies Act.

	£	£
Ordinary share capital		70,000
Share premium		5,000
Revaluation reserve		10,500
General reserve		6,000
Foreign exchange reserve		3,500
Profit and loss account		6,297
Patents, trade marks and licences	1,500	
Goodwill	17,500	
Land and buildings at cost	90,000	
Provision for depreciation: Land and buildings		17,500
Plant and machinery at cost	38,600	
Provision for depreciation: Plant and machinery		19,200
Stock of raw materials: 30 September 19X4	14,320	
Work in progress: 30 September 19X4	5,640	
Finished goods: 30 September 19X4	13,290	
Debtors: Trade	11,260	
Debtors: Other	1,050	
Prepayments and accrued income	505	
Debentures (redeemable in 6 months' time)		6,000
Debentures (redeemable in $4\frac{1}{2}$ years' time)		12,000
Bank overdraft (repayable in 3 months)		3,893
Trade creditors (payable in next 12 months)		11,340
Trade creditors (payable after 12 months)		1,260
Bills of exchange (payable within 12 months)		4,000
Corporation tax (payable in 9 months' time)		14,370
National insurance (payable in next month)		305
Pensions contribution owing		1,860
Deferred taxation		640
	193,665	193,665

10.3X The trial balance of Payne Peerbrook plc as on 31 December 19X6 is as follows:

	Dr £	Cr £
Preference share capital: £1 shares		50,000
Ordinary share capital: 50p shares		60,000
General reserve		45,000
Foreign exchange reserve		13,600
Profit and loss account as on 31 December 19X5		19,343
Stock 31 December 19X5	107,143	
Sales		449,110
Returns inwards	11,380	
Purchases	218,940	
Carriage inwards	2,475	
Wages (putting goods into a saleable condition)	3,096	
Wages: Warehouse staff	39,722	
Wages and salaries: Sales staff	28,161	
Wages and salaries: Administrative staff	34,778	
Motor expenses (*see* note ii)	16,400	
General distribution expenses	8,061	
General administrative expenses	7,914	
Debenture interest	10,000	
Royalties receivable		4,179
Directors' remuneration	18,450	
Bad debts	3,050	
Discounts allowed	5,164	
Discounts received		4,092
Plant and machinery at cost (*see* note (iii)	175,000	
Provision for depreciation: Plant and machinery		58,400
Motor vehicles at cost (*see* note (ii)	32,000	
Provision for depreciation: Motor vehicles		14,500
Goodwill	29,500	
Development costs	16,320	
Trade debtors	78,105	
Trade creditors		37,106
Bank overdraft (repayable any time)		4,279
Bills of exchange payable (all due within 1 year)		6,050
Debentures (redeemable in 5 years' time)		80,000
	845,659	845,659

Notes:

(i) Stock of finished goods on 31 December 19X6 £144,081.

(ii) Motor expenses and depreciation on motors to be apportioned: Distribution ¾ths, Administrative ¼th.

(iii) Plant and machinery depreciation to be apportioned. Cost of sales ⅓th: Distribution ⅓ths: Administrative ⅓th.

(iv) Depreciate the following fixed assets on cost: Motor vehicles 25 per cent, Plant and machinery 20 per cent.

(v) Accrue corporation tax on profits of the year £14,150. This is payable 1 October 19X7.

(vi) A preference dividend of £5,000 is to be paid and an ordinary dividend of £10,000 is to be proposed.

You are to draw up:

(*a*) A trading and profit and loss account for the year ended 31 December 19X6 for internal use, and

(*b*) A profit and loss account for publication, also a balance sheet as at 31 December 19X6.

10.4X The following financial information is available for Oakcroft plc, a retailing organisation, as at 31 March 19X0.

	£000
Aggregate depreciation on furniture and fittings at 1 April 19X9	31
Trade debtors	104
Trade creditors	86
Share premium account	50
Purchases	880
Sales	1,534
Issued share capital	370
Furniture and fittings at cost	395
Debenture interest	11
Cash at bank and cash in hand	328
Auditors' remuneration	30
Administration expenses	170
11% Debenture loan stock (19X8)	100
Distribution costs	110
Fixed assets: investments at cost	190
Hire charges: distribution equipment and vehicles	200
Interim dividend: paid 1 October 19X9	8
Profit and loss account: 1 April 19X9	320 Cr
Dividends received: 1 January 19X0	45
Stock in trade: 1 April 19X9	110

Additional information:
1 The authorised share capital is 450,000 ordinary shares of £1 each.
2 The directors have proposed that a final ordinary share dividend of 7 per cent be paid for the year ended 31 March 19X0.
3 Stock in trade was valued at £135,000 as at 31 March 19X0.
4 The market value of the investments at 31 March 19X0 was £208,000.
5 Depreciation of £28,000 is to be charged on furniture and fittings for the year to 31 March 19X0. One quarter of this depreciation is a distribution expense. There were no purchases or sales of furniture during the year.
6 Expenses in arrears as at 31 March 19X0:

	£000
Administration	12
Distribution	16

Required:

(a) A trading and profit and loss account for the year ended 31 March 19X0.   *(9 marks)*

(b) A profit and loss appropriation account for the year ended 31 March 19X0.   *(3 marks)*

(c) A balance sheet as at 31 March 19X0.   *(8 marks)*

(d) From the final accounts of Oakcroft plc give the minimum information required to be shown by the Companies Acts (including the relevant figures) for each of the following:
(i) The trading account.
(ii) The revenue expenditure of the profit and loss account.   *(5 marks)*

Note: Ignore all exemptions permitted for small and medium size companies.

(Associated Examining Board: GCE A-Level)

Chapter 11

Group Accounts: An Introduction

11.1 Shareholders and Their Rights

The owners of a company are its shareholders. When someone buys ordinary shares in a company then they are usually given three rights. These are:

- Voting rights at shareholders' meetings.
- A right to an interest in the net assets of the company.
- A right to an interest in the profits earned by the company.

Preference shareholders do not normally have such voting rights, but sometimes they can have such power. This could be when their dividends are in arrear, or their special rights are being changed by the company. Debenture holders have no rights at all to vote at general meetings.

By using their voting rights at shareholders' meetings, the shareholders are able to show their approval, or disapproval, of the election of directors. It is the directors who manage the affairs of the company. Therefore any group of shareholders, who between them own more than 50 per cent of the voting shares of the company, can control the election of directors. As a consequence they can therefore control the policies of the company through the directors. This would also be true if any one shareholder owned more than 50 per cent of the voting shares.

One company may hold shares in another company. Therefore, if one company wishes to obtain control of another company it can do so by obtaining more than 50 per cent of the voting shares in that company.

11.2 Parent Undertakings and Subsidiary Undertakings

- S Ltd has an issued share capital of 1,000 ordinary shares of £1 each.
- P Ltd now buys 501 of these shares from Jones, a shareholder, for £600.
- P Ltd will now have control of S Ltd because it has more than 50 per cent of the voting shares.
- P Ltd is now called the 'parent undertaking'.
- S Ltd is now called the 'subsidiary undertaking' of P Ltd.

Just because the identity of S Ltd's shareholders has changed it does not mean that the balance sheet of S Ltd will be drafted in a different fashion. Looking only at the balance sheet of S Ltd, no one would be able to deduce that P Ltd owned more than 50 per cent of the shares, or even that P Ltd owned any shares at all in S Ltd. After obtaining control of S Ltd both P Ltd and S Ltd will continue to maintain their own sets of accounting records and to draft their own balance sheets. In fact if the balance sheets of P Ltd and S

Ltd are looked at, both before and after the purchase of the shares, then any differences can be noted.

Exhibit 11.1

(a) Before P Ltd acquired control of S Ltd:

P Ltd Balance Sheet as at 31 December 19X5	£	£
Fixed assets		2,000
Current assets:		
Stock-in-trade	2,900	
Debtors	800	
Bank	1,300	
		5,000
		7,000
Share capital		5,000
Profit and loss account		2,000
		7,000

S Ltd Balance Sheet as at 31 December 19X5	£	£
Fixed assets		400
Current assets:		
Stock-in-trade	400	
Debtors	200	
Bank	100	
		700
		1,100
Share capital		1,000
Profit and loss account		100
		1,100

(b) After P Ltd acquired control of S Ltd the balance sheets would appear as follows before any further trading took place:

P Ltd Balance Sheet as at 1 January 19X6	£	£
Fixed assets		2,000
Investment in subsidiary undertaking		600
Current assets:		
Stock-in-trade	2,900	
Debtors	800	
Bank	700	
		4,400
		7,000
Share capital		5,000
Profit and loss account		2,000
		7,000

S Ltd Balance Sheet as at 1 January 19X6	£	£
Fixed assets		400
Current assets:		
Stock-in-trade	400	
Debtors	200	
Bank	100	
		700
		1,100
Share capital		1,000
Profit and loss account		100
		1,100

The only differences can be seen to be those in the balance sheets of P Ltd. The bank balance has been reduced by £600, this being the cost of shares in S Ltd, and the cost of the shares now appears as 'Investment in subsidiary undertaking £600'. The balance sheets of S Ltd are completely unchanged.

FRS 2 *'Accounting for Subsidiary Undertakings'* gives a much wider meaning to 'subsidiary undertaking' than we have seen so far. This has been deliberately excluded up to this point to let you see the basic structure without complicating it. Previously, a 'parent undertaking' was called a 'holding company', and a 'subsidiary undertaking' was a 'subsidiary company'. One reason for the change in terminology is that consolidated accounts used to be concerned only with companies but now 'subsidiary undertakings' can also include unincorporated businesses.

11.3 Profit and Loss Accounts

From the profit and loss account point of view the appropriation section of S Ltd would also be completely unchanged after P Ltd takes control. However, P Ltd would see a change in its profit and loss account when a dividend is received from S Ltd: in this case the dividends received would be shown as investment income on the credit side of the profit and loss account. Remember, dividends payable are charged to the appropriation section of the paying company's profit and loss account, while dividends received are in the main part of the receiving company's profit and loss account.

11.4 The Need for Consolidated Accounts

Imagine being a shareholder of P Ltd. Each year you would receive a set of P Ltd's final accounts. After P's acquisition of the shares in S Ltd then £600 would appear as an asset in the balance sheet of P Ltd. It would be normal for it to be shown at cost, £600, using the cost concept.

When you looked at the profit and loss account of P Ltd you would see the dividends received from S Ltd. This plus the cost of the investment in the balance sheet would therefore be the only things you would know about the subsidiary.

However, you have invested in P Ltd, and because of its majority shareholding in S Ltd you have in effect also invested in S Ltd as well. Just as you want to know how the assets and liabilities in P Ltd change over the years, you will now also like to know exactly the same for S Ltd.

You are not, however, a shareholder of S Ltd, and therefore you would not be sent a copy of its final accounts. If the situation were to stay like that, you could not get a proper view of your investment.

This would be even worse if in fact P Ltd was a parent undertaking with twenty subsidiaries, and held a different percentage stake in each of them. It would also be almost certain that the companies would trade with each other, and owe money to one another or be owed money by them. This would also raise complications.

Fortunately there is a remedy for this sort of problem. The Companies Acts provide for parent undertakings distributing to their shareholders a set of consolidated final accounts. These bring together all of the final accounts for the parent undertaking and its subsidiaries in such a way that the shareholders can get an overall view of their investments.

11.5 Different Methods of Acquiring Control of One Company by Another

So far the acquisition of control in S Ltd was by P Ltd buying more than 50 per cent of the shares in S Ltd from Jones, i.e. buying shares on the open maket. This is by no means the only way of acquiring control, so by way of illustration some of the other methods are now described:

(a) S Ltd may issue new shares to P Ltd amounting to over 50 per cent of the voting shares. P Ltd pays for the shares in cash.

(b) P Ltd could purchase over 50 per cent of the voting shares of S Ltd on the open market by exchanging for them newly issued shares of P Ltd.

Or, acting through another company:

(c) P Ltd acquires more than 50 per cent of the voting shares in S1 Ltd for cash, and then S1 Ltd proceeds to acquire all of the voting shares of S2 Ltd. S2 Ltd would then also be a subsidiary of P Ltd.

These are only some of the more common ways by which one company becomes a subsidiary undertaking of another company.

11.6 Control by Dominant Influence

The issue of FRS 2 in 1992 introduced a further way of looking at whether or not one company had control of another. If one company has *'the right to exercise a dominant influence'* over another undertaking, then the company with the dominating influence is deemed to have control of the other. A dominant influence means that the holder of it has a right to give directions with regard to the operating and financial policies of another undertaking, and that the directors of that latter undertaking are obliged to comply, whether or not they are for the benefit of the undertaking.

In other words, if one undertaking can tell another undertaking what to do, both from an operating and financial point of view, and the directors of that latter undertaking have to carry out such instructions, then such an undertaking will be a subsidiary undertaking. This is a much wider definition than merely looking at the amounts of the shareholdings.

11.7 The Nature of a Group

Wherever two or more companies are in the relationship of parent and subsidiary undertaking then a 'group' is said to exist.

Final accounts for such a group are known either as 'group accounts' or as 'consolidated accounts'. Both of the terms have exactly the same meaning.

11.8 Subsidiary Undertakings which are not Limited Companies

Prior to the release of FRS 2 in 1992, group accounts consolidated only those accounts which belonged to limited companies. A subsidiary undertaking now can be other than a limited company. Basically, share of ownership or the dominant influence approach will determine whether or not it can be called a subsidiary undertaking. These accounts are then consolidated in a similar fashion to those of limited companies.

11.9 FRS 2: Accounting for Subsidiary Undertakings

The main changes brought about by this FRS were as follows:

(a) The concept of 'dominant influence' widened the scope of which companies could be seen as subsidiary undertakings, rather than rely on share ownership.
(b) Unincorporated businesses (i.e. not companies) were brought into its scope and came to be classed as subsidiary undertakings which have to have their accounts consolidated with the rest of the group.

11.10 SSAP 1: Accounting for Associated Companies

Although, at present, the title of the SSAP has not changed, in fact the term *'associated undertakings'* would be more appropriate, as this is what they are defined as in the Companies Acts. Investments in such companies are too significant to be treated simply as trade investments, but on the other hand they do not qualify to be treated as investments in subsidiaries.

Basically, SSAP 1 says that B Ltd will be considered as an associated company of A Ltd if A Ltd can *significantly* influence the financial and operating decisions of B Ltd. As a normal rule the amount of B Ltd's equity shares that A Ltd would have to hold would be 20 per cent. This, however, is only a guideline. What is important is the presence or absence of significant influence.

The idea behind the SSAP was to ensure that if one company has invested in another company, and can significantly influence the affairs of that company, then ordinary investment accounting is not suitable. Rather than simply show dividends received as a measure of income, it would be much more realistic that the investing company's *full* share of the profit of that company should be incorporated in the investing company's accounts. The method of doing this is known as 'equity accounting'.

REVIEW QUESTIONS

Advice:

You are required to know about the basic features of group (or consolidated) accounts. It is not necessary to know all the details, for you will not be asked to draw up consolidated accounts in all but the simplest fashion.

11.1 What determines whether or not one company is a subsidiary undertaking of another company?

11.2 How are unincorporated businesses affected by the provisions of FRS 2?

11.3 What benefits accrue to the investor in a parent undertaking by the use of consolidated accounts?

11.4 In what ways did FRS 2 change the ways in which consolidated accounts should be drawn up?

Chapter 12

Group Accounts: Mechanics of Consolidation

12.1 The Principle of Cancellation

The various final accounts of the parent undertaking and its subsidiary undertakings have to be brought together and consolidated into one set of accounts for the whole of the group. Some items in one of the original sets of accounts will also be found to refer to exactly the same transactions in one of the other sets of original final accounts.

Let us look at some of the more common examples:

- An item which is a debtor in one balance sheet may be shown as a creditor in another balance sheet. If P Ltd had sold goods to S Ltd, its subsidiary, but S Ltd had not yet paid for them, then the item would be shown as a debtor in the balance sheet of P Ltd and as a creditor in the balance sheet of S Ltd.
- Sales by one of the group to another company in the group will appear as sales in one company's accounts and purchases in another company's accounts.
- Shares bought in one of the subsidiary undertakings by the parent undertaking will be shown as an investment on the assets side of the parent undertaking's balance sheet. In the balance sheet of the subsidiary, exactly those same shares will be shown as issued share capital.
- Dividends paid by a subsidiary undertaking to its parent undertaking will be shown as paid dividends in the final accounts of the subsidiary, and as dividends received in the final accounts of the parent undertaking.

The group or consolidated final accounts are supposed to show how the group as a whole has dealt with the world outside. Transactions which are simply within the group do not represent dealings with the outside world. When all of the separate accounts of the companies within the group are put together such items need to be deleted, and will not appear in the consolidated accounts of the group.

This therefore is the principle of cancellation. Like things in different final accounts within the group should be cancelled out from each to arrive at the group's final accounts. All of the items already listed will therefore not appear in the consolidated accounts.

This can be shown in the form of a diagram in Exhibit 12.1.

Exhibit 12.1 Consolidation of accounts of a group

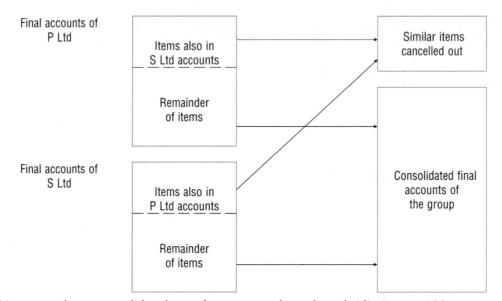

This means that a consolidated set of accounts, where the subsidiaries are 100 per cent owned by the parent undertaking will appear as follows:

Group Balance Sheet as at ......

	£	£
Fixed assets (*less* Cancelled items)		xxxx
Current assets (*less* Cancelled items)	xxxx	
Less Current liabilities (*less* Cancelled items)	xxxx	xxxx
		xxxx
Financed by		
Share capital (of the parent undertaking only, as the purchase of shares in the subsidiaries have cancelled out)		xxxx
Reserves (*less* Cancelled items)		xxxx
		xxxx

12.2 Goodwill and Capital Reserves

It may well have crossed your mind to enquire exactly what happens when the items to be cancelled out are not of the same amount. For instance if P Ltd pays £1,000 for all the shares in S Ltd which has shares and reserves at the time of purchase of £700. If the parent is paying more than the book value of the shares then the consolidated balance sheet will show the difference, i.e. £300 in this case, as 'goodwill'. Otherwise the consolidated balance sheet totals would not be of equal figures.

On the other hand, if £1,000 was paid for an investment of £1,200 book value in a subsidiary then the difference of £200 would be shown as a **'capital reserve'**. This would be shown on the capital and reserves side of the balance sheet.

12.3 Principles not Computations

The syllabuses for GCE A-Level examinations do not expect you to be able to perform all the computations necessary to draw up consolidated accounts. What they do ask for is that you should understand the principles involved in group accounts. This is what this book attempts to do.

12.4 Subsidiaries which Control other Companies

So far we have considered the case of parent undertakings having a direct interest in their subsidiaries. In each case the parent itself has bought the shares in its subsidiary undertakings. In each case over 50 per cent of the voting shares have been bought. In a straightforward case, where the parent P1 has bought shares in subsidiaries S1 and S2 it could be represented by a diagram (Exhibit 12.2).

Exhibit 12.2

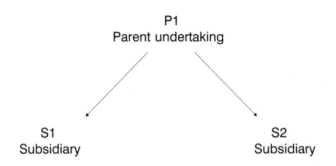

Suppose instead that P2 bought 100 per cent of the shares in S3, and that S3 then itself bought 100 per cent of the shares in S4. Because P2 controls S3 completely, and S3 controls S4 completely, therefore P2 controls both S3 and S4. This is shown as Exhibit 12.3.

If P3 owned S5 100 per cent, but S5 only owned 80 per cent of S6, then we can say that P3 owns 100% of 80% of S6 (*see* Exhibit 12.4). Similarly if in another case P4 owned 75% of S7, and S7 owns 80 per cent of S8, then P4 owns 75% × 80% = 60% (*see* Exhibit 12.5).

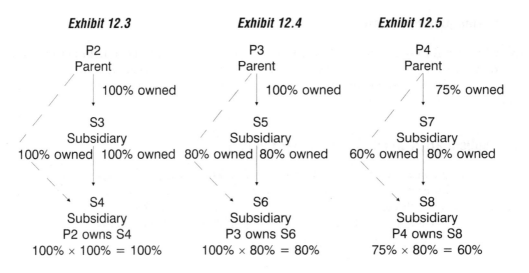

Exhibit 12.3

P2
Parent
100% owned
S3
Subsidiary
100% owned | 100% owned
S4
Subsidiary
P2 owns S4
100% × 100% = 100%

Exhibit 12.4

P3
Parent
100% owned
S5
Subsidiary
80% owned | 80% owned
S6
Subsidiary
P3 owns S6
100% × 80% = 80%

Exhibit 12.5

P4
Parent
75% owned
S7
Subsidiary
60% owned | 80% owned
S8
Subsidiary
P4 owns S8
75% × 80% = 60%

In Exhibits 12.3–12.5 the eventual ownership by P of each subsidiary exceeds 50 per cent.

There will be cases where the ownership of the subsidiary by the holding company is less than 50 per cent. Exhibit 12.6 shows where P5 owns 80 per cent of S9, and S9 owns 60 per cent of S10. This means that P5 owns 80% × 60% = 48% of S10. Exhibit 12.7 similarly shows where P6 owns 60 per cent of S11 and S11 owns 55 per cent of S12. Therefore P6 owns 60% × 55% = 33% of S13. Exhibits 12.6 and 12.7 illustrate the ownership.

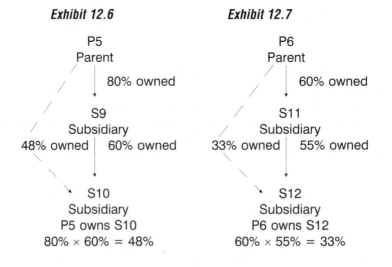

Exhibit 12.6

P5
Parent
80% owned
S9
Subsidiary
48% owned | 60% owned
S10
Subsidiary
P5 owns S10
80% × 60% = 48%

Exhibit 12.7

P6
Parent
60% owned
S11
Subsidiary
33% owned | 55% owned
S12
Subsidiary
P6 owns S12
60% × 55% = 33%

It might look as though S10 is not a subsidiary of P5, because P5 owns less than 50 per cent of S10. However, P5 controls S9 as its ownership is over 50 per cent, and in turn S9 controls S10 as it owns more than 50 per cent. Effectively, therefore, P5 controls S10, and as such S10 is its subsidiary.

12.5 Minority Interests

When a parent does not own 100 per cent of the shares of a subsidiary, then obviously outside shareholders own the shares not within the ownership of the parent. The name given to the collective value of the parts of the subsidiaries owned by outsiders is known as the 'minority interest'.

From the individual balance sheets of the subsidiaries you cannot tell how many of the shares are owned by people outside the group. All these balance sheets will show is the total amount of share capital.

However, in the consolidated balance sheet for the whole group it is necessary, and desirable, that the minority interests be shown. This is shown separately in the balance sheet showing the book values of the following:

	£
Total amount of shares held in subsidiaries by outside interests	xxx
Total amount of reserves in subsidiaries which is owned by outside interests	xxx
	xxx

The group balance sheet will therefore appear as:

Balance Sheet as at ....

	£	£
Fixed assets (*less* Cancelled items)		xxxx
Current assets (*less* Cancelled items)	xxxx	
Less Current liabilities (*less* Cancelled items)	xxxx	xxxx
		xxxx
Financed by:		
Share capital (of the parent only)		xxxx
Reserves owned by the group (excluding minority interests)		xxxx
		xxxx
Minority interests:		
Share capital in subsidiaries owned by outside interests	xxx	
Proportion of reserves in subsidiaries owned by outside interests	xxx	xxxx
		Xxxxx

12.6 Buying Shares to Become a Minority Interest Shareholder

When you buy shares in a company in which another company has a majority shareholding there are certain factors to be taken into account. These are:

- The parent will want to ensure that the subsidiary is operated to the better advantage of the shareholders of the parent. It will not put the welfare of the minority interest as its first priority.
- At shareholders' meetings the minority interest will be outvoted because the parent will have more votes.
- Shares held as part of a minority interest may not be so easily saleable because they are in a company controlled by another group.

- Policies regarding dividends may not suit you although they will suit the needs of the group as a whole.

REVIEW QUESTIONS

Advice:

If you can remember the basic outline of a consolidated balance sheet, as shown in Section 12.5, then you will probably be able to answer questions of a simple nature concerning the drawing up of such a balance sheet.

It is also important that you understand the principles of cancellation as described in Section 12.1.

Another point worth knowing is that of how 'goodwill' or 'capital reserves' occur in consolidated accounts, *see* Section 12.2.

Quite a common question, usually as part of a much larger question, is that of advising someone who is contemplating buying shares to become a minority interest shareholder. This is covered in Section 12.6.

12.1 Explain the reasons underlying the need for cancellation of like items when consolidating the accounts of a group.

12.2 Why is it necessary to calculate figures for goodwill or capital reserves when consolidating the accounts of a group?

12.3 Joan has asked your advice. She has been offered 25 per cent of the shares in B Ltd. The other shares are owned by: a friend of hers, 18 per cent, Joan's mother, 6 per cent, and K Ltd owns the remainder. She wants to buy the shares as a relatively short-term investment. Give her your advice.

12.4 The following are the balance sheets of G Ltd and H Ltd as on 31 December 19X9:

G Ltd

Balance Sheet as at 31 December 19X9

	£	£
Fixed assets		52,000
Investment in H Ltd		28,000
Current assets	45,000	
Less Current liabilities	15,000	
		30,000
		110,000
Financed by:		
Share capital		75,000
Reserves		35,000
		110,000

H Ltd
Balance Sheet as at 31 December 19X9

	£	£
Fixed assets		18,000
Current assets	11,000	
Less Current liabilities	4,000	
		7,000
		25,000
Financed by:		
Share capital		15,000
Reserves		10,000
		25,000

On the balance sheet date G Ltd owed H Ltd £800.

Draw up consolidated balance sheets as on 31 December 19X9, given the following possibilities:

(i)   It was on 31 December 19X9 that all the shares in H Ltd had been bought by G Ltd for £28,000.

(ii) 80 per cent of the shares of H Ltd were bought on 31 December 19X9 for £28,000.

(iii) 60 per cent of the shares of H Ltd were bought on 31 December 19X9 for £28,000.

12.5X In the annual report of a group of companies, you will find a consolidated balance sheet and a consolidated profit and loss account.
   Define each of the following terms which might be found within the annual report of a group of companies:

(*a*) Minority interests;

(*b*) Subsidiary company (also known as a subsidiary undertaking);

(*c*) Associated company (also known as an associated undertaking);

(*d*) Goodwill arising on consolidation.   *(20 marks)*

(University of London Examinations and Assessment Council: GCE A-Level)

Chapter 13

Social Accounting

13.1 Introduction

Over time, the objective of financial statements has changed. In addition to reporting to shareholders of the company, directors are aware of a wide range of other user groups who are interested in accounting information. These user groups include employees of the company and, more controversially, the public at large. The controversy arises when considering whether or not organisations are responsible for 'social actions', that is actions which do not have purely financial implications.

13.2 Costs and Measurement

One of the problems associated with actions of this type is the difficulty of identifying costs and measuring the effects of (often intangible) factors that contribute to the 'value' of an organisation. It is obvious that employee loyalty and commitment to quality performance increase this value, but how are such intangibles to be measured using objective and verifiable techniques?

Some of the input costs of 'social' activities can be evaluated reasonably accurately. Providing 'social' information required under the 1985 Companies Act is not particularly difficult – it requires information regarding employees to be presented in the accounts, including numbers of employees, wages and salaries data, and details regarding the company's policy on disabled persons. Also, even where 'social' actions are required by legislation, they can often be costed reasonably accurately. For example, there are a large number of European Community directives which have been implemented in the UK relating to social and environmental policies, including the monitoring and control of air and water pollution. The costs of complying with these disclosure requirements and operational control measures can be high and, as the numbers of regulations increase, these costs will become a basic and essential part of financial statements. It will become increasingly important that not only the costs are reported, but also the benefits, and this is where the difficulties arise – how can the benefits of controlling pollution from a factory be evaluated? Indeed, should an attempt be made to evaluate them at all? Would they be better reported in qualitative or non-financial quantitative terms?

As soon as a company seeks to incorporate social criteria alongside other more traditional performance measures, problems of objectivity, comparability and usefulness arise. For example, social criteria for a paper manufacturer may include environmental issues concerning reforestation. An oil extraction company would include the environmentally safe disposal of oil rigs at the end of their useful economic lives among its social criteria.

However, issues of this type become problematic when viewed using conventional capital appraisal techniques. Not only may the measurable financial payback be so long as to be immaterial – as in the case of an environmental project such as reforestation – it may be virtually non-existent, as in the case of the disposal of obsolete oil rigs. Assessment of issues of this type require different techniques from those traditionally used, and organisations' accounting information systems will need to take this into account, not just in terms of using more qualitative value criteria, but also in selecting the information which is sought in order to assist in the decision making process.

13.3 The Pressure for Social Actions and Social Accounting

Despite the existence of many environmental laws, much of the pressure for social actions comes from pressure groups like Greenpeace. These groups can have an enormous impact upon an organisation's profitability, in ways that governments have singularly failed to do. For example, an air pollution law may concentrate on monitoring the quality of air around a factory, rather than on measuring emissions from the factory, making it far more difficult to enforce action against the factory as it can always argue that another factory is the cause of any pollution found. Also, powerful cartels can influence legislation to create enormous delays in introducing socially responsible legislative controls. A pressure group, on the other hand, can stop demand for a company's products, make it difficult for it to send its products to its customers, and may give it so much negative publicity that it can find its public image materially and irreversibly altered in a very short time.

While pressure groups are not a new phenomenon, their power is now far greater than it has ever been. Organisations need to be aware of the social, particularly environmental issues inherent in and/or related to their activities, and must be in a position to assess how best to approach these issues. They can only do so if they identify all the variables, both quantitative and qualitative, and both the inputs (costs) and the outputs (effects) of these variables, and determine methods with which to determine what actions to take. Social accounting is concerned with how to report upon the application of the social policies adopted by an organisation, and upon how they have impacted upon the organisation and its environment. An organisation that does so effectively will not only be providing user groups with rich information from which to form a view concerning its social ethos, it will also be enhancing its ability to take decisions appropriate for its own longer-term survival and prosperity.

13.4 Corporate Social Reporting

The reporting of the social effects of a company's activities became an issue in the UK in the 1970s. The reporting of non-financial information usually takes the form of narrative disclosure, sometimes supported by a statistical summary. As much social reporting is non-mandatory, comparison with other companies is difficult, if not virtually pointless and misleading. This is partially due to a positive bias in what is reported – most companies tend to report only 'good news' in their social reports. It is also due to the lack of standards governing what to include and how to present social reports.

Environmental issues have been firmly on the political agenda since the early 1980s and large corporations have responded to public demands for more information about 'green issues'. Oil companies, in particular, produce a notable amount of additional information in their annual reports. This environmental information usually includes details about the company's waste disposal practices, attitudes towards pollution and natural resource depletion, as well as the overall corporate environmental policy. However, many continue to avoid any non-mandatory social reporting, and many instances have been reported of organisations claiming to be socially responsible, when they were, in fact, anything but.

13.5 Types of Social Accounting

Social accounting can be divided into five general areas:

- national social income accounting;
- social auditing;
- financial social accounting in profit-oriented organisations;
- managerial social accounting in profit-oriented organisations;
- financial and/or managerial social accounting for non-profit organisations.

13.6 National Social Income Accounting

Such accounts have now been in existence for many years. The measure of the nation's productivity recorded in the accounts – basically in sales terms – gives an income called the Gross National Product, usually referred to as GNP.

To an outsider an increase in GNP would seem to indicate a betterment or progress in the state of affairs existing in the country. This is not necessarily true. The following example illustrates this point.

A new chemical factory is built in a town. Fumes are emitted during production which cause houses in the surrounding areas to suffer destruction of paintwork and rotting woodwork, and it also causes extensive corrosion of bodywork on motor vehicles in the neighbourhood. In addition it also affects the health of the people living nearby. An increase in GNP results because the profit elements in the above add to GNP. These profit elements include:

- to construction companies and suppliers of building materials: profit made on construction of plant;
- to house paint dealers and paint manufacturers, painters and decorators, joiners and carpenters: profit made on all work effected in extra painting, woodwork, etc.;
- to garages and car paint manufacturers: profit made on all extra work needed on motor vehicles;
- to chemists and medical requirement manufacturers: profit made on dealing with effects on residents' health, because of extra medical purchases, etc.

However, in real terms one can hardly say that there has been 'progress'. Obviously the quality of life has been seriously undermined for many people.

As national income accounts do not record the 'social' well-being of a country, other national measures have been proposed. The one most often mentioned is a system of 'social indicators'. These measure social progress in such ways as:

- national life expectancies;
- living conditions;
- levels of disease;
- nutritional levels;
- amount of crime;
- road deaths.

Thus if national life expectancies rose, or road deaths per 100,000 people decreased, etc. there could be said to be social progress, while the converse would apply were the opposite signals found to be occurring.

The main difficulty with this approach is that (given present knowledge and techniques) it cannot be measured in monetary terms. Because of this, the national social income accounts cannot be adjusted to take account of social indicators. On the level of an individual organisation, however, social indicators similar to the above are used in planning, programming, budgeting systems (PPBS). This will be discussed later.

13.7 Social Auditing

Whilst national social accounting would measure national social progress, many individual people or organisations are interested in their own social progress. This form of social progress is usually called 'social responsibility'.

To discover which of their activities have to be measured a 'social audit' is required. This is an investigation into:

(*a*) which of their activities contribute to, or detract from, being socially responsible;
(*b*) measurement of those activities;
(*c*) a report on the results disclosed by the investigation.

An example of this might be to discover how the organisation had performed in respect of such matters as:

- employment of women;
- employment of disabled people;
- occupational safety;
- occupational health;
- benefits at pensionable age;
- air pollution;
- water pollution;
- charitable activities;
- help to third world countries.

Social audits may be carried out by an organisation's own staff or by external auditors. The reports may be for internal use only or for general publication.

13.8 Financial Social Accounting in Profit-Oriented Organisations

This is an extension to normal financial accounting. The objective may either be to show how the social actions have affected financial performance, or otherwise to put a social value on the financial statements of the organisations. The two main types of financial social accounting envisaged to date are those of human resource accounting and how the organisation has responded to governmental or professional bodies' regulations concerning environmental matters.

Human resource accounting

One of the main limitations of normal financial accounting is the lack of any inclusion of the 'value' of the workforce to an organisation. The value may be determined by either:

- capitalising recruitment and training costs of employees and apportioning value over employees' period of employment; or
- calculating the 'replacement cost' of the workforce and taking this as the value of human resources; or
- extending either of the above to include the organisation's suppliers and customers.

It is contended that such measurements have the benefits that (a) financial statements are more complete, and (b) managerial decisions can be made with a fuller understanding of their implications.

For instance, suppose that a short-term drop in demand for a firm's goods led to a manufacturer laying off part of the workforce. This might mean higher profits in the short term because of wages and salaries saved. In the long term it could do irreparable damage, because recruitment could then be made difficult in future, or because of the effect on the morale of the rest of the workforce, or changes in attitudes of suppliers and customers.

Compliance costs of statutory/professional requirements

As the effects of organisations upon societies are more widely recognised there will be more and more regulations with which to comply. The costs of compliance will obviously then become a basic and essential part of financial statements.

13.9 Managerial Social Accounting in Profit-Oriented Organisations

All that has been described has an effect upon the accounting information systems of an organisation. They will have to be established on an ongoing basis, rather than be based purely on adjustments to the financial accounts at the year end.

The information will be used to affect the day-to-day decisions needed to run the organisation.

13.10 Financial and/or Managerial Social Accounting for Non-Profit Organisations

As profit is not a measure in these organisations it can be difficult to measure how well they are performing. Two approaches to measurement have been used, **planning, programming, budgeting systems (PPBS)**, and **social programme measurement**.

Both of these approaches can be said to be part of what politicians in recent years have called 'value for money'. The general attitude is that whilst there may be a need for all sorts of social programmes, including health, there is a great need for ensuring that money is not wasted in doing this. The demand is that we should ensure that we get 'value for money' in that the outputs from such schemes should be worth the amount of money expended in carrying them out.

Planning, programming, budgeting systems (PPBS)

It has been said that in the past there was a great deal of confusion between planning and budgeting. Annual budgeting takes a short-term financial view. Planning on the other hand should be long-term and also be concerned with strategic thinking.

PPBS enables management of non-profit organisations to make decisions on a better-informed basis about the allocation of resources to achieve their overall objectives. PPBS works in four stages:

1   Review organisational objectives.
2   Identify programmes to achieve objectives.
3   Identify and evaluate alternative ways of achieving each specific programme.
4   On the basis of cost-benefit principles, select appropriate programme.

PPBS necessitates the drawing up of a long-term corporate plan. This shows the objectives which the organisation is aiming to achieve. Such objectives may not be in accord with the existing organisational structure.

For instance, suppose that the objective of a local government authority, such as a city, is the care of the elderly. This could include providing:

- services to help them keep fit;
- medical services when they are ill;
- old people's housing;
- 'sheltered' accommodation;
- recreational facilities;
- educational facilities.

These services will usually be provided by separate departments, e.g. housing, welfare, education. PPBS relates the total costs to the care of the elderly, rather than to individual departmental budgets.

Management is therefore forced by PPBS to identify exactly which services or activities should be provided, otherwise the worthiness of the programme could not be evaluated. PPBS also provides information which enables management to assess the effectiveness of their plans, such as giving them a base to decide whether for every thousand pounds they are giving as good a service as possible.

As the structure of the programme will not match up with the structure of the organisation, e.g. the services provided will cut across departmental borders, one particular individual must be made responsible for controlling and supervising the programme.

Social programme measurement

The idea that governmental social programmes should be measured effectively is, as yet, in its infancy.

A government auditor would determine whether the agency had complied with the relevant laws, and had exercised adequate cost controls. The auditor would determine whether or not the results expected were being achieved and whether there were alternatives to the programmes at a lower cost.

There should be cost-benefit analyses to show that the benefits are worth the costs they incur. However, the benefit side of the analysis is often very difficult to measure. How, for instance, do you measure the benefits of not dumping a particular substance or an obsolete oil rig into the sea?

As a consequence, so far most social programmes do not yet measure results (benefits). Instead they measure 'outputs', e.g. how many prosecutions for dumping waste. Therefore, a high number of prosecutions is 'good', a low number 'bad'. This is hardly a rational way of assessing results, and quite a lot of research is going into better methods of audit.

13.11 Conflict Between Shareholders' Interests and Social Considerations

Obviously, an organisation has to come to a compromise about how far it should look after the interests of its shareholders and how far it should bother about social considerations. For instance, a company could treat its employees so well in terms of pay, pensions and welfare that the extra costs would mean very low profits or even losses.

On the other hand there must be instances that, no matter what the effects on profits, the expenses just have to be incurred. If the company has a chemical plant which could easily explode, causing widespread destruction and danger to people, then there cannot be any justification for not spending the money either to keep the plant safe or to demolish it. The full severity of the law must bear down on transgressors of the law in such cases of wilful neglect.

All the facts of the particular case must be brought into account. Let us look at a typical case where the answer may seem obvious, but perhaps there may be other factors which may make the answer not so obvious. Workers in underdeveloped countries are usually paid far lower wages than those in the developed countries. What happens if a large multinational company pays its workers in a given country three or four times as much as home-based companies? Immediately everyone wants to work for the multinational company, which can afford high wages, and leave the home-based companies which cannot. Is that sensible? What chance is there for the development of the country's own home-based industries if the outside companies constantly take all the best brains and most able people?

In such a case it would probably make more sense for the multinational company to pay wages more in keeping with the particular economy, and to help that country in other ways such as by improving the health care generally for all, better education for all, and so on. Obviously a topic such as this will engender discussions and arguments for some considerable time.

13.12 Reports from Companies

Companies, mainly those in the USA at first, have begun to declare their philosophy towards such matters as the environment. These are usually included in the annual reports which accompany the accounts.

One company, for instance, has stated that it has ten principles of environmental policy. These, briefly, were as follows:

1 To comply with both governmental and community standards of environmental excellence.
2 To use only materials and packaging selected to be good for the health of consumers, and for the safety and quality of the environment.
3 To keep energy use per unit of output down to a low level.
4 To minimise waste.
5 To get to as low a level as possible the discharge of pollutants.
6 To use other firms in business which have shown commitment to environmental excellence.
7 To research fully the ecological effect of the company's products and packaging.
8 To carry on business operations in an open, honest and co-operative manner.
9 To make certain that on the board of directors there would be scientifically knowledgeable directors, and ensure that they were provided with environmental reports regularly.

10 To ensure that all the above principles are fully observed and that challenges posed by the environment are vigorously and effectively pursued.

REVIEW QUESTIONS

Advice:

Social accounting is as yet in its infancy. There is obviously a great difficulty in trying to put money values on the various aspects of being 'better off' or 'worse off'. There are also problems connected with exactly what 'better off' and 'worse off' means. One person's 'worsening' in some way may be someone else's 'betterment'.

13.1 Describe how an increase in Gross National Product may not have a positive effect on the well-being of the country.

13.2 What types of measures could be used to measure social well-being? What difficulties would be discovered in trying to use accounting in measuring these?

13.3 What aspects of an organisation's activities could be measured in a 'social audit'?

13.4 Describe how there could be conflicts between short-term and long-term benefits.

13.5 Describe how PPBS may conflict with departmental budgets.

13.6X The Board of Directors of a multinational chemical producing company are considering the final accounts for the year and are discussing the emphasis to be made in the Annual Report.

● The Financial Director claims that the main features should be the 20% increase in both the profit after tax and earnings per share plus the record dividend payout.

● The Production Director wants to highlight the massive amounts of capital expenditure this year on safety improvements at one of the chemical plants in Scotland. The plant had previously come under severe public pressure due to the potential health hazards to the local population.

● The Human Resources Director is concerned about the alarming increase in the rate of labour turnover. The trade unions claim that 20% of their workforce earn well below the European average.

● The Managing Director reminds the Board of the significant donations the company has made this year to overseas aid in the countries where they had previously been criticised for the exploitation of cheap labour.

(a) Suggest the ways in which companies are likely to experience conflicts between managing shareholders' interests and companies' social responsibilities. *(10 marks)*

(b) What might be the consequences for this company if it fails to address these issues? *(10 marks)*

(Total 20 marks)

(Northern Examinations and Assessment Board: GCE A-Level)

Chapter 14

Capital Expenditure Appraisal

14.1 Introduction

Let us assume that a man is to start a business making widgets (an imaginary product). If there is only one type of machine that will do the necessary work then that is the machine that he will have to buy. There is no alternative to this if he wants to conduct this type of business. On the other hand, suppose there were two different kinds of machine he could buy, then he would have to buy either machine A or machine B. If both machines were equally efficient, performed the same type of work and would be in use for the same length of time, then the decision would be an easy one. He would simply buy the machine which cost the least amount of money.

Such equality of cost and effective use would be rare. Usually there will be differences in the operation of the machines, what they cost, what they would cost to maintain, exactly what kind of work they could do, and how long they would last in service. Where these differences exist the proprietor could do with some advice that would help him decide, from a financial point of view, which machine should be chosen.

You should remember that the financial picture is only one aspect of the decision whether to undertake certain kinds of work or to buy a certain fixed asset. Other factors could be:

(*a*) Pollution. One machine may produce obnoxious fumes which might affect workers in the factory or people in the surrounding area. Such pollution might also include noise pollution.

(*b*) One machine might be more dangerous to use.

(*c*) Possibly one machine might be more compatible with other types of machinery which could be needed.

(*d*) Uncertainty as to whether any necessary repairs to the machinery would be done quickly or not by the supplier, as well as possible problems with spare parts for the machine.

(*e*) How quickly the machine could be delivered and installed.

(*f*) Whether or not the workforce would need training to use the machine. These are only some of the factors which could decide whether or not machine A or machine B is to be bought, and may override the answer which would be given if the decision were based simply on financial considerations.

There is obviously a strong link here between what has been written in this chapter and that in Chapter 13, *Social Accounting*.

So far we have looked at capital expenditure appraisal in a simple fashion, as though all we had to do was to decide whether to buy one machine or another. In fact the techniques of capital expenditure appraisal extend to issues much wider than that. Instances might be such as:

(a) Shall we build and operate a factory in Germany or should it be built in Spain instead?

(b) Shall we buy some expensive footballers for our football club and raise entrance fees to pay for them, or should we use the money to build a better stadium instead?

(c) Should we buy robot machinery to replace our present manually worked machines?

(d) Which site should we choose from the three available for the construction of a new theme park?

Sometimes therefore the decision will lie between changing something we are already doing, or deciding which of two or more additional projects should be undertaken without changing our basic existing business.

Remember that in appraising capital expenditure we are dealing with estimates of future costs and future cash inflows. Our assessment of projects will therefore only be as good as the accuracy of our estimates of these items.

We will first of all look at how the calculations are made for the various methods in use. Then we will examine the relative strengths and weaknesses of each of the methods used.

14.2 Accounting Rate of Return

In this method *profits* are used in the calculations. In the other methods shown in Sections 14.3, 14.4 and 14.7, it is *cash flows* that are used for the calculations.

The accounting rate of return as a percentage is calculated by using the following formula:

$$\text{Accounting rate of return} = \frac{\text{Average annual profits}}{\text{Average investment}} \times \frac{100}{1}$$

In calculating the average annual profits re the expenditure proposal, only the *additional* revenues and *additional* costs are used. The additional costs (we could call them incremental costs) include the total depreciation charges over the life of the asset.

The average investment figure to be used in the calculation will depend on the method of depreciation which has been used. Where straight-line depreciation is used, the figure is found as follows:

$$\frac{\text{Amount of initial investment} + \text{Scrap value at the end of its life}}{2}$$

At first sight it would be understandable if the reader was to think that the scrap value should be deducted, not added. Rather than elaborate on this point and possibly confuse quite a large number of readers, I would ask the more inquisitive reader to get hold of a more advanced book on the subject to confirm that it is true.

We can now work out the accounting rate of return on two possible projects, in both cases assuming that there is no scrap value.

		A		B	
		£		£	
Initial cost of investment		6,000		8,000	
Additional profits:	Year 1	2,000		2,600	
	Year 2	3,600		3,000	
	Year 3	4,000	9,600	4,000	
	Year 4			4,000	13,600

Average profits: A (9,600 – 6,000) ÷ 3 = £1,200
       B (13,600 – 8,000) ÷ 4 = £1,400

Average investment: A £6,000 ÷ 2 = £3,000: B £8,000 ÷ 2 = £4,000

Accounting rate of return: A $\dfrac{1,200}{3,000} \times \dfrac{100}{1}$ = 40%: B $\dfrac{1,400}{4,000} \times \dfrac{100}{1}$ = 35%

Using this form of assessment, project A is preferable to project B, as the rate of return is higher at 40 per cent.

14.3 Payback Method

This method is quite a simple one. It is also used by quite a lot of firms. It measures the length of time it takes to recover the original cash outlay from the stream of net cash proceeds from the investment.

Let us look at three possible projects, D, E and F. The initial costs and the cash inflows are now shown.

		D		E		F
	£	£	£	£	£	£
Initial cost		50,000		50,000		50,000
Cash inflows: Year 1	20,000		10,000		20,000	
Year 2	30,000		20,000		20,000	
Year 3	20,000		20,000		20,000	
Year 4	10,000		30,000		20,000	
		80,000		80,000		80,000

Each has had the same outflows and inflows of cash. However, the payback method will rank as the best choice as it is the one which recovers most quickly the cost of the original investment.

Payback method: D   2 years (£50,000 inflows during the first 2 years)
       E   3 years (£50,000 inflows during the first 3 years)
       F   2.5 years (£50,000 inflows during the first 2.5 years)

The payback method will therefore select project D.

With D and E, the initial cost is received back in an exact number of years. D took exactly 2 years to get back the cost, whilst E took exactly 3 years. Where the answer is not an exact number of years then in the final year during which costs are recovered it is assumed that the cash inflows are of an equal amount during each month of that final year. With F, £40,000 had been recovered by the end of year 2. In year 3, £10,000 still had to be recovered, and £20,000 was the total of cash inflows for year 3, therefore it is assumed that it took a 10,000/20,000 part of year 3, i.e. 0.5 year to recover the final

£10,000. If the final amount to be received during year 3 had been £15,000 then it would be taken as a 15,000/20,000 part of the year, i.e. 0.75 year.

It is quite possible that use of only the payback method can mean the selection of the (eventually) least profitable project. For instance:

		G			H		I
	£	£	£	£	£	£	
Initial cost		40,000		40,000		40,000	
Cash inflows: Year 1	20,000		10,000		10,000		
Year 2	20,000		25,000		10,000		
Year 3	10,000		15,000		10,000		
Year	–		5,000		30,000		
		50,000		55,000		60,000	

Payback method: G 2.00 years
H 2.33 years
I 3.33 years

If the payback method of selection was chosen the project G would be taken, although the overall profit during each project's life would be

G Revenue   £50,000 – cost £40,000 = profit £10,000
H Revenue   £55,000 – cost £40,000 = profit £15,000
I Revenue   £60,000 – cost £40,000 = profit £20,000

14.4 The Time Value of Money

The methods we have looked at so far have both contained defects. The accounting rate of return method ignored the 'time value' of money. The payback method ignored the cash flows which occurred after the investment costs had been recovered. The net present value method which we will look at in Section 14.7 does not have these defects.

You may well wonder what we mean by the 'time value' of money. If you were offered the choice of £1 now or £1 in a year's time, then obviously you would prefer to have £1 now. If you wanted to (assuming that you could invest such a small sum of money) you could invest the £1 now at (say) 10 per cent interest, and get back £1 + 10 per cent = £1.10 in one year's time. Therefore £1 now is better than £1 in a year's time.

Businesses adopt this same outlook when they are comparing the benefits to be gained from differing capital expenditures. They take into account the *time* value of future inflows of cash, rather than simply compare the actual amounts to be received. We can now start to look at how they arrive at an adjusted set of figures for comparison.

14.5 Cost of Capital

Before we can use the net present value method we will need to know the *cost of capital* for the firm. By this we mean the interest factor representing the cost of the funds needed to finance the projects.

This is based on the idea of *opportunity cost* which some readers will have studied in economics. Suppose you have the choice of investing in securities available on the stock markets, such as ordinary shares or government securities, or alternatively you can invest the funds in one of your own projects. Let us also imagine that the risks involved in the stock market shares or securities are exactly the same as those for your possible project. In that case you would not put your funds into your own project if the stock market investment would give you a higher return.

If you could get a 15 per cent return on your money from a stock market investment, you simply would not put your money into another project, with the same risk, which gave less than 15 per cent return. It would not make sense.

The rate of return we could get from an alternative investment, with the same degree of risk, is known as the cost of capital. In this chapter in most examples we are going to assume, from now on, that the cost of capital will be 10 per cent. It will make calculations easier to do and to understand. Following the same principle of trying to make things easier to understand for the reader, we are not going to use mathematical formulae but rely instead on basic arithmetical skills.

14.6 Present Values

The next step is to put calculations on to a common basis to make comparisons possible, as we can only compare like with like.

To do this we use a technique called 'discounted cash flow' abbreviated as DCF. To try to understand this, let us look at what would happen if we invested £10,000 in a security which was free from risk, and which yields a return of 10 per cent per annum. Exhibit 14.1 shows the increase in the value of the investment if it is allowed to accumulate at 10 per cent per annum.

Exhibit 14.1

Year end	Interest	Total value of investment £
0		10,000
	10% × £10,000	1,000
1		11,000
	10% × £11,000	1,100
2		12,100
	10% × £12,100	1,210
3		13,310

Now if we try to compare these figures we can say that, with 10 per cent interest, £13,310 at the end of year 3 is equivalent to £10,000 at the start of year 1. Similarly £12,100 at the end of year 2 is equivalent to £10,000 at the start of year 1, as also is £11,000 at the end of year 1.

Now different investments result in cash flows at different points in time. If we want to compare such cash flows we need somehow to be able to get a common measure.

We can do this by discounting the cash flows (DCF) of the future back to what the value of such cash flows were at the start of the investment, given the cost of capital, e.g. in Exhibit 14.1 £13,310 at the end of year 3 is equivalent, given the cost of capital, to £10,000 at the start of year 1. This means that if we are comparing different projects, one which has cash flows for three years, another for four years, and the final one for five years, then the thing which is common to them all is the present value at the start of year 1 for each investment.

What we need to help us is a set of tables which shows us, given the cost of capital, what the present value of £1 received x years hence is at the start of year 1. A table covering ten years is now shown as Exhibit 14.2.

Exhibit 14.2

Present Value of £1

Year	1%	2%	3%	4%	5%	6%	7%	8%	9%	10%	12%	14%	15%
1	0.990	0.980	0.971	0.961	0.952	0.943	0.935	0.926	0.917	0.909	0.893	0.877	0.870
2	0.980	0.961	0.943	0.925	0.907	0.890	0.873	0.857	0.842	0.826	0.797	0.769	0.756
3	0.971	0.942	0.915	0.889	0.864	0.840	0.816	0.794	0.772	0.751	0.712	0.675	0.658
4	0.961	0.924	0.889	0.855	0.823	0.792	0.763	0.735	0.708	0.683	0.636	0.592	0.572
5	0.951	0.906	0.863	0.822	0.784	0.747	0.713	0.681	0.650	0.621	0.567	0.519	0.497
6	0.942	0.888	0.838	0.790	0.746	0.705	0.666	0.630	0.596	0.564	0.507	0.456	0.432
7	0.933	0.871	0.813	0.760	0.711	0.665	0.623	0.583	0.547	0.513	0.452	0.400	0.376
8	0.923	0.853	0.789	0.731	0.677	0.627	0.582	0.540	0.502	0.467	0.404	0.351	0.327
9	0.914	0.837	0.766	0.703	0.645	0.592	0.544	0.500	0.460	0.424	0.361	0.308	0.284
10	0.905	0.820	0.744	0.676	0.614	0.558	0.508	0.463	0.422	0.386	0.322	0.270	0.247

Year	16%	18%	20%	24%	28%	32%	36%	40%	50%	60%	70%	80%	90%
1	0.862	0.847	0.833	0.806	0.781	0.758	0.735	0.714	0.667	0.625	0.588	0.556	0.526
2	0.743	0.718	0.694	0.650	0.610	0.574	0.541	0.510	0.444	0.391	0.346	0.309	0.277
3	0.641	0.609	0.579	0.524	0.477	0.435	0.398	0.364	0.296	0.244	0.204	0.171	0.146
4	0.552	0.516	0.482	0.423	0.373	0.329	0.292	0.260	0.198	0.153	0.120	0.095	0.077
5	0.476	0.437	0.402	0.341	0.291	0.250	0.215	0.186	0.132	0.095	0.070	0.053	0.040
6	0.410	0.370	0.335	0.275	0.227	0.189	0.158	0.133	0.088	0.060	0.041	0.029	0.021
7	0.354	0.314	0.279	0.222	0.178	0.143	0.116	0.095	0.059	0.037	0.024	0.016	0.011
8	0.305	0.266	0.233	0.179	0.139	0.108	0.085	0.068	0.039	0.023	0.014	0.009	0.006
9	0.263	0.226	0.194	0.144	0.108	0.082	0.063	0.048	0.026	0.015	0.008	0.005	0.003
10	0.227	0.191	0.162	0.116	0.085	0.062	0.046	0.035	0.017	0.009	0.005	0.003	0.002

Exhibit 14.2 is an extract from a full table which is shown as Exhibit 14.6 on page 166.

On looking at Exhibit 14.2 you can see that the present value of £1 received in five years' time, given a cost of capital of 10 per cent, is £0.621, i.e. line 5 under the column headed 10%. The tables show everything in terms of £1. If therefore £10,000 was received at the end of five years then the answer would be 10,000 × £0.621 = £6,210, or for £6,000 received at the end of five years it would be 6,000 × £0.621 = £3,726.

On the other hand if, given a cost of capital of 5 per cent, and if the cash flows from the investment would be £2,000 in two years' time, followed by £3,000 in three years' time, and a final £5,000 at the end of five years, the total present value of future cash inflows would be as follows:

		£
2,000 × £0.907	=	1,814
3,000 × £0.864	=	2,592
5,000 × £0.784	=	3,920
Total present value		8,326

In case you have had any problems in understanding that, you need to look at the columns under the heading 5%. The second line, which represents the present value based on receipt of £1 in two years' time, is £0.907. As there was £2,000 received rather than £1 it has been multiplied by 2,000 to give £1,814. For year 3 you look at the same column, line 3, £0.864 and then multiply by 3,000 as there was £3,000 received, to give £2,592. Then, under the same column, line 5 representing the end of year 5 the figure of £0.784 is taken and multiplied by 5,000, because the final sum received was £5,000, to give £3,920. Adding the figures together gives a present value for all the cash flows of £8,326.

14.7 Net Present Value

The difference between the amount invested and the present value of future cash flows is called the *net present value*. This can be either a positive net present value or a negative net present value. This can now be illustrated in Exhibit 14.3.

Exhibit 14.3

George is considering whether or not to invest in two alternative projects.

Details are as follows:

	Project K £	Project L £
Investment needed at start	10,000	10,000
Estimated future cash inflows:		
Year 1	4,000	1,000
Year 2	4,000	2,000
Year 3	4,000	2,000
Year 4	1,000	5,000
Year 5	–	4,000
	13,000	14,000

Cost of capital is 10 per cent.

You then perform the following calculations:

	Project K			Project L		
Year	Amount	Present value factors	Present value	Amount	Present value factors	Present value
	£		£	£		£
1	4,000	0.909	3,636	1,000	0.909	909
2	4,000	0.826	3,304	2,000	0.826	1,652
3	4,000	0.751	3,004	2,000	0.751	1,502
4	1,000	0.683	683	5,000	0.683	3,415
5	–		–	4,000	0.621	2,484
Total present value			10,627			9,962
Less initial outlay			10,000			10,000
Net present value			627			(38)

Project K has a positive net value of £627 as its total of present values exceeds the outlay by £627. Project L has a negative present value of £38, shown as being negative by being enclosed in brackets. Of the two projects Project K would be chosen for financial reasons, as it shows the largest net present value.

Even if Project L was the only project under consideration other than investing on the stock markets with a similar risk, it would still not be chosen because it shows a negative net present value, which means that it would bring back a lower return than from a stock market investment, so there would be no point in taking up project L.

14.8 Internal Rate of Return (IRR)

This is an alternative technique which also takes into account the time value of money. It uses as a measure the 'true' rate of interest which, when applied to the cash flows and discounted back to the initial outlay, will give a present value calculation of zero.

To find this 'true' rate involves trial and error methods. We proceed as follows:

1 Choose two rates for discounting back future receipts, one of the rates to give a positive net present value, and the other to give a negative net present value.
2 Calculate the net present values using the rates as per 1.
3 Then apply a formula which can be stated as:

$$\text{IRR} = \text{lower rate} + \left(\% \text{ difference between rates} \times \frac{\text{NPV using lower \% rate}}{\text{Total difference between the two NPVs}} \right)$$

Exhibit 14.4

A project involves an initial outlay of £10,000. It results in cash inflows of end of year 1 of £5,000, year 2 of £4,000, year 3 of £3,000.

Using discount rates of 10 and 12 per cent, obtaining the necessary figures from the tables in Exhibit 14.2, the NPVs are:

Discount rates	10%		12%	
		£		£
Cash inflows	£5,000 × 0.909 =	4,545	£5,000 × 0.893 =	4,465
	£4,000 × 0.826 =	3,304	£4,000 × 0.797 =	3,188
	£3,000 × 0.751 =	2,253	£3,000 × 0.712 =	2,136
		10,102		9,789
Less Investment		10,000		10,000
Net present value		102		(211)

The internal rate of return (IRR) is therefore:

$$10\% + \left(2\% \times \frac{102}{102 + 211} \right) = 10.65\%$$

The formula is an approximate one, it is not absolutely correct, but it gives an answer which is satisfactory for all normal practical purposes.

If we were now to repeat the calculations, taking the discount factor as 10.65 per cent we would see that they would give a net present value of zero.

Once calculated, the IRR is compared with the cost of capital. If the cost of capital is higher than the IRR then the project should not be taken up. If you are comparing two alternative projects the one with the highest IRR would be selected for investment, assuming that it was above the cost of capital.

14.9 Relevant and Irrelevant Costs

When decision making, some costs and revenues are relevant to a decision that is to be taken, whilst other costs and revenues are not, i.e. they are irrelevant. The *relevant costs* and revenues are those costs and revenues of the future that will be affected by the decision, whereas irrelevant costs and revenues will not be so affected.

Take as an example a decision as to whether or not we should telephone a lot of our customers or not in a sales campaign. The cost of the phone rental is irrelevant in the decision whether or not to conduct the campaign, as we will still have to pay exactly the same rental whether or not we engage in the campaign. On the other hand, the cost of making the extra phone calls will be a relevant cost as they would not have been incurred if the campaign had not gone ahead.

With revenues, take the case of buying a new car for a salesman. If the revenues he would help create by sales would remain unchanged no matter which car he were to have, then the revenues would be completely irrelevant in taking the decision as to the type of car to be bought.

However, to take the case of a salesman who sells some of his products to farmers. With a four-wheel drive car he could get to farms which would otherwise be inaccessible to an ordinary two-wheel drive car. In this case the revenues would be relevant to the decision as to the type of car to be bought, as they would be affected by the decision.

14.10 Sunk Costs

This is a term which can be confusing, since it really means an irrelevant cost which has already occurred. It is a past cost, not a future cost.

Let us take the case of a machine which was bought several years ago, and now has a written down value of £10,000. The scrap value is nil. We can either use the machine on a project we are considering or else we can scrap it. Let us suppose that the revenue from the project will be £25,000 and the future relevant costs will be £18,000. If we added the written down value of the machine to the £18,000 costs then we would make a loss of £3,000 (£25,000 – £28,000). Looking at it that way, we would not tackle the project.

However, the cost of the machine was a past cost. If we do not use the machine on this project the only other alternative is to scrap it. Such a past cost is said to be a *sunk cost* and is irrelevant to the decision to be taken. We therefore take on the project (assuming there is no better alternative project) and are better off by £7,000 (£25,000 – £18,000).

14.11 A Comparison of the Methods

We will now look at a case where each of the methods already described will be used to try to select the best investment. You will see that the different methods can give different answers as to which project should be chosen.

Exhibit 14.5

ABC Ltd is wondering whether or not to invest in one of three possible projects. The initial investment will be £10,000, and the cost of capital is 10 per cent. There is no scrap value for fixed assets used. Details of the net cash inflows are as follows:

	M	N	P
	£	£	£
Year 1	3,000	5,000	4,000
Year 2	6,000	5,000	5,000
Year 3	4,000	2,000	3,000
Year 4	–	1,600	1,000
Year 5	–	–	1,400
	13,000	13,600	14,400

1 Accounting rate of return method:

$$\frac{\text{Average yearly profit}}{\text{Average investment}} \times \frac{100}{1} \qquad \frac{1,000}{5,000} = 20\% \qquad \frac{900}{5,000} = 18\% \qquad \frac{880}{5,000} = 17.6\%$$

2 Payback method: 2.25 years   2 years $2\frac{1}{3}$ years

3 Net present value method (cost of capital 10%)

Discount factors per tables	M	N	P
		Present values in £s	
£0.909	× 3,000 = 2,727	× 5,000 = 4,545	× 4,000 = 3,636
£0.826	× 6,000 = 4,956	× 5,000 = 4,130	× 5,000 = 4,130
£0.751	× 4,000 = 3,004	× 2,000 = 1,502	× 3,000 = 2,253
£0.683		× 1,600 = 1,092	× 1,000 = 683
£0.621			× 1,400 = 869
Total value of present value	10,687	11,269	11,571
Less Investment	10,000	10,000	10,000
Net present values	687	1,269	1,571

4 Internal rate of return

Stage 1: Use a rate of return which will give negative net present values. In this instance it is taken to be 18%.

Discount factors per tables at 18%	M	N	P
		Present values in £s	
£0.847	× 3,000 = 2,541	× 5,000 = £4,235	× 4,000 = 3,388
£0.718	× 6,000 = 4,308	× 5,000 = 3,590	× 5,000 = 3,590
£0.609	× 4,000 = 2,436	× 2,000 = 1,218	× 3,000 = 1,827
£0.516		× 1,600 = 826	× 1,000 = 516
£0.437			× 1,400 = 611
Total of present value	9,285	9,869	9,932
Less Investment	10,000	10,000	10,000
Net present values	(715)	(131)	(68)

Stage 2: Calculate the internal rate of return (IRR), using figures for positive present value figures already calculated in **3** above.

M $\quad 10\% + \left(8\% \times \dfrac{687}{687 + 715} \right) \quad = 13.92\%$

N $\quad 10\% + \left(8\% \times \dfrac{1,269}{1,269 + 131} \right) \quad = 17.25\%$

P $\quad 10\% + \left(8\% \times \dfrac{1,571}{1,571 + 68} \right) \quad = 17.67\%$

If used on its own, without reference to the other methods:

1 Accounting rate of return would choose project M, as it gives highest rate of 20 per cent.
2 Payback would choose project N, as it pays back in the shortest time of two years.
3 Net present value would choose project P as it gives the highest net present value of £1,571.
4 Internal rate of return would choose project P, as it shows highest return of 17.67 per cent, which is itself higher than the cost of capital.

14.12 Merits and Demerits of the Techniques

Accounting rate of return

Although it is generally easy to calculate, ARR produces a percentage figure that is of little practical use. It cannot, for example, be compared to an organisation's cost of capital in order to assess whether a project would achieve a greater return than the cost of the capital that financed it. It also ignores the timing of cash flows – a project whose profits all arose at the start would be rejected in favour of one with a higher ARR whose profits all came at the end, even if inflation meant that those later period profits were worth significantly less in present value terms than the earlier profits of the rejected project.

Payback method

This method is easy to calculate, and is also easy for anyone to understand. As it concentrates on cash flows in the near future many people will tend to accept it, as they are more wary when the cash flows several years hence are used in the other methods. This is because the further away the estimates of cash flows are needed then the less accurate they will tend to be.

However, the method completely ignores the time value of money. It also ignores the cash flows received after the payback period has been reached.

There is no doubt that where there are severe cash-flow problems the payback method will be more appealing than the more theoretically correct present-value techniques.

Net present value

Theoretically this is the best method. It takes into account all the cash flows, the time value of money and the amounts involved.

Normally the IRR and the net present value method will rank the projects in the same order. For some rather complicated reasons which it is preferred not to examine here, the IRR does in certain cases give the wrong ranking compared with the net present value method.

Internal rate of return

This takes into account the time value of money and it is also easy for people to understand, as it is expressed as a percentage.

However, giving a return simply as a percentage can be misleading. Comparing a 50 per cent return which amounts to £100 with a 40 per cent return of £1,000, just looking at the percentage figures alone, would not be very sensible.

14.13 Surveys of Practice

The various surveys as to which techniques are used do vary somewhat, but there is a general picture available, although this varies between the UK and the USA.

1 Most firms use more than one method to evaluate an investment.
2 The payback method is that most frequently used, although it is less used in the USA than in the UK. The IRR method is the second most widely used method.
3 The use of both net present value method and of IRR is growing, although the IRR is preferred by more firms than the superior NPV method. This seems to be because managers can more easily understand the IRR method rather than the NPV method.

It would appear that the popularity of the payback method is due to the fact that most firms place undue emphasis on the short term, such an outlook not being too conducive to DCF methods.

Before we look at any of the methods in use we should bear in mind that estimates concerning cash flows in the very near future are normally more accurate than those for several years ahead. We do know what is going on at the present time, probably there will not be too much change very quickly, but we cannot pretend that we can be so certain about cash flows in five or six years' time.

There are mathematical methods dealing with probability that can help with this sort of problem. This is, however, outside the scope of the A-Level syllabuses and will not be included in this book.

Exhibit 14.6 For use with Review Questions

Year	1%	2%	3%	4%	5%	6%	7%	8%	9%	10%	12%	14%	15%
1	0.990	0.980	0.971	0.961	0.952	0.943	0.935	0.926	0.917	0.909	0.893	0.877	0.870
2	0.980	0.961	0.943	0.925	0.907	0.890	0.873	0.857	0.842	0.826	0.797	0.769	0.756
3	0.971	0.942	0.915	0.889	0.864	0.840	0.816	0.794	0.772	0.751	0.712	0.675	0.658
4	0.961	0.924	0.889	0.855	0.823	0.792	0.763	0.735	0.708	0.683	0.636	0.592	0.572
5	0.951	0.906	0.863	0.822	0.784	0.747	0.713	0.681	0.650	0.621	0.567	0.519	0.497
6	0.942	0.888	0.838	0.790	0.746	0.705	0.666	0.630	0.596	0.564	0.507	0.456	0.432
7	0.933	0.871	0.813	0.760	0.711	0.665	0.623	0.583	0.547	0.513	0.452	0.400	0.376
8	0.923	0.853	0.789	0.731	0.677	0.627	0.582	0.540	0.502	0.467	0.404	0.351	0.327
9	0.914	0.837	0.766	0.703	0.645	0.592	0.544	0.500	0.460	0.424	0.361	0.308	0.284
10	0.905	0.820	0.744	0.676	0.614	0.558	0.508	0.463	0.422	0.386	0.322	0.270	0.247
11	0.896	0.804	0.722	0.650	0.585	0.527	0.475	0.429	0.388	0.350	0.287	0.237	0.215
12	0.887	0.788	0.701	0.625	0.557	0.497	0.444	0.397	0.356	0.319	0.257	0.208	0.187
13	0.879	0.773	0.681	0.601	0.530	0.469	0.415	0.368	0.326	0.290	0.229	0.182	0.163
14	0.870	0.758	0.661	0.577	0.505	0.442	0.388	0.340	0.299	0.263	0.205	0.160	0.141
15	0.861	0.743	0.642	0.555	0.481	0.417	0.362	0.315	0.275	0.239	0.183	0.140	0.123
16	0.853	0.728	0.623	0.534	0.458	0.394	0.339	0.292	0.252	0.218	0.163	0.123	0.107
17	0.844	0.714	0.605	0.513	0.436	0.371	0.317	0.270	0.231	0.198	0.146	0.108	0.093
18	0.836	0.700	0.587	0.494	0.416	0.350	0.296	0.250	0.212	0.180	0.130	0.095	0.081
19	0.828	0.686	0.570	0.475	0.396	0.331	0.276	0.232	0.194	0.164	0.116	0.083	0.070
20	0.820	0.673	0.554	0.456	0.377	0.319	0.258	0.215	0.178	0.149	0.104	0.073	0.061
25	0.780	0.610	0.478	0.375	0.295	0.233	0.184	0.146	0.116	0.092	0.059	0.038	0.030
30	0.742	0.552	0.412	0.308	0.231	0.174	0.131	0.099	0.075	0.057	0.033	0.020	0.015

Year	16%	18%	20%	24%	28%	32%	36%	40%	50%	60%	70%	80%	90%
1	0.862	0.847	0.833	0.806	0.781	0.758	0.735	0.714	0.667	0.625	0.588	0.556	0.526
2	0.743	0.718	0.694	0.650	0.610	0.574	0.541	0.510	0.444	0.391	0.346	0.309	0.277
3	0.641	0.609	0.579	0.524	0.477	0.435	0.398	0.364	0.296	0.244	0.204	0.171	0.146
4	0.552	0.516	0.482	0.423	0.373	0.329	0.292	0.260	0.198	0.153	0.120	0.095	0.077
5	0.476	0.437	0.402	0.341	0.291	0.250	0.215	0.186	0.132	0.095	0.070	0.053	0.040
6	0.410	0.370	0.335	0.275	0.227	0.189	0.158	0.133	0.088	0.060	0.041	0.029	0.021
7	0.354	0.314	0.279	0.222	0.178	0.143	0.116	0.095	0.059	0.037	0.024	0.016	0.011
8	0.305	0.266	0.233	0.179	0.139	0.108	0.085	0.068	0.039	0.023	0.014	0.009	0.006
9	0.263	0.226	0.194	0.144	0.108	0.082	0.063	0.048	0.026	0.015	0.008	0.005	0.003
10	0.227	0.191	0.162	0.116	0.085	0.062	0.046	0.035	0.017	0.009	0.005	0.003	0.002
11	0.195	0.162	0.135	0.094	0.066	0.047	0.034	0.025	0.012	0.006	0.003	0.002	0.001
12	0.168	0.137	0.112	0.076	0.052	0.036	0.025	0.018	0.008	0.004	0.002	0.001	0.001
13	0.145	0.116	0.093	0.061	0.040	0.027	0.018	0.013	0.005	0.002	0.001	0.001	0.000
14	0.125	0.099	0.078	0.049	0.032	0.021	0.014	0.009	0.003	0.001	0.001	0.000	0.000
15	0.108	0.084	0.065	0.040	0.025	0.016	0.010	0.006	0.002	0.001	0.000	0.000	0.000
16	0.093	0.071	0.054	0.032	0.019	0.012	0.007	0.005	0.002	0.001	0.000	0.000	
17	0.080	0.060	0.045	0.026	0.015	0.009	0.005	0.003	0.001	0.000	0.000		
18	0.069	0.051	0.038	0.021	0.012	0.007	0.004	0.002	0.001	0.000	0.000		
19	0.060	0.043	0.031	0.017	0.009	0.005	0.003	0.002	0.000	0.000			
20	0.051	0.037	0.026	0.014	0.007	0.004	0.002	0.001	0.000	0.000			
25	0.024	0.016	0.010	0.005	0.002	0.001	0.000	0.000					
30	0.012	0.007	0.004	0.002	0.001	0.000	0.000						

REVIEW QUESTIONS

Advice:

The chances of your examinations containing a question on the appraisal of capital expenditure are quite high.

There will be occasions when you can bring in the factors other than financial ones which should be taken into account. This will gain you important marks, as examiners like to see answers which are not limited simply to computations. This is probably more true of A-Level examinations than in some other accounting examinations. Study the points raised in Section 14.1. Also think about it and bring in some points of your own.

Make certain that you can manage the computations required in Questions 14.1 and 14.2.

Make certain that you know 14.10, as the merits and demerits of the techniques used will often be asked.

When you see a set of net present value tables, such as those on page 166 you will need to perform calculations such as those shown in Section 14.7.

The payback method, net present value method, and the internal rate of return are all concerned with cash inflows and outflows. Remember that depreciation is neither of these; it should be adjusted to remove it from the calculations. On the other hand, the accounting rate of return includes depreciation as an expense.

In an examination you may well be given the task of comparing two projects, one costing less than the other. Frequently the more expensive project will give a slightly greater net cash flow. The examiner may well expect you to point out that if the project costing less had been taken up, it could be possible that the return from that project plus income earned by investing the difference in initial costs could result in a greater return than that from the more costly project.

14.1 RST Ltd has to decide which one of three projects should be taken up. The following information is available:

- The initial investment would be £20,000, and the cost of capital is 8 per cent. There is no scrap value for the fixed assets used.
- The net cash inflows from the three projects are estimated as:

	F £	G £	H £
Year 1	10,000	6,000	8,000
Year 2	8,000	5,000	9,000
Year 3	7,000	5,000	5,000
Year 4		5,000	4,000
Year 5		6,000	
	25,000	27,000	26,000

In respect of each project you are required to calculate the following:

(i) Accounting rate of return

(ii) Payback

(iii) Net present values

(iv) Internal rate of return.

14.2X Doldrums Ltd is trying to decide which project should be taken up, out of three possible investments.

- The initial investment would amount to £30,000. Scrap value at end of use would be nil. Cost of capital is 9 per cent.
- The net cash inflows from the three projects under consideration are:

	N £	V £	Q £
Year 1	7,000	12,000	10,000
Year 2	6,000	12,000	10,000
Year 3	8,000	15,000	10,000
Year 4	10,000		11,000
Year 5	12,000		
	43,000	39,000	41,000

Required:

For each possible project you are required to calculate:

(i) Accounting rate of return
(ii) Payback
(iii) Net present value
(iv) Internal rate of return

14.3 Two years ago Sandstone Ltd conducted market research at a cost of £16,000 to investigate the potential market for new products. They are now considering two new product developments, only one of which will be undertaken. The anticipated profitabilities of these two separate projects A and B are given below.

	Project A		Project B	
	£	£	£	£
Annual sales		80,000		100,000
Cost of sales	40,000		50,000	
Administration costs	15,000		10,000	
Depreciation	5,000		10,000	
		60,000		70,000
Net profit		20,000		30,000

It is expected that the above will continue for each year of each project's forecast life. The capital cost for Project A is £45,000 and for Project B £53,000.

The expected economic lives are

Project A	8 years
Project B	5 years

Depreciation has been calculated on a straight-line basis, and assumes estimated scrap values of £5,000 for Project A at the end of Year 8, and £3,000 for Project B at the end of Year 5. All costs and revenue take place at the end of each year. The cost of capital is 12 per cent.

Extract from Present Value Table of £1 @ 12 per cent

Year 1	0.893	Year 5	0.567
Year 2	0.797	Year 6	0.507
Year 3	0.712	Year 7	0.452
Year 4	0.636	Year 8	0.404

Required:

A   Calculate the payback period and net present value of each project. *(14 marks)*

B   State, with reasoning, which of the two projects you would recommend. *(3 marks)*

C   Briefly explain why net present value is considered a more meaningful technique compared to payback when making capital expenditure decisions. *(4 marks)*

D   Explain how you have treated the original market research costs in relation to the evaluation of the projects. *(2 marks)*

(Total marks 23)

(University of Oxford Local Delegacy Examinations: GCE A-Level)

14.4X Eastinteg plc, a major chemical company, had been invited to set up a plant in Eastern Europe in order to provide work in a region of high unemployment. The regional government also hoped that plant modernisation may be possible as well.

Eastinteg have the choice of two alternative plants:

(i)   *Plant A.* A modern complex from Japan; highly efficient but expensive. Its capital cost is £85m.

Its expected annual output is:

19X3	19X4	19X5	19X6
Tonnes	Tonnes	Tonnes	Tonnes
30,000	36,000	41,500	80,000

This plant produces a high quality output and fetches the following prices on the open market.

	19X3	19X4	19X5	19X6
	£	£	£	£
Price per tonne	1,000	1,100	950	1,150

(ii)   *Plant B.* This plant is manufactured locally in Eastern Europe and is relatively unsophisticated and inefficient. Many experts have reported that it pollutes the environment.

The plant will cost £45m, but since many regional government officials were keen to have locally provided plant, there would be a government grant for the initial capital cost of £20m.

In addition an annual subsidy would also be paid for the first four years of £5m per year. This is to offset some of the plant's running costs.

The expected annual output is:

19X3	19X4	19X5	19X6
Tonnes	Tonnes	Tonnes	Tonnes
26,000	28,000	27,000	60,000

The output quality of Plant B is relatively inferior to Plant A and is expected to fetch the following lower prices.

	19X3	19X4	19X5	19X6
	£	£	£	£
Price per tonne	600	650	570	750

Additional information

1 The forecast operating payments for the plants are as follows:

	Payments per tonne of output			
	19X3	19X4	19X5	19X6
	£	£	£	£
Plant A	400	450	460	500
Plant B	450	500	500	550

2 Both plants have an expected life of ten years, but it is known that Plant B becomes even less operationally efficient after six years.

3 Whilst the East European regional government is aware of the pollutive effect of Plant B, it feels that pollution is so common in the region that the additional amount caused by this plant can be ignored.

4 The company's cost of capital is 12 per cent per annum.

5 It should be assumed that all costs are paid and all revenues received at the end of each year.

6 The following is an extract from the present value table for £1:

	11%	12%	13%	14%
Year 1	£0.901	£0.893	£0.885	£0.877
Year 2	£0.812	£0.797	£0.783	£0.769
Year 3	£0.731	£0.712	£0.693	£0.675
Year 4	£0.659	£0.636	£0.613	£0.592

Required:

(a) The forecast revenue statements for each of the years 19X3–19X6 and for each of the plants being considered. Show the expected yearly net cash flows. *(8 marks)*

(b) Appropriate computations using the net present value method for each of the Plants A and B, for the first four years. *(6 marks)*

(c) A report providing a recommendation to the management of Eastinteg plc as to which plant should be purchased. Your report should include:
  (i) a critical evaluation of the method used to assess the capital project;
  (ii) a social accounting assessment of the effects of chemical pollution. *(11 marks)*

(Associated Examining Board: GCE A-Level)

14.5 Barchester United (a football club) is negotiating with an Italian club for the transfer of the noted player Luciano Gudshotti to the Barchester United team. It is now the start of the new season and you have been asked to advise on the financial aspects of the transfer negotiations.

The average home gate for Barchester is 30,000 people, 30 times a season and the spectator entrance fee is currently £2.50. The present team of 15 players earn on average a total of £6,000 per week (assume a 50-week year) and the existing team has cost £3,200,000 in transfer fees. At present and after all expenses, the Barchester United Football Club makes an annual profit of £150,000.

The directors consider that if an additional £240,000 is spent each year on new promotional activities and with Gudshotti in the team, it will be possible to increase the number of spectators to 33,000 per game and to raise the entrance fee to £3 per person. A new sponsorship deal to be agreed with a local company if Gudshotti joins the club would bring in an additional £50,000 a year in income.

The Italian club requires a transfer fee of £900,000 of which one half would have to be paid at once, and the balance payable equally in three annual instalments beginning at the end of year 1. Gudshotti requires a four-year contract paying him £50,000 a year plus a signing-on fee (payable at once on signing the contract) of £200,000. Additionally the rest of the team would expect a 20 per cent pay rise because more will be expected from the whole team in terms of performance.

The cost of capital to Barchester United is estimated to be 14 per cent and the club also expects a payback of not more than three years. You may assume that unless otherwise indicated all costs are to be paid and all revenues received at the end of each year and you are not required to consider the position beyond four years.

Required:

(a) Calculate the payback period over which the proposed expenditure will be recovered.

(5 marks)

(b) Calculate the net present value of the proposal using the discounted cash flow method.

(11 marks)

(c) Calculate the approximate internal rate of return of the proposal. (6 marks)

(d) Advise the directors as to whether or not they should sign Gudshotti and list two other factors which could have an effect on the decision. (3 marks)

Note: Table of present value factors:

Tn	i = 14%	18%	22%	26%	30%
t0	1.000	1.000	1.000	1.000	1.000
t1	0.877	0.847	0.820	0.794	0.769
t2	0.769	0.718	0.672	0.630	0.592
t3	0.675	0.609	0.551	0.500	0.455
t4	0.592	0.516	0.451	0.397	0.350

The above table shows the present value of £1 when received at time tn, where n is the number of years before payment is received and i is the rate of interest used in discounting.

(*Reproduced by permission of the University of Cambridge Local Examinations Syndicate*)

14.6X Richards Chemicals Ltd currently disposes of its waste material by using waste skips (large refuse containers) located around its site. The company has ten skips on site, with each skip being able to hold $16m^3$ of waste.

Each skip is only emptied when full, and there are an average of 12 collections in total for the company, each week throughout the year. The company pays a rental charge of £3 per day for each skip, and the collection charge for emptying is £10 per skip.

As part of its four-year plan from 1 January 19X3, the company is reviewing its waste disposal method, and wishes to evaluate alternatives. The amount of waste is expected to remain at current levels each year throughout the four-year period.

Option 1 – Current method
The current prices would remain fixed for the first two years (19X3 and 19X4), they would then be increased by 10 per cent and remain fixed for a further two years. All charges would be payable in arrears at the end of each year.

Option 2 – Waste Compactor
This would replace all skips on site, and waste would be put directly into a compactor (for compressing), and when full a collection would be made.

The price quoted from the supplier for a suitable compactor is £31,000, this including a delivery charge of £1,000. The full amount would be payable on 1 January 19X3.

The capacity of the compactor is the equivalent of $64m^3$ of waste, and the collection charge for emptying would be £17.50 per collection. This price would be fixed for the first two years, and would then be increased by 10 per cent and remain fixed for a further two years. These charges would be payable in arrears at the end of each year.

A maintenance contract would also be required, the charge is £500 p.a., payable in advance, and in addition to regular maintenance it includes all running costs throughout the year. The maintenance contract would be fixed in price for the first two years, but would increase by 10 per cent in year 3, with the new rate fixed until the end of the four-year period.

The compactor is expected to last four years, and would have a residual value of £400.

Option 3 – Gas Incinerator
This would again replace all skips on site, and would have the capacity to burn all the waste. The company had investigated this method in 19X0, and special gas pipes had been installed at a cost of £1,200. The project had been planned for the north end of the works overlooking a residential area. It did not continue at that time due to the possibility of toxic fumes and the concern of local residents. The new project would be located at the west end of the works overlooking open land and sports playing fields.

The price quoted from the supplier is £32,000, this includes a delivery charge of £1,000. The full amount would be payable on 1 January 19X3.

Installation of additional special gas pipes would cost £2,000. This would be payable on 1 January 19X3.

A maintenance contract would also be required, the charge is £500 p.a., payable in advance, and in addition to regular maintenance it includes the provision of smoke filters which would help reduce the smoke emissions given from the plant. The maintenance contract would be fixed in price for the first two years, but would increase by 10 per cent in year 3, with the new rate then fixed until the end of the four-year period.

The gas supply running costs would be £1,500 p.a., payable in arrears at the end of each year. These costs would be fixed for the first three years, but would then increase by 8 per cent in year 4.

The incinerator is expected to last four years and would not have any residual value at the end of the period.

One of the directors has already added up the various costs as listed, and states option 3 is the best.

The cost of capital for the company is 12 per cent.

Extract from Present Value Table of £1 @ 12%.

Year 1	0.893
Year 2	0.797
Year 3	0.712
Year 4	0.636
Year 5	0.567

Required:

A   A net present value evaluation of each of the three options (all calculations are to be rounded to the nearest £). *(23 marks)*

B   State with reasoning whether you agree with the comments of the director. What is your recommendation, giving brief reasons for your choice? *(3 marks)*

C   (i)   Outline the non-accounting factors which the company should consider when making its decision.
    (ii) What measures could a government take to deal with any environmental concerns?
(5 marks)
(Total marks 31)

(University of Oxford Local Delegacy Examinations: GCE A-Level)

14.7

(a) Why do ordinary shareholders usually expect a greater return than the holders of preference shares, and the holders of preference shares a greater return than the holders of debentures?

(3 marks)

(b) By carrying a lower rate of return, debentures may be regarded as a cheaper source of finance than are ordinary shares. What limits the amount of debentures a company can carry in its capital structure?

(3 marks)

(c)

Capital structure
(£000)

	Ajax	Borg
Ordinary shares (16%)	700	300
Preference shares (14%)	200	200
Debentures (12%)	100	500

   (i) Calculate the weighted average cost of capital for each of the companies above, on the assumption that debenture interest is an allowable expense against corporation tax, which stands at 40 per cent.

   (ii) Explain fully the reasons for any differences in the weighted average cost of capital for the two companies.

(9 marks)

(d) Ajax and Borg both have an opportunity to invest in project Cymberline which requires an initial investment of £300,000, and which is thought will generate the following net cash flows:

Cymberline
(£)

Year 1	55,000
Year 2	60,000
Year 3	145,000
Year 4	170,000

   (i) What is the maximum cost of financing that can be considered when investing in this project?

   (ii) From the information given, state with reasons whether you would advise either of the two companies to invest in Cymberline.

Note: Assume that the cash inflow arises at the end of each year.   *(10 marks)*

Present Value of 1
Period

	12%	13%	14%	15%	16%
1	0.893	0.885	0.877	0.870	0.862
2	0.797	0.783	0.769	0.756	0.743
3	0.712	0.693	0.675	0.658	0.641
4	0.636	0.613	0.592	0.572	0.552

(University of London: GCE A-Level)

14.8 The Grubby Brushes Co. Limited has the following capital structure:

	£000
Ordinary shares (fully paid)	1,000
Preference shares (11%)	400
Debentures (10%)	600

The holders of the ordinary shares expect a dividend of 14 per cent per annum. Debenture interest is an allowable charge against corporation tax which stands at 30 per cent.

The directors are considering the re-equipment of the production departments to enable the company to compete more effectively in overseas markets. Two schemes have been proposed, details of which are as follows:

	Scheme 1 £	Scheme 2 £
Initial capital cost	50,000	70,000
Estimated net cash flows:		
Year 1	14,000	14,000
Year 2	10,000	18,000
Year 3	19,000	27,000
Year 4	24,000	31,000

(a) Calculate the company's weighted average cost of capital (to nearest whole per cent).

(6 marks)

(b) Using your answer to (a) calculate the NPV (Net Present Value) of the two projects.

(8 marks)

(c) Using your answer to (b) state which project you would recommend and why.   *(5 marks)*

(d) Would your answer to (c) be different if you knew that the estimated net cash flows for the two projects in year 5 were (Scheme 1) £23,000 and (Scheme 2) £32,000? Give your reasons.

(6 marks)

Discount Factors

	9%	10%	11%	12%	13%	14%	15%
Year 1	0.917	0.909	0.901	0.893	0.885	0.877	0.870
2	0.842	0.826	0.812	0.797	0.783	0.769	0.756
3	0.772	0.751	0.731	0.712	0.693	0.675	0.658
4	0.708	0.683	0.659	0.636	0.613	0.592	0.572
5	0.650	0.621	0.594	0.567	0.543	0.519	0.497

(University of London: GCE A-Level)

14.9X A recent survey showed that in investment appraisal, the popularity of *payback* as an evaluation method continues to grow in spite of its known drawbacks. Of some 92 per cent of firms which use the method, approximately one half require its calculation for all projects.

(a) What are main drawbacks to payback in investment appraisal? Briefly examine two other methods that overcome these disadvantages.   *(8 marks)*

(b) Why do you think payback is so popular as a method as compared to the other methods you have examined in (a)?   *(12 marks)*

(University of London: GCE A-Level)

14.10X André Lefevre runs a car valeting business and now wishes to expand his operations into car hire. He is considering purchasing a small fleet of five identical cars. His accountant has provided him with the following information on each of the three models under consideration.

Model	Country of manufacture	Cost per car (£)
Armada	UK	7,000
Biarritz	Spain	12,000
Carioka	Japan	16,000

Additional information
(1) Dealers are prepared to allow the following discounts on the purchase of a fleet of five cars:

	%
Armada	5
Biarritz	10
Carioka	15

(2) Market research has indicated that likely demand for the hire of each fleet will yield the following total incomes per year:

	£
Armada	30,000
Biarritz	35,000
Carioka	44,000

(3) It is intended to sell the cars immediately at the end of three years. Estimated selling prices for each car then being:

	£
Armada	2,500
Biarritz	5,000
Carioka	7,000

(4) Insurance premiums are to be paid at the start of each year and are expected to rise over the next three years. Insurance for each fleet is expected to cost:

	Year 1 £	Year 2 £	Year 3 £
Armada	7,000	8,050	9,257
Biarritz	9,000	10,350	11,902
Carioka	10,500	12,075	13,886

(5) Servicing and fuel charges are also expected to rise over the next three years. Servicing and fuel charges for each fleet are expected to cost:

	Year 1 £	Year 2 £	Year 3 £
Armada	4,050	4,155	4,270
Biarritz	5,400	5,520	5,652
Carioka	6,700	6,870	7,057

(6) All cash flows except insurance arise at the end of the relevant year.

(7) The rate of interest applicable is 12% per annum.

(8) The following extract is from the present value table for £1:

Year	12%
1	0.893
2	0.797
3	0.712

Required:

(a) A financial statement using the net present value method for **each** fleet of cars being considered. (Workings to the nearest pound.) *(35 marks)*

(b) A report for André Lefevre advising him which fleet of cars should be purchased. Indicate any reservations you may have regarding the net present value method of evaluating a project. *(7 marks)*

(c) A discussion of any other factors which may influence André in his decision. *(8 marks)*

(Associated Examining Board: GCE A-Level)

Chapter 15

The Analysis and Interpretation of Accounting Statements

15.1 Introduction

When shareholders receive the annual financial statements of a business, many simply look to see whether it has made a profit, and then put the document away. They are aware of only one thing – that the company made a profit of £x. They do not know if it was a 'good' profit. Nor do they know whether it was any different from the profit earned in previous years. (Even if they had noticed the previous period's profit figure in the comparative column, they would be unaware of the equivalent figures for the periods that preceded it.) In addition, they would have no perception of how the performance compared to those of other companies operating in the same sector.

In order that performance within a period can be assessed, ratio analysis may be undertaken, as explained in Chapter 44 of *Frank Wood's Business Accounting 1*, seventh edition. However, such analysis is relatively useless unless a similar task is undertaken on the financial figures for previous periods. Trend analysis is very important in the interpretation of financial statements, for it is only then that the relative position can be identified, i.e. whether things are improving, etc.

Of similar importance if financial statements are to be usefully interpreted is comparison of the position shown with that of other companies operating in the same sector.

15.2 Sector Relevance

The importance of ensuring that any comparison of analysis between companies is between companies in the same sector can best be illustrated through an extreme example – that of the contrast between service companies and manufacturing companies.

Stating the obvious, a firm of consultants that advise their clients on marketing strategies will have far fewer tangible assets than a company with the same turnover which manufactures forklift trucks. The service industry will need premises, but these could easily be rented and, in addition, would need very little in the way of machinery. Some computer equipment and office equipment as well as motor cars would be all that would be needed.

Compared with the service industry firm, a manufacturing company, such as that making forklift trucks, would need a great deal of machinery as well as motor lorries and various types of buildings, and so on. The manufacturing firm would also have stocks of materials and unsold trucks. The service firm would have very little in the way of stocks of tangible assets.

Especially with the service industries, it is also likely that the number of people working for the firm, but who do most, sometimes all of their work in their homes will grow apace. The need for people to turn up at offices at given times every day is falling dramatically with the wider use of computers and various communication and link-up devices.

All of this has an effect on the ratios of performance calculated from the accounts of manufacturers and service industry firms. The figure of return on capital employed for a service firm, simply because of the few tangible assets needed, may appear to be quite high. For a manufacturing firm the opposite may well be the case.

If this distinction between these completely different types of organisation is understood, then the interpreter of the accounts will judge them accordingly. Failure to understand the distinction will bring forth some very strange conclusions.

15.3 Trend Analysis

What is important for a business is not just what the accounting ratios are for one year, but what the trend has been. In Chapter 44 of *Frank Wood's Business Accounting 1*, the example was introduced of two companies G and H. The example is now reintroduced and further developed: Exhibit 15.1 presents four ratios derived from the financial statements of G over the past five periods.

Exhibit 15.1

Period:	X1	X2	X3	X4	X5(now)
Gross profit as % of sales	40	38	36	35	34
Net profit as % of sales	15	13	12	12	11
Net profit as % of capital employed	13	12	11	11	10
Current ratio	3.0	2.8	2.6	2.3	2.0

If the trends in these four ratios are considered, it is clear that they are all deteriorating, but there is no indication whether there should be cause for concern as a result. For example, the industry may be becoming more competitive, causing margins to shrink, and the falling current ratio may be due to an increase in efficiency over the control of working capital.

A company with this trend of figures could state that these were the reasons for the decline in margins and for the reduction in liquidity. A reader of the financial statements could then accept the explanation and put the calculations away. However, there is no guarantee that an explanation of this kind actually indicates a beneficial situation, whether or not it is accurate. In order to gain a fuller view of the company, comparison with other comparable companies in the same sector is needed. Exhibit 15.2 presents the information from Exhibit 15.1 for company G plus information on another company of similar size operating in the same sector, company H.

Exhibit 15.2

Period:	X1	X2	X3	X4	X5(now)
Gross profit as % of sales	G 40	38	36	35	34
	H 30	32	33	33	34
Net profit as % of sales	G 15	13	12	12	11
	H 10	10	10	11	11
Net profit as % of capital employed	G 13	12	11	11	10
	H 8	8	9	9	10
Current ratio	G 3.0	2.8	2.6	2.3	2.0
	H 1.5	1.7	1.9	1.9	2.0

Another way in which these results may be compared is through graphs, as shown by the example in Exhibit 15.3 which compares the trend in gross profit as a percentage of sales of the two companies. (Note that the vertical axis does not show the percentage below 30 as there is no percentage below that amount. Omitting the lower figures on the graph allows for a more informative display of the information.)

Exhibit 15.3

The trend of gross profit as a percentage of sales

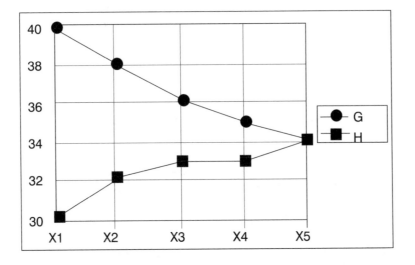

The companies have identical ratios for the current period – does that make them equally desirable as investments? Given one year's accounts it appears so, but the five-year trend analysis reveals a different picture.

From these figures, G appears to be the worse investment for the future, as the trend for it appears to be downwards, while that of H is upwards. It suggests that the explanation made earlier for the falling margins may not be valid. If the trend for G is continued it could be in a very dangerous financial situation in a year or two. H, on the other hand, is strengthening its position all the time.

While it would be ridiculous to assert that H will continue on an upward trend, or that G will continue downwards, a consistent trend of this type does suggest that the situation may well continue into the foreseeable future. It is certainly cause for further investigation

15.4 Comparisons Over Time

As shown in the previous section, one of the best ways of using ratios is to compare them with the ratios for the same organisation in respect of previous years. Take another example, the net profit percentage of a company for the past six years, including the current year 19X8:

Period:	19X3	19X4	19X5	19X6	19X7	19X8(now)
Net profit %	5.4	5.2	4.7	4.8	4.8	4.5

This could be graphed as in Exhibit 15.4.

Exhibit 15.4

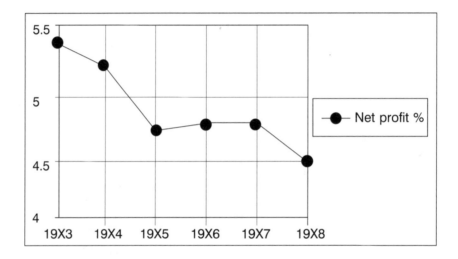

It is obvious that there is a long-term decline in net profit percentage. This prompts us to examine why this should be so. Without measuring against past years our understanding of the direction in which the business seems to be heading would be much diminished.

We would not look only at the long-term changes in net profit percentages, but would also compare similar long-term figures in relation to other aspects of the business.

In considering trends, problems may arise from the use of the historical cost accounting concept during a period of significant price increases because of inflation.

15.5 Comparisons with Other Businesses

No one can say in isolation that a firm is 'very profitable'. It could be the case that it has made £6 million a year, which to most people may seem profitable. On the other hand, if firms of a similar size in the same type of industry are making £20 million a year, then the firm making £6 million cannot be said to be 'very profitable'.

Ideally we would like to be able to compare the results of one firm with those of other similar firms in the same sort of industry. Then, and only then, would we really be able to judge how well, or how badly, it was doing.

The size of firm can have an important effect upon ratios. Just as we would not try to compare a chemist's shop with a building firm, it would also be wrong to judge a small supermarket against Sainsbury's, which owns hundreds of supermarkets.

Inter-firm comparisons are also sometimes misleading because of the different accounting treatment of various items, and the location and ages of assets. Some industries have, however, set up inter-firm comparisons with guidelines to the companies to ensure that the figures have been constructed using the same bases so that the information is properly comparable. The information does not disclose data which can be traced to any one firm, ensuring that full confidentiality is observed.

The information available may take the form shown in Exhibit 15.5.

Exhibit 15.5

Published ratios for the widget industry (extract)

	Solvency			Efficiency		
	Current	*Acid test*	*Asset T/O*	*Stock T/O*	*Debtor days*	*Creditor days*
19X6	2.4	0.7	5.4	8.2	56.4	80.4
19X7	2.2	0.8	5.7	9.3	52.6	66.8

The equivalent figures for the company being assessed can then be tabulated alongside the industry figures to enable comparisons to be made, as in Exhibit 15.6.

Exhibit 15.6

	Company ratios		Industry ratios	
	19X6	*19X7*	*19X6*	*19X7*
Current ratio	2.9	2.8	2.4	2.2
Acid test ratio	0.5	0.6	0.7	0.8
Asset turnover	5.2	5.3	5.4	5.7
Stock turnover	4.4	4.7	8.2	9.3
Debtor days	65.9	65.2	56.4	52.6
Creditor days	58.3	56.8	80.4	66.8

The financial status of the company is now much clearer. What appeared to be a situation of improving liquidity and efficiency is now clearly shown to be an increasingly poorer liquidity and efficiency position compared to the industry as a whole.

However, it should be borne in mind that the industry figures probably include many companies that are either much larger or much smaller than the company being assessed. To obtain a more complete picture, information is needed concerning companies of a similar size, such as in the comparison between G and H earlier in this chapter (section 15.3). This information may be available from the source of the inter-firm comparison. If not, other sources would need to be used, for example the published financial statements of appropriate companies.

The other information missing from the above comparison is data from previous periods. While not so relevant to the current position, it can be useful in explaining why a situation has developed, and in determining whether the current position is likely to persist into the future.

15.6 Pyramid of Ratios

Once ratios have been analysed and compared, explanations must be sought for the results obtained. Sometimes, it will be obvious why a certain result was obtained – for example, if a company has moved from traditional stock-keeping to a 'just-in-time' system during the period, its stock turnover will bear no resemblance to that which it had in the previous period.

For those inside the company – its directors and management – the management accounting records are available to assist in finding explanations, as are the company's staff. Outsiders – shareholders, analysts, lenders, suppliers, customers, etc. – do not have access to all this internal information (though some of these user groups will have access to more internal information than others – banks, for example, can usually obtain copies of a company's management accounts upon request). They must fall back upon other sources of information – newspaper reports and industry publications, for example. One source of additional information available to everyone is the **pyramid of ratios**. Most ratios can be further subdivided into secondary ratios, which themselves can also be subdivided. By following through the pyramid of a given ratio, the source of the original ratio can often be isolated, enabling a far more focused investigation than would otherwise be possible.

For example, one of the most important ratios is the return on the capital employed (ROCE). The ROCE comes about as a result of all the other ratios which have underpinned it. It is the final summation of all that has happened in the pyramid of ratios as shown in Exhibit 15.7.

Exhibit 15.7

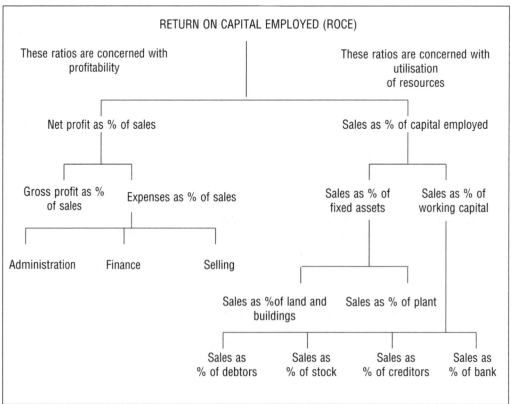

By itself the pyramid of ratios may not tell you much. It comes into full effect when compared with similar figures of the ratios for previous years, or with pyramids in respect of other firms. If the ROCE has been falling over the past year then a study of the pyramids for the two years may enable you to pinpoint exactly where the changes have been made to bring about the worsening position. Investigation of these matters may then give you some answers for action to be taken.

15.7 Return on Capital Employed: Company Policy

The pyramid of ratios in Exhibit 15.7 illustrates the interdependence of each ratio. This can be examined in greater detail by investigating the policies of two companies to achieve their desired return on capital employed.

The first part of the pyramid tells us that the ROCE is dependent on *both* net profit as a percentage of sales *and* also sales as a percentage of capital employed. This means that:

$$\text{ROCE} = \frac{\text{Net profit}}{\text{Capital employed}}$$

which by splitting the equation between profitability ratios and resource utilisation ratios means also that:

$$\text{ROCE} = \frac{\text{Net profit}}{\text{Sales}} \times \frac{\text{Sales}}{\text{Capital employed}}$$

This interrelationship of the subsidiary ratios can be illustrated through an example. At the same time, it can be seen that the result of computing a primary ratio is dependent upon the items comprising it; and that there is no guarantee that a value of x will be 'good', and y 'bad'. Whether the result obtained is 'good' or 'bad' depends on the underlying factors that give rise to the result obtained (what, for example, is the company's policy on depreciation and replacement of assets? This can significantly affect the ROCE), the sector in which the business operates and its relative size. Without knowledge of these items, comparison of the ratio analysis of two companies is likely to be misleading at best.

Two companies, both in the grocery business, may decide to aim for the same ROCE of 10 per cent. This can be achieved in completely different ways by the two companies.

A Ltd is a large company operating a supermarket. It seeks to attract customers by offering low prices and only makes a net profit of 1.25 per cent on sales. Its sales for the year are £8,000,000 on which its net profit is £100,000. Its capital employed is £1,000,000. The ROCE is, therefore, 10 per cent (i.e. £100,000 net profit on capital employed of £1,000,000). This can also be expressed as:

$$\frac{\text{Gross Profit}}{\text{Sales}} \times \frac{100}{1} = \text{Gross Profit as percentage of sales}$$

$$\text{ROCE} = \frac{\text{Net profit}}{\text{Sales}} \times \frac{\text{Sales}}{\text{Capital employed}}$$

$$= \frac{£100,000}{£8,000,000} \times \frac{£8,000,000}{£1,000,000} = 10\%$$

B Ltd, by comparison, is a small local retailer. It seeks a higher margin per £100 sales, but because of higher prices it will achieve a lower volume of business. It makes a net profit of 5 per cent on sales. Its sales for the year amount to £200,000 on which it makes net profit of £10,000. The capital employed is £100,000. The ROCE is therefore 10 per cent (i.e. £10,000 on capital employed of £100,000). This can also be expressed as:

$$\text{ROCE} = \frac{\text{Net profit}}{\text{Sales}} \times \frac{\text{Sales}}{\text{Capital employed}}$$

$$= \frac{£10,000}{£200,000} \times \frac{£200,000}{£100,000} = 10\%$$

We can therefore see that two firms, A Ltd and B Ltd, with different sizes of business, and operating different pricing policies, can finish up with the same ROCE.

15.8 Avoidance of Excessive Stocks

In your first-year studies you will have examined the different methods by which stocks are valued — see *Frank Wood's Business Accounting 1*, seventh edition, Chapter 28). Although this is important, it is also important for an accountant to ensure that the stocks being carried are not greater than they need be.

Let us look at how excessive stocks can have a detrimental effect upon the financial results of a firm:

1 Money tied up in unnecessarily large stocks is not earning anything. If, therefore, an extra £1 million is tied up in stocks which do not have to be so large, then the money which we could have earned from utilising that extra £1 million somewhere else has been lost. If we could have earned 10 per cent return on that money, then the unnecessary stocks have cost us £100,000 a year without any alternative benefit.

2 Too much stock needs extra storage space. Therefore the rent for the extra space, heating, lighting, insurance, wages of extra storekeepers, etc. is all money being spent for no benefit.

One thing that anyone should look for when examining the affairs of a business is to see if stocks are larger than they need be. For someone controlling the business there are three methods of cutting down on unnecessarily high stocks which have become much more popular in recent times. These are:

(a) Economic Order Quantity (EOQ). This is a mathematical method of deciding what is the lowest amount of stock that should be ordered at a time so that the costs of financing and keeping stock are kept down to the minimum.
The formula for this is:

$$\text{EOQ} = \sqrt{\frac{2CO}{S}}$$

where:

C = consumption (usage) per annum in units
O = cost of placing one order

S = cost of storage and holding of one unit per year

S will include the costs of operating the stores, transport and insurance, and also the costs concerned with interest on capital which has been invested in stock. We then take the square root of the above as the answer.

Exhibit 15.8 shows the calculation of the minimum order to be made.

Exhibit 15.8

Annual consumption = 800 units
Cost of reordering = £4
Storage and holding costs per unit = £1

$$\text{EOQ} = \sqrt{\frac{2 \times 800 \times £4}{£1}} = \sqrt{\frac{6,400}{1}} = 80 \text{ units (10 orders per year)}$$

(b) **Just-in-time** approach (JIT). This has been seen as one of the major factors which have resulted in the past success of Japanese manufacturers. It is not just an approach which is concerned with stock levels, but that is part of it.

   The JIT approach requires that delivery of materials should occur immediately before their use. If arrangements are made with suppliers for more frequent deliveries then stocks can be cut to a minimum. Getting suppliers to inspect the materials before they deliver them, and getting them to guarantee their quality, also cuts down on costs, including the need to keep larger stocks in case there are deficiencies.

   This sort of service is obtained by giving more business to fewer suppliers, and also placing longer-term orders. This enables the supplier to plan ahead more effectively to give you a better service.

(c) The last few years have also seen a new approach to the management of production called **optimised production technology** (OPT). The object is to distinguish between 'bottleneck' and 'non-bottleneck' resources. To give an example, the 'bottleneck' resource might be a machine which has a limited capacity. As a result, everything else can only be operated at that same level. Rather than other parts of the business produce more than the 'bottleneck' machine can absorb, a lower overall level of activity takes place. This needs less stocks.

   Of course if a 'bottleneck' can be eliminated it will be. The above applies when a bottleneck, for whatever reason, cannot be eliminated.

   It is better to have a smooth-running business, operating within its 'bottleneck' capacities, than to have one which operates very irregularly. One run irregularly would have to have parts of the business shut down at times. One running smoothly, besides all the other economies, needs fewer stocks.

REVIEW QUESTIONS

Advice:

Examiners at this level certainly do like to include a lot of questions concerned with the analysis and interpretation of accounting statements. This is almost certainly due to the fact that in no other topic can an examinee's *understanding* of accounts, as compared to his/her ability to *prepare* the accounts, be scrutinised so thoroughly.

   There is no one set pattern to the questions, which depend upon the examiner's ingenuity and background experience. The usual shortcomings in the answers handed in by examinees can be listed as:

1   Not following the instructions as laid down. If the question says 'list the' then the examiner expects a list as an answer, 'Discuss the' means exactly that, 'Write a report' needs a report as the answer, and so on. You will lose a lot of marks for not giving the examiner exactly what has been asked for.

2   Very often all the ratios, etc. are calculated, but then the candidate does not offer any comments even though they have been asked for. Make certain you cover this part of the question.

3   Even where students have written something about the ratios, they often repeat what the calculations are and offer nothing else, e.g. 'you can see that the gross profit ratio has increased from 18 to 20 per cent' and the answer has finished there. The examiner can already see from your calculations that the gross profit percentage has increased, and wants you to write about why it might have increased, what conclusions, if any, can be arrived at, or what further information may be needed to proceed with why it has changed.

4   Remember that when the examiner asks you 'what other information you would like to have' about a firm when trying to interpret the accounts so as to give advice to someone then, ideally, you would like to know more about the plans for the future of the business, how it compares with others in the same industry, whether or not there are going to be changes in the management and so on. We should not limit ourselves to information about the past, we really need to know as much about the future as we possibly can.

5   Do not restrict your examination answers to what you have read in a textbook. Keep your eyes and ears open as you go shopping, visit factories, do part-time work in the supermarket, buy petrol at the filling station, go to the theatre and so on. Also reading a 'quality' newspaper helps, as there are quite a lot of items about business. Bring all of this sort of knowledge and experience into your answers. You will impress the examiners. They are bored to death reading regurgitations of textbook learning with nothing else added.

6   Quite a few questions will concern the type of business you will have first hand experience of and can introduce your own personal knowledge into your answer. A typical instance would be comparing two grocery businesses. One would be a large supermarket and the other would be a small corner shop. The policies of the two firms would be quite different. The supermarket would have decided on a policy of attracting new customers by lowering sales margins and yet boosting ROCE. The corner shop might have a policy of high margins, but remain open on Sundays and late at nights, and thus be a 'convenience shop', i.e. customers might well go there when other shops are closed or are too far away to be worth the extra cost in petrol, etc. when compared with the extra cost of shopping at the corner shop.

7   Last, but not least, not showing your workings.

15.1 You are to study the following financial statements for two similar types of retail store and then answer the questions which follow.

Summary of Financial Statements

	A £	A £	B £	B £
Sales		80,000		120,000
Less Cost of goods sold				
Opening stock	25,000		22,500	
Add Purchases	50,000		91,000	
	75,000		113,500	
Less Closing stock	15,000	60,000	17,500	96,000
Gross profit		20,000		24,000
Less Depreciation	1,000		3,000	
Other expenses	9,000	10,000	6,000	9,000
Net profit		10,000		15,000

Balance sheets	A		B	
Fixed assets				
Equipment at cost	10,000		20,000	
Less Depreciation to date	8,000	2,000	6,000	14,000
Current assets				
Stock	15,000		17,500	
Debtors	25,000		20,000	
Bank	5,000		2,500	
	45,000		40,000	
Less Current liabilities				
Creditors	5,000	40,000	10,000	30,000
		42,000		44,000
Financed by				
Capitals				
Balance at start of year		38,000		36,000
Add Net profit		10,000		15,000
		48,000		51,000
Less Drawings		6,000		7,000
		42,000		44,000

Required:

(a) Calculate the following ratios:
- (i) gross profit as percentage of sales;
- (ii) net profit as percentage of sales;
- (iii) expenses as percentage of sales;
- (iv) stockturn;
- (v) rate of return of net profit on capital employed (use the average of the capital account for this purpose);
- (vi) current ratio;
- (vii) acid test ratio;
- (viii) debtor/sales ratio;
- (ix) creditor/purchases ratio.

(b) Drawing upon all your knowledge of accounting, comment upon the differences, and similarities of the accounting ratios for A and B. Which business seems to be the most efficient? Give possible reasons.

15.2X Study the following accounts of two companies and then answer the questions which follow. Both companies are stores selling textile goods.

Trading and Profit and Loss Accounts

	R Ltd £	R Ltd £	T Ltd £	T Ltd £
Sales		250,000		160,000
Less Cost of goods sold				
Opening stock	90,000		30,000	
Add Purchases	210,000		120,000	
	300,000		150,000	
Less Closing stock	110,000	190,000	50,000	100,000
Gross profit		60,000		60,000
Less Expenses				
Wages and salaries	14,000		10,000	
Directors' remuneration	10,000		10,000	
Other expenses	11,000	35,000	8,000	28,000
Net profit		25,000		32,000
Add Balance from last year		15,000		8,000
		40,000		40,000
Less Appropriations				
General reserve	2,000		2,000	
Dividend	25,000	27,000	20,000	22,000
Balance carried to next year		13,000		18,000
Balance sheets				
Fixed assets				
Equipment at cost	20,000		5,000	
Less Depreciation to date	8,000	12,000	2,000	3,000
Motor lorries	30,000		20,000	
Less Depreciation to date	12,000	18,000	7,000	13,000
		30,000		16,000
Current assets				
Stock	110,000		50,000	
Debtors	62,500		20,000	
Bank	7,500		10,000	
	180,000		80,000	
Less Current liabilities				
Creditors	90,000		16,000	
		90,000		64,000
		120,000		80,000
Financed by				
Issued share capital		100,000		50,000
Reserves				
General reserve	7,000		12,000	
Profit and loss	13,000	20,000	18,000	30,000
		120,000		80,000

Required:

(*a*) Calculate the following ratios for each of *R Ltd* and *T Ltd*:
    (i) gross profit as percentage of sales;   (vi) current ratio;
    (ii) net profit as percentage of sales;   (vii) acid test ratio;

(iii) expenses as percentage of sales;
(iv) stockturn;
(v) rate of return of net profit on capital employed
  (for the purpose of this question only, take capital as being total of share capitals +
  reserves at the balance sheet date);

(viii) debtor/sales ratio;
(ix) creditor/purchases ratio.

(*b*) Comment briefly on the comparison of each ratio as between the two companies. State which company appears to be the most efficient, giving what you consider to be possible reasons.

15.3X Following a particularly stormy board meeting several of the directors are having a private conversation, on the following lines:

(i) The sales director says, 'I think someone has been stealing cash. We have been making reasonable profits but we now have a bank overdraft. Surely that's impossible.'

(ii) The production director says, 'I don't think we should charge anything for depreciation this year. The machinery is in perfect condition because we have spent a lot of money on maintenance'.

(iii) 'I am stuck with a lot of outdated and unusable computer equipment', says the director of administration. 'However, the accountant won't let me scrap it as it still has a lot of book value'.

(iv) 'We badly need a new warehouse', says the merchandising director. 'We have got over £2 million in our general reserve. We should take the cash out of that to buy a new warehouse'.

Comment on each of these statements.

15.4 The following information had been prepared for the board of directors of Positive plc who were considering the financial position of another company Minus plc, in which they held ordinary shares as an investment.

Financial Information as at 31 December 19X0

	Positive plc £000	Minus plc £000
Issued share capital		
£1 ordinary shares fully paid	1,500	
25p ordinary shares fully paid		500
12% Preference shares fully paid £1 each		100
Share premium account	750	350
General reserve	350	50
Retained earnings	600	20
Investment in Minus plc:		
500,000 Ordinary shares	240	–
Current assets	1,360	320
Fixed assets	2,100	1,000
Current liabilities	300	300
11% Debentures 19X2–X6	200	–

Note: The net trading profits reported by Minus plc for the last five years were:

19X6	19X7	19X8	19X9	19X0
£125,000	£100,000	£75,000	£70,000	£10,000

Positive plc were considering the acquisition of further shares in Minus plc. The current ordinary share price was 30p. Positive plc wished to acquire sufficient shares to give them a 51 per cent stake in Minus plc.

Further investigation of the financial affairs of Minus plc by Positive plc revealed the following:

1 No dividends had been declared or paid for the year ended 31 December 19X0.

2 Raw material stocks held at 31 December 19X0 were valued at cost £160,000. Of these stocks £70,000 were redundant and of no value.

3   Cash and bank balances as at 31 December 19X0 amounted to £50,000.
4   Freehold land and buildings of £200,000 were included in the fixed assets. They had not been revalued for 11 years and the estimated market value was £2 million.

Required:

(a) A report on the financial position of Minus plc for the board of Positive plc. Your report should contain appropriate numerical analysis including an assessment of Minus plc's profitability and liquidity. *(9 marks)*

(b) A reasoned recommendation indicating whether or not Positive plc should increase its shareholding in Minus plc. *(6 marks)*

(c) If the board of Positive plc decided to acquire extra ordinary shares in Minus plc, explain the different ways in which Positive plc could, if need be, finance the acquisition of extra ordinary shares in Minus plc. *(5 marks)*

(d) Prepare a balance sheet for Positive plc as at 1 January 19X1, on the assumption that Positive plc purchased sufficient shares in Minus plc, for cash, at 30p per share on 1 January 19X1 to give them a 51 per cent stake. *(5 marks)*

(Associated Examining Board: GCE A Level)

15.5 Janet James is considering the investment of £50,000 which she recently inherited from her late father's estate. After much thought, Janet has decided that her legacy will be invested in one of the following propositions:

A   Placed on deposit with a building society; the interest rate being 10 per cent per annum.

B   The outright purchase of the business of Thomas Smith for £50,000. Thomas Smith has been involved full time in the management of the business; the business's accounts have shown a net profit of £20,000 for each of the last three financial years.

C   Purchase the entire ordinary share capital of Greater Deals Limited for £50,000. The share capital, reserves and loan capital of the company as shown in the company's last balance sheet are as follows:

	£	£
Ordinary share capital – ordinary shares of 50p each, fully paid up		30,000
10% Preference share capital – preference shares of £1.00 each, fully paid up		10,000
Reserves – Share premium	5,000	
General	10,000	
Retained earnings	8,000	
		23,000
10% Loan Stock		16,000

Note: The company's net profit, after taxation, for each of the last three years has been in the region of £7,000.

D   Purchase 20 per cent of the ordinary share capital of Central Traders Limited for £50,000. The company's issued capital is entirely in ordinary shares. The company's net profit, after taxation, for each of the last three years has been in the region of £32,000.

Required:

As her financial adviser, address a report to Janet James setting out the disadvantages and advantages of each of the four propositions so far as her proposed investment is concerned. Reports should indicate whether any further information is required before a final decision is made.

(25 marks)

(Reproduced by permission of the University of Cambridge Local Examinations Syndicate)

15.6X The following financial information was available on Tecopac plc.

Balance Sheets as at 31 December

19X8 £m		19X9 £m
8.0	Fixed assets	11.0
5.4	Current assets	7.0
13.4		18.0
3.4	*Less* Current liabilities	4.5
10.0		13.5
6.0	Called-up capital – £1 Ordinary shares fully paid	6.0
2.0	Share premium	2.0
2.0	Retained earnings 1 January 19X9	2.0
	Net profit for year ended 31 December 19X9	3.5
10.0		13.5

In respect of the financial year ended 31 December 19X9 the directors recommended the payment of a final ordinary dividend of 10p per share and the transfer of £3.0m to a general reserve. No interim dividend had been paid.

Hartington, an ordinary shareholder, purchased 30,000 shares at £1.50 per share on 1 January 19X9 (market value at 31 December 19X9 £1.80 per share). On receiving the company's annual statement he was disappointed to learn that he would only receive a final dividend of 10p a share, and he regarded the profit of £3.5m for 19X9 as unsatisfactory since the company employed a substantial amount of capital.

Hartington decided to write to the company's Chief Accountant with a number of suggestions which he hoped would increase the return to shareholders and improve the profitability of Tecopac plc. The suggestions were as follows:

1 The company should make a bonus issue of shares to keep the shareholders happy.
2 Use the share premium account to pay an increase in the dividend. This will also conserve cash resources.
3 Invest £3m of the company's retained earnings in 8 per cent per annum fixed interest government securities.

Required:

(a) A profit and loss appropriation account for Tecopac plc for the year ended 31 December 19X9. *(4 marks)*

(b) (i) Calculate **two** suitable accounting ratios to show Tecopac's level of profitability. Comment on the results.
   (ii) Calculate Hartington's 19X9 return on his investment distinguishing between the income return and the capital return. *(12 marks)*

(c) As Chief Accountant of Tecopac write a reply to Hartington commenting on each of the suggestions **1** to **3** above. *(9 marks)*

(Associated Examining Board: GCE A-Level)

15.7X A small limited company is hoping to expand its activities. It has approached a potential investor, Mr Abdul, regarding the possibility of his buying 90,000 ordinary shares in the company, at a premium of 50p each. Mr Abdul has been shown only the latest balance sheet of the company, together with that at the end of the previous financial year. They are as follows:

		19X1 £		19X2 £
Fixed assets:				
Land and buildings		506,000		405,000
Machinery		75,000		85,000
Computers		15,000		18,000
Motor vehicles		18,000		26,000
		614,000		534,000
Current assets:				
Stock	67,000		105,000	
Debtors	50,000		80,000	
Bank	–		–	
	117,0000		185,000	
Less: Current liabilities:				
Creditors	70,000		60,000	
Bank	8,000		50,000	
	78,000		110,000	
Net current assets		39,000		75,000
Total net assets		653,000		609,000
Share capital (£1)		100,000		100,000
Revenue reserves		363,000		319,000
		463,000		419,000
15% Debentures 20X0/20X5		190,000		190,000
		653,000		609,000

Annual net profit before debenture interest payments and dividends was £50,000 in 19X1 and £30,000 in 19X2.

You have been asked by Mr Abdul to comment on whether he should purchase shares in the company.

Write a report to Mr Abdul suggesting five areas of investigation prior to an investment decision being made.

(*University of London: GCE A-Level*)

15.8 Adrian Frampton was considering the purchase of one of two businesses. However Frampton had only been provided with limited information about the businesses, as follows:

Summarised financial information for the year ended 31 December 19X9

	Business X	Business Y
Cost of goods sold	£400,000	£600,000
Administrative expenses	£50,000	£60,000
Average stock at cost	£40,000	£50,000
Working capital as at 31 December 19X9	£90,000	£250,000
Selling and distribution expenses	£15,000	£35,000
Proprietor's capital at 1 January 19X9	£200,000	£350,000
Gross profit percentage mark-up on cost	20	25

Additional information
1   Average stock had been calculated by using the year's opening and closing stocks. Subsequently it was discovered that Business Y had overvalued its stock on 31 December 19X9 by £10,000.
2   Business X's administrative expenses included a payment for rent of £15,000 which covered a three-year period to 31 December 19X1.
3   A sum of £2,500 was included in the administrative expenses of Business Y in respect of a holiday taken by the owner and his family.
4   Cash drawings for the year ended 31 December 19X9 were:

	£
Business X	20,000
Business Y	25,000

5   The owners of the businesses had stipulated the following prices for their businesses:

	£
Business X	190,000
Business Y	400,000

Required:

(a) Based on the information available prepare comparative trading and profit and loss accounts for the year ended 31 December 19X9.   *(8 marks)*

(b) Using the information provided and the accounting statements prepared in (a), calculate relevant accounting ratios in order to give Frampton a basis for assessing the performances of the two businesses. Comment on the results.   *(11 marks)*

(c) What additional information is needed in order to assess more accurately:
(i)   the liquidity of the businesses;
(ii) the future prospects of the businesses?   *(6 marks)*

(Associated Examining Board: GCE A-Level)

15.9X The following information has been extracted from the final accounts of Dynamic Traders Limited:

Years ended 30 September	19X0	19X1	19X2
	£000	£000	£000
Sales	1,200	1,600	2,000
Cost of sales	800	1,000	1,200
Profit after tax	100	120	120
Dividends	60	60	–
As at 30 September	19X0	19X1	19X2
Fixed assets – Tangible	600	640	700
Current assets			
Stocks	60	90	260
Debtors	70	100	150
Bank	90	70	–
Current liabilities			
Bank overdraft	–	–	100
Creditors	16	36	26
Shareholders' funds			
Ordinary share capital	600	600	600
Retained earnings	204	264	384

John Thomas, a small shareholder in Dynamic Traders Limited has asked Andrew Sharp, a financial adviser, to prepare a report on the financial position and profitability of the company.

Required:

In the name of Andrew Sharp prepare a report for John Thomas. *(25 marks)*

Note: Make and state any necessary assumptions.

(Reproduced by permission of the University of Cambridge Local Examinations Syndicate)

15.10   The balance sheet of Trotwood Limited at 31 December 19X0 was as follows:

	£	£	£
Fixed assets (at book value)			
Freehold land and buildings			367,000
Machinery			35,000
Motor vehicles			120,000
Computer equipment			35,000
			557,000
Current assets			
Stock		34,000	
Debtors		7,000	
Bank		11,000	
		52,000	
Current liabilities			
Creditors	16,000		
Taxation	24,000		
Dividend	8,000		
	48,000		
		48,000	
			4,000
			561,000
Share capital			
Authorised and issued capital:			
1,600,000 Ordinary Shares of 25p			400,000
Reserves			
Retained earnings (P & L a/c)			61,000
			461,000
Long-term liabilities:			
20% Debentures (repayable in the next two years)			100,000
			561,000

The earnings per share figures were 0.9p in 19X7 0.7p in 19X8 and 19X9, and 0.6p in 19X0. Dividends per share in those years were 0.2p, 0.3p, 0.4p and 0.5p respectively.

You have been asked by a shareholder to prepare a report on the financial state of the company from the above information. The report should contain the following information.

(a) A comment on the company's working capital, liquidity and gearing position as shown on the balance sheet at 31 December 19X0.   *(8 marks)*

(b) The significance of the earnings per share and dividends per share figures.   *(8 marks)*

(c) Three questions which the shareholder could ask the company chairman at the Annual General Meeting in order to gain a fuller picture of the company's financial future.   *(9 marks)*

(*University of London: GCE A-Level*)

15.11X 'Service companies such as advertising agencies have few tangible assets. Their main assets are the copywriters and other creative people who win business from admiring clients, but who never appear in the balance sheet. Accounting was developed to serve companies which traded or made physical goods, not businesses which make advertisements or provide similar services.'

From *The Guardian*

(a) Is it possible for a 'service company' to show a realistic statement of its assets on its balance sheet? Discuss. *(12 marks)*

(b) A major advertising company showed the following position at its balance sheet date:

	£m
Tangible assets	215
Associate companies and investments	22
Net current liabilities	(130)
Total net assets	107
Less Net borrowings	186
Shareholder value (negative)	(79)
(Stock market value £136m)	

Give two reasons why the stock market value of the company is so much higher than the (negative) shareholder value. *(8 marks)*

(*University of London: GCE A-Level*)

15.12X The following are the summarised financial statements of Ball and Gregson Ltd, a trading company.

Trading and profit and loss account for the years ended 31 October

	19X4	19X5
	£000	£000
Sales	2,100	3,000
Less cost of sales		
Opening stock	350	420
Purchases	1,470	2,190
	1,820	2,610
Closing stock	420	510
	1,400	2,100
Gross Profit	700	900
Expenses	353	447
Net profit before tax	347	453
Taxation	87	113
	260	340
Dividends	90	120
Retained profit for the year	170	220

Balance sheets as at 31 October

	19X4		19X5	
	£000	£000	£000	£000
Fixed assets at net book value		1,700		2,100
Current assets				
Stock	420		510	
Debtors	400		450	
Bank and cash	100		120	
		920		1,080
Creditors less than one year				
Trade creditors	280		310	
Dividends	60		70	
Accruals	60		130	
Taxation	87		113	
		(487)		(623)
Creditors more than one year				
12% debentures 19X5		(400)		—
		1,733		2,557
£1 ordinary shares, fully paid		1,250		1,500
Share premium		250		604
Retained earnings		233		453
		1,733		2,557

Additional information

(1) 90% of all sales are on credit.

(2) All purchases were made on credit.

(3) Debtors and creditors figures at balance sheet dates may be taken as representative averages for each of the years in question.

Required:

(a) State and calculate **two** ratios relating to the profitability of Ball and Gregson Ltd for **each** of the years under review. *(6 marks)*

(b) State and calculate **two** ratios relating to the liquidity of Ball and Gregson Ltd for **each** of the years under review. *(6 marks)*

(c) Write a report using the ratios calculated in (a) and (b) to analyse the profitability and liquidity of Ball and Gregson Ltd over the two year period. The report should include an outline of major difficulties encountered in making inter-year comparisons. *(16 marks)*

(d) State **two** ways in which a business could increase its working capital. *(6 marks)*

(e) What are the disadvantages to a business of having:
  (i) excessive working capital *(6 marks)*
  (ii) limited working capital. *(6 marks)*

(f) Explain briefly how a business could be profitable yet encounter a liquidity problem. *(4 marks)*

(Associated Examining Board: GCE A-Level)

15.13X Study the passage below and then answer the questions which follow.

"...The Government should make auditors produce a standardised set of accounts on a single piece of paper aimed at shareholders — not finance directors. This would force all companies to report their profits on a common definition with suitable comparisons for previous years accompanied by a series of performance indicators like return on capital employed, profit margins, money spent on capital investment, research and development and so on."

(from an editorial in *The Guardian* newspaper)

(a) The author of this article appears to have made a fundamental error regarding the role of an *auditor* in relation to company accounting. What is the error? *(4 marks)*

(b) Explain how each of the four *"performance indicators"* mentioned in the article would assist shareholders in interpreting their company's financial results. *(12 marks)*

(c) Explain the significance of *Companies Act Formats* in helping to standardise company accounting. (You are *not* required to reproduce the formats as part of your answer.) *(4 marks)*

(University of London Examinations and Assessment Council: GCE A-Level)

Chapter 16

Accounting as an Information System

16.1 The Part Played by Financial Accounting

So far your studies have been concerned primarily with the recording function of accounting, often called bookkeeping, and the drafting of the final accounts of different types of organisations, such as partnerships or limited companies. The term generally used for your studies up to this point is that of **financial accounting**. Much of it is concerned with legal requirements, such as complying with the provisions of the Companies Acts when drafting final accounts, or keeping an accounting record of a customer's legal indebtedness, i.e. a debtor's account.

With companies the final accounts represent the account given to the shareholders by the directors of their running of the company during a particular year, in other words it is a statement of the directors' 'stewardship'. These accounts are also given to other interested parties such as the bankers to the firm, creditors, Inspectors of Taxes etc.

Whilst financial accounting is necessary from a legal point of view, it cannot be said to be ideal from the point of view of controlling the activities of a firm. Your studies would therefore be incomplete if you had seen only the 'stewardship' function of accounting. The use of accounting for controlling the activities of a firm is probably more important, therefore we can now move on to accounting for 'Management Control' purposes.

The word 'management' does not necessarily mean that the firm is a limited company, although most of the large organisations in the private sector of industry would in fact be limited companies. It means instead the people who are managing the affairs of the firm, whether they are directors, partners, sole traders or 'managers' classified as those employees who are in charge of other employees.

16.2 Deficiencies of Financial Accounting

Before starting to examine accounting for management control let us look first at the deficiencies of financial accounting when we want to control the activities of an organisation.

Its first deficiency is that it deals with operations that have already occurred: it deals with the past, not the future. It is possible to control something whilst it is happening, and control can be arranged for something that is going to happen, but when it has already happened without being controlled then the activity has ended and we are too late to do anything about control. In this way if a company incurs a loss and we do not realise it until long after the event then the loss cannot be prevented.

What we really want to do is to control affairs so that a loss is not incurred if at all possible, and we should be able to call on accounting techniques to help in the control of activities. However, it certainly does not mean that we are not interested in the past. We can learn lessons from the past which can be very useful in understanding what is going on now, and what is likely to be happening in the future.

The second deficiency of financial accounting is that it is concerned with the whole of the firm. Thus the trading account of a firm may show a gross profit of £60,000, and whilst it is better to know that than to have no idea at all of what the gross profit is, it does not tell management much about past transactions. Suppose that in fact the firm manufactures three products – watches, pens and cigarette lighters. Some possibilities of how much profit (or loss) was attributable to each of the products might be as in Exhibit 16.1

Exhibit 16.1

Various possibilities of profits and loss for each product

	1	2	3	4
Watches	20,000	5,000	30,000	(30,000)*
Pens	20,000	70,000	28,000	65,000
Lighters	20,000	(15,000)*	2,000	25,000
Total Gross Profit	£60,000	£60,000	£60,000	£60,000

*Losses are shown in brackets

These are only some of the possible figures of profit and loss for each product which could result in an overall gross profit of £60,000. Just the figure of total gross profit would give you very few clues as to what lessons can be learned from studying the past to help you control the firm in the future. If possibility number 2 was in fact the correct solution then it would stimulate further discussion and investigation as to why these results had occurred.

It could result in the closing down of the section of the firm which makes cigarette lighters if, after investigation, it was found to be in the interests of the firm to cease manufacturing them. Many more lessons can therefore be learned from events if the firms' activities can be examined for each part of its activities instead of just the whole of its activities.

This means that financial accounting is of little use by itself for management control purposes. It does not mean that it is of no use at all for control purposes, as for instance the financial accounting system may reveal that the debtors at a point in time are £50,000. Management need to know this if they are to control their finances properly, but although this is true of some accounting figures in financial accounting, many of the other accounting figures may not be much use in controlling the business. For example if a building was bought in 1930 for £20,000 it may well be worth £200,000 today, whilst if we rented a similar building now it might cost us £30,000 a year. We would surely not use the original cost of £20,000 as the deciding factor as to what we will do now with the building. The original cost is now completely irrelevant for the control of the business now or in the future.

16.3 Objectives of the Firm

If we want to discuss management control we must first of all ask ourselves what is its purpose. We can only have control if it is for a particular purpose, otherwise how can we possibly draw up any plans?

It might seem obvious to you that the objectives of an organisation should be spelled out clearly and unambiguously. In fact the writing down of objectives is not done by quite a few organisations. This means that all the employees of the firm could well be pulling in different directions, as they all have different ideas as to the firm's objectives.

Let us look at some of the possible objectives:

- To ensure that the maximum profit is made. This still is not clear; do we mean profits in the long term or the short term?
- To obtain a given percentage share of the market for our sort of goods or services.
- To achieve a high quality in the goods being manufactured or services offered.
- To ensure that our customers are fully satisfied with our goods and services.
- To ensure full employment for our employees.
- To ensure that our employees' welfare is maintained at a high level, in terms of back-up facilities and other things such as adequate pension schemes.
- To ensure that our employees receive the best training and are kept fully up to date with the latest technology for our sort of business.
- To cause as little damage as possible ecologically.

16.4 Conflicts between Objectives

Each objective of the firm is not 'mutually exclusive'. By that we mean that one objective may affect another objective, and that it cannot be considered completely on its own.

Let us take the case of the objective of maximum profit with that of causing as little damage as possible ecologically. We could have to spend a lot of money ensuring that dangerous chemical substances are not released into the atmosphere. This could mean less profits. There would be a conflict here if the improvements were being made voluntarily by the firm instead of being forced on it by the authorities.

Similarly, to maintain a very high quality of goods could mean lower profits if a large number of items manufactured are scrapped because they are not up to this standard. Lowering the quality could possibly increase profits.

This could again be interpreted in more than one way. Lowering the quality could possibly increase the profits in the short term, but it could mean less profits in the long term if our customers deserted us because our goods were second-rate. This could apply similarly to services.

It is thus essential to ensure that the objectives are very clearly spelled out. Otherwise people will easily misunderstand them and because of this the firm may not proceed in the direction that is desired.

16.5 People and Management Control

It is also important to point out that the most important resource of any firm is the people who work in it. A danger exists that a great deal of care and attention may be given to designing a management control system and operating it, but this is absolutely of no use to management if it does not result in action by the human beings in the firm. Systems and figures do not themselves do anything, instead it is the people in the firm who take (or do not take) the necessary action.

You must bear in mind that figures thrown up by systems are only part of the evidence available when a decision has to be made as to the necessary action. A particular department may be incurring losses now, but the sales manager may give as his considered opinion that sales will increase soon and that the department will become profitable. If people accepted accounting figures as the only criteria on which action should be based then there would be some very bad actions by management. Many of the now very successful products have started off by incurring losses in the early stages, and have been eventually successful because the firm has persevered with the product because it had the faith that it would eventually make the grade.

If it was possible to have exactly the same system of management control in three different firms, it might be found in firm A that the control system was useless because no one acted on the data produced. In firm B the control system might result in damage being done to the firm because management used the data as though it was the only criterion in gauging the actions it should take. In firm C it might be an extremely good system because the management saw the data as a useful guide in the planning and control of the firm, and had also made certain that the rest of the organisation took the same view.

How human beings react to a management control system is therefore right at the heart of the problem of ensuring that an effective management control system is in use.

16.6 Different Sizes of Organisations

Part of this book is about information which is intended to be used by the management of an organisation. For a small and simple organisation the information needs of management may be limited and can be obtained by direct observation – using eyes to look and the voice to ask questions. For example a person managing a greengrocer's stall on a market can often operate effectively without formal records to help him. What he buys is determined by the goods available in the local wholesale market and his personal knowledge of what his customers are prepared to buy at a given price. His records will probably centre around the recording of cash – the details of his sales and expenditures in order to prepare financial accounts. However, apart from the essential requirement of maintaining proper cash levels these records do not help him in the day-to-day management of his business operations.

If in contrast we look at the manager responsible for buying greengroceries for a large supermarket chain certain differences emerge. The basic decision about what to buy at a given price remains the same. However, in the large organisation there is a much wider choice of where and how to buy than in the small organisation. The large buyer may for example be able to enter into contracts directly with growers and to enter forward contracts for the supply of produce (for example a farmer agrees to sell all his potatoes at the end of the summer to the firm at a fixed price).

In the large organisation the buyer will not be in direct contact with the many different sales outlets and therefore needs written information to keep him in touch with demand. He does not have to listen to complaining customers! Similarly because the sources of supply are likely to be much wider for the big firm he needs more formal information to keep him in touch with market prices.

One of the other features about the large organisation which distinguishes it from the small, is that responsibility for running the business is shared between many different people. In order to ensure that the operations of the firm are carried out efficiently and effectively there needs to be some criterion to measure the performance of the managers. In a small firm the inadequate proprietor will either make a very poor living or become a bankrupt.

Thus his success or failure is clearly his own responsibility. In a large firm the same things can happen overall, but the situation may be obscured by a swings and roundabouts effect of some good sections making up for some bad. A management information system should help identify these problems in an organisation.

16.7 The Management Process

The way that management operates in an organisation may be conveniently described by a division into three areas:

(1) Forecasting and Planning
(2) Controlling Operations
(3) Evaluating Performance

1   Forecasting and Planning is the process by which senior management decide on major overall issues concerning what the business is going to do, and how it is going to do it. It involves an assessment of information about the future which is called forecasting. When the forecast has been prepared, then the company can plan how to achieve the objectives set by management based on the forecast. Planning is the process of co-ordinating the resources available to attain an objective.

2   Controlling Operations involves management in a number of processes and requires several different kinds of information. It involves converting top management plans into an operating pattern which matches the parts into which a company is divided. This changes the overall plan into detailed operating plans which relate to the management structure of the company. This process is called budgeting.

    When actual events occur, then the information recording the events needs to be measured in such a way that it can be compared with the plan. This important process of management gives a feedback on the success of the plan to those who set it up in the first instance.

    Controlling operations effectively also requires information designed to help managers take the decisions which their jobs require. For example, information about the profit produced by one product as compared to another will enable a decision about how many of each product to make.

3   Evaluating Performance involves the analysis and assessment of actual results. This is partly a process of comparison with plans but not exclusively. The information on which plans were based may have been wrong. Thus the analysis of performance whilst involving comparison of actual with planned results needs considerable judgement as to what the plans should have been had all the facts been known in advance.

The three elements we have described are by no means completely independent. One way of looking at them is as a cycle in which information is circulating continually from one area to another as in Exhibit 16.2.

In this diagram, information is shown to flow around from one part into the other. Thus, for example, forecasts in one period may be improved by taking account of the analysis of what happened last period.

The diagram which we have prepared only looks at internal information. In practice, information is being fed into the process from outside. Top management will have to take into account all the information it can about the outside environment such as competition, economic cutbacks, etc. The control of operations also receives information about actual events.

Exhibit 16.2

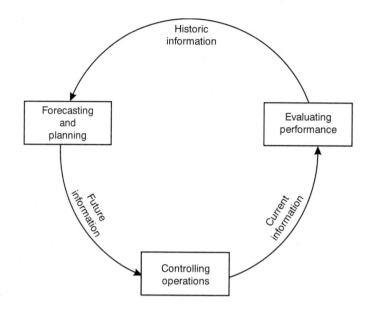

It is also useful to add to the diagram a time dimension as in Exhibit 16.3. Forecasting and planning must relate to the future. Controlling operations relates to concurrent events – the here and now. Evaluating performance can only be concerned with the past.

Exhibit 16.3

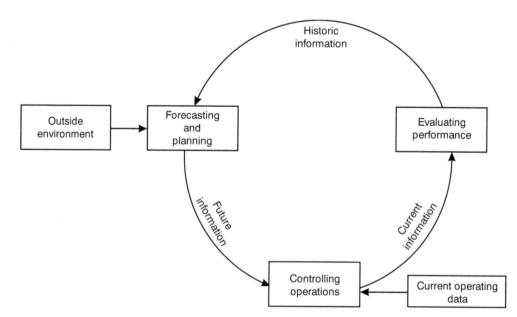

16.8 Types of Management Information

So far in this chapter no attempt has been made to describe the nature of the information which management requires. Information may come in many shapes and forms. In this chapter we are only concerned with information which is capable of being expressed in numerical terms, which in other words may be 'quantified'. Information of a more general nature about peoples' 'feelings' or 'views' may be very useful to management but cannot be quantified, and therefore is usually part of the informal rather than the formal information systems.

Within the body of quantified information it is normal to identify that part which can be measured in money terms. This is the part of the information system which is called 'accounting information'. Accounting information is a very important element in the whole system since the organisation is basically an economic unit which must survive in conditions of economic scarcity and competition. In other words an organisation which does not meet its economic objectives will eventually fail or be taken over, hence the central importance of accounting information.

However, other quantified information may be very important for management. For example, if you are a farmer you will measure the yield of milk from your cows in the first instance in litres. A production manager will be very concerned to monitor the tonnages produced on his machines.

16.9 Quantitative Methods in the Information System

A modern management information system collects all the data together (into what is called a data bank) and issues that part which is important to each manager. Thus the distinction between accounting and other types of management information has tended to become less meaningful in modern data processing systems. The techniques of quantitative analysis (or statistics) apply to all the data in this system whether it be accounting data or not.

REVIEW QUESTIONS

Advice:

Questions based on this chapter will be of the essay type. When answering, see how many marks are being awarded. The more the marks, the more substantial should be your answer.

16.1 'Financial accounting looks behind, whilst management accounting looks ahead.' To what extent does this quotation accurately reflect the role of the two branches of accountancy?

(20 marks)

(University of London: GCE A-Level)

16.2 'Financial accounting is non-dynamic, backward looking, conservative, as objective as possible, and subject to statutory and other regulation. Management accounting is future oriented, is dynamic, produces forward looking figures, should not be too concerned with objectivity, and is not generally subject to external regulation.'
(Prof. Michael Bromwich)
Justify this statement, giving examples to illustrate your answer. *(20 marks)*

(University of London: GCE A-Level)

16.3 What are some of the deficiencies of financial accounting?

16.4 Why is it important that the employees of an organisation should clearly understand what the objectives of the organisation are?

16.5 How can there be a conflict between the various objectives of an organisation?

16.6 Describe how the management process is carried out.

Chapter 17

Elements of Costing

17.1 Costs for Different Purposes

Cost accounting is needed so that there can be an effective management accounting system. Without a study of costs such a system could not exist. Before entering into any detailed description of costs it is better if we ask ourselves first of all what use we are going to make of information about costs in the business.

This can best be done by referring to something which is not accounting, and then relating it to accounting. Suppose that your employer asked you to measure the distance between Manchester and London, but walked away from you without giving any further information. As you thought about his request the following thoughts might go through your head:

1   *HOW* does he want the distance measured? Some possibilities are:
    - from the southern outskirts of Manchester to the northern outskirts of London.
    - from the accepted geographical centre of London to the accepted geographical centre of Manchester.
    - to the centres of the two cities calculated as mathematically precise points.
    - by road, this could be just major roads, just minor roads, or could be either major or minor roads the main requirement being the quickest route by road.
    - by canal.
    - by air; allowance may or may not be made for the distance covered by the aircraft which would include climbing to an altitude of 5,000 feet or perhaps 40,000 feet, or might ignore the distance travelling in achieving an altitude.

2   The *COST* of obtaining the information. Measuring distances (or measuring costs) is not costless itself. Using very sophisticated instruments to get accurate measurement can be very expensive indeed. On the other hand it might just be a matter of measuring the distance on a map with a rule and converting it into miles – this would cost hardly anything at all.

3   What is the *PURPOSE* for which the measurement will be used? This has been deliberately left as the last point, but in fact it should have been the first question that came into your mind. Illustrations of the use could have been as follows:
    - he is going to drive from Manchester to London by car and wants a rough idea of the mileage so that he can gauge what time to set off if he is to arrive before it goes dark in London.
    - he might conceivably want to walk it.
    - perhaps he wants to send goods by canal.
    - he might be an amateur pilot who wants to fly from Manchester Airport to London Airport.

- he might be submitting a tender for the building of a motorway by the shortest possible route, cutting tunnels through ranges of hills.

The lesson to be learned from this is that measurement depends entirely on the use that is to be made of the data. Far too often firms make measurements of financial and other data without looking first at the use that is going to be made of it. In fact it could be said that 'information' is useful data that is provided for someone.

Data given to someone which is not relevant to the purpose required is just not information. Data which is provided for a particular purpose, and which is completely wrong for the purpose, is worse than having no data at all. At least when there is no data the manager knows that he is making a guess. When useless data is collected it first of all has cost money to collect, in itself a waste of money; secondly it often gets taken to be useful data and misleads a manager into taking steps which are completely wrong and would not have happened if he had relied instead on his own hunches; thirdly, it clogs up the communication system within a firm, so that other data is not acted on properly because of the general confusion that has been caused.

How is all this reflected in a study of costs?

1   What is the data on costs wanted for? It might be needed for the financial accounts, for management control or for decision making. Different data on costs are wanted for different purposes.

2   How are the costs to be measured? Only when the purpose for which the costs are to be used has been decided can the measurement process be decided. Financial accounting for instance needs a certain precision in calculating costs which is often not needed in management accounting, where sometimes the nearest thousand pounds will be good enough for the purpose.

3   The cost of obtaining costing data should not exceed the benefits to be gained from having it. This does not refer to some cost data which is needed to comply with various provisions of the law. We can, however, look at several cases to illustrate the cost/benefit factor:

    - Spending £100 to obtain costs which will be used as a basis for pricing many of the products of the firm. If the costs had been 'guessed' an error could have meant large losses for the firm.

    - Spending £10,000 to find data on sales which the sales manager will toss into the wastebasket, because it is not the sort of data he wants, is obviously money wasted.

    - Spending a lot of time and money to find out that the stock values on a particular day were £2,532,198, when such precision was not needed. Perhaps the chairman was having a general chat with the bank manager, and all he needed to know was an approximate figure for stock of £2,500,000. The approximate figure could have been found easily and at little cost, so here costs have exceeded benefits.

When it is known what the costs are for, and how much is to be spent on studying them, the appropriate method for measuring them can be decided.

17.2 Past Costs in Trading Companies

Past costs – often aptly called historic costs – are part of the ordinary financial accounting done in firms. Here the 'original cost' concept is used. A diagram – Exhibit 17.1 – shows costs flowing through financial accounts.

Exhibit 17.1

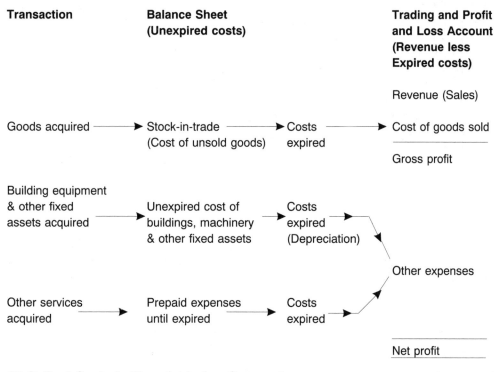

17.3 Past Costs in Manufacturing Companies

You have probably already covered the topic of manufacturing accounts earlier in your studies. In this chapter we will examine some of the detailed aspects of them a little further, as this is essential for a study of costing.

Exhibit 17.2 shows costs flowing through a manufacturing company.

Exhibit 17.2

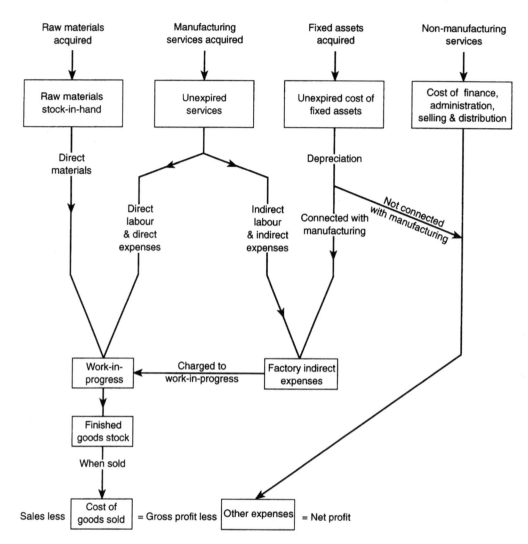

The following is a more detailed description of costs than you will have encountered previously.

- *Direct materials* are those materials which become part of the finished goods, subject to the proviso that the expense involved in tracing the cost is worth while. Some items, usually of insignificant amounts, are treated as indirect materials even though they are part of the finished product because the cost cannot be ascertained easily.

- *Direct labour* are those labour costs which are applied to convert the direct materials into the finished goods, also subject to the proviso that the expense involved in tracing this cost is worth while.

- *Direct expenses* are those expenses which can be traced directly to the product being manufactured. These are fairly rare, but an instance would be a royalty where the production of each item resulted in say £1 being due to the owner of a patent.

• *Prime cost:* The total of Direct materials + Direct labour + Direct expenses is called prime cost.

   Naturally there will be disagreement between accountants as to whether certain costs are worth tracing as being of a direct type, as it will often be a matter of judgement which defies any easy proof whether or not the expense of tracing the cost exceeds the benefit from so doing. You should get used to the idea in accounting that disagreement will often occur, which will only be settled by a compromise or appeal to someone in higher authority to settle the argument. This obviously relates to many things in accounting beside the decision as to whether an item is of a direct type or not.

• *Factory indirect expenses or manufacturing overheads* are all those other expenses concerned with the manufacturing process which have not been treated as of the direct type. Because there is no easily traceable direct connection with the goods being manufactured these costs must be apportioned between the goods being manufactured in a logical fashion.

• *Production cost:* The total of Prime cost + Factory indirect expenses is called production cost.

• *Administration, selling and distribution and finance expenses* are common to both trading and manufacturing firms.

• *Total cost:* If we add together production cost and administration, selling and distribution, and finance expenses, the resultant figure is known as total cost. To summarise:

	Direct materials
ADD	Direct labour
ADD	Direct expenses
Gives:	PRIME COST
ADD	Factory indirect expenses
Gives:	PRODUCTION COST
ADD	Administration expenses
ADD	Selling and distribution expenses
ADD	Finance expenses
Gives:	TOTAL COST

Exhibit 17.3 is a list of typical types of expenses found in a manufacturing firm. These can be analysed as to whether they are direct materials, direct labour, direct expenses, factory indirect expenses, administration expenses, selling and distribution expenses, or finance expenses. See how well you can do yourself by covering up the right-hand column with a piece of paper, then sliding your paper down to reveal one answer at a time after you have mentally analysed it yourself.

Exhibit 17.3

	Cost	Cost Analysis
1	Raw materials for goods – identifiable with product made.	Direct materials
2	Rent of factory buildings.	Factory indirect expenses
3	Sales staff salaries.	Selling and distribution
4	Wages of machine operators in factory.	Direct labour
5	Wages of accounting machine operators in office.	Administration expenses
6	Depreciation of lathes in factory.	Factory indirect expenses
7	Depreciation of typewriters in office.	Administration expenses
8	Depreciation of fixtures in sales showrooms.	Selling and distribution expenses
9	Supervisors' wages in factory.	Factory indirect expenses
10	Royalty paid for each item manufactured.	Direct expenses
11	Works manager's salary: he reckons that he spends $\frac{3}{4}$ of his time in the factory and $\frac{1}{4}$ in general administration of the firm.	$\frac{3}{4}$ Factory indirect expenses $\frac{1}{4}$ Administration expenses
12	Raw materials incorporated in goods sold, but too difficult to trace to the goods being made.	Indirect expenses
13	Depreciation of motor vehicles used for delivery of finished goods to customers.	Selling and distribution expenses
14	Interest on bank overdraft.	Finance expenses
15	Wages of crane drivers in factory.	Factory indirect expenses
16	Discounts allowed.	Finance expenses
17	Company secretary's salary.	Administration expenses
18	Advertising.	Selling and distribution expenses
19	Wages of staff of canteen used by factory staff only.	Factory indirect expenses
20	Cost of hiring special machinery for use in manufacturing one special item.	Direct expenses

17.4 Product Costs and Period Costs

Product costs are those costs which are allocated to the units of goods manufactured. In fact product costs make up production cost. Such costs are charged up to the cost of goods manufactured in the trading account, and would normally be part of the valuation of unsold goods if the goods to which they refer had not been sold by the end of the period. Product costs are therefore matched up against revenue as and when the goods are sold and not before.

   Period costs are those of a non-manufacturing nature and represent the selling and distribution, administration and the financial expenses. They are treated as expenses of the period in which they were incurred irrespective of the volume of goods sold.

17.5 Advantages of a Costing System

You have now looked at the various elements of cost as far as the whole of the firm is concerned. Such a classification of costs is necessary so that the overall production cost can be ascertained in the case of a manufacturing company with its effect on the valuation of the closing stock of finished goods and of work-in-progress. What most businesses want to know is how much each item has cost to make. This means that the total costs for the whole firm are not sufficient, and so these costs must be analysed further.

Any costing system must bring about the better control of the firm in guiding it towards its objectives, and the benefits to be derived from the costing system must be greater than the expense of operating the costing system. We must, therefore, look at the possible advantages to be gained in carrying on further analyses of cost:

(a) Because expenditure is traced down to each item produced, or each batch of items, it becomes possible to ascertain the contribution of each item to the profitability of the business. The desirability of stopping unprofitable activities can then be assessed.

(b) Once the profitability of each item is known, the reasons for increases or decreases in profits can be seen more clearly.

(c) It becomes easier to forecast future results if we know more about the operations of all the various parts of the business. When forecasted results are not achieved it becomes possible to highlight the reasons for the failure to achieve the forecasted results.

(d) Estimates and tenders can be prepared in future with far greater confidence – previously such calculations as were done must have been largely guesswork. Fewer errors should be made because of the greater knowledge gained via the costing system.

(e) Improvements in various activities of the firm may come about because of the more relevant information that can be supplied. Thus a machine which had always been thought to be quite cheap to use may turn out to be very expensive to use. This may bring about an investigation which would not otherwise have happened, and it may consequently be found that a simple attachment to the machine costing £10 brings about a saving of £100 a year.

(f) As we will see, a very important advantage is the control of expenditure, and it can be achieved because an individual can be made responsible for the expenditure under his/her control.

The possible advantages which can be gained from having a costing system can be seen to be quite considerable. It is, however, now a convenient point to remind you that accounting techniques themselves do not solve problems. Instead it is people within the firm who, when armed with the information that accounting techniques can provide, are far more able to make sensible decisions about what should be done to aid the progress of the firm towards its objectives.

Imagine trying to decide which item to stop producing out of twelve items made by a firm if you have little information as to the contribution of each item towards the profitability of the firm. Very often the solution will be that a new layout in the factory is needed; special training given to certain employees; changes made in the system of remunerating employees, and so on. The information provided by accounting is, therefore, only one part of the whole story for any problem. It is important to remember that often it will be the least important information available to the decision-taker.

17.6 The Control of Costs

One of the most important features of cost accounting is its use for control purposes, meaning in this context the control of expenditure. But control of expenditure is possible only if you can trace the costs down to employees who are responsible for such costs. A convenient area for collecting costs is called a 'cost centre'. In a manufacturing firm all direct materials, direct labour and direct expenses are traced to cost centres, in this case they would be known as 'product centres'. A product centre may be such as a single machine used for jobbing work, i.e. quite a lot of separate jobs performed specially to conform with the customer's specifications. It could, however, be a group of similar machines or a production department.

By comparison factory indirect expenses by definition, i.e. because they are 'indirect' expenses, cannot be traced (or it is not worth while tracing them) to product centres. These are traced to cost centres which give service rather than being concerned with work directly on the products, and such cost centres are, therefore, known as 'service centres'. Examples of service centres would be the factory canteen or the maintenance department. The costs from these service centres will then need allocating to the product centres in a logical fashion.

In practice there are a number of possible ways of allocating costs to cost centres. What must not be lost sight of is the endeavour to trace costs to a person responsible for the expenditure so that the costs can be controlled.

17.7 Costing: Manufacturing Firms Compared with Retailing or Wholesale Firms

It is quite wrong to think that costing is concerned only with manufacturing firms. Both textbooks and examination papers often give the impression that only in manufacturing is costing needed or found. This is quite incorrect, as costing is just as relevant to retailing and wholesaling firms and service industries as it is to those in manufacturing. It is simply that manufacturing, which usually has more complex sorts of activities because of the manufacturing element, has attracted greater attention than other types of firms. There are, in addition, many other forms of organisations such as farming, shipping, banking and even charitable organisations where costing can aid management control. It would indeed be difficult to find any organisation which could not use some form of costing system profitably.

REVIEW QUESTIONS

Advice:

This chapter is basically for background information. As such, there have not been any A-Level questions simply concerned with the contents of this chapter.

17.1 Analyse the following costs between:
(i) Direct materials
(ii) Direct labour
(iii) Factory indirect expenses
(iv) Administration expenses
(v) Selling and distribution expenses
(vi) Finance expenses

(a) Wages for staff maintaining machines in factory
(b) Wages for staff maintaining accounting machinery
(c) Expenses of canteen run exclusively for factory workers
(d) Expenses of canteen run exclusively for administrative workers
(e) Grease used for factory machinery
(f) Cost of raw materials
(g) Carriage inwards on fuel used in factory boiler-house
(h) Carriage inwards on raw material
(i) Wages of managing director's chauffeur
(j) Wages of cleaners in factory
(k) Discounts allowed
(l) Rent of salesrooms
(m) Wages of lathe operators in factory
(n) Wages of security guards; the area of the factory buildings is four times as great as the other buildings
(o) Debenture interest
(p) Rent of annexe used by accounting staff
(q) Managing director's remuneration
(r) Sales staff salaries
(s) Running costs of sales staff cars
(t) Repairs to factory buildings
(u) Audit fees
(v) Power for machines in factory
(w) Rates: ¾ for factory buildings and ¼ for other buildings
(x) Rent of internal telephone system in factory
(y) Bank charges
(z) Costs of advertising products on television.

17.2X Analyse the following costs between
(i)   Direct materials
(ii) Direct labour
(iii) Factory indirect expenses
(iv) Administration expenses
(v)   Selling and distribution expenses
(vi) Finance expenses
    (a) Interest on bank overdraft
    (b) Factory storekeepers' wages
    (c) Hire of Rolls-Royce for managing director's use
    (d) Repairs to factory roof
    (e) Hotel bills incurred by sales staff
    (f) Motor tax for vans used for delivering goods to customers
    (g) Chief accountant's salary
    (h) Lubricants for factory machinery
    (i) Cost of disks for firm's computer
    (j) Helicopter hire charges re special demonstration of company's products
    (k) Debt collection costs
    (l) Costs of painting advertising signs on London buses
    (m) Cost of aeroplane tickets for sales staff
    (n) Wages of painters engaged in production
    (o) Wages of timekeepers in factory
    (p) Postal charges for letters

(q) Wages of office boy in general office
(r) Postal charges – parcels sent to customers
(s) Repairs to vans used for taking goods to customers
(t) Cost of raw materials included in product
(u) Wages for cleaners engaged in administration block
(v) Carriage inwards on raw materials
(w) Repairs to neon sign in Piccadilly Circus
(x) Advertising agency fees
(y) Wages of crane drivers in factory
(z) Power costs of accounting machinery.

17.3 From the following information work out:

(a) Prime cost
(b) Production cost
(c) Total cost

Wages and salaries of employees:

	£	£
In factory (70 per cent is directly concerned with units being manufactured)		220,000
Salaries: Sales staff		8,000
Commission on sales paid to sales staff		1,400
Salaries of administrative staff		72,000
Travelling expenses:		
Sales staff	2,900	
Factory workers not directly concerned with production	100	
Administrative staff	200	
		3,200
Haulage costs on raw material bought		4,000
Carriage costs on goods sold		7,800
Depreciation:		
Factory machinery	38,000	
Accounting and office machinery	2,000	
Motor vehicles:		
Sales staff	3,800	
Administrative staff	1,600	
Sales display equipment	300	
		45,700
Royalties payable per unit of production		1,600
Canteen costs used by all the workers, ⅔ work in the factory, ⅓ in other parts of the firm		6,000
Raw materials:		
Stock at start of period		120,000
Stock at close of period		160,000
Bought in the period		400,000
Interest on loans and overdrafts		3,800
Other factory indirect expenses		58,000
Other administrative expenses		42,000
Other selling expenses		65,000

17.4X From the following information work out:

(a) Prime cost
(b) Production cost
(c) Total cost

	£	£
Wages and salaries of employees:		
In factory (60 per cent is directly concerned with units being manufactured)		150,000
In sales force		15,000
In administration		26,000
Carriage costs:		
On raw materials brought into the firm		1,800
On finished goods delivered to customers		1,100
Rent and rates:		
Of factory block	4,900	
Of sales department and showrooms	1,000	
Of administrative block	1,100	
		7,000
Travelling expenses:		
Sales staff	3,400	
Administrative staff	300	
Factory workers not connected directly with production	200	
		3,900
Raw materials:		
Stock at start of period		11,400
Bought in the period		209,000
Stock at close of the period		15,600
Royalties: payable per unit of production		400
Depreciation:		
Sales staff cars	500	
Vehicles used for deliveries to customers	300	
Cars of administrative staff	400	
Machinery in factory	1,800	
Office machinery	200	
		3,200
Interest costs on borrowed money		800
Other factory indirect expenses		6,000
Other administrative expenses		4,000
Other selling expenses		1,000

17.5X

(a) The terms *cost behaviour* and *analysis of total cost* are regularly used in cost accounting to classify costs. Distinguish between the two terms. *(12 marks)*

(b) Explain how the following costs will:
(i) behave;
(ii) be analysed.

- Factory Power and Lighting
- Production Line Workers' Wages
- Sales Manager's Salary
- Office rent *(8 marks)*

(University of London Examinations and Assessment Council: GCE A-Level)

Chapter 18

Absorption and Marginal Costing

18.1 Allocation of Factory Indirect Expenses

The most commonly accepted cost accounting theory used for purposes of the determination of profit is where all the factory indirect expenses are allocated to the products manufactured. The factory indirect expenses are seen as adding to the value of work-in-progress and thence to finished goods stock. The production cost of any article is thus comprised of direct materials, direct labour, any direct expenses and a share of factory indirect expense.

After the financial year it is possible to look back and calculate exactly what the factory indirect expenses were. This means that this figure is used when calculating the valuation of the closing stock. For a firm which had produced 1,000 units, of which 200 units have not yet been sold, with a total production cost of £100,000, the closing stock valuation becomes:

$$\frac{\text{Unsold units}}{\text{Total units produced}} \times \text{Production cost of goods completed} = \frac{200}{1,000} \times £100,000$$

= £20,000 closing stock valuation

Cost data is, however, used for purposes other than that of valuing stock. The question is, therefore, whether or not this method is suitable for all costing purposes. The method we have just used above, of allocating all factory indirect expenses to products is known as absorption costing, sometimes called full costing.

18.2 Absorption Costing: Effect upon Future Action

We can now look at a decision we might have to come to about a future action. Exhibit 18.1 shows a firm which has to make a decision about whether or not to take on an extra order.

Exhibit 18.1

Donald Ltd's factory has been making 1,000 units annually of a particular product for the past few years. Last year costs were:

	£
Direct labour	2,000
Direct materials	3,000
Factory indirect expenses	4,000
Production cost	9,000
Administration and other expenses	1,000
	10,000

The units, 1,000 had been sold for £12 each = £12,000

The production cost per unit can be seen to be $\dfrac{£9,000}{1,000} = £9$.

The current year is following exactly the same pattern of production and costs. Suddenly, part-way through the year, a foreign buyer says he will take 200 units if the price for him can be cut from £12 each to £8 each. A meeting is held and the managing director says, 'What a pity. This could have been our first export order, something we have been waiting to happen for several years. The selling price overseas has no bearing on our selling price at home. But it costs us £9 a unit in production costs alone. We just cannot afford to lose money so as to export. Our shareholders would not tolerate the profits of the company falling to less than £2,000.'

'I think that you are wrong,' says John the accountant. 'Let's look at this year's results (*a*) if we do not accept the order and (*b*) if the order is accepted.' He then drafts the following:

	(a) Order not taken		(b) Order taken	
	£		£	
Sales 1,000 × £12		12,000		
1,000 × £12 + 200 × £8				13,600
Less Expenses:				
Direct labour	2,000		2,400	
Direct materials	3,000		3,600	
Factory indirect expenses	4,000		4,200	
Other expenses	1,000	10,000	1,000	11,200
Net profit		2,000		2,400

'More profit. This means that we take the order,' says the sales director enthusiastically.

'Surely you've got your figures wrong, John,' says the managing director. 'Check your arithmetic.'

'There's nothing wrong with my arithmetic,' says John, 'but perhaps it will be a little more enlightening if I draft (*b*) Order taken, more fully.'

(b) *Order taken*

Sales		13,600
Less Costs which vary with production: Direct labour. The men are on piece work of a type that means 20 per cent more production brings 20 per cent more wages (i.e. £2,000 for 1,000 units, £2,400 for 1,200 units).	2,400	
Direct materials. 20 per cent greater production gives 20 per cent more materials (£3,000 + £600).	3,600	
Factory indirect expenses: Some would not change at all, e.g. factory rent, factory rates. Some would alter, e.g. cost of electric power because machines are used more. Of the factory indirect expenses one-quarter is variable. For this part £1,000 costs for 1,000 units means £1,200 costs for 1,200 units.	1,200	7,200
Sales *less* Variable costs		6,400
Costs: i.e. costs which will not alter at all if 200 more units are produced:		
Factory indirect expenses; fixed part	3,000	
Administration and other expenses	1,000	4,000
Net profit		2,400

'We can do all this without borrowing any money,' says the managing director, 'so I'll phone now to tell them we will start production immediately. By the way, John, come to my office this afternoon and tell me more about variable and fixed costs.'

18.3 The Lesson to be Learned

We must not get lost in the technicalities of accounting. It is easy to think that calculations which look complicated must give the right answer. Logic must be brought to bear on such problems. This last case shows that different costs will often be needed when making decisions about the future than the costs which were used for calculating profit earned in the past. £9 per unit had been taken for stock valuation, but this case proves that a firm could still manufacture units and sell at less than £9 each and still increase profits. The reason for this state of affairs is the very essence of the differences between fixed and variable costs which we will now consider.

18.4 Fixed and Variable Costs

The division of costs into those that are fixed and those that are variable is not an easy matter. Even factory rent is not always a fixed cost, for if production had to be increased to a certain figure the firm might have to rent further premises. Such a change would not usually happen in the short term, it would take a while to rent and set up a new factory or extra premises before production could start. When fixed costs are mentioned it is normally assumed that this means costs which are fixed in the short term.

In the firm Donald Ltd, Exhibit 18.1 assumed that variable costs were 100 per cent variable, by this meaning that if production rose 20 per cent then the cost would rise 20 per cent, if the production rose 47 per cent then the cost would also rise 47 per cent. This is not necessarily true. The cost of power may rise 20 per cent if production rose 20 per cent, but the cost of repairing and maintaining the machines may rise by only 10 per cent if production rose 20 per cent. In this case the machine maintenance would be a semi-variable cost, this being the term for a cost which varies with production but not at a proportionate rate.

18.5 Cost Behaviour

Intelligent cost planning and control is dependent on the knowledge of how costs behave under certain conditions. What is important is how costs behave in a particular firm; there is no substitute for experience in this respect.

Raw materials are examples of variable costs which normally vary in strict proportion to the units manufactured. Labour costs, on the other hand, usually move in steps, thus the name 'step-variable' costs. For instance, a job may be done by two men, and then a slight increase in activity means that the two men, cannot manage it so that a third man is added. In fact it may represent only $2\frac{1}{3}$ men's work, but the acquisition of workers come in indivisible chunks. There can still be a further increase in activity without any more workers, but then the time will come when a fourth man is needed. This is shown on the two graphs in Exhibit 18.2

Exhibit 18.2

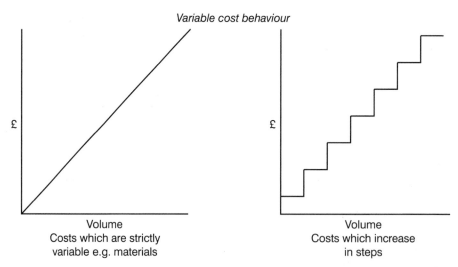

Variable cost behaviour

Volume
Costs which are strictly
variable e.g. materials

Volume
Costs which increase
in steps

18.6 Marginal Costing and Absorption Costing Contrasted

Where costing is used which takes account of the variable cost of products rather than the full production cost, then this is said to be marginal costing. We have seen that a marginal costing approach to the decision as to whether or not to accept the foreign order by Donald Ltd gave us the answer which increased the firm's profitability, whereas to use absorption costing of £9 a unit in a blind fashion would have meant our rejecting the order and therefore passing up the chance to increase profits and break into the foreign market. Let us look now at what would happen if we used either marginal costing or absorption costing in the calculation of profits for a whole firm, i.e. income determination.

Exhibit 18.3

The final accounts of a firm, Burke Ltd, are now shown drafted as if (A) marginal costing had been used, (B) absorption costing had been used. The following information is available:

1 All fixed factory overheads amounted to £4,000 per annum.
2 Variable overheads amounted to £2 per unit.
3 Direct labour and direct materials total £3 per unit.
4 Sales remain constant at 1,000 units per annum at £12 per unit.
5 Production in year 1 is 1,200 units, year 2 is 1,500 units and year 3 is 900 units.

Year 1	(A) Marginal costing		(B) Absorption costing	
	£	£	£	£
Sales		12,000		12,000
Less Variable costs:				
Direct labour and material, 1,200 × £3	3,600		3,600	
Variable overheads, 1,200 × £2	2,400		2,400	
Total variable cost	6,000			
Less in (A) Valuation closing stock				
$\frac{200}{1,200} \times £6,000$	1,000*			
	5,000			
Fixed factory overhead	4,000	9,000	4,000	
Total production costs			10,000	
Less in (B) Valuation closing stock				
$\frac{200}{1,200} \times £10,000$			1,666*	8,334
Gross profit		3,000		3,666
Year 2				
Sales		12,000		12,000
Less Variable costs:				
Direct labour and material 1,500 × £3	4,500		4,500	
Variable overheads, 1,500 × £2	3,000		3,000	
Total variable cost	7,500			
Add in (A) Opening stock b/fwd	1,000			
	8,500			
Less in (A) Closing stock				
$\frac{700}{1,500} \times £7,500$	3,500*			
	5,000			
Fixed factory overhead	4,000	9,000	4,000	
Total production costs			11,500	
Add opening stock in (B) b/fwd			1,666	
			13,166	
Less Closing stock in (B)				
$\frac{700}{1,500} \times £11,500$			5,366*	7,800
Gross profit		3,000		4,200

*See note

Year 3	(A) Marginal costing		(B) Absorption costing	
	£	£	£	£
Sales		12,000		12,000
Less Variable costs:				
Direct labour and material, 900 × £3	2,700		2,700	
Variable overheads, 900 × £2	1,800		1,800	
Total variable cost	4,500			
Add in (A) Opening stock b/fwd	3,500			
	8,000			
Less in (A) Closing stock $\frac{600}{900}$ × £4,500	3,000*			
	5,000			
Fixed factory overheads	4,000	9,000	4,000	
			8,500	
Add in (B) Opening stock b/fwd			5,366	
			13,866	
Less in (B) Closing stock $\frac{600}{900}$ × £8,500			5,666*	8,200
Gross profit		3,000		3,800
	*See note			

Note: The closing stock each year for (A) is made up of:

$$\frac{\text{Unsold units}}{\text{No. of units produced in year}} \times \text{Total variable cost of that year}$$

Units produced year 1   1,200 − 1,000 = Closing stock 200 units

Units produced year 2   1,500 + 200 opening stock − sales 1,000 = Closing stock 700 units

Units produced year 3   900 + 700 opening stock − sales 1,000 = Closing stock 600 units

So in year 1 unsold units are 200 units; units produced 1,200; total variable cost is £6,000, therefore stock valuation is:

$$\frac{200}{1,200} \times £6,000 = £1,000$$

The closing stock each year for (B) is made up of:

$$\frac{\text{Unsold units}}{\text{No. of units produced in year}} \times \text{Total production cost of that year.}$$

So in year 1 stock valuation becomes $\frac{200}{1,200} \times £10,000 = £1,666.$

Exhibit 18.4 shows in diagrammatic form the reported profits shown in Exhibit 18.3.

Exhibit 18.4

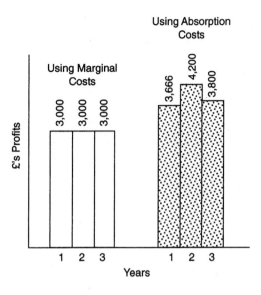

18.7 Comparison of Reported Profits – Constant Sales and Uneven Production

Exhibits 18.3 and 18.4 have illustrated that Burke Ltd, a firm which has had the same amount of sales each year at the same prices, and the same variable costs per unit have not changed at all, shows quite different profit figures using a marginal costing approach compared with absorption costing. As these were the gross profits that were calculated let us assume that the selling, distribution, administration and finance expenses were £1,000 for each of these years. The net profits would therefore be as follows:

	(A) Marginal costing	(B) Absorption costing
	£	£
Year 1	2,000	2,666
Year 2	2,000	3,200
Year 3	2,000	2,800

Because of the absorption costing approach, year 2 shows the biggest profit. As sales etc. are the same, only production being different, this means that the year which has the greatest closing stock has shown the greatest profit. Because of greater production, the amount of fixed factory overhead per unit is less. For instance in year 1 with 1,200 units produced and £4,000 fixed factory overhead this means $\dfrac{£4,000}{1,200}$ = £3.3 per unit, year 2 $\dfrac{£4,000}{1,500}$ = £2.7 per unit, year 3 $\dfrac{£4,000}{900}$ = £4.4 per unit (only taken to one decimal place).

By calculating the value of closing stock to include the fixed factory overhead means that less gets charged per unit for fixed factory overhead when production is greatest, and thus there is a tendency for a greater profit to be shown.

Of course the situation gets more complicated because the closing stock of one year is the opening stock of the next year, and under absorption costing, the values of units of stock will vary. Look at year 3: the opening stock of 700 units is shown as £5,366 = £7.7 approximately; the closing stock of 600 units is shown as £5,666 = £9.4 approximately. Yet these are exactly the same kind of things, and because we have made costs the same each year we have been ignoring inflation. To show a higher profit in a year when the closing stock is higher than usual is often dangerous. In fact the stock may be rising because we cannot sell the goods, we are really getting into trouble, yet the accounts sublimely show a higher profit!

Many experts have argued for or against the marginal and the absorption approach in income determination. The marginal approach really states that fixed factory overhead is a function of time and should not be carried forward to the next period by including it in stock valuations. The absorption approach states that such overhead is concerned with production and therefore the goods produced in that year, but not yet sold, should have such overhead brought into the calculation of their value carried forward to the next period. Put bluntly – do such costs 'attach' to the product or to time? Accountants are divided on this issue, perhaps what has been written in this chapter may have brought you down in favour of one side or the other. It does seem that the marginal approach will become used much more frequently than in the past.

Of course, during the complete life of a business the recorded profits of a firm will be the same in total whichever method is in use. If A Ltd exists for 20 years before it closes down, the profits as calculated for each year using the different methods will result in different recorded profits year by year (except by coincidence). The total profit during the complete life of the business of (say) £20 million will, however, be the same. However, the intermediate reporting of profits may induce decisions which may change the pattern of activities.

18.8 Marginal Costing and Pricing Policy

A more detailed examination as to how marginal costing can be used when setting prices is to be found in Chapter 28.

REVIEW QUESTIONS

Advice:

The use of marginal costs in taking decisions is one which figures in quite a lot of A-Level examinations. The idea of the 'contribution' which a project might make towards covering overheads and potential profits is one which has many applications in accounting. You have already seen it applied in Chapter 2, on branch accounts.

18.1 Drake Ltd's cost and revenues for the current year are expected to be:

		£
Direct labour		6,000
Direct materials		7,000
Factory indirect expenses:		
Variable	4,500	
Fixed	500	
		5,000
Administration expenses		1,200
Selling and distribution expenses		600
Finance expenses		200
		£20,000

It was expected that 2,000 units would be manufactured and sold, the selling price being £11 each.

Suddenly during the year two enquiries were made at the same time which would result in extra production being necessary. They were:

(A) An existing customer said that he would take an extra 100 units, but the price would have to be reduced to £9 per unit on this extra 100 units. The only extra costs that would be involved would be in respect of variable costs.

(B) A new customer would take 150 units annually. This would mean extra variable costs and also an extra machine would have to be bought costing £1,500 which would last for 5 years before being scrapped. It would have no scrap value. Extra running costs of this machine would be £600 per annum. The units are needed for an underdeveloped country and owing to currency difficulties the highest price that could be paid for the units was £10 per unit.

On this information, and assuming that there are no alternatives open to Drake Ltd, should the company accept or reject these orders? Draft the memo that you would give to the managing director of Drake Ltd.

18.2X Hawkins Ltd expects its cost per unit – assuming a production level of 100,000 per annum – to be:

	£
Direct materials	2.8
Direct labour	2.4
Factory indirect expenses: Variable	0.8
Fixed	0.4
Selling and distribution expenses	0.2
Administration expenses	0.3
Finance	0.1
	£7.0

Selling price is £7.5 per unit.

The following propositions are put to the managing director. Each proposition is to be considered on its own without reference to the other propositions.

(a) If the selling price is reduced to £7.4 per unit, sales could be raised to 120,000 units per annum instead of the current 100,000 units. Apart from direct materials, direct labour and factory variable expenses there would be no change in costs.

(b) If the selling price is put up to £7.7 per unit, sales would be 80,000 per annum instead of 100,000. Apart from variable costs there would also be a saving of £2,000 per annum in finance costs.

(c) To satisfy a special order, which would not be repeated, 5,000 extra units could be sold at £6.3 each. This would have no effect on fixed expenses.

(d) To satisfy a special order, which would not be repeated, 3,000 extra units could be sold for £5.9 each. This would have no effect on fixed expenses.

Draft a memo stating what you would advise the managing director to do giving your reasons and workings.

18.3 Assume that by coincidence two firms have exactly the same costs and revenue, but that Magellan Ltd uses a marginal costing approach to the valuation of stock-in-trade in its final accounts, whilst Frobisher Ltd has an absorption cost approach. Calculate the gross profits for each company for each of their first three years of operating from the following:
(a) All fixed factory overhead is £9,000 per annum.

(b) Direct labour costs over each of the three years – £3 per unit.
(c) Direct material costs over each of the three years – £5 per unit.
(d) Variable overheads which vary in direct ratio to production were £2 per unit.
(e) Sales are: Year 1 900 units: Year 2 1,200 units: Year 3 1,100 units.
    The selling price remained constant at £29 per unit.
(f) Production is at the rate of: Year 1 1,200 units: Year 2 1,300 units: Year 3 1,250 units.

18.4X Your firm has been trading for three years. It has used a marginal costing approach to the valuation of stock-in-trade in its final accounts. Your directors are interested to know what the recorded profits would have been if the absorption cost approach had been used instead. Draw up the three years' accounts using both methods.

(a) Fixed factory overhead is £16,000 per annum.
(b) Direct labour costs per unit over each of the three years £4 per unit.
(c) Direct material costs over each of the three years £3 per unit.
(d) Variable overheads which vary in direct ratio to production were £5 per unit.
(e) Sales are: Year 1 9,000 units; Year 2 10,000 units; Year 3 15,000 units. All at £16 per unit.
(f) Production is at the rate of: Year 1 10,000 units; Year 2 12,000 units; Year 3 16,000 units.

18.5 Greatsound Ltd manufactures and sells compact disc players, the cost of which is made up as follows:

	£
Direct material	74.80
Direct labour	18.70
Variable overhead	7.50
Fixed overhead	30.00
Total cost	131.00

The current selling price is £187.

Greatsound Ltd works a day shift only, at present producing 120,000 compact disc players per annum, and has no spare capacity.

Market research has shown that there is a demand for an additional 60,000 compact disc players in the forthcoming year. However, these additional sales would have a selling price of £150 each. One way of achieving the extra production required is to work a night shift. However, this would increase fixed costs by £2,500,000 and the labour force would have to be paid an extra 20 per cent over the day shift rate.

The company supplying the materials to Greatsound Ltd has indicated that it will offer a special discount of 10 per cent on total purchases if the annual purchases of materials increase by 50 per cent.

The selling price and all other costs will remain the same.

Assuming that the additional purchases will only be made if the night shift runs, you are required to:

(a) advise Greatsound Ltd whether it should proceed with the proposal to commence the night shift, based on financial considerations.

(8 marks)

(b) calculate the minimum increase in sales and production required to justify the night shift.

(4 marks)

(c) give **four** other matters which should be taken into consideration when making a decision of this nature.

(8 marks)

(Total marks 20)

(Northern Examinations and Assessments Board: GCE A-Level)

18.6X

(a) What is meant by the terms *contribution* and *marginal cost*? (*4 marks*)

(b) Barton & Co Ltd make and sell 2,000 units per month of a product 'Barco'. The selling price is £65 per unit, and unit costs are: direct labour £8; direct materials £17; variable overheads £11. Fixed costs per month are £29,400.

The company receives two export orders for completion in September 19X2. Order A requests 600 items at a special total price of £20,000; order B requires 750 items at a total price of £34,000. Order A will require no special treatment, but order B will demand extra processing at a cost of £6 per item. The company has sufficient capacity to undertake *either* A *or* B in addition to its current production, but only by paying its direct labour force an overtime premium of 25 per cent.

Calculate the company's contribution and the profits for the month if:

(i) normal production only takes place;
(ii) order A is accepted in addition to normal production;
(iii) order B is accepted in addition to normal production. (*16 marks*)

(c) Use your answer to (b) to demonstrate that a company will normally accept an order which produces a *contribution* towards overheads. (*5 marks*)

(*Total marks 25*)

(*University of London: GCE A-Level*)

18.7 Arncliffe Limited manufactures two types of product marketed under the brand names of 'Crowns' and 'Kings'. All the company's production is sold to a large firm of wholesalers.

Arncliffe is in something of a crisis because the chief accountant has been taken ill just as the company was about to begin negotiating the terms of future contracts with its customer. You have been called in to help and are given the following information relating to each product for the last year. This information has been prepared by a junior assistant.

Report on revenues/costs for the year just ended:

	Crowns £	Kings £
Sales	60,000	25,000
Floor space costs (rent and rates)	10,000	5,000
Raw materials	8,000	2,000
Direct labour	20,000	10,000
Insurances	400	200
Machine running costs	12,000	3,000
Net profit	9,600	4,800

The junior assistant says in his report. 'As you can see, Crowns make twice as much profit as Kings and we should therefore stop manufacturing Kings if we wish to maximise our profits. I have allocated floor space costs and insurances on the basis of the labour costs for each product. All other costs/revenues can be directly related to the individual product.'

Further investigation reveals the following information:

(i) The wholesaler bought all the 20,000 Crowns and 10,000 Kings produced last year, selling them to their customers at £4 and £3 each respectively. The wholesaler is experiencing an increasing demand for Crowns and intends to raise his price next year to £4.50 each.
(ii) Crowns took 8,000 hours to process on the one machine the company owns, whereas Kings took 2,000 hours. The machine has a maximum capacity of 10,000 hours per year.

(iii) Because all production is immediately sold to the wholesaler no stocks are kept.

Required:

(*a*) Prepare the revenue/cost statement for the year just ended on a marginal cost basis, and calculate the rate of contribution to sales for each product. *(8 marks)*

(*b*) You are told that in the coming year the maximum market demand for the two products will be 40,000 Crowns and 36,000 Kings and that the wholesaler wishes to sell a minimum of 6,000 units of each product. Calculate the best product mix and resulting profit for Arncliffe Limited. *(6 marks)*

(*c*) Calculate the best product mix and resulting profit for Arncliffe Limited if another machine with identical running costs and capacity can be hired for £20,000 per annum. Floor space and insurance costs would not change and the maximum and minimum conditions set out in (*b*) above continue to apply. *(6 marks)*

(*d*) What points does Arncliffe Limited need to bear in mind when negotiating next year's contract with the wholesaler? *(5 marks)*

(Total marks 25)

(Reproduced by permission of the University of Cambridge Local Examinations Syndicate)

18.8X Reed Ltd manufactures three products A, B and C. Budgeted costs and selling prices for the three months ending 30 September 19X2 are as follows:

	A	B	C
Sales (units per month)	6,000	8,000	5,000
	£	£	£
Selling price per unit	45	44	37
Unit costs			
Direct labour	6	9	6
Direct materials*	20	24	16
Variable overhead	4	3	2
Fixed overhead	5	5	6

Labour costs are £3 per hour, and material costs are £4 per kilo for all products. The total fixed costs are of a general factory nature, and are unavoidable.

The company has been advised by its supplier that due to a material shortage, its material requirement for the month of September will be reduced by 15 per cent. No other changes are anticipated.

Required:

A   A statement to show the maximum net profit for the three months ending 30 September 19X2, taking into account the material shortage for the month of September. *(15 marks)*

B   Explain how the fixed cost element is dealt with in marginal costing and in absorption costing. Briefly explain how this affects any closing stock valuation. *(8 marks)*

(Total marks 23)

(University of Oxford Delegacy of Local Examinations: GCE A-Level)

*Authors' note : Assume that the materials used in each product are of the same kind.

18.9 Paul Wagtail started a small manufacturing business on 1 May 19X8. He has kept his records on the double entry system, and has drawn up a trial balance at 30 April 19X9 before attempting to prepare his first final accounts.

Extract from the trial balance of Paul Wagtail at 30 April 19X9

	£	£
Purchases of raw materials	125,000	
Sales		464,360
Selling expenses	23,800	
Insurance	4,800	
Factory repairs and maintenance	19,360	
Carriage on raw materials	1,500	
Heating and lighting	3,600	
Direct factory power	12,430	
Distribution expenses	25,400	
Production wages	105,270	
Factory supervisor's wages	29,600	
Administration expenses	46,700	
Plant and machinery at cost	88,000	
Delivery vehicles at cost	88,000	
Raw materials returned to supplier	2,100	

At 30 April 19X9, he has closing stocks of raw materials costing £8,900. He has manufactured 9,500 completed units of his product, and sold 8,900. He has a further 625 units that are 80 per cent complete for raw materials and production labour, and also 80 per cent complete for factory indirect costs.

He has decided to divide his insurance costs and his heating and lighting costs 40 per cent for the factory and 60 per cent for the office/showroom.

He wishes to depreciate his plant and machinery at 20 per cent p.a. on cost, and his delivery vehicles using the reducing balance method at 40 per cent p.a.

He has not yet made up his mind how to value his stocks of work-in-progress and finished goods. He has heard that he could use either marginal or absorption costing to do this, and has received different advice from a friend running a similar business and from an accountant.

Required:

(a) Prepare Paul Wagtail's manufacturing, trading and profit and loss accounts for the year ended 30 April 19X9 using *both* marginal and absorption costing methods, preferably in columnar format. *(14 marks)*

(b) Advise Paul Wagtail of the advantages and disadvantages of using each method. *(6 marks)*

(Total marks 20)

(University of Oxford Local Delegacy Examinations: GCE A-Level)

18.10X The figures given below are all that could be salvaged from the records after a recent fire in the offices of Firelighters Limited. The company manufactures a single product, has no raw materials or work-in-progress and values its stocks at marginal cost (i.e. at variable manufacturing cost) using the FIFO basis. It is known that the unit closing stock valuation in 19X0 was the same as in 19X9.

	19X0	19X1
Selling price per unit	£10.00	£10.00
Variable manufacturing cost (per unit produced)	£4.00	£4.00
Variable selling cost (per unit sold)	£1.25	?
Quantity sold (units)	100,000	?
Quantity manufactured (units)	105,000	130,000
Contribution	?	£585,000
Fixed manufacturing costs	£105,000	£117,000
Other fixed costs	£155,000	?
Operating profit before interest charges	?	£292,000
Interest charges	£70,000	?
Opening finished stock (units)	?	?
Closing finished stock (units)	20,000	20,000
Net profit for the year	?	£210,000

Required:

Prepare a revenue statement for management showing contribution, operating profit and net profit for each year in as much detail as the information given above permits.

(Reproduced by permission of the University of Cambridge Local Examinations Syndicate)

18.11X Gainford Ltd is a manufacturing company which produces three specialist products – **A, B** and **C**. For costing purposes the company's financial year is divided into thirteen periods of four weeks. There is always sufficient raw material in stock to meet any planned level of production but there is a maximum number of labour hours available to the company. The production of each product requires a different physical layout of the factory equipment although the labour tasks are broadly similar. For this reason the company only produces one type of product at any time, and the decision as to which product to manufacture is taken before each four week period commences.

A forty hour working week is in operation and the following factory staff are employed:

Grade 1	28 staff paid at a rate of £8 per hour
Grade 2	12 staff paid at a rate of £6 per hour

In addition, a limited number of qualified part-time staff can be employed when required. Both full-time and part-time staff are paid at the same rate. The next four week period is number 7 and the following maximum part-time hours are available for that period:

Grade 1	2,240 hours
Grade 2	1,104 hours

The production costs and selling costs per unit for each product are:

		A	B	C
		£	£	£
Direct raw material		147	87	185
Direct labour:	Grade 1	64	56	60
	Grade 2	24	27	21
Variable overheads		15	10	15
Fixed Overheads		12	12	12
Selling price of each product		400	350	450

There is a strong demand for all three products and every unit produced is sold.

Required:

(a) Explain the terms:
  (i) 'contribution' *(4 marks)*
  (ii) 'key factor' *(4 marks)*
(b) Calculate the contribution and profit obtained when **each** product is sold. *(7 marks)*
(c) Prepare a statement from the available information, for each period number 7 which will assist management to decide which product to produce in order to maximise contribution. This statement should include details of the:
  (i) total production labour hours available *(4 marks)*
  (ii) number of hours required to produce one unit of **each** type of product *(6 marks)*
  (iii) maximum production (in units) possible of **each** type of product *(6 marks)*
  (iv) product which will give the greatest contribution in period number 7 *(4 marks)*
(d) Outline the main steps in the manufacturing decision making process which ought to be adopted by a business. *(15 marks)*

(Associated Examining Board: GCE A-Level)

18.12X Vale Manufacturing started in business on 1 April 19X3, and incurred the following costs during its first three years.

Year ending 31 March	19X4	19X5	19X6
	£	£	£
Direct materials	60,000	49,900	52,200
Direct labour	48,000	44,000	45,000
Variable overheads	24,000	30,000	40,000
Fixed costs	40,000	40,600	41,300

Sales during the first three years were all at £20 per unit.

	19X4	19X5	19X6
Production each year (units)	16,000	14,000	14,000
Sales each year (units)	14,000	14,000	15,000

Required:

(a) Prepare a statement showing the gross profit for each of the three years if the company used:
  (i) the marginal costing approach to valuing stock;
  (ii) the absorption costing approach to valuing stock. *(17 marks)*
(b) Advise the company of the advantages and disadvantages of using each method *(6 marks)*
(Total marks 23)

(University of Oxford Delegacy of Local Examinations: GCE A-Level)

Chapter 19

Job and Process Costing

19.1 Introduction

The earlier chapters on costing have been concerned mainly with the firm as a whole. You have seen the effects of marginal and absorption costing if applied to the firm, and you have seen the flow of costs through manufacturing and retail businesses. Now we have to consider the use of these concepts in the application of costing in firms. So far there has been a certain amount of simplification just so that the concepts could be seen without too much detail obscuring your view. For instance, it has been usually assumed in most of the Exhibits that the firms have been making only one kind of product, and that there has really been only one cost centre. Without stretching your imagination greatly you will realise that firms manufacture many different types of goods, and that there are many cost centres in most firms.

When looking at the costing systems in use it can be seen that they can usually be divided into two main types, (a) job costing, (b) process costing. These two main types have either an absorption or marginal costing approach, they use FIFO or LIFO or AVCO methods of pricing issues etc. It is important to realise that marginal costing is not a costing system, it is instead an approach to costing which is used when job or processing costing systems are used. The same applies to absorption costing.

19.2 The Choice of Job Costing or Process Costing

Process costing is relevant where production is regarded as a continuous flow, and would be applicable to industries where production is repetitive and continuous. One example would be an oil refinery where crude oil is processed continually, emerging as different grades of petrol, paraffin, motor oil, etc. Another instance would be a salt works where brine (salt water) is pumped into the works, and the product is slabs or packets of salt. Salt works and oil refineries will have a repetitive and continuous flow of production and would, therefore, use process costing.

Contrasted with this would be production which consisted of separate jobs for special orders which could be just one item or of a batch of items. For instance where bodies of Rolls-Royce cars are made to each customer's specifications, each car can be regarded as a separate job. Compared with this would be a printer's business where books are printed, so that the printing of say 5,000 copies of a book can also be regarded as a job. The 'job' can thus be one item or a batch of similar items.

We can compare the two approaches by using diagrams of the different types of costing. These are shown as Exhibit 19.1.

Exhibit 19.1

Process costing

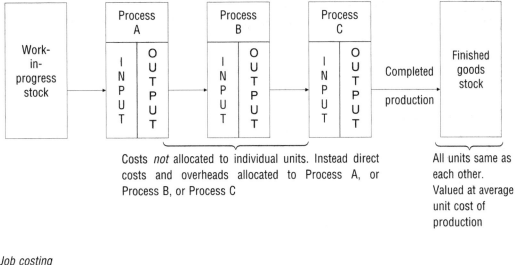

Costs *not* allocated to individual units. Instead direct costs and overheads allocated to Process A, or Process B, or Process C

All units same as each other. Valued at average unit cost of production

Job costing

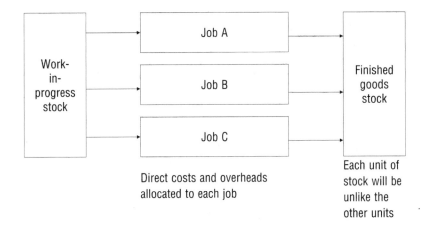

Direct costs and overheads allocated to each job

Each unit of stock will be unlike the other units

19.3 Job Costing

Each job will be given a separate job number, and direct materials and direct labour used on the job will be charged to the job. The accumulation of the costs will be done on a 'job cost sheet'. The materials will have been charged to the job on FIFO, or LIFO, or AVCO, etc., basis. The direct labour costs will be found by recording the number of direct labour hours of each type of direct worker, and multiplying by the labour cost per hour for each type.

The job is thus the cost centre, and direct labour and direct materials can be charged direct to the cost centre. The indirect expenses cannot be charged direct to the job, such costs are charged instead to a service cost centre and the cost of the service centre is then apportioned between the various jobs to give the cost of each job including indirect expenses. Now it is only after the accounting period is over that the exact costs of each service centre are known, but you will want to know how much each job costs as it is finished. You will not want to wait months to find out the cost of each job. This is solved by estimating the indirect expenses, and then fixing the method of apportioning these estimated expenses as will be seen in Exhibit 19.2.

Suppose there are three jobs being performed and these are in separate production departments, Departments A, B and C. There are also two service centres, Departments G and H. Some of the indirect labour expenses and other indirect expenses can be allocated direct to the production departments – for instance the wages of the foremen of each of Departments A, B and C, or items such as lubricating materials if each department used quite different lubricants. Other indirect labour can be traced to the two centres G and H as well as expenses. The problem then is that of apportioning the costs of G and H between Departments A, B and C. We can now look at Exhibit 19.2, and see what answer this firm came up with.

Exhibit 19.2

Indirect labour costs and other indirect expenses have been allocated to Production Departments A, B and C and Service Departments G and H as follows:

| | Production Departments | | | Service Departments | |
	A	B	C	G	H
Indirect labour	2,000	3,000	4,000	500	1,000
Other expenses	1,000	2,000	3,000	1,500	2,000
	£3,000	£5,000	£7,000	£2,000	£3,000

The problem is to apportion the costs of G and H to the production departments. G was a department which maintained factory buildings whilst H maintained factory machinery. A study of the costs of G produced a very easy answer. There was no doubt that the costs were in direct relationship to the floor space occupied by each department. But it must not be overlooked that department H also needed the attention of G's workforce so that part of the costs of G would have to be apportioned to H. These costs would then increase the total of costs of department H which would then need apportioning to the production departments. Floor space in square feet was A 2,000, B 4,000, C 3,000, and H 1,000. The £2,000 costs of department G were therefore apportioned:

$$\text{Each department:} \quad \frac{\text{Its floor space}}{\text{Total floor space}} \times £2,000$$

Therefore:

A $\dfrac{2,000}{10,000} \times £2,000 = £400$ 　　　　 B $\dfrac{4,000}{10,000} \times £2,000 = £800$

C $\dfrac{3,000}{10,000} \times £2,000 = £600$ 　　　　 H $\dfrac{1,000}{10,000} \times £2,000 = £200$

(Department H's costs have now increased by £200 and become £3,200)

Department H's costs presented a far more difficult problem. Consideration was given to apportionment based on numbers of machines, volumes of production, and types of machinery. It was, however, felt that there was a high relationship in this case (although this would certainly not always be true in other firms) between the values of machinery in use and the costs of maintaining them. The more costly equipment was very complicated and needed a lot of attention. Consequently it was decided to apportion H's costs between A, B and C on the basis of the value of machinery in each department. This was found to be A £3,000; B £6,000; C £7,000. The costs were therefore apportioned:

$$\frac{\text{Value of machinery in department}}{\text{Total value of machinery in all 3 departments}} \times £3,200$$

Therefore

$$\text{A} \quad \frac{3,000}{16,000} \times £3,200 = £600 \qquad\qquad \text{B} \quad \frac{6,000}{16,000} \times £3,200 = £1,200$$

$$\text{C} \quad \frac{7,000}{16,000} \times £3,200 = £1,400$$

The costs and their apportionment can, therefore, be shown:

	Production Departments			Service Departments	
	A	B	C	G	H
Indirect labour	2,000	3,000	4,000	500	1,000
Other expenses	1,000	2,000	3,000	1,500	2,000
	3,000	5,000	7,000	2,000	3,000
Department G's costs apportioned	400	800	600	(2,000)	200
					3,200
Department H's costs apportioned	600	1,200	1,400		(3,200)
	£4,000	£7,000	£9,000	–	–

This method of apportioning service department overheads is sometimes called the repeated distribution method. (See Question 19.7 for a discussion of this and another method.)

Now we have the estimated overhead for each department for the ensuing accounting period. We now have another problem as to how the overhead is going to be taken into the calculation of the cost of each job in these departments. After investigation the conclusion is that in departments A and B there is a direct relationship between direct labour hours and overhead, but in department C the guiding fact is machine hours. If the total overheads of departments A and B are therefore divided by the estimated number of direct labour hours this will give the overhead rate per direct labour hour, whilst in department C the total overhead will be divided by the estimated machine hours. The calculation of the overhead rates are therefore:

	Production Departments		
	A	B	C
Direct labour hours	5,000	4,000	
Machine hours			6,000
Overhead rate per direct labour hour	$\dfrac{£4,000}{5,000}$ = £0.8	$\dfrac{£7,000}{4,000}$ = £1.75	
Overhead rate per machine hour			$\dfrac{£9,000}{6,000}$ = £1.5

We can now calculate the costs of four jobs performed in this factory:

Job A/70/144 | *Department A*
Started 1.7.19X2. Completed 13.7.19X2
Cost of direct materials £130
Number of direct labour hours 100
Cost rate of direct labour per hour £0.9

Job B/96/121 | *Department B*
Started 4.7.19X2. Completed 9.7.19X2
Cost of direct materials £89
Number of direct labour hours 40
Cost rate of direct labour per hour £1.1

Job C/67/198 | *Department C*
Started 8.7.19X2. Completed 16.7.19X2
Cost of direct materials £58
Number of direct labour hours 50
Cost rate of direct labour per hour £1.0
Number of machine hours 40

Job AC/45/34 | *Departments A and C*
Started in A 3.7.19X2. Passed on to C 11.7.19X2. Completed in C 16.7.19X2
Cost of materials £115
Number of direct labour hours (in Dept. A) 80
(in Dept. C) 90
Cost rate per direct labour hour (in Dept. A) £0.9
(in Dept. C) £1.0
Number of machine hours (in Dept. C) 70

The job cost sheets for these four jobs are shown below. At no point during this Exhibit has it been stated whether a marginal costing or an absorption costing approach has been adopted. If an absorption costing approach had been used, overhead would include both fixed and variable overheads. If a marginal costing approach had been used, the overhead brought into the calculations of job costs would exclude fixed overhead, so that the overhead rate would be a variable overhead rate.

```
┌─────────────────────────────────────────────────────────────────────┐
│                    Job Cost Sheet. Job No. A/70/144                    │
│                                                                       │
│  Started 1.7.19X2                          Completed 13.7.19X2         │
│                                                              £         │
│  Materials                                                  130        │
│                              Hours        Rates £                     │
│  Direct labour                100          0.9              90         │
│  Factory overhead             100          0.8              80         │
│  Total job cost                                            £300        │
└─────────────────────────────────────────────────────────────────────┘
┌─────────────────────────────────────────────────────────────────────┐
│                    Job Cost Sheet. Job No. B/96/121                    │
│                                                                       │
│  Started 4.7.19X2                          Completed 9.7.19X2          │
│                                                              £         │
│  Materials                                                   89        │
│                              Hours        Rates £                     │
│  Direct labour                40           1.1              44         │
│  Factory overhead             40           1.75            70          │
│  Total job cost                                            £203        │
└─────────────────────────────────────────────────────────────────────┘
┌─────────────────────────────────────────────────────────────────────┐
│                    Job Cost Sheet. Job No. C/67/198                    │
│                                                                       │
│  Started 8.7.19X2                          Completed 16.7.19X2         │
│                                                              £         │
│  Materials                                                   58        │
│                              Hours        Rates £                     │
│  Direct labour                50           1.0              50         │
│  Factory overhead             40           1.5              60         │
│  Total job cost                                            £168        │
└─────────────────────────────────────────────────────────────────────┘
┌─────────────────────────────────────────────────────────────────────┐
│                    Job Cost Sheet. Job No. AC/45/34                    │
│                                                                       │
│  Started 3.7.19X2                          Completed 16.7.19X2         │
│                                                              £         │
│  Materials                                                  115        │
│                              Hours        Rates £                     │
│  Direct labour (Dept. A)      80           0.9              72         │
│  Direct labour (Dept. C)      90           1.0              90         │
│  Factory overhead (Dept. A)   80           0.8              64         │
│  Factory overhead (Dept. C)   70           1.5             105         │
│  Total job cost                                            £446        │
└─────────────────────────────────────────────────────────────────────┘
```

19.4 Cost Centres – Job Costing and Responsibility

It must be pointed out that a cost centre for job costing is not necessarily the same as tracing the costs down to the individual who is responsible for controlling them. There are two questions here: (*a*) finding the cost of a job to check on its profitability and

(b) controlling the costs by making someone responsible for them so that he/she will have to answer for any variations from planned results. Many firms therefore keep separate records of costs to fulfil each of these functions.

19.5 Process Costing

Job costing treats production as a number of separate jobs being performed, whereas process costing sees production as a continuous flow. In process costing there is correspondingly no attempt to allocate costs to specific units being produced.

There is, however, usually more than one process in the manufacture of goods. We can take for an example a bakery producing cakes. There are three processes: (a) the mixing of the cake ingredients, (b) the baking of the cakes, (c) the packaging of the cakes. Each process is treated as a cost centre, and therefore costs for (a), (b) and (c) are collected separately. Overhead rates are then calculated for each cost centre in a similar fashion to that in job costing.

In the case of the bakery, each accounting period would probably start and finish without any half-mixed or half-baked cakes, but some types of firms which use process costing have processes which take rather longer to complete than baking cakes. A typical case would be the brewing of beer. At the beginning and end of each period there would be partly processed units. It is a matter of arithmetic to convert production into 'equivalent production'. For instance, production during a particular period may be as in Exhibit 19.3.

Exhibit 19.3

Started in previous period and $\frac{3}{4}$ completed then, and $\frac{1}{4}$ completed in current period, 400 units, 400 $\times$ $\frac{1}{4}$	100
Started and completed in current period	680
Started in current period and $\frac{1}{8}$ completed by end of period, 160 units, 160 $\times$ $\frac{1}{8}$	20
Equivalent production	800 units

If the total costs of the cost centre amounted to £4,000 then the unit cost would be $\frac{£4,000}{800}$ = £5.

In fact, process costing can become very complicated because some of the part-produced items are complete in terms of say, materials, but incomplete in terms of labour, or else say $\frac{2}{3}$ complete for materials and $\frac{1}{4}$ complete for labour. Although the situation becomes complicated, the principles are no different from those described for calculating equivalent production.

We can now look at an example of process costing in Exhibit 19.4. So that we do not get involved in too many arithmetical complications, we will assume that there are no partly completed goods in each process at the start and end of the period considered.

Exhibit 19.4

A bakery making cakes has three processes, process (A) The mixing of the cake ingredients, (B) The baking of the cakes, (C) The packaging of the cakes.

January activity was as follows:

Materials used:	£
Process (A)	4,000
Process (B)	–
Process (C)	1,000
Direct labour:	
Process (A)	1,500
Process (B)	500
Process (C)	800
Factory overhead:	
Variable:	
Process (A)	400
Process (B)	1,300
Process (C)	700
Fixed: (allocated to processes)	
Process (A)	600
Process (B)	500
Process (C)	400

During January 100,000 cakes were made.
The process cost accounts will appear as:

Process (A)

	£		£
Materials	4,000	Transferred to Process (B)	
Direct labour	1,500	100,000 units at £0.065	6,500
Variable overhead	400		
Fixed overhead	600		
	£6,500		£6,500

Process (B)

	£		£
Transferred from Process (A)		Transferred to Process (C)	
100,000 units at £0.065	6,500	100,000 units at £0.088	8,800
Direct labour	500		
Variable overhead	1,300		
Fixed overhead	500		
	£8,800		£8,800

Process (C)

	£		£
Transferred from Process (B)		Transferred to finished goods stock	
100,000 units at £0.088	8,800	100,000 units at £0.117	11,700
Materials	1,000		
Direct labour	800		
Variable overhead	700		
Fixed overhead	400		
	£11,700		£11,700

19.6 Normal and Abnormal Losses

There are some losses that are basically part of the production process and cannot be eliminated. For instance, when printing books, losses occur in the cutting of paper, when brewing beer there will be losses due to evaporation, when cutting steel there will be losses. These losses are inevitable, even in the most efficient firms, and as such they are called normal or uncontrollable losses.

On the other hand, there are losses which should be avoided if there are efficient operating conditions. Such things as the incorrect cutting of cloth so that it is wasted unnecessarily, not mixing ingredients properly so that some of the product is unusable, and the use of inferior materials so that much of the product cannot pass production tests and is wasted. These are abnormal or controllable losses.

The accounting treatment varies between these two sorts of losses:

Normal losses: These are not transferred from the process account but are treated as part of the process costs.

Abnormal losses: These are transferred from the process account to an abnormal loss account. The double entry is:

> *Dr* Abnormal loss account
> *Cr* Process account

The abnormal loss is then treated as a period cost. Accordingly it is written off to the debit of the profit and loss account at the end of the period.

19.7 Under/Over Absorption of Overheads

When an overhead rate is based on estimated annual overhead expenditure and estimated activity, it would be very rare for it to be exactly the same as the actual overhead incurred. Either the costs themselves will have changed, or the activity, or both.

If therefore £300,000 has been allocated to the year's production, but actual costs were £298,000 then too much has been allocated; in other words, it is a case of over-absorption of overheads amounting to £2,000. If on the other hand £305,000 had been allocated but the actual costs were £311,000 then too little has been allocated, and this is an under-absorption of overheads amounting to £6,000.

At the closing balance sheet date the stock-in-trade has been valued and this will include something for overheads. In the case of an under-absorption the question arises as to whether the closing stock valuation should be amended to include something for the under-absorbed overheads. The accounting answer is that no adjustment should be made to the stock valuation. Similarly the stock valuation should not be reduced to take account of over-absorption of overheads.

Exhibit 19.5 shows how the costs should be treated for underabsorption of overheads.

Exhibit 19.5

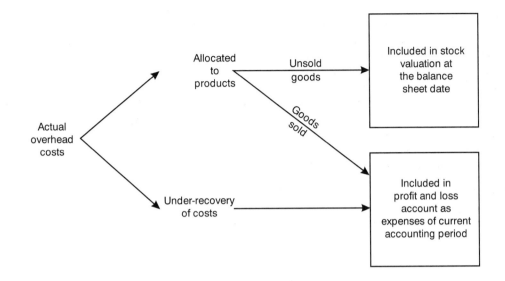

19.8 Other Kinds of Firms

Process costing is found most often in industries such as oil, canning, paint manufacture, steel, textiles, and food processing.

19.9 The Problem of Joint Costs

Usually a manufacturing operation results in one simple product. Any excess is regarded as scrap, and the small cost that could be traced to it is ignored, e.g. the manufacture of a suit where the cost is traced to the suit, the small unusable bits of cloth being ignored.

This is not always the case, and where a group of separate products is produced simultaneously, each of the products having relatively substantial sales values, then the products are called 'joint products'. Thus crude oil taken into an oil refinery is processed and the output is in terms of different grades of petrol, paraffin, motor oil, etc. This means that in costing terms the costs of the materials and processes, etc. have to be split between the joint products.

Many problems exist in this area. Perhaps you will see why when the problem of allocating costs between joint products is concerned with the cutting up of a cow for beef. From a cow there is rump steak, the fillet steaks, the T-bone steaks, sirloin, silverside, brisket, etc. If the cow costs the butcher £300, then how would you allocate the cost between all of these various joint products? This gives you some idea of the problem which exists; in many industries this becomes involved with complex technological problems.

REVIEW QUESTIONS

Advice:

Questions on job and process costing are usually fairly easy to answer and it is also relatively simple to gain quite high marks by tackling them.

19.1 In a firm there are four types of jobs performed in separate production departments A, B, C and D. In addition there are three service departments, K, L and M. Costs have been allocated to the departments as follows:

	Production Departments				Service Departments		
	A	B	C	D	K	L	M
	£	£	£	£	£	£	£
Indirect labour	4,000	6,000	8,000	2,000	1,500	3,000	4,100
Other expenses	2,700	3,100	3,600	1,500	4,500	2,000	2,000

The expenses of the service departments are to be allocated between other departments as follows:

Dept K to Depts A 25 per cent: B 30 per cent: C 20 per cent: D 10 per cent: M 15 per cent.
Dept L to Depts A 60 per cent: C 30 per cent: D 10 per cent.
Dept M to Depts B 30 per cent: C 50 per cent: D 20 per cent.

In departments A and C the job costing is to use an overhead rate per direct labour hour, whilst in B and D a machine hour rate will be used. The number of direct hours and machine hours per department is expected to be:

	A	B	C	D
Direct labour hours	2,000	4,000	4,450	2,700
Machine hours	1,900	2,600	2,900	2,400

You are required to calculate:

(*a*) The overhead rates for departments A and C.
(*b*) The overhead rates for departments B and D.

(Keep your answer – it will be used as a basis for the next question.)

19.2 In the firm mentioned in Question 19.1 what would be the costs of the following jobs given that the direct labour costs per hour are: Dept A £2.1; B £1.7; C £2.4; D £2.3?

Job 351: Dept A	Direct materials cost	£190
	Number of direct labour hours	56
	Number of machine hours	40
Job 352: Dept B	Direct materials cost	£1,199
	Number of direct labour hours	178
	Number of machine hours	176
Job 353: Dept C	Direct materials cost	£500
	Number of direct labour hours	130
	Number of machine hours	100
Job 354: Dept D	Direct materials cost	£666
	Number of direct labour hours	90
	Number of machine hours	64
Job 355: Dept C	Direct materials cost	£560
	Number of direct labour hours	160
	Number of machine hours	150
	Job passed on to Dept B where additional direct materials cost	£68
	Number of direct labour hours	30
	Number of machine hours	20

19.3X In a firm there are five types of jobs performed in separate production departments P, Q, R, S and T. In addition there are two service departments F and G. Costs have been allocated to the departments as follows:

	Production Departments					Service Departments	
	P	Q	R	S	T	F	G
	£	£	£	£	£	£	£
Indirect labour	5,000	7,000	3,000	6,000	8,000	10,000	9,000
Other expenses	500	1,800	1,000	1,200	1,300	6,000	7,000

The expenses of the service departments are to be allocated between other departments as follows:

Dept F to Depts P 10 per cent: Q 20 per cent: S 30 per cent: T 15 per cent: G 25 per cent.

Dept G to Depts P 12.5 per cent: Q 20 per cent: R 25 per cent: S 30 per cent: T 12.5 per cent.

In departments R and T the job costing is to use an overhead rate per direct labour hour, whilst in the other production departments a machine hour rate will be used. The number of direct labour hours and machine hours per department are expected to be:

	P	Q	R	S	T
Direct labour hours	4,000	5,000	3,600	10,000	3,550
Machine hours	3,000	4,000	3,000	8,000	2,800

You are required to calculate:

(a) The overhead rates for departments R and T.
(b) The overhead rates for departments P, Q and S.

(Keep your answer – it will be used for Question 19.4.)

19.4X In the firm mentioned in Question 19.3X what would be the costs of the following jobs, given that the direct labour rate per hour is Dept P £1.9: Q £2.5: R £2.0: S £2.7: T £2.4?

Job 701: Dept R	Direct materials cost	£115
	Number of direct labour hours	35
	Number of machine hours	29
Job 702: Dept T	Direct materials cost	£1,656
	Number of direct labour hours	180
	Number of machine hours	160
Job 703: Dept P	Direct materials cost	£546
	Number of direct labour hours	100
	Number of machine hours	90
Job 704: Dept S	Direct materials cost	£65
	Number of direct labour hours	250
	Number of machine hours	60
Job 705: Dept Q	Direct materials cost	£4,778
	Number of direct labour hours	305
	Number of machine hours	280
Job 706: Dept P	Direct materials cost	£555
	Number of direct labour hours	200
	Number of machine hours	180
	Then passed to Dept T for completion where direct materials cost	£11
	Number of direct labour hours	18
	Number of machine hours	2

19.5

(a) Define the term *equivalent production* and state when the principle is used. *(4 marks)*

(b) During May 19X1, M Wurzel & Co. Limited's output was 4,000 finished items plus 600 partly finished items. There was no work-in-progress on 1 May 19X1.

	Materials	Labour	Overheads	Total
Total cost (£)	8,172	7,120	5,196	20,488
WIP degree of completion %	90	75	55	–

Calculate for the month of May 19X1:

(i) the total equivalent production for each cost element;
(ii) the cost per complete unit;
(iii) the value of the work-in-progress. *(11 marks)*

(*University of London: GCE A-Level*)

19.6X

(a) What is meant by the term *equivalent production*? *(3 marks)*

(b) At Earith Industries at the beginning of April there were no partially finished goods on hand. During the month, 6,000 completed units were produced, together with 800 units partially completed. Details of the partially finished items were:

	Total Cost (£)	Percentage completed
Materials	12,540	75
Labour	8,476	65
Overheads	7,084	55

Calculate:
(i) the total equivalent production,

(ii) the cost per complete unit,

(iii) the total value of work-in-progress. *(12 marks)*

(*University of London: GCE A-Level*)

19.7

(a) Explain the difference between the terms *overhead allotment, overhead apportionment,* and *overhead absorption*. *(5 marks)*

(b) Why are *estimated* figures used in calculating overhead absorption rates? *(2 marks)*

(c) The following information relates to the Flyby Knight Plc for the six months ended 31 December 19X1:

	Production Departments			Service Departments	
	A	B	C	X	Y
Overheads (£)	14,000	12,000	8,000	4,000	3,000
Overheads to be apportioned:					
Dept X (%)	35	30	20	–	15
Dept Y (%)	30	40	25	5	–

(i) Use the continuous apportionment (repeated distribution) method to apportion the service departments' overheads between each other.

(ii) Apportion the service departments' overheads calculated in (i) to the production departments.
(iii) Show how the overheads apportioned to the production departments would have differed if the elimination method had been used for the service departments.
(iv) State how far it is true to say that the elimination method produces an inaccurate answer, and is therefore not to be recommended. *(18 marks)*

(University of London: GCE A-Level)

19.8X Kalmo Ltd offers a subcontracting service in assembly, painting and packing. Components are supplied by customers to the company, the required operations are then carried out, and the completed work returned to the customer. The company is labour intensive, with only a relatively small amount of materials purchased.

Currently, one factory overhead recovery rate is used which is a percentage of total direct labour costs. This is calculated from the following budgeted costs.

Department	Direct labour costs £	Direct labour hours	Machine hours	Factory overheads £
Assembly	450,000	150,000	6,000	180,000
Painting	500,000	140,625	–	225,000
Packing	250,000	100,000	8,000	75,000

The cost sheet for Job 131190 shows the following information:

Department	Direct labour costs £	Direct labour hours	Machine hours	Direct material costs £
Assembly	2,500	1,000	120	100
Painting	2,200	900	–	400
Packing	4,800	960	80	500

General administration expenses of 20 per cent are added to the total factory costs, and then a further 25 per cent of the total cost is added as profit, to arrive at the selling price.

Although the company has been using the blanket factory overhead recovery rate for a number of years, one of the directors has questioned this method, and asks if it would be possible to apply overhead recovery rates for each department.

Required:

A Calculate the current factory overhead recovery rate, and apply this to arrive at the selling price for Job 131190. *(4 marks)*

B In line with the director's comments, calculate overhead recovery rates for each department, using two alternative methods, and apply both to arrive at new selling prices for Job 131190. *(10 marks)*

C Briefly evaluate the methods you have used for the recovery of factory overheads, justifying which one you consider to be most appropriate. *(6 marks)*

D Outline how an unsatisfactory method of overhead absorption can affect the profits of a business. *(3 marks)*

(Total marks 23)

(University of Oxford Delegacy of Local Examinations: GCE A-Level)

19.9

(a) What is meant by the term, 'specific order costing'? *(3 marks)*

(b) In what ways does specific order costing differ from process costing? *(6 marks)*

(c) The Acme Shelving Co. Ltd manufactures shelving brackets in batches of 300. During May, Batch No. 23 was machined at a rate of 15 per hour. Sixty of the brackets failed to pass inspection, but of these, 40 were thought to be rectifiable. The remaining 20 were scrapped, and the scrap value was credited to the batch cost account. Rectification work took nine hours.

Batch No. 23

	£
Raw materials per bracket	1.60
Scrap value per bracket	0.86
Machinists' hourly rate	4.20
Machine hour overhead rate	3.60
(running time only)	
Setting up of machine: normal machining	21.00
rectification	18.00

Calculate:

(i) the cost of Batch No. 23 in total and per unit, if all units pass inspection;

(ii) the *actual* cost of Batch No. 23, in total and per unit, after crediting the recovery value of the scrapped components, and including the rectification costs;

(iii) the loss incurred because of defective work. *(16 marks)*

(University of London: GCE A-Level)

19.10X Horden Products Ltd manufactures goods which could involve any or all of three production departments. These departments are simply entitled **A**, **B** and **C**. A direct wages cost percentage absorption rate for the recovery of production overheads is applied to individual job costs.

Details from the company's budgets for the year ended 31 March 19X5 are as follows:

	Dept A	Dept B	Dept C
Indirect materials	£23,000	£35,000	£57,000
Indirect wages	£21,000	£34,000	£55,000
Direct wages	£140,000	£200,000	£125,000
Direct labour hours	25,000	50,000	60,000
Machine hours	100,000	40,000	10,000

The following information is also available for the production departments:

	Dept A	Dept B	Dept C
Area (square metres)	30,000	20,000	10,000
Cost of machinery	£220,000	£160,000	£20,000
Horse power of machinery	55	30	15

Other budgeted figures are:

	£
Power	120,000
Rent, rates, light, heat	90,000
Insurance (machinery)	20,000
Depreciation	80,000

Machinery is depreciated on the basis of 20% on cost.
Job No 347 passed through all three departments and incurred the following actual direct costs and times:

	Direct Materials £	Direct Wages £	Direct Labour Hours £	Machine Hours £
Dept A	152	88	35	60
Dept B	85	192	90	30
Dept C	52	105	45	10

A sum amounting to 30% of the production cost is added to every job to enable a selling price to be quoted.

Required:

(a) A statement to show the total production overheads per department and calculate the absorption rate which the company has adopted. *(8 marks)*

(b) Calculate the selling price to be quoted for Job No 347. *(8 marks)*

(c) Using the available data, calculate absorption rates when based on:
   (i) direct labour hour rate *(3 marks)*
   (ii) machine hour rate. *(3 marks)*

(d) Explain clearly the meaning of the following terms relating to overheads:
   (i) allotment *(3 marks)*
   (ii) allocation *(3 marks)*
   (iii) apportionment. *(2 marks)*

(Associated Examining Board: GCE A-Level)

19.11X

(a) Explain the following terms as used in process costing:
   (i)   normal losses
   (ii) abnormal losses
   (iii) equivalent production
   (iv) joint cost
   (v)   split-off point   *(10 marks)*

(b) In process costing, it is neither the technology nor the costs incurred, but the market price of the item, which determines whether an item is classed as:
   (i)   scrap or waste; and
   (ii) a joint product or a by-product.

   How far do you agree?   *(10 marks)*

(University of London Examinations and Assessment Council: GCE A-Level)

Chapter 20

Budgeting and Budgetary Control

20.1 Financial Budgets

In Chapter 16 of this book it was stated that management control was needed to try to ensure that the organisation achieved its objectives. Once the objectives have been agreed, plans should be drawn up so that the progress of the firm can be directed towards the ends specified in the objectives. Now it must not be thought that plans can be expressed only in accounting terms, for example quality of the product might be best shown in engineering terms, or social objectives shown in a plan concerned with employee welfare. But some of the objectives, such as the attainment of a desired profit, or of the attainment of a desired growth in assets can be expressed in accounting terms. When a plan is expressed quantitatively it is known as a 'budget' and the process of converting plans into budgets is known as 'budgeting'. In this book we are concerned primarily with budgets shown in monetary terms, i.e. financial budgets.

The budgeting process may be quite formal in a large organisation with committees set up to perform the task. On the other hand in a very small firm the owner may jot down his budget on a piece of scrap-paper or even on the back of a used envelope. Some even manage without writing anything down at all, they have done the budgets in their heads and can easily remember them. This book is concerned with budgeting in a formal manner.

20.2 Budgets and People

Probably in no other part of accounting is there a greater need for understanding other people than in the processes of budgeting. Budgets are prepared to try to guide the firm towards its objectives. There is no doubt that some budgets that are drawn up are even more harmful to a firm than if none were drawn up at all.

Budgets are drawn up for control purposes, that is an attempt to control the direction that the firm is taking. Many people, however, look upon them, not as a guide, but as a straitjacket. We can look at a few undesirable actions that can result from people regarding budgets as a straitjacket rather than as a guide.

(a) The sales manager refuses to let a salesman go to Sweden in response to an urgent and unexpected request from a Swedish firm. The reason – the overseas sales expenses budget has already been spent. The result – the most profitable order that the firm would have received for many years is taken up instead by another firm.

(b) The works manager turns down requests for overtime work, because the budgeted overtime has already been exceeded. The result – the job is not completed on time, and the firm has to pay a large sum under a penalty clause in the contract for the job which stated that if the job was not finished by a certain date then a penalty of £200,000 would become payable.

(c) Towards the end of the accounting year a manager realises that he has not spent all of his budget for a particular item. He then launches on a spending spree, completely unnecessary items being bought, on the basis that 'If I don't spend this amount this year they will cut down next year when I will really need the money'. The result: a lot of unusable and unnecessary equipment.

(d) The education budget has been spent, therefore the education manager will not let anyone go on courses for the rest of the year. The result: the firm starts to fall behind in an industry which is highly technical, the staff concerned become fed up, and the better ones start to look for jobs in other firms which are more responsive to the need to allow personnel to keep in touch with changing technology.

Studies have shown that the more that managers are brought into the budgeting process, then the more successful budgetary control is likely to be. A manager on whom a budget is imposed, rather than a manager who had an active part in the drafting of his budget, is more likely to pay less attention to the budget and use it unwisely in the control process.

Having sounded the warning that needs to be borne in mind constantly when budgeting, we can now look at the positive end of budgeting – to see the advantages of a good budgetary control system.

20.3 Budgets, Planning and Control

The methodology of budgetary control is probably accountancy's major contribution to management. Before we get down to the mechanics of constructing budgets we should first of all look at the main outlines of drafting budgets.

When the budgets are being drawn up the two main objectives must be uppermost in the mind of top management, that is that the budgets are for:

(a) **Planning.** This means a properly co-ordinated and comprehensive plan for the whole business. Each part must interlock with the other parts.

(b) **Control.** Just because a plan is set down on paper does not mean that the plan will carry itself out. Control is exercised via the budgets, thus the name budgetary control. To do this means that the responsibility of managers and budgets must be so linked that the responsible manager is given a guide to help him to produce certain desired results, and the actual achieved results can be compared against the expected, i.e. actual compared with budget.

20.4 Preparation of Estimates

The first thing to establish is what the limiting factors are in a firm. It may well be the fact that sales cannot be pushed above a certain amount, otherwise it might be the fact that the firm could sell as much as it can produce, but the productive capacity of the firm sets a limit. Whatever the limiting factor is, there is no doubt that this aspect of the firm will need more attention than probably any other. There would not, for instance, be much point in budgeting for the sale of 1,000 units a year if production could not manufacture more than 700, or to manufacture 2,000 a year if only 1,300 of them could be sold.

There is no doubt that usually the most difficult estimate to make is that of sales revenue. This can be done by using one of two methods:

(i) Make a statistical forecast on the basis of the economic conditions applying to the goods sold by the company, and what is known about the actions of competitors.
(ii) The opposite is to make an internal forecast. This is usually done by asking each member of the sales staff, or group of salespeople, to estimate the sales in their own areas, and then total the estimates. Sometimes the sales staff are not asked at all.

Now we should remember that much of the subject matter that you have read about, or are currently reading in Economics, is very relevant here. A knowledge of elasticity of demand, whether the product is a complementary product, e.g. the price of egg-cups is linked to the demand for eggs, whether it is a substitute, e.g. that a rise in the price of butter may induce housewives to turn to other commodities instead, is very relevant in this area. Factors such as whether the firm has a monopoly, whether the firm has many small customers, a few large customers, or even one large customer, are of crucial importance. Estimating sales revenue is very much a matter of taking all the economic factors into account allied to other factors.

The sales budget is, however, more than just a sales forecast. Budgets should show the actions that management is taking to influence future events. If an increase in sales is desired the sales budget may show extra sales, which may well be an indication of the action that management is going to take by means of extra television advertising, making a better product, or to give retailers better profit margins and push up sales in that way.

20.5 The Production Budget

The production budget stems from the sales budget, but the first question that has to be settled is that of the level of the stock of finished goods which will be held by the firm.

If sales are even over the year, then production can also be in keeping with the sales figure, and the stock figure can remain constant. Suppose that the firm sells 50 units every month, then the firm can produce 50 units per month. In almost every firm, a minimum stock level will have to be maintained. The amount of stock will be dependent on factors such as amount of storage space, the estimated amount needed to cater for breakdowns in production or for delays in receiving raw materials, etc. Nonetheless, if the stock level was to be a minimum of 70 units it would still mean that production was at the rate of 50 units per month.

On the other hand, sales may not be constant. Sales may average 50 units per month, but the figures may well be as follows:

| January | 20 units | February | 30 units | March | 60 units |
| April | 80 units | May | 70 units | June | 40 units |

This would mean that if production levels were kept at 50 units per month, there would be a shortage of 10 units in November – when 70 were demanded but only 60 were available for sale (10 left over from October plus 50 produced in November). An extra 10 units would need to be held to cover this shortfall. If production each month is to be the same, 10 units would need to be held at the beginning of the year.

Any calculation of minimum stock levels must include these 10 units. For example, if minimum stock of 100 is required, stock at the beginning of the year would need to be 110 units.

However, instead of producing the same number of units each month, the monthly production could be set to equal the sales figures. If a minimum stock level of 100 units is required, the number of units held at the beginning of the year would then be 100.

We can now compare the two levels of production in Sections 20.6 and 20.7.

20.6 Even Production Flow

The problem here is to find the stock level that the firm would need on 1st January if (i) sales are as shown, (ii) the stock must not fall below 100 units, (iii) production is to be 50 units per month. It can be found by trial and error. For instance, if you decided to see what would happen if the firm started off with 100 units in stock at 1st January you would find that, after adding production and deducting sales each month, the stock level would fall to 90 units in May. As 100 units of stock is the minimum needed you would need to start off on 1st January with 110 units. The method is that if you start off your calculation with an estimated figure of stock, which must at least be the minimum figure required, then if you find that the lowest figure of stock shown during the period is 10 units less than the minimum stock required, go back and add 10 units to the stock to be held on 1st January. If the lowest figure is 30 units less than required add 30 units to the 1st January stock, and so on. We can now look at the figures in Exhibit 20.1.

Exhibit 20.1

Units	January	February	March	April	May	June
Opening stock	110	140	160	150	120	100
Add Units produced	50	50	50	50	50	50
	160	190	210	200	170	150
Less Sales	20	30	60	80	70	40
Closing stock	140	160	150	120	100	110

Before we look at the implications of maintaining an even production flow we can look at another example. Try and work it out for yourself before looking at the answer in Exhibit 20.2. The sales are expected to be January 70, February 40, March 50, April 120, May 140 and June 70. The stock level must not fall below 120 units and an even production flow of 80 units is required. What would be the stock level on 1st January?

Exhibit 20.2

Units	January	February	March	April	May	June
Opening stock	140	150	190	220	180	120
Add Units produced	80	80	80	80	80	80
	220	230	270	300	260	200
Less Sales	70	40	50	120	140	70
Closing stock	150	190	220	180	120	130

It is more important in many firms to ensure a smooth production flow than to bother unduly about stock levels, assuming that the minimum stock level is always attained. If the work is skilled then that type of labour force may take several years to become trained, and skilled labour in many industries does not take kindly to being sacked and re-employed as the demand for the goods fluctuates. This is not always true with skilled labour; for instance in the building industry such craftsmen as bricklayers may go to a builder until he has completed a contract such as building a college, a hospital, or a housing estate, and then leave and go to another employer on the completion of the job.

On the other hand, a skilled engineer concerned with the manufacturer of say, diesel engines, would not expect to be fired and re-employed continuously. The bricklayer has a skill that is easily transferable to many other building employers in an area, whereas the diesel engineer may have only one firm within fifty miles of his home where he can perform his skills properly. A man employed as a labourer might work on a building site in one part of the year and then transfer as a labourer to an engineering factory in another part of the year.

Whether a firm could carry on production with widely uneven production levels depends so much on the type of firm and the type of labour involved. A firm would only sack skilled labour which it needed again shortly if it could persuade the men or women to come back when required. If the people who had been sacked were likely to find other employment, and not return to the firm when required, then this would mean that the firm would probably keep them on its payroll and production would continue and stocks of finished goods would begin to pile up.

Many firms do in fact realise their social obligations by only laying off workers when no other alternative is at all reasonable. In some organisations there are probably more workers from time to time than the firm actually needs – this is known as 'organisational slack', so that there is a leeway between the increasing of production and having to take on extra workers.

20.7 Uneven Production Levels

Some firms by their very nature will have uneven production levels, and this will be accepted by their labour force. An ice-cream firm would find sales at the highest levels in summer, tailing off in winter. It is not really possible to build up stock of ice-cream in the winter for summer sales! Even if it could be done technically, the costs of refrigerating large quantities of ice-cream for several months could hardly be economic. The large labour force used in the summer months will probably include students occupying their vacation periods profitably, and not able anyway to work at the job all the year round even if they wanted to. Such a kind of firm will normally have a far greater relationship between current stock levels and current sales than a firm which has even production levels. The calculation of the quantity to be produced is then:

$$\text{Sales} - (\text{Opening stock} + \text{Closing stock}) = \text{Production}$$

This can also be stated as:

$$\text{Opening stock} + \text{Units produced} - \text{Sales} = \text{Closing stock}$$

If the opening stock is 80 units, the sales are expected to be 100 units and the desired closing stock is 50 units, it becomes:

	Units
Opening stock	80
Add Production	?
Less Sales	100
Closing stock	50

Production will, therefore, be the missing figure, i.e. 70 units (80 + Production 70 = 150 less actually sold 100 = closing stock 50).

Exhibit 20.3 shows the units to be produced if the following information is known – Stock required 1st January 40, at end of each month, January 60, February 110, March 170, April 100, May 60, June 20. Sales are expected to be January 100, February 150, March 110, April 190, May 70, June 50.

Exhibit 20.3

Units	January	February	March	April	May	June
Opening stock	40	60	110	170	100	60
Production required	120	200	170	120	30	10
	160	260	280	290	130	70
Less Sales	100	150	110	190	70	50
Closing stock	60	110	170	100	60	20

Linked with the production budget will be a materials purchase budget. It may well be that an order will have to be placed in January, received in March and issued to production in April. The purchase of materials will have to be planned as scientifically as possible.

REVIEW QUESTIONS

Advice:

It is unlikely that a full question will be devoted to the contents of this chapter. What is far more likely is that this will be part of a larger question.

20.1 For the year ended 31 December 19X6 the sales of units are expected to be:

January	70	July	20
February	90	August	30
March	60	September	60
April	40	October	70
May	30	November	90
June	20	December	50

The opening stock at 1 January 19X6 will be 120 units. The closing stock desired at 31 December 19X6 is 150 units.

(a) What will production be per month if an even production flow is required and stock levels during the year could be allowed to fall to zero?

(b) Given the same information plus the constraint that stock levels must never fall below 110 units, and that extra production will be undertaken in January 19X6 to ensure this, what will the January production figure be?

20.2 A firm wants to maintain an even production flow for the first six months of 19X4 followed by an even production flow of 20 units per month greater for the last six months of 19X4.

Opening stock of units at 1 January 19X4 are	50
Closing stock of units wanted at 31 December 19X4	120
Sales of units during the year	650

How many units should be manufactured per month (*a*) January to June 19X4, (*b*) July to December 19X4?

20.3X What stock should be held by a firm on 1 July 19X7 if the following data is available:

	Jul	*Aug*	*Sept*	*Oct*	*Nov*	*Dec*
(i) Sales expected to be	100	140	180	270	190	130
(ii) Production expected to be	160	200	220	250	210	180

(iii) Desired stock level at 31 December 19X7 is 320 units.

20.4X What would the production levels have to be for each month if the following data was available:

	Jan	*Feb*	*Mar*	*Apr*	*May*	*Jun*
(i) Stock levels wanted at the end of each month	690	780	1,100	1,400	1,160	940
(ii) Expected sales each month	800	920	1,090	1,320	1,480	1,020

(iii) The stock level at 1 January 19X5 will be 740 units.

Chapter 21

Cash Budgets

21.1 The Need for Cash Budgets

It is no use budgeting for production and for sales if sometime during the budget period the firm runs out of cash funds. When talking about cash in budgets we are also usually including bank funds, and therefore in this book we will not be differentiating between cash and cheque payments or between cash and cheques received. Cash is, therefore, also budgeted for, so that any shortage of cash can be known in advance and action taken to obtain permission for a loan or a bank overdraft to be available then, rather than wait until the shortage or deficiency occurs. Bank managers, or anyone concerned with the lending of money, certainly resent most strongly one of their customers needing a bank overdraft without prior warning, when in fact the customer could have known if he had drawn up a cash budget in advance which revealed the need for cash funds on a particular date.

The finance needed may not just be by way of borrowing from a bank or finance house, it may well be a long-term need that can only be satisfied by an issue of shares or debentures. Such issues need planning well in advance, and a cash budget can reveal (a) that they will be needed (b) how much is needed and (c) when it will be needed.

We can now look at a very simple case. Without being concerned in this first exhibit with exactly what the receipts and payments are for, just to keep matters simple at this stage, we can see the dangers that are inherent in not budgeting for cash.

Exhibit 21.1

Mr Muddlem had a meeting with his accountant on 1st July, 19X3. He was feeling very pleased with himself. He had managed to get some very good orders from customers, mainly because he was now allowing them extra time in which to pay their accounts. Sprite, the accountant, said, 'Can you afford to do all that you are hoping to do?'

Muddlem laughed, 'Why, I'll be making so much money I won't know how to spend it.'

'But have you got the cash to finance everything?', asked Sprite.

'If I'm making a good profit then of course I'll have the cash,' said Muddlem. 'I know the bank manager says that any bank overdraft could not be more than £1,000, but I doubt if I need it.'

'Don't let us rely on guesses,' says Sprite. 'Let's work it out.'
   After an hour's work the following facts emerge.

(a) Present cash balance (including bank balance) £800.
(b) Receipts from debtors will be: July £2,000, August £2,600, September £5,000, October £7,000, November £8,000, December £15,000.

(c) Payments will be: July £2,500, August £2,700, September £6,900, October £7,800, November £9,900, December £10,300.

This is then summarised:

	Jul £	Aug £	Sep £	Oct £	Nov £	Dec £
Balance at start of the month:	+800	+300	+200			
Deficit at the start of the month:				−1,700	−2,500	−4,400
Receipts	2,000	2,600	5,000	7,000	8,000	15,000
	2,800	2,900	5,200	5,300	5,500	10,600
Payments	2,500	2,700	6,900	7,800	9,900	10,300
Balance at end of the month:	+300	+200				+300
Deficit at the end of the month:			−1,700	−2,500	−4,400	

'I'm in an awkward position now,' says Muddlem. 'I just cannot borrow £4,400 nor can I cut down on my sales, and anyway I don't really want to as these new sales are very profitable indeed. If only I'd known this, I could have borrowed the money from my brother only last week but he's invested it elsewhere now.'

'Come and see me tomorrow,' says Sprite. 'There may well be something we can do.'

Fortunately for Muddlem his luck was in. He arrived to see his accountant the following morning, waving a cheque. 'My wife won £5,000 on a bingo jackpot last night,' he said.

'Thank goodness for that, at least in future you'll learn to budget ahead for cash requirements. You can't be lucky all the time,' says Sprite.

21.2 Timing of Cash Receipts and Payments

In drawing up a cash budget it must be borne in mind that all the payments for units produced would very rarely be at the same time as production itself. For instance the raw materials might be bought in March, incorporated in the goods being produced in April, and paid for in May. On the other hand the raw materials may have been in hand for some time, so that the goods are bought in January, paid for in February, and used in production the following August. Contrary to this, the direct labour part of the product is usually paid for almost at the same time as the unit being produced. Even here a unit may be produced in one week and the wages paid one week later, so that a unit might be produced on say 27th June and the wages for the direct labour involved paid for on 3rd July.

Similarly the date of sales and the date of receipt of cash will not usually be at the same time, except in many retail stores. The goods might be sold in May and the money received in August, or even paid for in advance so that the goods might be paid for in February but the goods not shipped to the buyer until May. This is especially true, at least for part of the goods when a cash deposit is left for specially-made goods which will take some time to manufacture. A simple example of this would be a made-to-measure suit on which a deposit would be paid at the time of order, the final payment being made when the completed suit is collected by the buyer.

Exhibit 21.2

A cash budget for the six months ended 30th June 19X3 is to be drafted from the following information.

(a) Opening cash balance at 1st January 19X3 £3,200.

(b) Sales; at £12 per unit: cash received three months after sale.

Units: 19X2   19X3

	Oct	Nov	Dec	Jan	Feb	Mar	Apr	May	Jun	Jul	Aug	Sep
	80	90	70	100	60	120	150	140	130	110	100	160

(c) Production: in units.

   19X2   19X3

	Oct	Nov	Dec	Jan	Feb	Mar	Apr	May	Jun	Jul	Aug	Sep
	70	80	90	100	110	130	140	150	120	160	170	180

(d) Raw materials used in production cost £4 per unit of production. They are paid for two months before being used in production.

(e) Direct labour: £3 per unit paid for in the same month as the unit is produced.

(f) Other variable expenses: £2 per unit, ¾ of the cost being paid for in the same month as production, the other ¼ paid in the month after production.

(g) Fixed expenses of £100 per month are paid monthly.

(h) A motor van is to be bought and paid for in April for £800.

Schedules of payments and receipts are as follows:

Payments: (The month shown in brackets is the month in which the units are produced)

	January		£		February		£
Raw ×materials:	130	(March) × £4	520	140	(April) × £4		560
Direct labour:	100	(January) × £3	300	110	(February) × £3		330
Variable:	100	(January) × ¾ × £2	150	110	(February) × ¾ × £2		165
	90	(December) × ¼ × £2	45	100	(January) × ¼ × £2		50
Fixed:			100				100
			£1,115				£1,205

	March		£		April		£
Raw materials:	150	(May) × £4	600	120	(June) × £4		480
Direct labour:	130	(March) × £3	390	140	(April) × £3		420
Variable:	130	(March) × ¾ × £2	195	140	(April) × ¾ × £2		210
	110	(February) × ¼ × £2	55	130	(March) × ¼ × £2		65
Fixed:			100				100
Motor van							800
			£1,340				£2,075

	May		£		June		£
Raw materials:	160	(July) × £4	640	170	(August) × £4		680
Direct labour:	150	(May) × £3	450	120	(June) × £3		360
Variable:	150	(May) × ¾ × £2	225	120	(June) × ¾ × £2		180
	140	(April) × ¼ × £2	70	150	(May) × ¼ × £2		75
Fixed:			100				100
			£1,485				£1,395

Receipts: (The month shown in brackets is the month in which the sale was made)

				£
January	80 (October)	×	£12	960
February	90 (November)	×	£12	1,080
March	70 (December)	×	£12	840
April	100 (January)	×	£12	1,200
May	60 (February)	×	£12	720
June	120 (March)	×	£12	1,440

Cash Budget

	Jan £	Feb £	Mar £	Apr £	May £	Jun £
Balance from previous month	3,200	3,045	2,920	2,420	1,545	780
Add Receipts (per schedule)	960	1,080	840	1,200	720	1,440
	4,160	4,125	3,760	3,620	2,265	2,220
Less Payments (per schedule)	1,115	1,205	1,340	2,075	1,485	1,395
Balance carried to next month	3,045	2,920	2,420	1,545	780	825

21.3 Advantages of Cash Budgets

These can be said to be:

1 Having to think ahead and plan for the future and express the plans in figures, focuses one's mind in a way that thinking in a general fashion about the future will not do. A general optimistic feeling that 'all will be well' will often not stand up to scrutiny when the views of the future are expressed in a cash budget.

2 Seeing that money will have to be borrowed at a particular date will mean that you can negotiate for a loan in advance, rather than at the time when you have actually run out of cash. Bankers and other lenders do not like someone attempting to borrow money in a panic, and which has to be instantly available.

   In borrowing money you have to give the lender the confidence that the loan will be repaid at the proper time, plus any interest and charges that may accrue. Attempted last-minute borrowing, probably not substantiated by any calmly thought-out plan will not inspire such confidence, and will often lead to the loan being refused as the lender may think that the risk is too great.

   It is not only that you risk the loan being refused. Lenders will often realise that they have you at their mercy, and will charge much higher rates of interest and impose other conditions that otherwise they would not have done.

3 Knowing about the need to borrow in advance also widens the possible pool of lenders. Such people as friends, relations, and businessmen or investors other than bankers rarely have large sums of cash quickly available. They need time to turn their own investments into cash before they can lend to you.

4 Alternatively you may find that you will have cash funds surplus to requirements. Knowing this in advance will enable you to investigate properly how you can invest this surplus cash until required, thus earning interest or other investment income. Surplus cash lying in bank current accounts very often earns absolutely no interest at all, no matter how large the amount. Banks often have deposit accounts into which

surplus current account cash can be invested to earn interest, then transferring the necessary sums back into the current account when required by the business. There are also other sorts of short-term investments which your bank or accountant can advise you to put your surplus cash into at appropriate times.

21.4 Profits and Shortages of Cash Funds

Just because a firm is making good profits it does not mean that it will not be short of cash funds. Let us look at how some firms may have good profits and yet still be short of cash funds, possibly having bank overdrafts or loans which are getting steadily bigger.

1   Firm A has increased its sales by 50 per cent, is making the same percentage gross profit and its expenses have hardly increased, yet its overdraft has got bigger. The reason is that it increased its sales by giving all of its customers four months to pay instead of the usual one month. This has attracted a lot of new customers.

   This means that the debtors are increasing by very large amounts, as they can wait another three months in which to pay their bills. Thus the equivalent of three months' cash receipts have not come into the bank. Meanwhile the firm is making extra purchases for goods for the new customers, with a consequent outflow of more cash than usual, especially if it has not got longer credit terms from its suppliers. So hardly any cash is coming in in the short term, whilst more cash than usual is going out.

   The answer to this is: large increase in profits and fewer cash funds probably resulting in higher bank overdrafts or loans.

2   Firm B has the same sales, purchases and expenses as usual. However, the proprietor, for whatever reason, is now taking much higher drawings than before. In fact his drawings are exceeding the profits he is making.

   Such a situation cannot go on for ever. He will start to find his cash funds in the business are decreasing, possibly meaning higher loans or overdrafts being needed.

3   Firm C has just spent a lot of money on fixed assets. It will be several years before the firm recoups the money it has paid out. In the meantime only the depreciation provisions are charged against profits. However, the cash funds have seen the disappearance of the whole amount paid for fixed assets. The net result is that profits may be recorded but the firm is hard-up for cash funds.

4   Firm D is going through a bad patch in that sales are very difficult to make, but it does not want to get rid of any of its workforce. Production is kept going at normal rates, and the products not sold are simply kept in stock. Thus the stock is increasing at an alarming rate.

   If stock is not being sold then cash obviously is not being received in respect of such production. Meanwhile all the expenses and wages are still being paid for. This can result in a severe shortage of funds if carried on for long if no further finance is received.

5   A long-term loan has been paid off but no extra finance from anywhere else has been received. This could equally apply to a partner retiring and the balance due to him being paid out of the firm's funds, without a new partner being introduced. Similarly a company buying back its shares without a new issue of shares could face the same situation.

In the long term there is a connection between profits and cash funds available, even though it may not be that marked. In the short term you can see that there may be no relationship at all. This simple fact is one that surprises most people. It is because the calculation of profits follows one set of concepts, whereas the calculation of cash funds follows a completely different set of rules.

REVIEW QUESTIONS

Advice:

Cash budgeting is an extremely important part of accounting. Questions on this topic are relatively easy to do, and high marks can be gained quite easily.

21.1 Ukridge comes to see you in April 19X3. He is full of enthusiasm for a new product that he is about to launch on to the market. Unfortunately his financial recklessness in the past has led him into being bankrupted twice, and he has only just got discharged by the court from his second bankruptcy.

'Look here laddie,' he says, 'with my new idea I'll be a wealthy man before Christmas.'

'Calm down,' you say, 'and tell me all about it.'

Ukridge's plans as far as cash is concerned for the next six months are:

(a) Present cash balance (including bank) £5.

(b) Timely legacy under a will – being received on 1 May, 19X3, £5,000. This will be paid into the business bank account by Ukridge.

(c) Receipts from debtors will be: May £400, June £4,000, July £8,000, August £12,000, September £9,000, October £5,000.

(d) Payments will be: May £100, June £5,000, July £11,000, August £20,000, September £12,000, October £7,000.

You are required:

(a) To draw up a cash budget, showing the balances each month, for the six months to 31 October 19X3.

(b) The only person Ukridge could borrow money from would charge interest at the rate of 100 per cent per annum. This is not excessive considering Ukridge's past record.

Advise Ukridge.

21.2X Draw up a cash budget for N. Morris showing the balance at the end of each month, from the following information for the six months ended 31 December 19X2:

(a) Opening cash (including bank) balance £1,200

(b) Production in units:

19X2									19X3	
Apr	May	Jun	Jul	Aug	Sep	Oct	Nov	Dec	Jan	Feb
240	270	300	320	350	370	380	340	310	260	250

(c) Raw materials used in production cost £5 per unit. Of this 80 per cent is paid in the month of production and 20 per cent in the month after production.

(d) Direct labour costs of £8 per unit are payable in the month of production.

(e) Variable expenses are £2 per unit, payable one-half in the same month as production and one-half in the month following production.

(f) Sales at £20 per unit:

19X2

Mar	Apr	May	Jun	Jul	Aug	Sep	Oct	Nov	Dec
260	200	320	290	400	300	350	400	390	400

Debtors to pay their accounts three months after that in which sales are made.

(g) Fixed expenses of £400 per month payable each month.

(h) Machinery costing £2,000 to be paid for in October 19X2.

(i) Will receive a legacy £2,500 in December 19X2.

(j) Drawings to be £300 per month.

21.3 Herbert Limited make a single product, whose unit budget details are as follows:

	£	£
Selling price		30
Less Costs		
Direct material	9	
Direct labour	4	
Direct production expenses	6	
Variable selling expenses	4	23
Contribution		7

Additional information

1   Unit sales are expected to be:

June	July	August	September	October
1,000	800	400	600	900

2   Credit sales will account for 60 per cent of total sales. Debtors are expected to pay in the month following sale for which there will be a cash discount of 2 per cent.

3   Stock levels will be arranged so that the production in one month will meet the next month's sales demand.

4   The purchases of direct materials in one month will just meet the next month's production requirements.

5   Suppliers of direct materials will be paid in the month following purchase.

6   Labour costs will be paid in the month in which they are incurred. All other expenses will be paid in the month following that in which they are incurred.

7   Fixed expenses are £2,000 per month and include £180 for depreciation.

8   The bank balance at 1 July 19X9 is £3,900 favourable to the business.

Required:

(a) A cash budget for Herbert Limited for the three month period ending on 30 September 19X9 showing the balance of cash at the end of each month. *(16 marks)*

(b) List and explain **three** ways in which the preparation of a cash flow budget could be of advantage to the management of Herbert Limited. *(6 marks)*

(Associated Examining Board: GCE A-Level)

21.4X Mtoto Ltd operate as wholesale 'cash and carry' stores and in addition to its main store have two other depots.

The company's summarised balance sheet as at 31 August 19X1 was as follows.

	£	£		£	£
Fixed assets			*Authorised and issued capital*		
(at net book value)		549,600	450,000 £1 *Ordinary shares*		
Current assets			Fully paid		450,000
Stock	399,900		Retained earnings at		
Trade debtors	21,000	420,900	1 Sept 19X0	300,000	
			Less Current year ended		
			31 Aug 19X1 loss.	130,000	170,000
			Current liabilities		
			Trade (and other)		
			creditors	110,500	
			Bank overdraft	240,000	350,500
		970,500			970,500

- Over the past year the company has experienced increased competition and as a consequence reported a net trading loss for the year ended 31 August 19X1.
- The company has decided that in the new financial year tighter control must be exercised over cash resources.
- The following information is available:

1 All goods are purchased by the main store.

Purchases 19X1

Actual		*Forecast*			
Jul	*Aug*	*Sep*	*Oct*	*Nov*	*Dec*
£	£	£	£	£	£
55,800	61,200	64,300	41,000	46,000	41,800

- Mtoto Ltd pays suppliers two months after the month of purchase.
- Forecast purchases are being reduced since the managing director regarded current stock levels as too high.
- In addition, shop-soiled stock which cost £20,000 is to be sold for cash in October. It is anticipated that this stock will be sold for £17,000. This sale is not included in the sales of note 2 below.

2 All sales are on a cash basis only except for several important customers who trade only with Mtoto's main store.

Sales 19X1

		Actual			Forecast		
		Jul	Aug	Sep	Oct	Nov	Dec
		£	£	£	£	£	£
Mainstore:							
Cash sales		21,500	21,600	18,000	26,300	19,200	24,700
Credit sales		24,000	21,000	32,500	26,000	25,400	27,800
Depot	1	15,500	17,400	19,700	18,000	17,600	17,900
Depot	2	21,000	24,000	26,300	19,700	21,000	19,100

3 Mtoto Ltd pays £9,500 fixed overhead costs per month.

4 Wages and salaries are paid each month through a centralised payroll system.

Wages and salaries 19X1

Actual		Forecast			
Aug		Sep	Oct	Nov	Dec
£		£	£	£	£
16,000		17,000	19,000	13,000	12,000

In October, 10 staff were made redundant and are to receive their redundancy compensation of £12,000 in December. This amount is not included in the above figures.

5 Other variable overhead charges are paid by Mtoto Ltd in the month following the month they are incurred.

Variable overhead charges 19X1

Aug	Sep	Oct	Nov	Dec
£	£	£	£	£
5,600	6,800	6,100	7,400	6,900

6 Plant surplus to requirement is to be sold in September for £26,500 cash. The plant cost £55,000 and depreciation to date is £20,000.

Required:

(a) A detailed cash budget, on a month by month basis, for the first four months of the financial year ending 31 August 19X2 for Mtoto Ltd.   (13 marks)

(b) A report commenting on:
  (i)   the current and forecast liquidity position.   (7 marks)
  (ii) the action that Mtoto Ltd could take to attempt a return to a profit situation.   (5 marks)

(*Associated Examining Board: GCE A-Level*)

21.5 David Llewelyn has been advised by his bank manager that he ought to provide a forecast of his cash position at the end of each month. This is to ensure that his cash inputs will be sufficient to allow a bank loan to be repaid when due and to check that his outgoings are properly controlled. It is estimated that at 30 June 19X0 his current account will be £5,000 in credit, whereas the amount owing in respect of the bank loan taken out on 1 March 19X0 will be £15,000. Monthly deductions from the current account balance amount to £242 including interest charges on account of this loan. In addition to these outgoings, David has to allow for the following:

(i) The payment of wages of £2,000 per month.
(ii) Personal drawings of £500 per month.
(iii) On average David earns a margin of 15 per cent (of sales) and expects to sell stocks purchased in the previous month. Of the sales in any one month, 20 per cent are paid for within that month, 70 per cent the following month and the remainder two months after sale.

    Other receipts from debtors are expected to be £40,000 in July 19X0, £32,000 in August 19X0 and £4,000 in September 19X0.
(iv) Purchases of supplies will amount to £38,250 per month from July 19X0 payable one month in arrears. In addition, purchases of £7,500 to increase stocks will be delivered in September 19X0 and must be paid for in October 19X0. Creditors of £34,000 for purchases made in June 19X0 are to be paid in July 19X0.
(v) Monthly payments to the Inland Revenue for the taxation on his employees' earnings will amount to £500 per month.
(vi) Rent which has to be paid quarterly in advance amounts to £5,000 per annum. These payments commenced in January 19X0.
(vii) Business rates are to be paid in two instalments as due in October 19X0 and in March 19X1. This estimated expenditure will amount to £4,500 per annum.
(viii) Payment of Value Added Tax to H.M. Customs and Excise of £5,000 in July 19X0 and every third month thereafter (but see also (ix)).
(ix) David intends to purchase a van for £8,150 in August 19X0. He will then be entitled to deduct £1,050 from the VAT payment due to H.M. Customs and Excise in October 19X0.

Required:

A forecast cash flow statement in columnar form showing the estimated current account balance at the close of each of the four months ending 31 October 19X0.   *(28 marks)*

(Welsh Joint Education Committee: GCE A-Level)

21.6 The managing director of Pumpkin Ltd was reviewing the results of the company for the financial year ended 31 March 19X0. The following summarised information was available:

	£
Balances as at 1 April 19X9	
Issued ordinary share capital:	
£1 fully paid shares	150,000
Share premium account	100,000
Balance of retained earnings	40,000

Balances as at 31 March 19X0

Net profit for year 19X9/X0	70,000
Fixed assets	300,000
Bank overdraft	150,000
Other net current assets	210,000

Note: There were no other accounts with balances. The balances as at 1 April 19X9 had remained unchanged throughout the year.

The managing director was pleased that the company had made a good profit, but he was rather concerned that a healthy bank balance at the beginning of the year had now become a large bank overdraft.

Consequently he asked the company accountant to prepare forecast information for 19X0/X1 in order that the cash situation could be improved.

The following information was prepared by the accountant:

1 Company sales – March 19X0

	£
Cash sales	30,000
Credit sales	65,000

In each month April to September (inclusive) the sales per month would be:

	£
Cash sales	40,000
Credit sales	70,000

All credit sales are settled the month after the sale.

2 All goods purchased are from a single supplier. The goods are purchased on credit and each month's purchases are paid for three months after the month of purchase.

The following purchase schedule had been prepared for the first 9 months of 19X0:

	January	February	March
Purchases	£60,000	£58,000	£61,000

Purchases in April, May and June: £55,000 in each month
Purchases in July, August and September: £45,000 in each month

Note: The company had successfully negotiated lower prices from its supplier commencing 1 July 19X0.

3 Dividends would be paid as follows:
   (i) Final ordinary dividend of 5p per share payable on 31 May 19X0 in respect of financial year 19X9/X0.
   (ii) Interim ordinary dividend of 2p per share payable on 31 July 19X0 in respect of financial year 19X0/X1.

4 Selling and distribution expenses are expected to be 6 per cent of a given month's total sales. They are paid one month in arrears.

5 Administration charges would be incurred as follows:

19X0 February, March, April	£10,000 per month
19X0 May to September (inclusive)	£13,500 per month

Administration charges are settled two months after the month in which they were incurred.

6 The company had decided to make a bonus issue of shares of one share for every three held. The issue would be made on 30 April 19X0. The bonus shares would not qualify for the final dividend of 19X9/X0, but would qualify for the interim dividend to be paid on 31 July 19X0.

Required:

(a) Comment on the liquidity of the company as at 31 March 19X0 and explain to the managing director why a company can apparently make a good profit but have no cash in the bank.

(8 marks)

(b) Prepare a cash budget for each of the four months ending 31 July 19X0. (12 marks)

(c) Comment on the forecast bank balance as shown by your cash budget. Identify ways in which the bank overdraft could be reduced over the last five months of 19X0. (5 marks)

(*Associated Examining Board: GCE A-Level*)

21.7X Belinda Raglan owns a clothing factory. Trading over the last two years has been very successful and she feels that having achieved good results it is now time to request an increase in the overdraft facility.

● In the past the bank has been willing to offer business overdraft facilities and at present there is an agreed limit of £15,000.
● On 1 May 19X4 the overdraft stands at £5,000.
● In order to support her request for the increased facility, she has produced a forecast profit statement for the four months ended 31 August 19X4 as follows:

	May		June		July		August	
	£000	£000	£000	£000	£000	£000	£000	£000
Sales		74		28		116		168
Cost of sales		51		12		78		101
Gross Profit		23		16		38		67
Less: Rent	4		4		4		4	
Other expenses	8		3		10		14	
Depreciation	5	17	5	12	5	19	5	23
Net profit		6		4		19		44

Although Belinda thought these figures would be sufficient to satisfy the requirements of the bank, the manager has asked for a cash budget for the period concerned to be submitted.

The following additional information concerning the business is available.

(1) Rent is paid quarterly in advance on the first day of May, August, November and February.
(2) All other expenses are payable in the month in which they are incurred.
(3) Purchases for the period are expected to be — May £60,000; June £120,000; July £40,000 and August £43,000. These will be paid for in the month of purchase. Purchases will be unusually high in May and June because they will be subject to a special reduction of 3% of the amounts quoted.
(4) 80% of the sales are on a credit basis payable two months later. Sales in March and April were £88,000 and £84,000 respectively.
(5) A compensation payment of £10,000 to a former employee for an industrial injury, not covered by insurance, is due to be paid in May.

Required:

(a) Prepare a forecast cash budget on a month by month basis for the period May to August 19X4. (15 marks)
(b) Discuss the advantages and disadvantages of cash budgeting. (10 marks)
(c) Draft notes, to be used by the bank manager for a letter to Ms Raglan, indicating why the request for an increased overdraft facility may be refused. (9 marks)

(*Associated Examining Board: GCE A-Level*)

Chapter 22

Co-ordination of Budgets

22.1 Master Budgets

The various budgets have to be linked together and a 'master budget', which is really a budgeted set of final accounts drawn up. We have in fact looked at the sales, production and cash budgets. There are, however, many more budgets for parts of the organisation, for instance there may be:

(i)   A selling expense budget,
(ii) An administration expense budget,
(iii A manufacturing overhead budget,
(iv) A direct labour budget,
(v)   A purchases budget,

and so on. In this book we do not wish to get entangled in too many details, but in a real firm with a proper set of budgeting techniques there will be a great deal of detailed backing for the figures that are incorporated in the more important budgets.

Now it may be that when all the budgets have been co-ordinated, or slotted together, the master budget shows a smaller profit than the directors are prepared to accept. This will mean recasting budgets to see whether a greater profit can be earned, and if at all possible the budgets will be altered. Eventually there will be a master budget that the directors can agree to. This then gives the target for the results that the firm hopes to achieve in financial terms. Remember that there are other targets such as employee welfare, quality product, etc. that cannot be so expressed.

The rest of this chapter is concerned with the drawing up of budgets for an imaginary firm, Walsh Ltd, culminating in the drawing up of a master budget.

To start with we can look at the last balance sheet of Walsh Ltd as at 31 December 19X4. This will give us our opening figures of stocks of raw materials, stock of finished goods, cash (including bank) balance, creditors, debtors etc.

Walsh Ltd
Balance Sheet as at 31 December 19X4

Assets Employed:

Fixed assets	Cost	Depreciation to date	Net
	£	£	£
Machinery	4,000	1,600	2,400
Motor vehicles	2,000	800	1,200
	6,000	2,400	3,600

Current assets

Stocks: Finished Goods (75 units)	900	
Raw materials	500	
Debtors (19X4 October £540 + November £360 +		
December £450)	1,350	
Cash and bank balances	650	3,400
		£7,000

Financed by:

Share Capital, 4,000 shares of £1 each	4,000
Profit and loss account	2,600
	6,600

Current liabilities

Creditors for raw materials		
(November £120 + December £180)	300	
Creditors for fixed expenses (December)	100	400
		£7,000

The plans for the six months ended 30 June, 19X5 are as follows:

(i)   Production will be 60 units per month for the first four months, followed by 70 units per month for May and June.

(ii)   Production costs will be (per unit):

	£
Direct materials	5
Direct labour	4
Variable overhead	3
	£12

(iii)   Fixed overhead is £100 per month, payable always one month in arrears.

(iv)   Sales, at a price of £18 per unit, are expected to be:

	January	February	March	April	May	June
No. of units	40	50	60	90	90	70

(v)   Purchases of direct materials (raw materials) will be:

	January	February	March	April	May	June
	£	£	£	£	£	£
	150	200	250	300	400	320

(vi)   The creditors for raw materials bought are paid two months after purchase.

(vii)   Debtors are expected to pay their accounts three months after they have bought the goods.

(viii) Direct labour and variable overhead are paid in the same month as the units are produced.

(ix)   A machine costing £2,000 will be bought and paid for in March.

(x)   3,000 shares of £1 each are to be issued at par in May.

(xi)   Depreciation for the six months: machinery £450, motor vehicles £200.

We must first of all draw up the various budgets and then incorporate them into the master budget. Some of the more detailed budgets which can be dispensed with in this illustration will be omitted.

Materials Budget

	Jan	Feb	Mar	Apr	May	Jun
Opening stock £	500	350	250	200	200	250
Add Purchases £	150	200	250	300	400	320
	650	550	500	500	600	570
Less Used in production:						
Jan.–April 60 × £5	300	300	300	300		
May and June 70 × £5					350	350
Closing stock £	350	250	200	200	250	220

Production Budget (in units)

	Jan	Feb	Mar	Apr	May	Jun
Opening stock (units)	75	95	105	105	75	55
Add Produced	60	60	60	60	70	70
	135	155	165	165	145	125
Less Sales	40	50	60	90	90	70
Closing stock	95	105	105	75	55	55

Production Cost Budget (in £'s)

	Jan	Feb	Mar	Apr	May	Jun	Total
Materials cost £	300	300	300	300	350	350	1,900
Labour cost £	240	240	240	240	280	280	1,520
Variable overhead £	180	180	180	180	210	210	1,140
	720	720	720	720	840	840	4,560

Creditors Budget

	Jan	Feb	Mar	Apr	May	Jun
Opening balance £	300	330	350	450	550	700
Add Purchases £	150	200	250	300	400	320
	450	530	600	750	950	1,020
Less Payments £	120	180	150	200	250	300
Closing balance £	330	350	450	550	700	720

Debtors Budget

	Jan	Feb	Mar	Apr	May	Jun
Opening balances £	1,350	1,530	2,070	2,700	3,600	4,320
Add Sales £	720	900	1,080	1,620	1,620	1,260
	2,070	2,430	3,150	4,320	5,220	5,580
Less Received £	540	360	450	720	900	1,080
Closing balances £	1,530	2,070	2,700	3,600	4,320	4,500

Cash Budget

	Jan	Feb	Mar	Apr	May	Jun
Opening balance £	+650	+550	+210			+1,050
Opening overdraft £			−2,010	−2,010		
Received (see Schedule) £	540	360	450	720	3,900	1,080
	1,190	910	660	1,290	1,890	2,130
Payments (see Schedule) £	640	700	2,670	720	840	890
Closing balance £	+550	+210			+1,050	+1,240
Closing overdraft £			−2,010	−2,010		

Cash Payments Schedule

	Jan	Feb	Mar	Apr	May	Jun
Creditors for goods bought two months previously £	120	180	150	200	250	300
Fixed overhead £	100	100	100	100	100	100
Direct labour £	240	240	240	240	280	280
Variable overhead £	180	180	180	180	210	210
Machinery £			2,000			
	640	700	2,670	720	840	890

Cash Receipts Schedule

	Jan	Feb	Mar	Apr	May	Jun
Debtors for goods sold three months previously £	540	360	450	720	900	1,080
Shares issued £					3,000	
					3,900	

Walsh Ltd: Master Budget
Forecast Operating Statement for the six months ended 30 June 19X5

			£
Sales			7,200
Less Cost of goods sold:			
Opening stock of finished goods		900	
Add Cost of goods completed		4,560	
		5,460	
Less Closing stock of finished goods		660	4,800
Gross profit			2,400
Less:			
Fixed Overhead		600	
Depreciation:			
Machinery	450		
Motors	200	650	1,250
Net profit			1,150

Walsh Ltd
Forecast Balance Sheet as at 30 June 19X5

Assets employed:
Fixed assets

	Cost	Depreciation to date	Net
	£	£	£
Machinery	6,000	2,050	3,950
Motor vehicles	2,000	1,000	1,000
	8,000	3,050	4,950

Current assets
Stocks:

Finished goods		660	
Raw materials		220	
Debtors		4,500	
Cash and bank balances		1,240	
		6,620	

Creditors

Amounts falling due within one year	720		
Trade creditors			
Creditors for overheads	100	820	5,800
			10,750

Financed by:
Capital and Reserves

Called up share capital	7,000
Profit and loss account (2,600 + 1,150)	3,750
	10,750

22.2 Capital Budgeting

The plan for the acquisition of fixed assets such as machinery, buildings etc. is usually known as a capital budget. Management will evaluate the various possibilities open to it, and will compare the alternatives. This is a very important part of budgeting. So far in this book it has been assumed that any capital budgeting has already been done (see Chapter 14).

22.3 The Advantages of Budgeting

The process of budgeting with the necessary participation throughout management, finally producing a profit plan, is now a regular feature in all but the smallest firms. Very often budgeting is the one time when the various parts of management can really get together and work as a team rather than just as separate parts of an organisation. When budgeting is conducted under favourable conditions, there is no doubt that a firm which budgets will tend to perform rather better than a similar firm that does not budget. Budgeting means that managers can no longer give general answers affecting the running of the firm, they have to put figures to their ideas, and they know that in the end their estimated figures are going to be compared with what the actual figures turn out to be.

It has often been said that the act of budgeting is possibly of more benefit than the budgets which are produced. However, the following benefits can be claimed for good budgeting:

(a) The strategic planning carried on by the board of directors or owners can be more easily linked to the decisions by managers as to how the resources of the business will be used to try to achieve the objectives of the business. The strategic planning has to be converted into action, and budgeting provides the ideal place where such planning can be changed into financial terms.

(b) Standards of performance can be agreed to for the various parts of the business. If sales and production targets are set as part of a co-ordinated plan, then the sales department cannot really complain that production is insufficient if they had agreed previously to a production level and this is being achieved, nor can production complain if its production exceeds the amount budgeted for and it remains unsold.

(c) The expression of plans in comparable financial terms. Some managers think mainly in terms of, say, units of production, or of tonnes of inputs or outputs, or of lorry mileage, etc. The effect that each of them has upon financial results must be brought home to them. For instance a transport manager might be unconcerned about the number of miles that his haulage fleet of lorries covers until the cost of doing such a large mileage is brought home to him, often during budgeting, and it may be then and only then that he starts to search for possible economies. It is possible in many cases to use mathematics to find the best ways of loading vehicles, or of the routes taken by vehicles so that fewer miles are covered and yet the same delivery service is maintained. This is just one instance of many when the expression of the plans of a section of a business in financial terms sparks off a search for economies, when otherwise such a search may never be started at all.

(d) Managers can see how their work slots into the total activities of the firm. It can help to get rid of the feeling of 'I'm only a number not a person', because they can identify their position within the firm and can see that their jobs really are essential to the proper functioning of the firm.

(e) The budgets for a firm cannot be set in isolation. This means that the situation of the business, the nature of its products and its workforce, etc., must be seen against the economic background of the country. For instance, it is no use budgeting for extra labour when labour is in extremely short supply, without realising the implications, possibly that of paying higher than normal wage rates. Increasing the sales target during a 'credit squeeze' needs a full investigation of the effect of the shortage of money upon the demand for the firm's goods and so on.

The charges made against budgeting are mainly that budgets bring about inflexibility, and that managers will not depart from budget even though the departure would bring about a more desirable result. Too many budgets are set at one level of sales or production when in fact flexible budgets (discussed later in this chapter) ought to be used. It is very often the case that budgeting is forced upon managers against their will, instead the firm should really set out first of all to do a 'selling job' to convince managers that budgets are not the monsters so often thought. A trial run for part of a business is far superior than starting off by having a fully detailed budget set up right away for the whole of the business.

Learning to use budgets is rather like learning to swim. Let a child get used to the water first and remove its fear of the water, then it will learn to swim fairly easily. For most children (but not all), if the first visit to the baths meant being pushed into the deep end immediately, then reaction against swimming would probably set in. Let a manager become used to the idea of budgeting, without the fear of being dealt with severely during a trial period, and most managers will then become used to the idea and participate properly.

22.4 The Use of Computers in Budgeting

Years ago budgeting was a task which most accountants hated doing. It was not the concept of budgeting that accountants disliked; far from it, as it suited their needs perfectly. Instead it was the multitude of numerical manipulations that had to be performed that made the task a formidable one.

Those of you who have done some of the exercises in this book manually know the feeling when after a lot of work your master budget simply will not balance. Searching through to find the error(s) can be a daunting prospect. Imagine how much more complicated it is in a real firm dealing with real figures rather than with the simple sets of data which form your exercises. Also imagine the feeling when the managing director used to say to the accountant 'What if we increased our prices by 5 per cent and took an extra month to pay creditors?' The accountant would then have to plough his way through a large number of extra calculations.

Most of that is now a thing of the past. Computers are used instead. They either have a computer program specially written for the task, or else commercial spreadsheets can be used. By keying in the necessary basic figures or 'what if' amendments the computer will automatically produce the budgets or the amended budgets within a very short space of time.

This enables management to see the results that would be expected to be obtained from many separate propositions, thus enhancing the chance of choosing the best solution. Also as the accounting year unfolds the changes that have occurred since the year started can be incorporated very easily so as to adjust the budgets as the year progresses.

22.5 Flexible Budgets

So far in this book budgets have been drawn up on the basis of one set of expectations, based on just one level of sales and production. Later, when the actual results are compared with the budgeted results expected in a fixed budget, they will have deviated for two reasons:
1   Whilst the actual and budgeted volumes of production and sales may be the same there may be a difference in actual and budgeted costs.
2   The volumes of actual and budgeted units of sales and production may vary, so that the costs will be different because of different volumes.

The variations, or variances as they are more commonly known, are usually under the control of different managers in the organisation. Variances coming under 1 will probably be under the control of the individual department. On the other hand variances under 2 are caused because of variations in plans brought about by top management because of changing sales, or at least the expectation of changing sales.

Budgets are used for control purposes, therefore a manager does not take kindly to being held responsible for a variance in his spending if the variance is caused by a type 2 occurrence if he is working on a fixed budget. The answer to this is to construct budgets at several levels of volume, and to show what costs, etc. they should incur at different levels. For instance, if a budget had been fixed at a volume of 500 units and the actual volume was 550, then the manager would undoubtedly feel aggrieved if his costs for producing 550 units are compared with the costs he should have incurred for 500 units. Budgets which do allow for changing levels are called 'flexible budgets'.

To draft a full set of flexible budgets is outside the scope of this book, but an instance of one department's flexible budget for manufacturing overhead can be shown in Exhibit 22.1.

Exhibit 22.1

Data Ltd

Budget of Manufacturing Overhead, Department S.
(This would in fact be in greater detail)

Units	400	450	500	550	600
	£	£	£	£	£
Variable overhead	510	550	600	680	770
Fixed overhead	400	400	400	400	400
Total overhead (A)	£910	£950	£1,000	£1,080	£1,170
Direct labour hours (B)	200	225	250	275	300
Overhead rates (A) divided by (B)	£4.55	£4.22	£4.00	£3.92	£3.90

Notice that the variable costs in this case do not vary in direct proportion to production. In this case, once 500 units production has been exceeded, they start to climb rapidly. The flexible budget makes far greater sense than a fixed budget. For instance if a fixed budget had been agreed at 400 units, with variable overhead £510, then if production rose to 600 units the manager would think the whole system unfair if he was expected to incur only £510 variable overhead (the figure for 400 units). On the contrary, if the comparison was on a flexible budget then costs at 600 units production would instead be compared with £770 (the figure at 600 units).

REVIEW QUESTIONS

Advice:

In many ways drawing up a budgeted set of final accounts is very much like drawing up accounts from single-entry records. Accounts from single-entry records concern the past; budgeted accounts from estimates concern the future.

22.1 D Smith is to open a retail shop on 1 January 19X4. He will put in £25,000 cash as capital. His plans are as follows:

(i)   On 1 January 19X4 to buy and pay for premises £20,000, shop fixtures £3,000, motor van £1,000.
(ii) To employ two assistants, each to get a salary of £130 per month, to be paid at the end of each month. (PAYE tax, National Insurance contributions, etc. are to be ignored.)
(iii) To buy the following goods (shown in units):

	Jan	Feb	Mar	Apr	May	Jun
Units	200	220	280	350	400	330

(iv) To sell the following number of units:

	Jan	Feb	Mar	Apr	May	Jun
Units	120	180	240	300	390	420

(v) Units will be sold for £10 each. One-third of the sales are for cash, the other two-thirds being on credit. These latter customers are expected to pay their accounts in the second month following that in which they received the goods.

(vi) The units will cost £6 each for January to April inclusive, and £7 each thereafter. Creditors will be paid in the month following purchase. (Value stock-in-trade on FIFO basis.)

(vii) The other expenses of the shop will be £150 per month payable in the month following that in which they were incurred.

(viii) Part of the premises will be sublet as an office at a rent of £600 per annum. This is paid in equal instalments in March, June, September and December.

(ix) Smith's cash drawings will amount to £250 per month.

(x) Depreciation is to be provided on shop fixtures at 10 per cent per annum and on the motor van at 20 per cent per annum.

You are required to:

(a) Draw up a cash budget for the six months ended 30 June, 19X4, showing the balance of cash at the end of each month.

(b) Draw up a forecast trading and profit and loss account for the six months ended 30 June 19X4 and a balance sheet as at that date.

22.2X B. Cooper is going to set up a new business on 1 January 19X8. He estimates that his first six months in business will be as follows:

(i) He will put £10,000 into a bank account for the firm on 1 January 19X8.

(ii) On 1 January 19X8 he will buy machinery £2,000, motor vehicles £1,600 and premises £5,000, paying for them immediately out of the business bank account.

(iii) All purchases will be effected on credit. He will buy £2,000 goods on 1 January and he will pay for these in February. Other purchases will be rest of January £3,200, February, March, April, May and June £4,000 each month. Other than the £2,000 worth bought on 1 January all other purchases will be paid for two months after purchase.

(iv) Sales (all on credit) will be £4,000 for January and £5,000 for each month after that. Debtors will pay for the goods in the third month after purchase by them.

(v) Stock-in-trade on 30 June 19X8 will be £2,000.

(vi) Wages and salaries will be £150 per month and will be paid on the last day of each month.

(vii) General expenses will be £50 per month, payable in the month following that in which they were incurred.

(viii) He will receive a legacy of £5,500 on 21 April 19X8. This will be paid into the business bank account immediately.

(ix) Insurance covering the 12 months of 19X8 will be paid for by cheque on 30 June 19X8, £140.

(x) Rates will be paid as follows: for the three months to 31 March 19X8 by cheque on 28 February 19X8: for the 12 months ended 31 March 19X9 by cheque on 31 July 19X8. Rates are £360 per annum.

(xi) He will make drawings of £80 per month by cheque.

(xii) He has substantial investments in public companies. His bank manager will give him any overdraft that he may require.

(xiii) Depreciate motors 20 per cent per annum, machinery 10 per cent per annum.

You are required to:

(a) Draft a cash budget (includes bank) month by month showing clearly the amount of bank balance or overdraft at the end of each month.

(b) Draft the projected trading and profit and loss account for the first six months' trading, and a balance sheet as at 30 June 19X8.

22.3 Draw up a cash budget for N. Morris showing the balance at the end of each month from the following information for the six months ended 31 December 19X2:

(a) Opening cash (including bank) balance £1,200.

(b) Production in units:

19X2									19X3	
Apr	May	Jun	Jul	Aug	Sep	Oct	Nov	Dec	Jan	Feb
240	270	300	320	350	370	380	340	310	260	250

(c) Raw materials used in production cost £5 per unit. Of this 80 per cent is paid in the month of production and 20 per cent in the month after production.

(d) Direct labour costs of £8 per unit are payable in the month of production.

(e) Variable expenses are £2 per unit, payable one-half in the same month as production and one-half in the month following production.

(f) Sales at £20 per unit:

19X2									
Mar	Apr	May	Jun	Jul	Aug	Sep	Oct	Nov	Dec
260	200	320	290	400	300	350	400	390	400

Debtors to pay their accounts three months after the month in which sales are made.

(g) Fixed expenses of £400 per month payable each month.

(h) Machinery costing £2,000 to be paid for in October 19X2.

(i) Will receive a legacy £2,500 in December 19X2.

(j) Drawings to be £300 per month.

22.4X

(a) What is meant by the terms:
  (i) Budget
  (ii) Operating budget
  (iii) Master budget? *(8 marks)*

(b) The information below relates to the business of Madingley Ltd:

Balance Sheet as at 30 May 19X0

	Cost	(£000) Aggregate depreciation	Book value
Fixed assets			
Land and buildings	134.00	–	134.00
Plant and machinery	9.40	3.76	5.64
Fixtures and fittings	2.30	1.05	1.25
	145.70	4.81	140.89
Current assets			
Stocks: Raw materials	91.70		
Finished goods	142.40		
Debtors	594.40		
Bank	12.40		
		840.90	
Less: Current liabilities			
Creditors: Raw materials	82.20		
Overheads	127.40		
		209.60	
Working capital			631.30
			772.19
Financed by:			
Share capital		500.00	
Profit and loss account		272.19	
			772.19

The following is a schedule of the budgeted income and expenditure for the six months ended 30 November 19X0 (£000):

	Sales	Materials	Wages	Overheads
June	193.20	41.20	7.60	123.00
July	201.40	42.40	7.90	119.20
August	216.10	49.60	8.80	131.40
September	200.50	31.40	6.10	91.50
October	190.30	21.20	3.70	59.30
November	183.70	19.80	2.60	42.60

Notes:
(i) Generally, materials are paid for two months after receipt, and customers pay on average after three months.
(ii) Payments outstanding for materials at 1 June 19X0 were: April £38,500; May £43,700.
(iii) Debtors were: March £194,300; April £203,600; May £196,500.
(iv) Wages are to be paid in the month in which they fall due.
(v) Overheads are to to be paid one month after they are incurred: the figure for May was £127,400.

(vi) Stocks of raw materials are to be kept at £91,700.

(vii) The stocks of finished goods at 30 November 19X0 are to be £136,200.

(viii) There are no stocks of semi-finished items on 31 May 19X0, and none are expected in stock on 30 November.

(ix) Forty per cent of the overheads are to be considered as fixed.

(x) Depreciation on plant and machinery is to be allowed at 10 per cent *per annum* on cost; the fixtures and fittings are thought to have a value at 30 November of £980.

(xi) There are no sales of finished goods or purchases of raw materials for cash planned during the period.

Prepare:

(*a*) A forecast operating statement for the period June to November 19X0; and

(*b*) A forecast balance sheet as at 30 November 19X0.   (*17 marks*)

(*University of London: GCE A-Level*)

22.5 The following information has been extracted from the books of Issa Ltd for the financial year ended 31 December 19X0.

Trading and Profit and Loss Account
for the year ended 31 December 19X0

	£000s		£000s
Opening stock	90	Sales	750
Purchases	490		
	580		
Less Closing stock	80		
Cost of goods sold	500		
Gross profit	250		
	750		750
Administration expenses	60	Gross profit	250
Selling and distribution expenses	50		
Financial charges	20		
Depreciation of fixed assets	20		
Net profit	100		
	250		250

Balance Sheet as at 31 December 19X0

	£000s	£000s		£000s	£000s
Fixed assets			£1 Ordinary shares:		
At cost		750	Fully paid		200
Less Aggregate depreciation		144	9% £1 Preference shares Fully paid.		100
		606			
Current assets			Share premium		150
Stock		80	Retained earnings		350
Trade debtors	75				800
Less Provision for			*Current liabilities*		
doubtful debtors	5	70	Trade creditors	50	
Balance at bank		100	Accrued expenses	6	56
		250			856
		856			

The company had commenced the preparation of its budget for the year ending 31 December 19X1 and the following information is the basis of its forecast.

1 An intensive advertising campaign will be carried out in the first six months of 19X1 at a cost of £15,000. It is anticipated that as a result of this, sales will increase to £900,000 in 19X1.
2 The gross profit/sales ratio will be increased to 35 per cent.
3 A new stock control system is to be installed in 19X1 and it is expected that the stock level will be reduced by £15,000 as compared to the 19X0 closing stock.
4 Land and buildings which cost £50,000 (nil depreciation to date) will be sold in 19X1 for £200,000 cash. Half of the proceeds will be used to buy ordinary shares in another company, Yates Ltd, at an agreed price of £4 per share. (Ignore share commission etc.)
5 The company planned to capitalise some of its reserves on 1 April 19X1. New ordinary shares are to be issued on a 1 for 2 basis. Half the funds required will be drawn from the share premium account and the remainder will be taken from retained earnings.
6 Preference share dividends will be paid on 1 May 19X1 and 1 November 19X1. The company planned to pay an interim ordinary share dividend on the increased share capital of 2.5p per share on 1 July 19X1. No final dividend is proposed.
7 Owing to inflation revenue expenses are expected to rise as follows:
Administration expenses will increase by 6 per cent.
Selling and distribution expenses will increase by 8 per cent.
The advertising campaign expenses are in addition to the increase above.
Financial charges will increase by 4 per cent.
These percentage increases are based on the figures for the year ended 31 December 19X0.
8 With the projected sales increases trade debtors are expected to rise to £100,000 by 31 December 19X1. The provision for doubtful debts is to be adjusted to $7\frac{1}{2}$ per cent of forecast trade debtors.
9 Other forecast figures as at 31 December 19X1:

	£000s
Balance at bank	350.1
Trade creditors	56.0
Expense creditors	15.0

10 Depreciation of 10 per cent per annum on cost is to be provided on £600,000 of the company's fixed assets.

Required:

(a) A budgeted trading, profit and loss and appropriation account for the year ending 31 December 19X1. Show the full details of the trading account. (10 marks)

(b) A budgeted balance sheet as at 31 December 19X1. (8 marks)

(c) What advantages accrue to a business by preparing a budget with respect to:
  (i) forecast profitability;
  (ii) forecast liquidity? (7 marks)

(Associated Examining Board: GCE A-Level)

22.6X The balance sheet of Gregg Ltd at 30 June 19X6 was expected to be as follows:

Balance Sheet 30 June 19X6

Fixed assets	Cost	Depreciation to date	Net
Land and buildings	40,000	–	40,000
Plant and machinery	10,000	6,000	4,000
Motor vehicles	6,000	2,800	3,200
Office fixtures	500	220	280
	56,500	9,020	47,480

Current assets			
Stock-in-trade: Finished goods		1,800	
Raw materials		300	
Debtors (May £990 + June £900)		1,890	
Cash and bank balances		7,100	11,090
			£58,570

Financed by		
Share capital		50,000
Profit and loss account		7,820
		57,820

Current liabilities			
Creditors for raw materials			
(April £240 + May £140 + June £160)		540	
Creditors for variable overhead		210	750
			£58,570

The plans for the six months to 31 December 19X6 can be summarised as:

(i) Production costs per unit will be:

	£
Direct materials	2
Direct labour	5
Variable overhead	3
	£10

(ii) Sales will be at a price of £18 per unit for the three months to 30 September and at £18.5 subsequently. The number of units sold would be:

Jul	Aug	Sep	Oct	Nov	Dec
60	80	100	100	90	70

All sales will be on credit, and debtors will pay their accounts two months after they have bought the goods.

(iii) Production will be even at 90 units per month.

(iv) Purchases of direct materials – all on credit – will be:

	Jul £	Aug £	Sep £	Oct £	Nov £	Dec £
	220	200	160	140	140	180

Creditors for direct materials will be paid three months after purchase.

(v) Direct labour is paid in the same month as production occurs.

(vi) Variable overhead is paid in the month following that in which the units are produced.

(vii) Fixed overhead of £90 per month is paid each month and is never in arrears.

(viii) A machine costing £500 will be bought and paid for in July. A motor vehicle costing £2,000 will be bought and paid for in September.

(ix) A debenture of £5,000 will be issued and the cash received in November. Interest will not start to run until 19X7.

(x) Provide for depreciation for the six months: motor vehicles £600, office fixtures £30, machinery £700.

You are required to draw up as a minimum:

(a) Cash budget, showing figures each month.
(b) Debtors' budget, showing figures each month.
(c) Creditors' budget, showing figures each month.
(d) Raw materials budget, showing figures each month.
(e) Forecast operating statement for the six months.
(f) Forecast balance sheet as at 31 December 19X6.

In addition you may draw up any further budgets you may wish in order to show the workings behind the above budgets.

22.7 The following information relates to the actual sales of Griffton Ltd during the last four months of its financial year.

	March	April	May	June
Quantity (units)	900	900	900	1,000
Price each	£55	£55	£55	£55

The budgeted information below relates to the next financial year commencing 1 July 19X2:

(i) The company forecasts that sales quantity will decrease in July by 10 per cent of the level in June. The reduced quantity will remain for August and September, but will then increase by 10 per cent in October, and remain fixed for the next three months.

The sales price will remain at £55 each until 1 September when it will be increased to £60 per unit, this price will be effective for a minimum of six months.

50 per cent of sales are on a cash basis and attract a 2 per cent cash discount, the remaining 50 per cent of sales are paid two months in arrears.

The company arranges its purchases of raw materials such that the closing stock at the end of each month exactly meets the requirement for the following month's sales. Each unit sold requires 2 kg of material at £15 per kg; this price is fixed until December 19X3.

(ii) As a separate exercise, the managing director asks for stock levels to be reviewed, and asks you about the use of Economic Order Quantities at some time in 19X3. The following budgeted data would apply to this exercise:

Material	2,000 kg per month
Price	£15 per kg
Stockholding costs	20% p.a. on average stock value
Ordering costs	£10 per order

Required:

A Draw up monthly budgets for the four-month period commencing 1 July 19X2 for:
   (a) Debtors in £s
   (b) Raw material purchases in kg.   *(19 marks)*

B From the budgeted information given in note (ii) calculate the Economic Order Quantity for the company. Briefly outline the limitations of this ordering method.   *(4 marks)*
                                                                          (Total marks 23)

(University of Oxford Delegacy of Local Examinations: GCE A-Level)

22.8 Bedford Ltd is a manufacturing business with several production departments. Benjamin Kent, the manager of the machining department, submitted the following figures for the firm's annual budget for his department:

Units produced	64,000
	(Normal
	production
	level)
	£
Raw materials	294,400
Direct labour	236,800
Power	38,400
Repairs and maintenance (25% variable at this level of budgeted cost)	51,200
Insurance	1,300
Heating and lighting	1,250
Indirect wages (15% variable at this level of budgeted cost)	64,000
Total cost	687,350
Total capacity for machining department	80,000 units

Actual production for the period is 68,000 units, and costs are:

Materials	310,750
Direct labour	249,100
Power	39,800
Repairs and maintenance	53,050
Insurance	1,350
Heating and lighting	1,200
Indirect wages	65,250
Total cost	720,500

   Benjamin is being criticised for overspending £33,150 compared with his normal budget. It is appreciated that he has made a saving on heating and lighting, but concern is being expressed over the spending on materials and labour. Benjamin feels that he has been able to control the department's costs efficiently.

Required:

A   Construct a flexible budget for 60 per cent, 70 per cent, 75 per cent, 85 per cent and 90 per cent of production capacity, calculate any savings or overspending by Benjamin's department and comment on its efficiency.   *(17 marks)*

B   Describe the operation of an efficient system of budgetary control.   *(6 marks)*
   (Total marks 23)

(University of Oxford Delegacy of Local Examinations: GCE A-Level)

Chapter 23

Contract Accounts

23.1 Accounts and the Business Cycle

The span of production differs between businesses, and some fit into the normal pattern of annual accounts more easily than others do. Farmers' accounts are usually admirably suited to the yearly pattern, as the goods they produce are in accordance with the seasons, and therefore repeat themselves annually. With a firm whose production span is a day or two the annual accounts are also quite suitable.

On the other hand, there are businesses whose work does not conform to a financial year's calculation of profits. Assume that a firm of contractors has only one contract being handled, and that is the total construction of a very large oil refinery complex. This might take five years to complete. Not until it is completed can the actual profit or loss on the contract be correctly calculated. However, if the company was formed especially with this contract in mind, the shareholders would not want to wait for five years before the profit could be calculated and dividends paid. Therefore an attempt is made to calculate profits yearly. Obviously, most firms will have more than one contract under way at a time, and also it would be rare for a contract to take such a long time to complete.

23.2 Opening Contract Accounts

For each contract an account is opened. It is, in fact, a form of trading account for each contract. Therefore if the firm has a contract to build a new technical college it may be numbered Contract 71. Thus a Contract 71 Account would be opened. All expenditure traceable to the contract will be charged to the contract account. This is far easier than ascertaining direct expenses in a factory, as any expenditure on the site will be treated as direct, e.g. wages for the manual workers on the site, telephone rental for telephones on the site, hire of machinery for the contract, wages for the timekeepers, clerks, etc., on the site.

23.3 Certification of Work Done

The contractor is paid by agreement on the strength of architects' certificates in the case of buildings, or engineers' certificates for an engineering contract. The architect, or engineer, will visit the site at regular intervals and will issue a certificate stating his estimate of the value of the work done, in terms of the total contract price (the sale price of the whole contract). Thus he may issue a certificate for £10,000. Normally the terms governing the contract will contain a clause concerning retention money. This is the amount, usually stated as a percentage, which will be retained, i.e. held back, in case the contract is not completed by a stated date, or against claims for faulty workmanship, etc. A 10 per cent retention in the case already mentioned would lead to £9,000 being payable by the person for whom the contract was being performed.

23.4 Allocation of Overheads

The administration overhead expenses not traceable directly to the sites, are sometimes split on an arbitrary basis and charged to each contract. Of course, if there were only one contract then all the overhead expenses would quite rightly be chargeable against it. On the other hand if there are twenty contracts being carried on, any apportionment must be arbitrary. No one can really apportion on a 'scientific' basis the administration overhead expenses of the managing director's salary, the cost of advertising to give the firm the right 'image', the costs of running accounting machinery for the records of the whole firm, and these are only a few of such expenses. Any attempt at apportionment is likely to give misleading results, and it is therefore far better left for the administrative overhead expenses which are obviously not chargeable to a contract to be omitted from the contract accounts. The surplus left on each contract account is thus the 'contribution' of each contract to administrative overhead expenses and to profit.

23.5 Example

Exhibit 23.1

Contract 44 is for a school being built for the Blankshire County Council. By the end of the year the following items have been charged to the contract account:

Contract 44

	£
Wages – Labour on site	5,000
Wages – Foreman and clerks on the site	600
Materials	4,000
Subcontractors on the site	900
Other site expenses	300
Hire of special machinery	400
Plant bought for the contract	2,000

The entries concerning expenditure traceable direct to the contract are relatively simple. These are charged to the contract account. These can be seen in the contract account on the next page.

Architects' certificates have been received during the year amounting to £14,000, it being assumed for this example that the certificates related to all work done up to the year end. (It is not always the case that engineers or architects will certify the work done up to the financial year end. They may call several days earlier than the year end. The cost of work done, but not certified at the year end, will therefore need carrying down as a balance to the next period when certification will take place.) A retention of 10 per cent is to be made, and the Blankshire County Council has paid £12,600. The £14,000 has been credited to a holding account called an Architects' Certificates Account and debited to the Blankshire County Council Account. The total of the Architects' Certificates Account now needs transferring to the Contract 44 Account. It is, after all, the 'sale' price of the work done so far, and the contract account is a type of trading account. The £12,600 received has been debited to the cash book and credited to Blankshire County Council Account, which now shows a balance of £1,400, this being equal to the retention money.

The cost of the stock of the materials on the site unused is not included in the value of the architects' certificates and is therefore carried forward to the next year at cost price. The value of the plant at the end of the year is also carried forward. In this case the value of the cost of the plant not yet used is £1,400. This means that £2,000 has been debited for the plant and £1,400 credited, thus effectively charging £600 for depreciation. Assume that the stock of unused materials cost £800.

The Contract 44 Account will now appear:

Contract 44

	£		£
Wages – Labour on site	5,000	Architects' certificates	14,000
Wages – Foreman and clerks on the site	600	Stock of unused materials c/d	800
Materials	4,000	Value of plant c/d	1,400
Subcontractors on the site	900		
Other site expenses	300		
Hire of special machinery	400		
Plant bought for the contract	2,000		

23.6 Profit Estimation

The difference between totals of the two sides (Credit side £16,200; Debit side £13,200) can be seen to be £3,000. It would be a brave person indeed who would assert that the profit made to date was £3,000. The contract is only part completed, and costly snags may crop up which would dissipate any potential profit earned, or snags may have developed already, such as subsidence, which has remained unnoticed as yet. The concept of prudence now takes over. For many years, the normal custom, barring any evidence to the contrary, was for the apparent profit (in this case £3,000) to have the following formula applied to it:

$$\text{Apparent profit} \times \tfrac{2}{3} \times \frac{\text{Cash received}}{\text{Work certified}} = \text{Amount which can be utilised for dividends, etc.}$$

In this case this turns out as $£3,000 \times \tfrac{2}{3} \times \dfrac{12,600}{14,000} = £1,800.$

The Contract 44 Account can now be completed.

Profit and Loss Account

	£
Profits from contracts: (See section 23.8)	
Contract 43	
Contract 44	1,800
Contract 45	

Contract 44

	£		£
Wages – Labour on site	5,000	Architects' certificates	14,000
Wages – Foreman and clerks on the site	600	Stock of unused materials c/d	800
Materials	4,000	Value of plant c/d	1,400
Subcontractors on the site	900		
Other site expenses	300		
Hire of special machinery	400		
Plant bought for the contract	2,000		
Profit to the profit and loss account	1,800		
Reserve (the part of the apparent profit not yet recognised as earned) c/d	1,200		
	16,200		16,200
Stock of unused materials b/d	800	Reserve b/d	1,200
Value of plant b/d	1,400		

23.7 Anticipated Losses

In the case shown there has been an apparent profit of £3,000, but the action would have been different if instead of revealing such a profit, the contract account had in fact shown a loss of £3,000. In such a case it would not be two-thirds of the loss to be taken into account but the whole of it. Thus £3,000 loss would have been transferred to the profit and loss account. This is in accordance with the concept of prudence which states that profits may be underestimated but never losses.

23.8 SSAP 9

When a revised version of SSAP 9: *Stocks and long-term contracts* was issued in 1988, this custom-based *rule of thumb* was replaced with a far more complex calculation that focuses upon turnover and the work certified valued in relation to the overall contract amount.

SSAP 9 requires that long-term contracts should be assessed on a contract-by-contract basis. They should be reflected in the profit and loss account by recording turnover and related costs as contract activity progresses. Turnover should be ascertained in a manner appropriate to the stage of completion of the contract, the business and the industry in which it operates. Where the outcome of the contract can be assessed with reasonable accuracy, profit should be recognised (so far as prudence permits) as the difference between recognised turnover and related costs. As previously, any foreseeable losses identified should be immediately recognised.

The amount of long-term contracts, at costs incurred, net of amounts transferred to cost of sales, after deducting foreseeable losses and payments on account not matched with turnover should be classified as 'long term contract balances' and separately disclosed within the balance sheet heading of 'stocks'. The balance sheet note should disclose separately the balances of 'net cost less foreseeable losses' and 'applicable payments on account'.

However, this topic is really beyond the scope of most A-Level syllabuses, and therefore of this book. Instead, this chapter is intended to provide an introduction to the subject of accounting for long-term contracts. Students who require a sound understanding of the

SSAP 9 rules concerning long-term contracts should refer to the standard, where the appendix covers the topic in detail, or to a specialised text on the subject.

REVIEW QUESTIONS

Advice:

As you can see, each contract account is a type of profit and loss account for each contract. The profit to date on contract which can be taken to the main profit and loss account is calculated per Section 23.6, unless the examiner gives you another method of calculating it.

23.1 Barley Construction plc are the contractors for the building of a replacement high technology factory for a multinational company. The total value of the contract is £8,500,000 over a three-year period. The contract commenced on 1 March 19X0, and the following details are available as at 28 February 19X1.

	£
Materials purchased	765,000
Material transfers in from another site	23,000
Material transfers out to another site	8,000
Materials on site, not yet used	38,000
Direct labour	448,000
Direct labour accrued	19,500
Indirect labour	63,000
Indirect labour accrued	2,400
Plant delivered to site	120,000
Hire of equipment	57,000
Hire charges owing	3,200
Head office charges	48,000
Cost of work not yet certified	86,000

Barley Construction plc have received payment of £1,555,500 which represents work certified as completed by the architects as at 28 February 19X1, less a 15 per cent retention. The company takes credit for two thirds of the profit on work certified (less retention).

The plant is estimated to last the life of the contract, and no residual value is expected.

Required:

A The contract account for the year ended 28 February 19X1, together with a calculation of the value of work in progress as at that date.   *(15 marks)*

B Briefly explain the accounting concept involved in the calculation of profit to be credited to the accounts for the year ended 28 February 19X1.
   In the event of a loss being made, how would this be dealt with?   *(3 marks)*

C It is intended that the new factory be fully automated with the consequence of a number of redundancies amongst existing employees. From the social responsibility viewpoint, what factors should the company consider, and what assistance could it give to employees who will eventually be made redundant at the site (the majority of whom it is anticipated will be taking early retirement)?   *(5 marks)*
                                                                              (Total marks 23)

(University of Oxford Delegacy of Local Examinations: GCE A-Level)

23.2X The final accounts of Diggers Ltd are made up to 31 December in each year. Work on a certain contract was commenced on 1 April 19X5 and was completed on 31 October 19X6. The total contract price was £174,000, but a penalty of £700 was suffered for failure to complete by 30 September 19X6.

The following is a summary of receipts and payments relating to the contract:

	During 19X5	During 19X6
	£	£
Payments:		
Materials	25,490	33,226
Wages	28,384	45,432
Direct Expenses	2,126	2,902
Purchases of plant on 1 April 19X5	16,250	–
Receipts		
Contract price (*less* Penalty)	52,200	121,100
Sale, on 31 October 19X6, of all plant purchased on 1 April 19X5	–	4,100

The amount received from the customer in 19X5 represented the contract price of all work certified in that year less 10 per cent retention money.

When the annual accounts for 19X5 were prepared it was estimated that the contract would be completed on 30 September 19X6, and that the market value of the plant would be £4,250 on that date. It was estimated that further expenditure on the contract during 19X6 would be £81,400.

For the purposes of the annual accounts, depreciation of plant is calculated, in the case of uncompleted contracts, by reference to the expected market value of the plant on the date when the contract is expected to be completed, and is allocated between accounting periods by the straight-line method.

Credit is taken, in the annual accounts, for such a part of the estimated total profit, on each uncompleted contract, as corresponds to the proportion between the contract price of the work certified and the total contract price.

Required:

Prepare a summary of the account for this contract, showing the amounts transferred to profit and loss account at 31 December 19X5 and 31 December 19X6.

23.3 Skimpy plc is a construction company currently undertaking three large construction contracts in its South West Division. Information relating to these three contracts for the year ended 31 October 19X9 is as follows:

	Plymouth contract £000	Torquay contract £000	Truro contract £000
Fixed contract price	600	800	1,200
Balances brought forward at 1 November 19X8			
Cost of work completed	240	80	–
Materials on site	18	6	–
Plant at written down value	90	25	–
Transactions during year			
Materials delivered to site	60	130	80
Wages	75	105	30
Payments to subcontractors	10	46	–
Salaries and other direct costs	18	32	8
Plant at written down value			
–issued to sites	6	115	77
–transferred to other sites	13	–	–
Balances carried forward at 31 October 19X9			
Materials on site	12	28	35
Plant at written down value	55	80	52
Value of work certified at end of year	500	450	125

Skimpy operates a local head office in the South West Division, the costs of which totalled £70,000 in the year ended 31 October 19X9. These costs are to be apportioned over the three construction contracts in the region in proportion to the wages paid.

The Plymouth contract is nearing completion and the site architect estimates that the additional costs to complete the contract will total £60,000. This sum includes an allowance for all anticipated costs including overheads and contingencies.

Required:

(a) Prepare a cost account for each of the three contracts for the year ended 31 October 19X9 and show the cost of the work completed at the end of the year. *(16 marks)*

(b) For each contract recommend, giving reasons, how much profit or loss should be taken for the year ended 31 October 19X9. *(9 marks)*

(Reproduced by permission of the University of Cambridge Local Examinations Syndicate)

23.4X

(a) How and why do companies account for profits on uncompleted contracts? *(8 marks)*

(b) From the following information prepare a contract account for the year ending 31 December 19X0. Show clearly the amount of profit that may prudently be taken.

Paddy Quick Construction Co

Contract No. 1234 (Start date 1 January 19X0)

	£
Contract price	850,000
Materials issued to site during 19X0	120,480
Materials returned to stores	1,460
Materials on site, 31 December, 19X0	15,340
Direct wages	134,200
Wages owing at 31 December, 19X0	5,220
Plant issued to contract (at cost)	82,600
Plant value at 31 December, 19X0	63,200
Subcontractors' charges	27,560
Head office expenses charged to contract	71,430
Direct expenses (site expenses)	42,570
Direct expenses owing at 31 December, 19X0	2,840
Work certified by architect	500,000
Cost of work not yet certified	27,350

The money received from the client (£425,000) was equivalent to the value of work certified less the agreed 15 per cent retention. Paddy Quick uses the fraction $\frac{2}{3}$ in calculating the profits on uncompleted contracts. *(17 marks)*

(University of London: GCE A-Level)

23.5X

(a) Define the term *contract costing* and explain what differences exist between contract and job costing. *(8 marks)*

(b) If a lengthy contract is being undertaken, profit must be accounted for in different accounting periods. A common formula for that allocation is:

$$\frac{2}{3} \times \frac{notional\ profit}{1} \times \frac{cash\ received}{work\ certified}$$

(i) Clearly explain the terms *notional profit* and *work certified* *(4 marks)*
(ii) As prudence is a fundamental accounting concept, how can it allow profit to be taken during the contract period rather than on its completion. *(8 marks)*

(University of London Examinations and Assessment Council: GCE A-Level)

Chapter 24

Standard Costing

24.1 Comparison with Actual Costs

A cost accounting system can be said to be either an actual cost system or a standard cost system. The difference is not in the systems themselves but rather on the kind of costs that are used. In the costing systems already shown we have seen that they have consisted of the actual costs for direct materials and direct labour, and overhead has been charged by reference to a predetermined overhead rate. Standard costing uses instead the costs that should have been incurred. So standard costing has costs that should have been incurred, whilst other systems use costs that have been incurred.

In an actual cost accounting system, costs are traced through the records as product costs. On the other hand, standard costing uses standards of performance and of prices derived from studying operations and of estimating future prices. Each unit being produced can have a standard material cost, a standard direct labour cost and a standard overhead cost. As with any form of management accounting, this does not in fact have to be carried out fully, for instance some companies will use standard labour and standard overhead costs but may use actual material costs. In the rest of this chapter we will consider firms that use a standard costing system for all items.

As with all management accounting, the benefits flowing from using standard costing should exceed the costs of operating it, so that there should be advantages accruing from having a standard costing system, and these are:

1 Usually it is simpler and needs less work than an actual cost system. This is because once the standards have been set they are adhered to, and the standard costs will remain unchanged for fairly long periods. Other systems need constant recalculations of cost. For instance the average cost method of pricing issues of materials needs a recalculation of the price each time there are further receipts, whereas standard cost of materials will remain at a constant figure. This can bring about a reduction in the costs of clerical work.

2 The unit costs for each identical product will be the same, whereas this may not be the same with actual costing systems. For instance, in an actual cost system two men making identical units may be paid at different wage rates, the materials issued to one man may have come from a slightly later lot of raw materials received which cost more than the previous lot and therefore the issue price may be higher, and so on. In a standard costing system the same amount would be charged for each of these men, until such time as the standards were altered.

3 A standard cost system provides a better means of checking on the efficiency with which production is carried on, in that the differences between the standard costs and the actual costs, i.e. the variances, throw up the changes in efficiency.

4 One important advantage may be that standard costing might make faster reporting available. This is certainly most important, as generally the later information is received the less useful it will be. Standard costing has a great deal of predetermined data when compared with an actual costing system; therefore entering up job order sheets, job sheets and many other tasks can be speeded up if the actual costs do not have to be waited for.

The costs that will have been flowing through the standard costing system are those of standard costs and as actual costs will normally be different, then the difference or variance if adverse (i.e. actual costs have exceeded standard costs) will be debited to the profit and loss account. If the variance is a favourable one (i.e. actual costs have been less than standard costs) then this would be credited to the profit and loss account. This must be done, as all the costs used for the calculation of gross profit, etc. have been standard costs, and if the variances were not put in the profit and loss account then the net profit would not be the net profit actually made.

24.2 Setting Standards

Standard cost accounting is a classic case of the use of the principle of 'management by exception'. Put roughly this means that when things are going according to plan leave them alone, and concentrate instead on the things that are deviating from planned results. With standard costing the actual results that conform to the standards require little attention. Instead management's interest is centred on the exceptions to standards.

Getting the 'right' standards is, therefore, of prime importance. If the 'wrong' standards are used, not only will a lot of time and money have been wasted, but it may bring worse results than if no standard had been set at all. Standards may be unsuitable because they were not set properly, or because conditions have changed greatly since they were set.

Standards of one of two types can be used: ideal standards and attainable standards. These are as follows:

1 **Ideal standards.** These are set at a maximum level of efficiency, and thus represent conditions that really can very rarely be attained. This approach can be seriously objected to, in that if standards are too high, employees who might otherwise be motivated by standards which are possible to achieve may become discouraged.

2 **Attainable standards.** It is simple for someone to say that individuals will be motivated to attain standards that they are capable of, that they will not exert very much effort to exceed standards, and that standards outside their capabilities will not motivate them. From this follows the also easy conclusion that standards should be neither 'too easy' nor 'too difficult' but should be 'just right'. The difficult part of this is in saying what the 'just right' figures are to ask as standards. There is no doubt that the work of behavioural scientists in this area has brought about a far greater insight into such problems. In a very large firm such specialists may be members of the team setting the standards.

The standards for materials and for labour can be divided between those which are concerned with (i) prices and (ii) quantities. Standard overhead costs are divided between standard variable overhead costs, and standard fixed overhead costs. The standard fixed overhead costs will be used in absorption costing only, as marginal costing does not bring the fixed costs into its figures.

REVIEW QUESTIONS

Advice:

This is a chapter giving background information only. You will not find many computational questions limited to the contents of the chapter.

24.1 Rimham plc prepares its budgets annually and as the accountant you are responsible for this task. The following standard data is available:

Material content	Product X	Product Y	Product Z
	kg	kg	kg
Material 1	–	18	24
Material 2	4	14	–
Material 3	12	10	6
Material 4	8	–	18

Material prices	Price per kg
	£
Material 1	0.1
Material 2	0.15
Material 3	0.25
Material 4	0.05

Labour content	Product X	Product Y	Product Z
	hours	hours	hours
Department A	2.5	1.5	3
Department B	2.5	1.5	3

Labour rates	Rate per hour
	£
Department A	1.6
Department B	1.2

Additional budgeted information	
Direct labour hours	635,000
Production overheads	£1,143,000

- Production overheads are absorbed on the direct labour hour rate method.

- Administration and selling overheads are absorbed as a percentage of production cost at the rates of 50 per cent and 25 per cent, respectively.

- Profit is estimated at 12½ per cent on budgeted selling price.

- Sales, at standard selling price, for the following year are budgeted as follows:

Product	£
X	800,000
Y	1,280,000
Z	2,400,000

● In order to meet the needs of an expansion programme the company considers it necessary to increase stocks as follows:

Material 1	90,000 kg
Material 2	36,000 kg
Material 3	42,000 kg
Material 4	54,000 kg
Finished goods	
Product X	5,000 units
Product Y	10,000 units
Product Z	10,000 units

You are required to prepare the following:

(a) A schedule giving a detailed standard cost and standard selling price per unit for **each** product,

(20 marks)

(b) The sales budget in units, *(3 marks)*

(c) The production budget in units, *(3 marks)*

(d) The direct material purchases budget in both units and value. *(14 marks)*

(Total marks 40)

(Northern Examination and Assessments Board: GCE A-Level)

24.2X

(a) Define the terms:

    (i)   standard costing

    (ii)   standard cost

    (iii) standard hours

    (iv) variance. *(5 marks)*

(b) The following diagram reflects costs under a standard costing system. Assume that all the variances are *unfavourable*. State, with reasons, which rectangle(s) represent:

(i) the standard cost

(ii) the actual cost

(iii) the total labour cost variance

(iv) the efficiency variance

(v) the wage rate variance

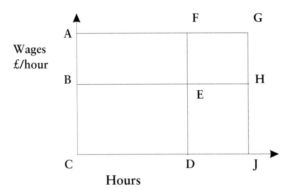

(10 marks)

(University of London Examinations and Assessment Council: GCE A-Level)

Chapter 25

Variance Analysis: Material and Labour Variances

25.1 Introduction

Variance analysis is a means of assessing the difference between a predetermined cost and the actual cost. It can improve the operating efficiency of a business by first of all setting up the predetermined standard cost structures and then measuring actual costs against them in order to measure production efficiency.

It also makes use of the principle of management by exception. When things are going according to plan they can be left alone. Management can then concentrate on the things that deviate from the planned results.

25.2 Adverse and Favourable Variances

The difference between standard cost and actual cost has already been stated to be a variance. Remember these are classified:

> Adverse: Actual cost greater than standard cost.
> Favourable: Actual cost less than standard cost.

The use of the words favourable and adverse should not be confused with their meaning in ordinary language usage, they are technical terms. Whether a variance is 'good' or 'bad' can only be determined after the cause(s) of the variance have been fully investigated and ascertained.

25.3 Computation of Variances

There is a great deal of difference between the *computation* of the variances and their *analysis*. The computation is simply the mathematical calculation of the variance. The analysis of the variance is a matter requiring a fair amount of judgement, it just cannot be performed in a mechanical fashion.

We can now look at some computations of variances. In fact there are many variances which can be computed, but we will concentrate on a few of the more important ones. In order that sense can be made of the computations and a reasonable job of analysis done, it will be assumed that the standards set were calculated on a rational basis.

NB In the computations of variances which follows this, there are diagrams to illustrate the variances which have been calculated. The lines drawn on the diagrams will be as follows:

Representing standard costs — — — — — —
Representing actual costs - - - - - - - - -
Where actual costs and standard costs are the same —·—·—·—·—·—·—·—·

(a) Material price variances

(i) Favourable variance:

Material J

Standard price per foot	£4
Standard usage per unit	5 feet
Actual price per foot	£3
Actual usage per unit	5 feet

Usage is the same as standard, therefore the only variance is that of price, calculated:

	£
Actual cost per unit 5 × £3	15
Standard cost per unit 5 × £4	20
Variance (favourable)	£5

The diagram illustrates this in that the variance is represented by the shaded area. This is £1 by a quantity of 5, therefore the variance is £5. The variance extends to the price line and not the quantity line, therefore it is a price variance.

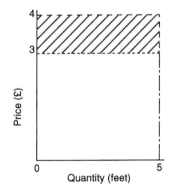

(ii) Adverse variance:

Material K

Standard price per foot	£9
Standard usage per unit	8 feet
Actual price per foot	£11
Actual usage per unit	8 feet
Variance computed:	£
Actual cost per unit 8 × £11	88
Standard cost per unit 8 × £9	72
Variance (adverse)	£16

The shaded part of the diagram is the variance, this extends £2 times a quantity of 8, therefore the variance is £16. Notice that the shaded area is outside the lines marked - - - - - - - - - - - - - representing standard costs. In the diagrams, when the variance is outside the standard cost area as marked by the standard cost lines, it will be an adverse variance. When it is inside the standard cost area as marked by the standard cost lines, it will be a favourable variance.

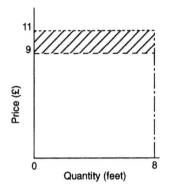

(b) Material usage variances

(i) Favourable variance:

Material L

Standard price per ton	£5
Standard usage per unit	100 tons
Actual price per ton	£5
Actual usage per unit	95 tons

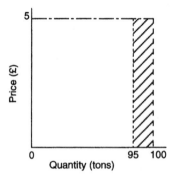

Cost is the same as standard, therefore the only variance is that of usage, calculated:

	£
Actual cost per unit 95 × £5	475
Standard cost per unit 100 × £5	500
Variance (favourable)	25

(ii) Adverse variance:

Material M

Standard price per yard	£8
Standard usage per unit	11 yards
Actual price per yard	£8
Actual usage per unit	13 yards
Variance computed:	£
Actual cost per unit 13 × £8	104
Standard cost per unit 11 × £8	88
Variance (adverse)	16

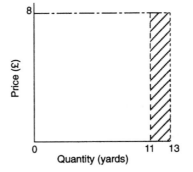

Here again the variances for Materials L and M are shown in diagrams by means of shaded areas. The variances extend to the quantity lines and are, therefore, usage variances. With material L the variance is shown inside the standard cost area, and is, therefore, a favourable variance, whereas Material M shows an adverse variance as it is outside the standard cost area.

(c) Combinations of material price and usage variances

Most variances are combinations of both material price and usage variances. Sometimes one variance will be favourable whilst the other is adverse, sometimes both will be adverse variances, and at other times both will be favourable variances.

(i) Favourable and adverse variances combined:

Material N

Standard price per metre	£6
Standard usage per unit	25 metres
Actual price per metre	£7
Actual usage per metre	24 metres

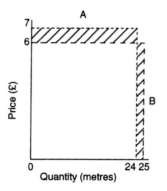

The net variance is calculated as:

	£
Actual cost per unit 24 × £7	168
Standard cost per unit 25 × £6	150
Variance (adverse)	£18

As the diagram shows, this is in fact made up of two variances. The first variance, shown as the shaded portion A, is an adverse price variance (i.e. it is outside the standard cost lines, therefore actual cost has exceeded standard cost). The second variance, shown as the shaded portion B, is a favourable usage variance (i.e. it is inside the standard cost lines, therefore actual usage has been less than standard usage).

The adverse price variance can therefore be seen to be £1 by a quantity of 24 = £24. The favourable usage variance can be seen to be a length of 1 metre by a price of £6 = £6. The net (adverse) variance is therefore made up:

	£
Adverse material price variance	24
Favourable material usage variance	6
Net (adverse) variance	£18

(ii) Both adverse variances combined:

Material O

Standard price per kilo.	£9
Standard usage per unit	13 kilos
Actual price per kilo.	£11
Actual usage per unit	15 kilos

The net variance is computed:

	£
Actual cost per unit 15 × £11	165
Standard cost per unit 13 × £9	117
Variance (adverse)	£48

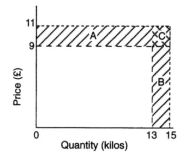

The diagram shows the shaded area A which is definitely a price variance of £2 × 13 = £26 adverse. Shaded area B is definitely a usage variance of 2 × £9 = £18 adverse. This makes up £44 of the variance, but there is the double shaded area, C, of 2 × £2 = £4. This is really an area which is common to both usage and price. Sometimes, although not very often, this would be treated as a separate variance, but as detail is necessarily limited, in this book we will just add it to the price variance, making it £26 + £4 = £30, the usage variance being left at £18.

(iii) Both favourable variances combined:

> *Material P*
> Standard price per ton   £20
> Standard usage per unit   15 tons
> Actual price per ton   £19
> Actual usage per unit   13 tons

The net variance is computed:

	£
Actual cost per unit 13 × £19	247
Standard cost per unit 15× £20	300
Variance (favourable)	£53

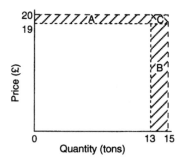

The diagram shows the shaded area A which is definitely a price variance of £1 × 13 = £13 favourable. Shaded area B is a usage variance of 2 × £19 = £38 favourable. The double shaded area C of £1 × 2 = £2, making up the total variance of £53 would normally be added to the usage variance to make it £38 + £2 = £40.

25.4 Materials Variances – Analysis

(a) Price variances

The price variance is a simple one in that it is obvious that the purchasing department has not been able to buy at the anticipated price. How far this is completely outside the powers of the purchasing department depends entirely on the facts. It may simply be that the rate of inflation is far greater than it had been possible to foresee, or that special forms of extra taxes have been introduced by the government. No one can surely blame the purchasing department for not knowing the secrets of the government's budget each year!

On the other hand, it may have been that poor purchasing control has meant that orders for materials have been placed too late for the firm to manage to get the right price in the market, or that materials which ought to have been bought in bulk have been in fact bought in small lots at uneconomic prices. If there are regular suppliers, a short-term gain by buying a cheaper lot from somewhere else could militate against the firm's benefit in the long run if the firm's regular suppliers took umbrage.

Buying the cheapest materials does not always bring about the achievement of the greatest profit. It may result in more wastages, a greater amount of labour time because the men take longer to do the job with inferior materials, and a unit made up of poor materials may well damage the image of the firm because its products do not last as long as they used to do.

All the same, there must be someone to whom the responsibility for the price variance can be traced and who is then accountable for it.

(b) Usage variances

There are many reasons for excessive use of material. Inferior materials can bring about a lot of waste, so can workers who are not as skilled as they ought to be. Perhaps the machinery is not suitable for the job, or there might even be deliberate wastage of material, e.g. wood wasted so that it can be taken home by workers as fuel etc. The theft of material obviously aggravates a usage variance. Here again responsibility must be traced.

25.5 Key Questions of Variances

Before we look at the computation or analysis of any further variances this is a convenient point to raise some fundamental questions about variances. They are:
1   Why do we wish to calculate this particular variance?
2   When it has been calculated what action are we going to take about it?
3   If we are not going to make an effective use of the variance, then why bother at all to calculate it?

25.6 Formulas for Material Variances

We have deliberately waited until now to give you the formula for calculating each variance. We wanted you to understand what the variances were, rather than simply give you the formula to calculate them. They are as follows:

Materials price variance = (Standard price – Actual price per unit) × Quantity purchased
= (SP – AP) × QP

Materials usage variance = (Standard quantity required – Actual quantity)
× Standard price (per unit)
= (SQ – AQ) × SP

25.7 Inventory Records under Standard Costing

It is worth noting at this point that when a firm adopts a standard costing system it avoids the difficulties involving FIFO, LIFO or average stock methods. In a standard costing system all materials received and issued are valued at the standard cost in the inventory account. There is no recording problem associated with changing prices during the period since they are separately recorded as variances.

Provided that standards are reviewed sufficiently often this system should ensure that the values of inventories are maintained close to their current value.

25.8 Disposition of Variances

The question arises as to how the variances are to be brought into the final accounts of the business. There are, in fact, several methods of dealing with them.

They can be treated entirely as costs (if adverse variances) which are period costs and are, therefore, not included in the valuation of closing stocks of finished goods or work in progress. Alternatively they may be brought in as product costs and therefore used in the valuation of closing stocks. Another variation is to treat those variances which are controllable as period costs, but the uncontrollable variances be treated as product costs. All of these methods are acceptable for the final accounts which are used for external reporting.

Before you read further, now attempt Questions 25.1 and 25.2X.

25.9 Labour Variances

The computation of labour variances is similar to that of material variances. With labour variances the analysis can be broken down into:

(a) Wage rate variances.
(b) Labour efficiency variances.

Because the computation of labour variances is so similar to that of material variances only a few examples will be given.

(a) Wage rate variance

Product A	
Standard hours to produce	100
Actual hours to produce	100
Standard wage rate per hour	£0.9
Actual wage rate per hour	£1.0

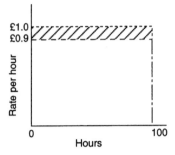

As the actual and standard hours are the same, then the only variance will be a wage rate variance, computed as follows:

	£
Actual cost per unit 100 × £1.0	100
Standard cost per unit 100 × £0.9	90
Variance (adverse)	£10

The diagram illustrates this in that the variance is represented by the shaded area. This is £0.1 by a quantity of 100, therefore the variance is £10. The variance extends to the wage rate line and it is thus a wage rate variance, and as the shaded area is outside the standard cost lines, indicated by lines marked – – – – – – –, then it is an adverse variance.

(b) Labour efficiency variance

Product B

Standard hours to produce	400
Actual hours to produce	370
Standard wage rate per hour	£1.0
Actual wage rate per hour	£1.0

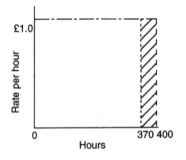

As the actual and standard wage rates are the same, then the only variance will be a labour efficiency variance, computed as follows:

	£
Actual cost per unit 370 × £1.0	370
Standard cost per unit 400 × £1.0	400
Variance (favourable)	£30

The diagram illustrates this in that the variance is represented by the shaded area. This is a quantity of 30 by a rate of £1.0, therefore the variance is £30. The variance extends to the time line, therefore this is an efficiency variance, as the job has been completed in a different number of hours than standard. As the shaded area is inside the standard cost lines, indicated by lines marked – – – – – –, then it is a favourable variance.

(c) Combined wage rate and efficiency variance

Product C

Standard hours to produce	500
Actual hours to produce	460
Standard wage rate per hour	£0.9
Actual wage rate per hour	£1.1

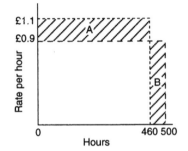

The net variance can be computed as:

	£
Actual cost per unit 460 × £1.1	506
Standard cost per unit 500 × £0.9	450
Variance (adverse)	£56

The diagram shows that this is made up of two variances. The first variance, shown as the shaded portion A, is an adverse wage rate variance (it is outside the standard cost lines, therefore it is an adverse variance because actual cost for this has exceeded standard cost). The second variance, shown as the shaded portion B, is a favourable labour efficiency variance (it is inside the standard cost lines, therefore actual hours have been less than standard hours).

The adverse wage rate variance can, therefore, be seen to be £0.2 by a quantity of 460 = £92. The favourable efficiency variance is a quantity of 40 by a price of £0.9 = £36. The net adverse variance is, therefore, made up of:

	£
Adverse wage rate variance	92
Favourable labour efficiency variance	36
	£56

25.10 Labour Variances – Analysis

Labour wage rates will probably be set in conjunction with the trade unions involved, so that this variance may not really be subject to control at any other level other than at the bargaining table with the unions involved. Nevertheless such a variance could arise because a higher grade of labour was being used than was necessary, even taking into account trade union needs. It might reflect a job running behind schedule that had to be finished off quickly even though higher grade labour was used. It might have been a rush job that also meant bringing in a higher grade of labour as well. The staffing policy of the firm may have come adrift because the firm had not recruited sufficient numbers of the various grades of labour.

Labour efficiency variances can be caused by a great number of things. Using unsuitable labour, unsuitable machinery, workers trying to slow work up so that more overtime rates of pay are earned, the day after a bank holiday, or the day before it, can affect performance. The morale of workers, the physical state of workers, using poor materials which slows up production, hold-ups because of bottlenecks in production and so on. The possibilities are almost endless. At the same time, if the variance was worth calculating then some form of action should follow, as otherwise there is no point at all in doing the accounting work of calculating such variances.

25.1 Formulas for Labour Variances

Wage rate variance $\quad$ = (Standard wage rate per hour – Actual wage rate) × Actual hours worked

$\qquad\qquad\qquad\quad$ = (SR – AR) × AH

Labour efficiency variance $\quad$ = (Standard labour hours for actual production – Actual

$\qquad\qquad\qquad\qquad\quad$ labour hours worked) × Standard wage rate per hour

$\qquad\qquad\qquad\qquad$ = (SH – AH) × SR

REVIEW QUESTIONS

Advice:

Work carefully through Questions 25.1 and 25.3. If you have any difficulty repeat them in 24 hours' time. Once you get into the swing of doing this type of question, it is quite easy to tackle them and get high marks.

25.1 Calculate the materials variances from the following data.

(i)	Material Q:	Standard price per tonne	£20	
		Standard usage per unit	34	tonnes
		Actual price per tonne	£18	
		Actual usage per unit	37	tonnes
(ii)	Material R:	Standard price per yard	£17	
		Standard usage per unit	50	yards
		Actual price per yard	£19	
		Actual usage per unit	46	yards
(iii)	Material S:	Standard price per metre	£12	
		Standard usage per unit	15	metres
		Actual price per metre	£14	
		Actual usage per unit	18	metres
(iv)	Material T:	Standard price per roll	£40	
		Standard usage per unit	29	rolls
		Actual price per roll	£37	
		Actual usage per unit	27	rolls

(v)	Material U:	Standard price per kilo	£7	
		Standard usage per unit	145	kilos
		Actual price per kilo	£8	
		Actual usage per unit	154	kilos
(vi)	Material V:	Standard price per litre	£25	
		Standard usage per unit	10,000	litres
		Actual price per litre	£22	
		Actual usage per unit	9,850	litres

25.2X Calculate the materials variances from the following data.

(i)	Material E:	Standard price per metre	£6	
		Standard usage per unit	88	metres
		Actual price per metre	£6	
		Actual usage per unit	85	metres
(ii)	Material F:	Standard price per tonne	£117	
		Standard usage per unit	30	tonnes
		Actual price per tonne	£123	
		Actual usage per unit	30	tonnes
(iii)	Material G:	Standard price per litre	£16	
		Standard usage per unit	158	litres
		Actual price per litre	£16	
		Actual usage per unit	165	litres
(iv)	Material H:	Standard price per cm	£16	
		Standard usage per unit	92	cm
		Actual price per cm	£19	
		Actual usage per unit	92	cm
(v)	Material I:	Standard price per tonne	£294	
		Standard usage per unit	50	tonnes
		Actual price per tonne	£300	
		Actual usage per unit	50	tonnes
(vi)	Material J:	Standard price per kilo	£27.5	
		Standard usage per unit	168	kilos
		Actual price per kilo	£27.5	
		Actual usage per unit	156	kilos

25.3 Calculate the labour variances from the following data:

		Standard hours	Actual hours	Standard wage rate	Actual wage rate
(i)	Job A	220	218	£2.1	£2.1
(ii)	Job B	115	115	£1.7	£1.9
(iii)	Job C	200	240	£1.8	£1.8
(iv)	Job D	120	104	£2.0	£2.0
(v)	Job E	68	68	£1.8	£1.5
(vi)	Job F	30	34	£1.7	£1.7
(vii)	Job G	70	77	£1.6	£1.6
(viii)	Job H	100	100	£1.9	£2.0

25.4X Calculate the labour variances from the following data:

		Standard hours	Actual hours	Standard wage rate	Actual wage rate
(i)	Job I	150	142	£2.0	£2.2
(ii)	Job J	220	234	£1.9	£1.7
(iii)	Job K	50	48	£2.0	£1.9
(iv)	Job L	170	176	£2.0	£2.2
(v)	Job M	140	149	£2.1	£1.8
(vi)	Job N	270	263	£1.6	£2.0

25.5 The company for which you are the accountant manufactures three related, but different, products. These are dishwashers, washing machines and refrigerators.
   Each product has a standard time per unit of production. These are:

Dishwashers	10 hours
washing machines	12 hours
Refrigerators	14 hours

In the month of March the actual production was:

Dishwashers	150
washing machines	100
Refrigerators	90

and the labour details were:

actual hours worked	4,100
standard hourly rate of pay	£4
actual wages incurred	£18,450

You are required to:

(a) Explain the term 'standard hour'   *(2 marks)*

(b) Calculate the standard hours produced in the month of March   *(2 marks)*

(c) Calculate the following variances, using the above data:
   (i)   total direct labour variance
   (ii) direct labour rate variance
   (iii) direct labour efficiency variance   *(12 marks)*

(d)   Give **two** possible causes for **each** of the labour rate and efficiency variances in (c).   *(4 marks)*
                                                                                         (Total marks 20)

(Northern Examinations and Assessments Board: GCE A-Level)

25.6X Central Grid plc manufactures tungsten parts which pass through two processes, machining and polishing, before being transferred to finished goods. The management of the company have in operation a system of standard costing and budgetary control. The standard cost and budget information for April 19X8 has been established by the management accountant as follows:

Standard cost and budget details for April 19X8

	Machining	Polishing
Standard cost per unit:		
Direct material	£5	–
Direct labour	£12	£4.50
Budgeted output – units	16,000	16,000
(*See* Note below)		
Budgeted direct labour hours	48,000	24,000

Note: Output passes through both processes and there is no opening or closing work in progress.

Additional information

1 The actual production costs and details for April 19X8 are as follows:
   (i) The output that passed through the two processes was 12,000 units and there was no opening or closing work-in-progress.
   (ii) Direct material used at standard prices was £64,150.
   (iii) Direct material used at actual prices was £60,390.
   (iv) The direct wages bill and the direct labour hours clocked for the machining department were:

	£	Hours
Machining department	153,000	34,000

2 Variances for the polishing department have been calculated and reveal the following:

Labour efficiency variance	£3,000 Adverse
Labour rate variance	Nil

Required:

(a) Calculate the total direct material variance and its analysis into:
   (i) direct material usage variance
   (ii) direct material price variance.   *(6 marks)*
(b) Calculate the overall direct labour variance for the machining department and analyse this variance into:
   (i) direct labour efficiency variance
   (ii) direct labour rate variance.   *(6 marks)*
(c) Identify the possible reasons for each of the variances calculated for the machining department in (a) and (b) above and also for the variances given for the polishing department.   *(5 marks)*
(d) Discuss possible interrelationships between these variances.   *(5 marks)*

(*Associated Examining Board: GCE A-Level*)

25.7 Borrico Ltd manufacture a single product and they had recently introduced a system of budgeting and variance analysis.
   The following information is available for the month of July 19X1:

1

	Budget	Actual
	£	£
Direct materials	200,000	201,285
Direct labour	313,625	337,500
Variable manufacturing overhead	141,400	143,000
Fixed manufacturing overhead	64,400	69,500
Variable sales overhead	75,000	71,000
Administration costs	150,000	148,650

2 Standard costs were:
   Direct labour 48,250 hours at £6.50 per hour.
   Direct materials 20,000 kilograms at £10 a kilogram.

3 Actual manufacturing costs were:
   Direct labour 50,000 hours at £6.75 per hour.
   Direct materials 18,900 kilograms at £10.65 a kilogram.

4 Budgeted sales were 20,000 units at £50 a unit.
   Actual sales were
       15,000 units at £52 a unit
       5,200 units at £56 a unit

5 There was no work-in-progress or stock of finished goods.

Required:

(a) An accounting statement showing the budgeted and actual gross and net profits or losses for July 19X1.   (6 marks)

(b) The following variances for July 19X1:
     (i) Direct material cost variance, direct material price variance and direct material usage variance.
     (ii) Direct labour cost variance, direct labour rate variance and direct labour efficiency variance.   (6 marks)

(c) What use can the management of Borrico Ltd make of the variances calculated in (b) above?
                                                                                (3 marks)

(*Associated Examining Board: GCE A-Level*)

25.8X

(a) How does a system of standard costing enable a business to operate on the principle of management by exception?   (3 marks)

(b) Some of the following materials and labour variances have been wrongly calculated, although the figures used are correct. Recalculate the variances, showing clearly the formulae you have used, and state whether the variances are adverse or favourable.

     (i) *Total Materials Variance*
              (Standard price   –   Actual price)   (Standard quantity   –   Actual quantity)
          = (£8.42   –   £8.24)   (1,940 litres   –   2,270 litres)
          = (£0.18)   (– 330 litres)
          = £59.40 *adverse*

     (ii) *Materials Price Variance*
              (Standard price   –   Actual price)   Standard quantity
          = (£8.42   –   £8.24   1,940
          = £349.20 *favourable*

     (iii) *Materials Usage Variance*
              (Standard quantity – Actual quantity   Standard price
          = (1,940   –   2,270)   £8.42
          = £2,778.6 *adverse*

(iv) *Total Labour Variance*

        (Actual hours   – Standard hours   (Actual rate   –   Standard rate)

  = (860   800)   (£6.14   –   £6.53)

  = (60 hours)   (– £0.39)

  = £23.4 *adverse*

(v) *Wage Rate Variance*

        (Standard rate   –   Actual rate   Actual hours

  = (£6.53   –   £6.14)   860

  = £335.4 *favourable*

(vi) *Labour Efficiency Variance*

        (Actual hours   – Standard hours)   Standard rate

  = (860   800)   £6.53

  = £391.80 *favourable*   (12 marks)

(*University of London: GCE A-Level*)

25.9X Makers Ltd assembles computer games machines. Standard costs have been prepared as follows:

		GAMESMASTER	GOTCHYA
		£	£
standard cost:			
direct material:	boards	5	10
	components	20	30
direct labour:	assembly	5	5
	testing	5	10
overheads charged at 200%		20	30
		55	85
profit margin		11	15
standard selling price		66	100

The standard direct labour rate is £5 per hour.
During May 19X5, 5,000 Gamesmasters were sold at £60 each and 2,000 Gotchyas at £110 each. Actual costs were incurred as follows:

	£
5,050 Gamesmaster boards	26,000
5,060 sets Gamesmaster components	75,000
2,010 Gotchya boards	28,390
2,025 sets Gotchya components	56,409
10,000 assembly labour hours @ £4.90	49,000
7,000 testing labour hours at £5.10	35,700
Overheads	160,000
	430,499

    There are no opening or closing stocks.

Required:

A schedule of direct material and direct labour variances for the month.   *(20 marks)*

(*Welsh Joint Education Committee: GCE A-Level*)

Chapter 26

Variance Analysis: Overhead and Sales Variances

26.1 Management Overheads

In Chapter 19 the problem of allocating manufacturing overheads to jobs or processes, was introduced. In the first instance the costs were collected in cost centres – normally recognisable departments of the organisation. The total costs of these centres is then applied to products or jobs as they pass through the operations of the cost centre.

Suppose that a firm collects costs into three manufacturing departments with the results as in Exhibit 26.1.

Exhibit 26.1

Department	A	B	C
	£	£	£
Fixed overhead cost	50,000	40,000	20,000
Variable overhead cost	30,000	35,000	40,000
Total overhead	80,000	75,000	60,000
Direct labour hours	10,000	30,000	15,000
Direct labour cost	£22,000	£59,000	£35,000
Machine hours	20,000	2,000	10,000

A decision has to be taken as to which activity, either labour of machine time, is the dominant factor in the department and will provide the most sensible basis for allocating the overhead.

In the case of Department A machine hours appear to be the major factor and therefore overheads will be charged on the basis $\frac{£80,000}{20,000}$ hours = £4 per machine hour. The firm will record for each job or process the number of machine hours taken and the overheads allocated on this total of hours at £4 per hour.

In Department B labour appears to be the dominant factor and therefore overheads will be charged on a labour hour rate calculated at $\frac{£75,000}{30,000}$ hours = £2.50 per hour.

Department C does not exhibit any dominant activity and could either be expressed in a machine hour rate or a labour hour rate. Some firms where rates of pay in a department are stable and the mix of labour at different rates of pay stays the same prefer to express the overheads as a percentage of labour cost. In Department C it could be $\dfrac{£60,000}{£35,000} = 171$ per cent. Thus the labour cost for all work going through department C would be collected and overheads allocated at 171 per cent of this labour cost figure.

26.2 Predetermined Rates

The usual procedure whether using standard costing or not is to predetermine the overhead absorption rates using budgeted figures both for the overhead costs and for the activity measure, whether machine or labour hours or cost. This process has a number of advantages – since not only does it allow proper current estimates to be made for things such as price quotations – but also it avoids the problem of fluctuating overhead rates at different times of the year due to seasonal variations. For example an ice-cream manufacturer is likely to be much more active in the summer months than in the winter. Because activity is low in winter the rate of absorption is likely to rise steeply since costs will not reduce proportionately. It makes more sense to view the overheads in this type of business on an annual cycle and recover the same amount of overhead in both summer and winter.

26.3 Variances in Overhead Recovery

As in all situations where budgeted figures are used there are almost certainly going to be variances at the end of a period. Take figures from Exhibit 26.1 for Department A as the budget, and compare them with actual performance (*see* Exhibit 26.2).

Exhibit 26.2

	Department A	
	Budget figures	Actual figures
	£	£
Fixed overhead	50,000	52,000
Variable overhead	30,000	37,000
Total overhead	80,000	89,000
Machine hours	20,000	25,000
Machine hour rate £4		

The actual machine hours worked of 25,000 will have been used to allocate overheads to production at the rate of £4 per hour and therefore £100,000 will have been allocated. Compared to actual overheads of £89,000 this represents an over-absorption of £11,000. Only if 22,250 machine hours had been worked would the recovery have been exactly equal to actual overhead costs.

In a cost accounting system not using standard costing the over or under absorption of overheads would be either:

1 transferred wholly to cost of goods sold in the profit and loss account for the period.
2 allocated between closing inventories and cost of goods sold.
3 carried forward to the net period.

The first choice would be used if the difference was felt to represent a shortfall in achievement; for example, if the number of hours worked had dropped due to bad management planning. The second would be applied if the differences were felt to be due to poor estimates of the original budgets. The third would only apply to interim accounts – not those at a year end.

Analysing the variances

The variance between the amount recovered of £100,000 and the actual overhead cost of £89,000 can be analysed into a number of constituent variances in the normal manner of standard costing. In the example we have used the variance can be due to:

1   the prices paid for goods and services being different from original estimates or standards.

2   the volume of activity during the period being different from the original estimate.

These are known as the budget or spending variance for the first and a volume variance for the second reason.

Budget or spending variance

This represents the difference between the actual cost of overhead and the budgeted overhead cost adjusted to the actual level of operational activity. From Exhibit 26.2 the budget figures need to be increased to take account of the fact that activity measured in machine hours has increased from 20,000 to 25,000 hours. This will not, of course, increase the fixed overhead – only the variable overheads which we will assume increase by 25 per cent in line with the hours. This is shown as Exhibit 26.3.

Exhibit 26.3

	a	b	c	b – c
	Original Budget	Adjusted budget	Actual	Variance
Fixed overhead	50,000	50,000	52,000	(2,000)
Variable overhead	30,000	37,500	37,000	500
	80,000	87,500	89,000	(1,500)

The actual expenditure exceeds the adjusted budget by £1,500 which represents an adverse budget or spending variance.

Volume variance

The other factor apart from the cost of the overheads which was budgeted in developing the predetermined standard was the number of machine hours. In the example we estimated that 20,000 machine hours would be worked whereas 25,000 were actually worked. This difference would not matter if all the overheads were variable since the rate per hour would be constant at different activities. Where fixed costs are concerned, however, increasing the activity will increase the amount recovered above the level required, and if activity is below budget insufficient overhead will be recovered.

In the example the rate is split:

$$\text{Fixed} \quad \frac{50{,}000}{20{,}000} = \quad £2.50$$

$$\text{Variable} \quad \frac{30{,}000}{20{,}000} = \quad £1.50$$

$$\underline{£4.00}$$

When the machine hours increase from 20,000 to 25,000 we recover 5,000 × £2.50 = £12,500 more than required.

An alternative way of viewing this is to compare the amount of overheads recovered at 25,000 hours with the flexible budget for this level of activity:

Recovered 25,000 × £4 =		100,000
Budget variable cost 25,000 × £1.50	37,500	
Fixed cost	50,000	87,500
Volume variance		12,500

This variance shows that by increasing the utilisation of the fixed resources in a business considerable savings are made. The £12,500 is a favourable variance in terms of the original standard.

Summary of variances

The analysis so far shows:

	£
Standard overhead recovered at actual level of activity (25,000 × £4)	100,000
Budget or spending variance – adverse	1,500
	101,500
Volume variance – favourable	12,500
Actual level of manufacturing overheads	89,000

26.4 Assessing Variances

In standard costing in an organisation where products are being manufactured it is common for the cost of the overheads to be related to the product. If in the example a Superwidget is manufactured in Department A which it is estimated requires 2 machine hours per widget then the standard cost of overhead per Superwidget will be 2 × £4 = £8.

If in the actual period a Superwidget takes less than two hours to make there will be a favourable variance which will be costed at £4 per hour. Similarly if more than two hours are taken there will be an unfavourable variance.

Using the example and assuming Department A exclusively manufactures Superwidgets, the original budget is to make 10,000 Superwidgets and the actual production of Superwidgets is 12,000.

	Department A	
	Original budget	Actual
	£	£
Total overhead	80,000	89,000
Machine hours	20,000	25,000
Hours per superwidget	2	
Number of units	10,000	12,000

To produce 12,000 widgets should take 24,000 hours at the standard rate. Since the actual hours are 25,000 there is an adverse variance of 1,000 hours which costs £4 per hour (note this is both fixed and variable overhead in effect as it is money wasted through operating at below expected efficiency). Relating this adverse £4,000 variance to the other overhead variances we get:

	£
Standard cost of overheads for 12,000 actual Superwidgets produced × £8 =	96,000
Efficiency variance – adverse	4,000
Standard overhead recovered at actual level of activity	100,000
Budget variance – adverse	1,500
	101,500
Volume variance – favourable	12,500
Actual level of manufacturing overhead	89,000

26.5 Formulas for Variances

The formula for each overhead variance is as follows:

Budget or spending variance = Budgeted fixed overheads – Actual fixed overheads

= BFO – AFO

Volume variance = (Actual production – Budgeted production) × Standard fixed overhead rate

= (AP – BP) × SR

Efficiency variance = (Standard hours of output – Actual hours) × Standard variable overhead rate

= (SH – AH) × SR

26.7 A Comprehensive Example

The data set out below refers to a cost centre for a particular period:

Budget

Variable overheads (extract)

	Output		Cost
In units	In standard hours		£
9,800	49,000		98,000
9,900	49,500		99,000
10,000	50,000		100,000
10,100	50,500		101,000
10,200	51,000		102,000
Fixed overheads			150,000

Budgeted volume of production 10,000 units

Standard Labour Hours/Unit = 5

Actual

Variable overhead	£104,000	
Fixed overhead	£160,000	
Direct labour hours worked	49,000	hours
Units of production	9,900	units

9,900 units of production is the equivalent of 9,900 × 5 = 49,500 standard direct labour hours.

Before making the variance calculations it will be helpful to make some observations on the data given. The flexible budget shows that each unit of production has a standard variable overhead cost of £10. Alternatively, this can be expressed as £10 ÷ 5 = £2 per standard hour of labour. It should not be assumed that this rate of £2 would also apply to levels of production outside the range shown. These may well be step costs, such as additional supervision, which would alter the standard variable overhead rate at higher levels of output.

The fixed costs are thought likely to remain fixed provided the range of output does not extend too far above or below the budgeted volume of production. The fixed standard rate is £150,000 ÷ 50,000 = £3 per standard hour of labour, or £150,000 ÷ 10,000 = £15 per unit.

The standard unit cost for overhead is thus £10 + £15 = £25 per unit and £2 + £3 = £5 per labour hour.

This budgeted volume of production is likely to be the level of output thought of as being normal and acceptable in the long run. It is frequently referred to as the normal volume of production.

Calculation of variances

Firstly it is helpful to calculate the net variance which is to be analysed. This is developed from the standard cost of the actual units produced:

Standard cost of actual production 9,900 × £25 =		£247,500
Actual overhead costs total		£264,000
Total variance –	Adverse	16,500

This is broken down into efficiency, budget and volume variances as follows.

Efficiency variance

Actual units produced 9,900 × 5 hours =	49,500	(standard labour hours)	
Actual labour hours	49,000		
Labour hours saved	500		
Efficiency variance at the overhead rate per labour hour £5		Favourable	2,500

Budget variance

Budgeted overheads at actual labour hours			
worked of 49,000 – Variable	98,000		
Fixed	150,000		248,000
Actual overheads			264,000
Budget variance –		Adverse	16,000

Volume variance

Budgeted recovery of fixed overheads at standard activity 50,000 hrs × £3		150,000
Actual recovery of fixed overheads at actual activity 49,000 hrs × £3		147,000
Volume variance –	Adverse	3,000

Summary of variances

Efficiency	Favourable	2,500
Budget	Adverse	16,000
Volume	Adverse	3,000
	Net Adverse	16,500

Reconciliation of standard and actual cost

Standard cost of actual production 9,900 units × £25	247,500
Efficiency variance – favourable	2,500
Budgeted level of overhead cost on actual labour hours at standard 49,000 × £5	245,000
Budget variance – adverse	16,000
	261,000
Volume variance – adverse	3,000
Actual cost of overheads	264,000

26.6 Variances and Management Action

The calculation of variances and their explanation to managers is of no value unless the information so revealed is put to use in making decisions which change subsequent activities. The question then arises as to whether every variance needs some form of action. It is not possible to be dogmatic here, it really does depend on circumstances. In some cases, a fairly large variance may be fairly insignificant, whereas in others even a small amount may call for urgent action.

There is no doubt that variance calculations of the right type, transmitted to the right people at the right time, and which have an effect upon subsequent operations, can be of immense use. On the other hand, much of the effort put into variance calculation in many firms just goes to waste, as managers do not act on the information. This is very often because a poor 'selling' job has been done by the accounting staff to the managers concerned, in that they have not either been able to convince the managers that variance analysis is worth while, or possibly that the information provided is not really what the managers require to enable them to tackle their jobs properly.

26.8 Sales Variances

The analysis of the difference between budgeted sales levels and actual levels can have an important bearing on the understanding of results. The main factors which are important in analysing sales are:

(a) selling price variances
(b) volume variances
(c) mix variances.

The selling price variance measures the overall profit difference caused by budgeted unit selling price and actual unit selling price being different. If the budget was to sell 100 widgets at £5 each and the actual sales were 100 widgets of £4.50 each, there will be a profit reduction of £50 due to the adverse selling price variance of 50p per unit on the 100 units sold.

The volume variances in sales will be measured in terms of the difference in the total quantity being sold between budget and actual. The impact of changes in volume of sales on profit can only be measured if we know the profitability of the sales. This will be dealt with at gross profit level. Thus if the budget is to sell 100 widgets with a unit gross margin of £2 and the actual sales achieved are only 90 widgets then there is an adverse variance of 10 units at the margin of £2 which represents a loss of profit of £20. If several products are being sold the variance will be worked on total units actually sold in the proportion originally budgeted.

Exhibit 26.4

Product	Budget sales units	%	Budget gross margin £	Total budget margin £	Actual sales units	Actual sales in budget %
X	200	33.3	1.00	200	250	240
Y	200	33.3	1.50	300	190	240
Z	200	33.3	3.50	700	280	240
	600	100.0		1,200	720	720

The volume variance is calculated by company actual sales in budget percentage mix with the original budget at budget margins:

Product	Budget sales units	Actual sales in budget % units	Variance units	Budget margin £	Volume variances £
X	200	240	40	1.00	40.00
Y	200	240	40	1.50	60.00
Z	200	240	40	3.50	140.00
	600	720	120		240.00

The mix variance arises where more than one product is being sold and the different products have differing profit margins. If the proportions in which the actual sales of the products varies from budget then the overall profit will vary as a consequence.

In the example on volume variance the original budget was compared with actual sales split in the budget mix. For the mix variance these figures of actual sales in budget mix are compared with the actual sales and the differences evaluated at the budgeted gross profit margin.

Product	Actual sales in budget % units	Actual sales units	Variance units	Budget gross margin £	Mix variance £
X	240	250	+10	1.00	+10
Y	240	190	−50	1.50	− 75
Z	240	280	+40	3.50	+140
	720	720	−		+ 75

The difference in mix between budget and actual has increased profit by £75 due to the influence of more sales of product Z, i.e. there is a favourable mix variance of £75.

Exhibit 26.5

Product	%	Units	Budget Unit selling price £	Budget Unit gross profit £	Budget Total profit £	Units	Actual Unit selling price £	Actual Unit gross profit £	Actual Total profit £
A	16.7	100	20	5	500	90	21	6	540
B	33.3	200	25	10	2,000	220	24	9	1,980
C	50	300	10	2	600	350	10	2	700
	100	600			3,100	660			3,220

Total variance =		
Actual profit	3,220
Budget profit	3,100
Favourable variance	120

Firstly eliminate the price variance using the actual units sold as the basis.

	Actual units sold	Budget price	Actual price	Unit variance	Total price variance
	1	2	3	3 − 2 = 4	1 × 4 = 5
		£	£	£	£
A	90	20	21	+1	+90
B	220	25	24	−1	−220
C	350	10	10	−	−
	Adverse price variance				−130

Secondly eliminate the volume variance using the unit budgeted gross profit to evaluate the variance.

	Actual units sold	Actual units in budget %	Budget units sold	Variance in units	Budget unit gross profit	Total value variance
	1	2	3	2 − 3 = 4	5	4 × 5 = 6
					£	£
A	90	110	100	+ 10	5	+ 50
B	220	220	200	+ 20	10	+ 200
C	350	330	300	+ 30	2	+ 60
	660	660	600	+ 60		
			Favourable volume variance			+ 310

Finally eliminate the mix variance. This is done by comparing the actual total units sold in the mix as originally budgeted with the actual sales.

	Budget %	Actual total sales split in budget %	Actual sales units	Difference units	Budget unit gross profit	Mix variance
	1	2	3	3 − 2 = 4	5	4 × 5 = 6
A	16.7	110	90	− 20	5	−100
B	33.3	220	220	−	10	−
C	50.0	330	350	+ 20	2	+ 40
		660	660			
		Adverse mix variance				− 60

Summary of variance:

Adverse price variance	− 130
Favourable volume variance	+ 310
Adverse mix variance	− 60
Favourable total sales variance	+ 120

The gross profit margin may change for reasons other than changes in sales – for example, if the cost of materials varies from budgets or wage rates change. This type of variance has, however, already been dealt with under material and labour variances.

REVIEW QUESTIONS

Advice:

Remember that the overhead variances consist of the difference between the standard costs at the actual level of activity and the actual costs. Remember also that sales variances consist of those for price, volume and mix.

It is important that you answer the parts of the questions that ask you to comment on exactly what might be behind the variances and what action is needed.

26.1 Calculate the overhead variances from the following data:

(a) Budgeted for £6,000 variable overhead and 1,000 machine hours.

Actual overhead	£5,840
Actual machine hours	1,000

(b) Budgeted for £20,000 variable overhead and 5,000 machine hours.

Actual overhead	£21,230
Actual machine hours	5,000

(c) Budgeted for £12,000 fixed overhead and the actual overhead is found to be £11,770.

(d) Budgeted for £40,000 fixed overhead and the actual overhead is found to be £41,390.

(e) Budgeted production of 2,000 units in 8,000 hours. Standard variable overhead rate is £3 per hour. In fact 2,000 units are produced in 7,940 hours.

(f) Budgeted production of 5,000 units in 15,000 hours. Standard variable overhead rate is £4 per hour. In fact 4,860 units are produced in 15,000 hours.

26.2X Calculate the overhead variances in the following cases:

(a) Budgeted for £37,000 fixed overhead. The actual fixed overhead turns out to be £36,420.

(b) Budgeted for production of 500 units in 250 hours. The variable overhead rate is £6 per hour. In fact 500 units are produced in 242 hours.

(c) Budgeted for £18,000 variable overhead and 9,000 machine hours. Actual overhead is £18,000 and actual machine hours 8,820.

(d) Budgeted for £9,000 variable overhead and 3,000 machine hours. Actual overhead is £8,790 and actual machine hours 3,000.

(e) Budgeted for £120,000 fixed overhead. The actual fixed overhead turns out to be £129,470.

(f) Budgeted for production of 10,000 units in 30,000 hours. Standard variable overhead rate is £8 an hour. In fact 9,880 units are produced in 30,000 hours.

26.3 You are required to calculate the overhead variances of Joseph Ltd. The budget is prepared as:

(a) Total budgeted variable overhead £400,000.

(b) Total budgeted fixed overhead £160,000.

(c) Budgeted volume of production 80,000 direct labour hours for 40,000 units.

The actual results turn out to be:

(d) Actual variable overhead £403,600.

(e) Actual fixed overhead £157,200.

(f) Actual volume 78,500 direct labour hours which resulted in 42,000 units of production.

26.4X You are required to calculate the overhead variances of Raymond Ltd. The budget is prepared as:

(a) Total budgeted variable overhead £100,000.

(b) Total budgeted fixed overhead £125,000.

(c) Budgeted volume of production 50,000 direct labour hours of 250,000 units.

The actual results turn out to be:

(d) Actual variable overhead £96,500.

(e) Actual fixed overhead £129,400.

(f) Actual volume 52,000 direct labour hours which resulted in 244,000 units.

26.5 The Grange Company had the following results for the year to 31 March 19X1. A single product – a toggle – was made by the company.

	Budget	Actual
Sales in units	125,000	150,000
Sales in £	312,500	356,250

The standard cost of manufacturing each unit was £1.50.

What are the price and volume variances on sales in 19X1?

26.6X Corporec PLC manufactures a detergent in one of its plants. The information for the year to 30 September 19X2 was as follows:

	Budget	Actual
Sales in litres	180,000	170,000
Sales in £	540,000	527,000

The standard cost of manufacturing a litre was £2.

Calculate the price and volume variances for 19X2.

26.7 The following data was collected for Molton Ltd for the year ended 31 March 19X3.

Product	Budget Selling price	Budget sales units	%	Budget gross profit per unit	Budget gross profit total	Actual selling price	Actual sales units	%	Actual gross profit per unit	Actual gross profit total
	£			£	£	£			£	£
M	5	800	25	1.00	800	5.10	840	30	0.90	756
N	8	1,600	50	1.50	2,400	7.90	1,680	60	1.40	2,352
P	7	800	25	1.20	960	7.30	280	10	1.20	336
		3,200	100		4,160		2,800	100		3,444

Calculate price, volume and mix variances for 19X3.

26.8X The following information relates to Burton Company for the year to 30 June 19X6.

Product	Budget Units	Sales %	Budget selling price unit	Budget gross profit per unit	Actual units	Sales %	Actual unit selling price	Actual unit gross profit
			£	£			£	£
A	400	14.3	30	5	500	20.8	29	4
B	600	21.4	25	4	400	16.7	27	5
C	1,800	64.3	40	10	1,500	62.5	39	9
	2,800	100.0			2,400	100.0		

Calculate price, volume and mix variances for 19X6.

26.9 Singleton has been operating for some years as a manufacturer of a single product, and after several years' growth has decided to form a company, Singleton Ltd.

His accountant advised him that in an increasingly competitive world he really should achieve greater financial control of his business, and to assist Singleton in this objective the accountant prepared a simple manufacturing budget for the financial year ending 31 August 19X9.

The following schedule provides the detail of the budget and the actual results for the year ended 31 August 19X9. The actual results have been extracted from the ledger as at that date without any adjustments made.

	Budget £	Actual £
Raw materials consumed	80,000	90,000
Factory rent	10,000	12,500
Factory maintenance expenses	6,700	6,100
Heating and lighting	2,900	3,000
Direct labour wages	120,000	110,500
Direct expenses	5,800	6,000
Depreciation of plant and machinery	8,900	10,500
Wages, maintenance labour	18,000	24,000
Other factory overheads	12,700	9,600

Additional information

1   At 31 August 19X9 the following amounts were still owing:

	£
Direct labour wages	5,100
Heating and lighting	900
Other factory overhead	400

2   The factory rent paid covered the period from 1 September 19X8 to 30 November 19X9.
3   During the year the firm sold 90,000 units of its product at £4.50 a unit.

4   There was no work-in-progress. The stocks of finished goods were:

	£
1 September 19X8	28,900
31 August 19X9	35,000

Required:

(a) What is variance analysis and how can it contribute to the operating efficiency of Singleton's business?   *(4 marks)*

(b) For the year ended 31 August 19X9 prepare:
   (i) A manufacturing account and a schedule of the relevant variances;
   (ii) A trading account.   *(13 marks)*

(c) Write a report to advise Singleton whether the principles of budgeting can be applied to:
   (i) Non-manufacturing costs;
   (ii) The control of cash resources.

Your report should indicate in each case the potential benefits that the firm could achieve through extending its use of budgeting.   *(8 marks)*

(Associated Examining Board: GCE A-Level)

26.10X Flint Palatignium Ltd calculates the prices of its output by adding a mark-up of 15 per cent to standard costs. These standard costs are arrived at by reference to budgeted outputs and estimated direct costs as follows:

	£ each	Standard price/rate
Materials	5.00	£1.00 per unit
Direct labour	2.50	£1.25 per hour
Overheads	7.50	£3.75 per direct labour hour
	15.00	
Mark-up	2.25	
Selling price	17.25	

Management accounts for April 19X8 provide an analysis of operations as follows:

	£
Sales – at standard price	534,750
Standard margin on sales	69,750
Favourable sales price variance	8,691
	78,441
Other favourable variances:	
Material price	4,662
Labour rate	600
Overhead expenditure	147
	83,850
Adverse variances:	
Material usage	1,743
Labour efficiency	292
Overhead capacity	9
Actual operating profit	81,806

Materials in stock are valued at standard cost. At 1 April, 1,000 units of material were held, whereas at 30 April the stock of this material increased to 1.750 units.

Required:

(i) A trading account for the month of April, 19X8 comparing the budgeted income and expenditure appropriate to actual output, to actual income and expenditure. *(10 marks)*

(ii) An explanation of the value of standard costing and variance analysis to a service business whose custom is to negotiate fixed price contracts. *(8 marks)*

(Welsh Joint Education Committee: GCE A-Level)

26.11X *(Note: this question covers material from both Chapters 25 and 26.)* HGW Limited produces a product called a Lexton. The standard selling price and the manufacturing costs of this product are as follows:

		£
Standard selling price per unit		86

Standard production costs:

Direct material	1.5 kilos at £12 per kilo	18
Direct labour	4.4 hours at £7.50 per hour	33
Variable overheads	4.4 hours at £5 per hour	22
		73

The projected production and sales for March 19X4 were 520 units.
On 1 April 19X4 the following actual figures were determined.

Sales	550 units at £85 each
Production	550 units
Direct material	785 kilos at £12.40 per kilo
Direct labour	2,400 hours at £7.80 per hour
Overheads	£12,500 (overall variance £400 adverse)

There was no opening stock of the product Lexton.

Required:

(a) Prepare an actual profit and loss statement for HGW Ltd for March 19X4. *(8 marks)*

(b) Calculate the following variances and their respective sub-variances:
   (i) sales — price and volume *(6 marks)*
   (ii) direct material — price and usage *(6 marks)*
   (iii) direct labour — rate and efficiency. *(6 marks)*

(c) Prepare a statement reconciling the actual profit calculated in part (a) with the budgeted profit on actual sales. (Use the variances calculated in part (b) and the given overhead variance.) *(10 marks)*

(d) Write a report to the management outlining the factors that need to be considered when standards are being established. *(9 marks)*

(Associated Examining Board: GCE A-Level)

Chapter 27

Break-even Analysis

27.1 Introduction

The level of activity achieved by a firm is of paramount importance in determining whether the firm is making a profit or loss, and the size of such profits or losses. Let us take an example to which the answer is obvious. If a firm has fixed costs of £10,000 and its total revenue is £8,000, then, no matter how much the variable costs are, the firm is bound to make a loss. A firm has to cover both its fixed costs plus its variable costs before it can make a profit. With very low revenue, as in the case already stated, a loss would be bound to be incurred.

There is, therefore, a great deal of interest in exactly how much revenue (i.e. sales) has to be earned before a profit can be made. If revenue is below fixed costs then a loss will be incurred: if revenue is below fixed costs + variable costs then a loss will still be incurred. Where revenue is greater than fixed costs plus variable costs then a profit will have been made. The question then arises – at what point does the firm stop incurring a loss and with the next unit of revenue make a profit, i.e. at what point does the firm break even or make neither a profit nor a loss?

Fixed costs stay unchanged over stated ranges in the volume of production, but variable costs are those that change with volumes in production. As revenue increases so do variable costs, so that the only item that remains unchanged is that of fixed costs. Let us look at an example of a firm showing the changing costs and revenue over differing volumes of production.

Apollo Ltd has fixed costs of £5,000. The variable costs are £2 per unit. The revenue (selling price) is £3 per unit. Looking at production in stages of 1,000 units, we can see that the figures emerge as in Exhibit 27.1.

Exhibit 27.1

No. of units	Fixed cost	Variable cost	Total cost: Variable + Fixed	Revenue (Sales)	Profit	Loss
	£	£	£	£	£	£
0	5,000	Nil	5,000	Nil		5,000
1,000	5,000	2,000	7,000	3,000		4,000
2,000	5,000	4,000	9,000	6,000		3,000
3,000	5,000	6,000	11,000	9,000		2,000
4,000	5,000	8,000	13,000	12,000		1,000
5,000	5,000	10,000	15,000	15,000	Nil	Nil
6,000	5,000	12,000	17,000	18,000	1,000	
7,000	5,000	14,000	19,000	21,000	2,000	
8,000	5,000	16,000	21,000	24,000	3,000	
9,000	5,000	18,000	23,000	27,000	4,000	

With activity of 5,000 units the firm will break even, it will make neither a profit nor a loss. Above that the firm moves into profit, below that the firm would never make a profit.

We could have calculated the break-even point without drawing up a schedule of costs, etc. as in Exhibit 27.1. Instead we could have said that for one unit the revenue is £3 and the variable cost is £2, so that the remaining £1 is the amount out of which the fixed costs have to come, and anything left over would be profit. The £1 is thus the 'contribution' towards fixed costs and profit. Now if the contribution was only just enough to cover fixed costs then there would be no profit, but neither would there be any loss. There are £5,000 fixed costs, so that with a contribution of £1 per unit there would have to be 5,000 units to provide a contribution of £5,000 to cover fixed costs. It could be stated as:

$$\text{Break-even point} = \frac{\text{Fixed costs}}{\text{Selling price per unit} - \text{Variable costs per unit}}$$

i.e. in the case of Apollo Ltd $\dfrac{£5,000}{£3 - £2} = \dfrac{5,000}{1} = 5,000 \text{ units}$

27.2 The Break-Even Chart

The information given in Exhibit 27.1 can also be shown in the form of a chart. Many people seem to grasp the idea of break-even analysis rather more easily when they see it in chart form. This is particularly true of people who are not used to dealing with accounting information. We will, therefore, plot the figures from Exhibit 27.1 on a chart which is shown as Exhibit 27.2.

The use of the chart can now be looked at. It would be extremely useful if you could draw the chart as shown in Exhibit 27.2 on a piece of graph paper. The larger the scale that you use the easier it will be to take accurate readings. Plot the lines from the figures as shown in Exhibit 27.1.

Exhibit 27.2

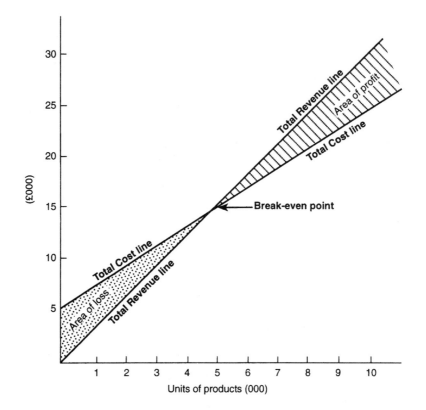

To find the break-even point in terms of units of product, draw a line straight down from the break-even point so that it meets the base line at right angles. This is shown in Exhibit 27.3 as line A, which when read off on the base line gives units of products and sales as 5,000 units. Now draw a line direct to the vertical £s line so that it meets that at a right angle. This is line B and shows £15,000. This means that according to the chart the break-even point is shown at 5,000 units where both costs and revenue are equal at £15,000. This is naturally the same answer as given by ordinary means in Exhibit 27.1.

As production and sales go above 5,000 units, the firm makes profits. When production and sales are above 5,000 units, the difference represents the 'safety margin', as this is the number of units in excess of the break-even point, below which the firm would incur losses.

Look at the chart again, and without consulting the book attempt to answer the following; answer by taking readings off your chart:

(i) What would the total costs of the firm be at (a) 2,000 units, (b) 7,000 units, (c) 8,500 units?

(Remember: take a line up from the product line for the figure needed, then from where the cost line is bisected draw a line to the £s line to meet it at right angles.)

(ii) What is the revenue for (a) 3,000 units, (b) 6,000 units, (c) 7,500 units?

Exhibit 27.3

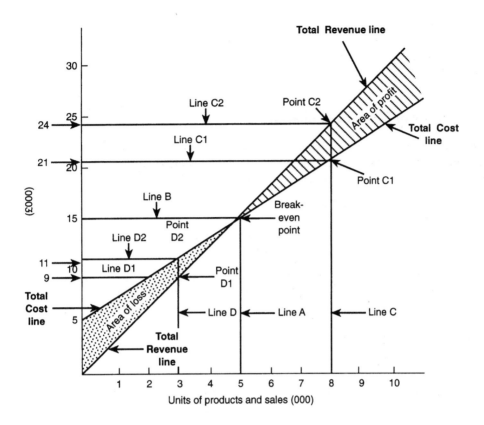

Before proceeding further now look at the answers which are shown at the end of this section.

Now we will try to find the amount of profit or loss at various levels by looking at the chart in Exhibit 27.3. First let us calculate the profit made if 8,000 units are going to be made and sold. Draw a line up from the product line at right angles (shown as line C) until it bisects both the Total Cost line and the Total Revenue line, the points of intersection being shown as C1 for the Total Cost line and C2 for the Total Revenue line. Read off the amounts in £s by taking lines across to the £s vertical line until they meet it at right angles. These are shown as lines C1 and C2. The line from C1 will give a reading of £21,000 and from C2 of £24,000. As the Total Revenue exceeds the Total Costs there is a profit, and in this case the profit is £3,000.

If we now try for 3,000 units, the line drawn up from the product line will meet the Total Revenue line at point D1 and the Total Cost line at D2. Reading off to the £s line D1 shows as £9,000 whilst D2 shows as £11,000. In this case the Total Cost exceeds the Total Revenue by £2,000 and there is, therefore, a loss of £2,000.

Before you proceed further, attempt to find from your own chart the profit or loss recorded at (i) 1,000 units, (ii) 4,000 units, (iii) 6,500 units and (iv) 8,500 units.

The answers can now be checked.

Answers
(i) (a) £9,000 (b) £19,000 (c) £22,000
(ii) (a) £9,000 (b) £18,000 (c) £22,500
(i) Loss £4,000 (ii) Loss £1,000
(iii) Profit £1,500 (iv) Profit £3,500

27.3 Changes and Break-Even Charts

The effect of changes on profits can easily be shown by drawing fresh lines on the chart to show the changes, or intended changes, in the circumstances of the firm. Let us first of all consider what factors can bring about a change in the profits of a firm. These are:

(a) The selling price per unit could be increased (or decreased).
(b) A possible decrease (or increase) in fixed costs.
(c) A possible decrease (or increase) in variable costs per unit.
(d) Increase the volume of production and sales.

We will investigate these by starting with the same basic information for a firm and then seeing what would happen if each of the changes (a) to (d) were to happen.
   The basic information, before suggested changes, is shown in Exhibit 27.4.

Exhibit 27.4

No. of units	Fixed cost	Variable cost	Total costs: Variable + Fixed	Revenue (Sales)	Profit	Loss
	£	£	£	£	£	£
100	2,000	400	2,400	900		1,500
200	2,000	800	2,800	1,800		1,000
300	2,000	1,200	3,200	2,700		500
400	2,000	1,600	3,600	3,600	Nil	Nil
500	2,000	2,000	4,000	4,500	500	
600	2,000	2,400	4,400	5,400	1,000	
700	2,000	2,800	4,800	6,300	1,500	
800	2,000	3,200	5,200	7,200	2,000	
900	2,000	3,600	5,600	8,100	2,500	

The above table shows that variable costs are £4 per unit and selling price £9 per unit. We can draw a chart to incorporate this information before considering the changes being contemplated. This is shown in Exhibit 27.5.

Exhibit 27.5

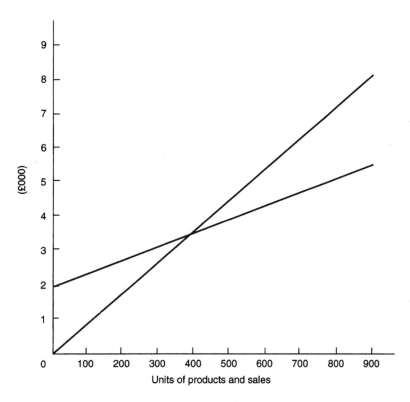

(a) Increase selling price

Taking a copy of the old chart as a base, we can now draw an extra line on it to represent an increase in selling price. Let us suppose that the selling price could be increased by £2 per unit. This can now be shown on a break-even chart, see Exhibit 27.6. The line shown as 'New Total Revenue' could then be added. This would mean that the break-even point would change as the increased revenue would mean that costs were covered sooner. The dotted area shows the reduction in the loss area that would be incurred at the same volume of sales, whilst the shaded area shows the increase in profit at the various volumes of sales.

Exhibit 27.6

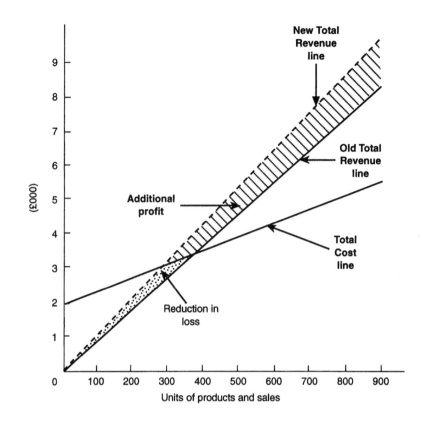

(b) Reduce fixed costs

Again taking a copy of the old chart we can now draw extra lines etc. on it (*see* Exhibit 27.7). The reduction of £800 in fixed costs results in a new line being drawn for New Total Costs. The reduction in loss if sales were at a low volume is represented by the dotted area whilst the shaded area shows the additional profit at various volumes of activity. The change in profit or loss will be constant at £800 over these volumes.

Exhibit 27.7

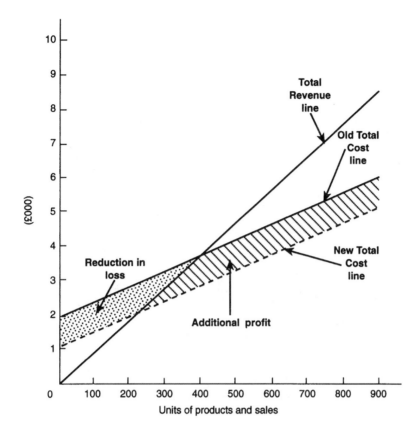

(c) Reduce variable costs

Exhibit 27.8 shows the position when variable costs per unit are reduced, the particular example being a reduction of £2 per unit. The dotted area shows the reduction in loss compared with the position if the costs had not changed, whilst the shaded area shows the additional profit at different levels of activity. A reduction in fixed costs in Exhibit 27.7 showed a constant difference of £800 compared with previously over the whole range of activity, whereas a reduction in variable costs as in Exhibit 27.8 brings about different increases of profit, or reduction of loss, over the whole range of activity. The greater the activity the greater the gain with variable cost savings, whereas the gain remains constant with fixed cost savings.

Exhibit 27.8

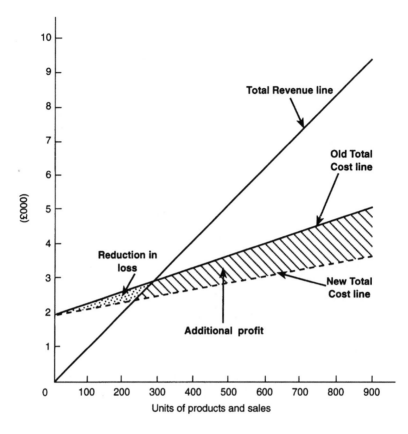

(d) Increased production and sales

In this case it is merely a matter of extending the lines for Total Revenue and of Total Costs. Exhibit 27.9 shows this for an increase of 300 units. The new profit indicated will be greater than the old profit because all extra units are being sold at a profit.

Exhibit 27.9

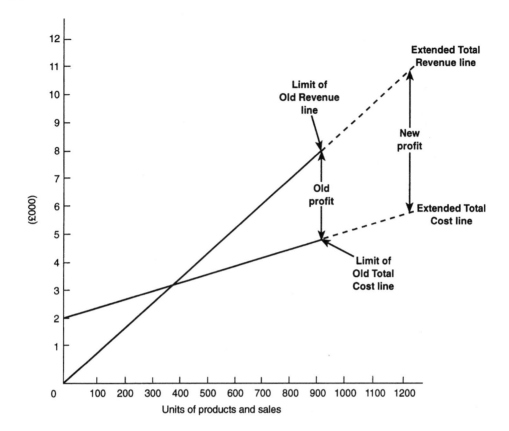

27.4 The Limitations of Break-Even Charts

In each of the cases looked at it has been assumed that only one of the factors of variable cost, fixed cost, selling price, or volume of sales has in fact altered. Usually this is not the case. An increase in price may well reduce the number sold. There may well be an increase in fixed cost which has an effect which brings down variable costs. The changes in the various factors should, therefore, be studied simultaneously rather than separately.

In addition, where there is more than one product, the proportions in which the products are sold, i.e. the product mix, can have a very important bearing on costs. Suppose that there are two products, one has a large amount of fixed costs but hardly any variable costs, and the other has a large amount of variable costs but little fixed costs. Therefore if the proportions in which each are sold change very much this could mean that the costs and profit could vary tremendously, even though the total figures of sales stayed constant. An illustration of this can be seen in Exhibit 27.10.

Exhibit 27.10

In considering the break-even analysis we may expect that the following will occur:

Fixed costs £1,000, Variable costs: Product A £5 per unit, B £20 per unit.

Selling prices: A £10 per unit, B £30 per unit.

Expected sales: A 150, B 50. Actual sales: A 30, B90.

The expected sales are A 150 × £10 + B 50 × £30 = £3,000.

The actual sales are A 30 × £10 + B 90 × £30 = £3,000.

The actual and expected sales are the same, but the costs and profit are quite different.

Expected:		Sales		£ 3,000
Less Variable costs:	A 150 × £5 =	750		
	B 50 × £20 =	1,000	1,750	
	Contribution		1,250	
	Less Fixed costs		1,000	
	Net profit		£250	

Actual:		Sales		£ 3,000
Less Variable costs:	A 30 × £5 =	150		
	B 90 × £20 =	1,800	1,950	
	Contribution		1,050	
	Less Fixed costs		1,000	
	Net profit		£50	

Variable costs are usually taken to be in direct proportion to volume, so that 1,000 units means (say) £5,000 variable costs and therefore 2,000 units would mean £10,000 variable costs, 3,000 units equal £15,000 variable costs and so on. This is often a reasonable estimation of the situation, but may well hold true only within fairly tight limits. For instance 3,100 units could mean £16,000 costs instead of the £15,500 that it would be if a linear relationship existed. This is also true of sales, because to increase sales beyond certain points some units may be sold cheaply. Thus 1,000 units might be sold for £9,000; 2,000 units sold for £18,000; but to sell 2,200 units the revenue might be only £19,100 instead of the £19,800 (2,200 × £9) that might be expected if a linear relationship existed over all ranges.

It is assumed that everything produced is sold, and that stocks-in-trade remain constant. It would be difficult to do otherwise as both sales revenue and costs relate to one and the same measure of volume.

27.5 Contribution Graph

This is an alternative method of presentation. It highlights the fact that the total contribution is emphasised in the graph. Exhibit 27.5 is now redrafted as a contribution graph in Exhibit 27.11.

Exhibit 27.11

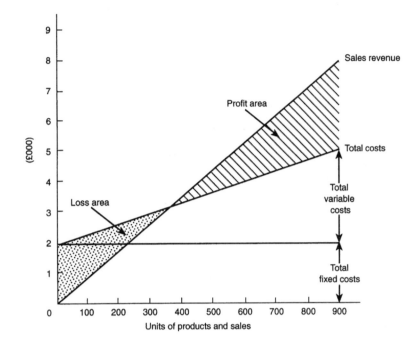

REVIEW QUESTIONS

Advice:

The very important concept of 'break-even' attracts quite a large number of questions. Be careful when drawing any charts, as a faulty chart will give you wrong answers for every part of your answer. You cannot expect examiners to assume that your faulty drawing of a graph was a simple error of draughtsmanship instead of being conceptual. They will not give you the marks.

27.1 Hedges Ltd has fixed costs of £8,000. The variable costs are £4 per unit. The revenue (selling price) is £6 per unit. You are required (i) to draft a schedule as follows filling in the columns (a) to (f) for each stage of 1,000 units up to 10,000 units.

No. of units	(a) Fixed cost £	(b) Variable cost £	(c) Total cost £	(d) Revenue £	(e) Profit £	(f) Loss £
0						
1,000						
2,000						
3,000						
4,000						
5,000						
6,000						
7,000						
8,000						
9,000						
10,000						

(ii) You are also required to draw a break-even chart from the data in this schedule. Draw it carefully to scale on a piece of graph paper. Retain your answer, you will need it for some questions which follow later.

27.2 Cover up the schedule you constructed as your answer to 27.1(i) and look instead at the break-even chart constructed as the answer to 27.1(ii). Answer the following:

(a) What are the total costs at production levels of (i) 4,000 units, (ii) 7,000 units, (iii) 9,000 units, (iv) 5,500 units?

(b) What is the total revenue at (i) 3,000 units, (ii) 8,000 units, (iii) 5,500 units?

27.3X Look at your schedule in answer to 27.1(i) and answer the following:

(a) What are the total costs at production levels of (i) 4,000 units, (ii) 7,000 units, (iii) 9,000 units, (iv) 5,500 units? You will have to deduce this amount as it is not shown as a figure on the schedule.

(b) What is the total revenue at (i) 3,000 units, (ii) 8,000 units, (iii) 5,500 units?

27.4 From your break-even chart for 27.1(ii) calculate the profit or loss that will be made at levels of (i) 3,000 units, (ii) 10,000 units, (iii) 4,000 units, (iv) 7,000 units, (v) 8,500 units.

27.5X From the schedule in 27.1(i) calculate the profit or loss that would be made at levels of (i) 3,000 units, (ii) 10,000 units, (iii) 4,000 units, (iv) 7,000 units, (v) 8,500 units (this last figure will have to be deduced as it is not a figure on the schedule).

27.6 Polemic Ltd manufacture and sell a single product. The following information is available for three financial years ending 30 September.

	Price per unit £	Unit volume 000s
Sales		
Actual 19X1	130	50
Forecast 19X2	129	52
Forecast 19X3	128.5	53

Costs per unit produced	Actual 19X1 £	Forecast 19X2 £	Forecast 19X3 £
Direct materials	50	55	55
Direct labour	30	31.5	33
Variable production overhead	10	11	12
Direct expenses	5	5	6
Variable sales overhead	15	16	16

Other costs for the year	£ 000s	£ 000s	£ 000s
Fixed production overhead	50	55	55
Other fixed overhead	200	220	220

Additional information
1   When the management of Polemic prepared its direct labour forecast unit cost for 19X2 and 19X3, direct wages were increased only by the forecast rate of inflation.

2   The trade union representatives of the production workers wished to press for a greater wage increase. They suggested that:

   (i)   Direct wages be increased at twice the rate of inflation. The effect of this would be to increase direct labour costs per unit as follows:

	19X2 £	19X3 £
Direct labour	33	35

   (ii) Unit selling prices be increased in order to cover the increased labour costs.

3   It is to be assumed that all expense and revenue relationships will be unchanged except where indicated.

Required:

(a) A schedule for 19X1, 19X2 and 19X3 for Polemic Ltd showing:

   (i)   the break-even points;
   (ii) the net profit for each year.

   Base your calculations on the original labour costs.   *(8 marks)*

(b) A graph showing a break-even point for 19X2.   *(5 marks)*

(c) Advise Polemic Ltd's management as to their response to the trade union's claim for higher wages. Include relevant financial analysis.   *(7 marks)*

(d) Explain the limitation of break-even analysis   *(5 marks)*

(Associated Examining Board: GCE A-Level)

27.7X The relationship between income/cost/volume suggests that there are four ways by which profit can be increased. These are:

1   Increase unit selling price.
2   Decrease unit variable cost.
3   Decrease fixed costs.
4   Increase volume.

Assume that the current situation for a product is as follows:

Sales volume	1,000 units
Selling price	£2 each
Variable cost	£1 per unit
Fixed costs	£500

You are required to:

(a) draw **four** separate break-even charts showing the effect of the following changes on the current situation:

   (i)   a 10 per cent increase in volume,
   (ii) a 10 per cent increase in unit selling price,
   (iii) a 10 per cent decrease in unit variable cost,
   (iv) a 10 per cent reduction in fixed costs.   *(16 marks)*

(b) Use your charts to state the additional profit resulting from **each** change.   *(4 marks)*
                                                                                          (Total marks 20)

(Northern Examinations and Assessments Board: GCE A-Level)

27.8 At the monthly senior management meeting of Hampshire plc on 1 May 19X0, various suggestions were made to improve the profit to be made by selling the firm's single product in the last quarter of the year ending 30 September 19X0. The product is not subject to seasonal demand fluctuations, but there are several competitors producing similar items. In the first quarter of the year a suggestion was made that profit could be improved if the selling price were reduced by 5 per cent, and this was put into effect at the beginning of the second quarter. As the new price undercut that of the rival firms, demand increased, and the firm's break-even point was reduced.

The following suggestions have now been raised:

(i)   Differentiate the product from its rivals by giving it a more distinctive shape, colour and packaging. This would increase material costs per unit by £0.30, but selling price would not be raised. Demand is then predicted to rise by 10 per cent;

(ii) Improve the quality of the product by strengthening it and giving it a one-year guarantee – material costs would then increase by £0.15 per unit and labour costs by £0.30 per unit. Selling price would rise by £0.40 per unit, and demand increase by 7 per cent;

(iii) Further reduce the selling price by 10 per cent – demand to rise by 20 per cent;

(iv) Pay commission plus salaries instead of fixed salaries only to all sales staff. Variable selling costs would then rise by £0.20 per unit, but fixed costs would fall by £4,100 per quarter;

(v)   Subcontract the making of some components, and close the department responsible, making six staff redundant at an estimated cost to the firm of £12,000. 30,000 components are currently made per quarter. Each component's variable cost is £0.55. They can be bought from a recently established firm for £0.60 per unit. The department's share of the firm's fixed costs is 20 per cent and £2,500 fixed costs per quarter would cease to arise if the department were to be closed.

Data for:	First quarter	Second quarter
Number of units produced and sold	9,000	10,800
	£	£
Selling price per unit	14.00	13.30
Materials per unit	3.65	3.65
Labour per unit	2.10	2.10
Variable factory overhead per unit	1.40	1.40
Variable selling costs per unit	0.85	0.85
Fixed factory overhead	21,375	21,375
Fixed selling and administration costs	16,125	16,125

Required:

A   Calculate the profit made in each of the first and second quarters, showing clearly the contribution per unit in each case. *(4 marks)*

B   Draw one break-even chart showing the total costs and total revenues for the first and second quarters. You should label clearly the two break-even points and margins of safety. *(7 marks)*

C   Taking each suggestion independently, calculate the profit that might be made in the last quarter if each of them were to be implemented. *(9 marks)*

D   Discuss the implications for the firm of undertaking suggestions (i–iv), and for the firm and the local community of undertaking suggestion (v). *(8 marks)*

E   Explain to the senior managers how, while break-even analysis is useful, it has limitations.
(3 marks)
(Total marks 31)

(University of Oxford Delegacy of Local Examinations: GCE A-Level)

27.9X You are employed by Monarch Ltd which manufactures specialist hydraulic seals for the aircraft industry. The company has developed a new seal with the following budgeted data:

	£
Variable cost per unit	
Direct materials	8
Direct labour	4
Variable overheads	4
	16

The draft budget for the following year is as follows:

Production and sales	60,000 units

		£
Fixed cost:	Production	260,000
	Administration	90,000
	Selling, marketing and distribution	100,000
Contribution		840,000

Certain departmental managers within the company believe there is room for improvement on the budgeted figures, and the following options have been suggested.

(i) The sales manager has suggested that if the selling price was reduced by 10 per cent, then an extra 30 per cent units could be sold. The purchasing manager has indicated that if material requirements were increased in line, then a material price reduction of 6.25 per cent could be negotiated. With this additional output, fixed production costs would increase by £30,000, administration by £5,000 and selling, marketing and distribution by £10,000. Other costs would remain unchanged.

(ii) The export manager has suggested that if the company increased overseas marketing by £15,000 then exports would increase from 15,000 units to 17,000 units. With this suggestion, distribution costs would increase by £12,000, and all other costs would remain unchanged.

(iii) The marketing manager has suggested that if an extra £40,000 were spent on advertising, then sales quantity would increase by 25 per cent. The purchasing manager has indicated that in such circumstances, material costs would reduce by £0.30 per unit. With this suggestion fixed production costs would increase by £25,000, administration by £4,000 and other selling, marketing and distribution costs by £7,000. All other costs would remain unchanged.

(iv) The managing director believes the company should be aiming for a profit of £486,000. He asks what the selling price would be per unit if marketing were increased by £50,000, this leading to an estimated increase in sales quantity of 30 per cent? Other fixed costs would increase by £67,000, whilst material prices would decrease by 6.25 per cent per unit. All other costs would remain unchanged.

Required:

A Taking each suggestion independently, compile a profit statement for options (i) to (iii), showing clearly the contribution per unit in each case. For suggestion (iv), calculate the selling price per unit as requested by the managing director. *(13 marks)*

B Calculate the break-even quantity in units if the Managing Director's suggestion were implemented. Draw a contribution/sales graph to illustrate your calculations.
   Read from the graph the profit if 60,000 units were sold. *(6 marks)*

C Whilst marginal costing has a number of applications, it also has disadvantages. In a report to the managing director, outline the main applications of marginal costing and explain its disadvantages. *(12 marks)*
   (Total marks 31)

(University of Oxford Delegacy of Local Examinations: GCE A-Level)

27.10 Magwitch Limited's finance director produced the following forecast break-even chart for the year ending 31 May 19X1:

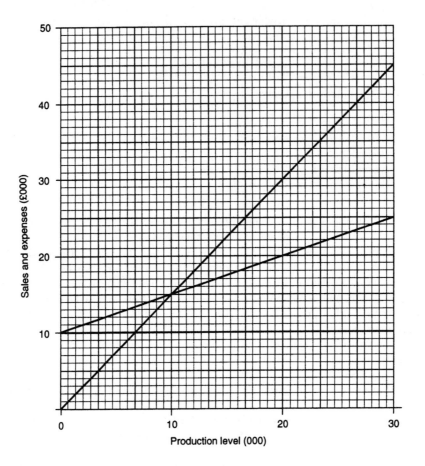

During the year the company produced and sold 20,000 units, and both revenue and expenses were 10 per cent higher than forecast.

Compeyson plc has made an agreed takeover bid for the company at a value of twelve times the net profit for the year ending 31 May 19X1.

Magwitch's assets and liabilities are to be taken over at their balance sheet values, with the exception of fixed assets, which are to be revalued at £40,000.

The summarised balance sheets of Magwitch Limited and Compeyson plc at the takeover date of 31 May 19X1 are as follows:

	Magwitch £000	Compeyson £000
Fixed assets	32	160
Current assets	65	340
Short-term liabilities	(26)	(110)
	71	390
Share capital (£1 shares)	40	200
Reserves	31	190
	71	390

The terms of the takeover are that Compeyson plc will give three of its shares (value £1.80 each) for every two shares in Magwitch Limited, plus a cash payment to make up the total agreed takeover price.

Magwitch Limited will cease to trade on 31 May 19X1, and its assets and liabilities will be assumed by Compeyson plc. Any goodwill arising is to be written off immediately against reserves.

(a) Draw up a summarised profit and loss account for Magwitch Limited for the year ended 31 May 19X1. *(5 marks)*

(b) Draw up a balance sheet for Compeyson plc after the takeover of Magwitch Limited has taken place. *(15 marks)*

(c) Calculate how many shares and how much cash would be received by a holder of 6,000 shares in Magwitch Limited as a result of the takeover. *(5 marks)*

(University of London: GCE A-Level)

27.11X

(a) How far is it true to state that a company's break-even point occurs where the contribution just equals the fixed costs? *(5 marks)*

(b) A company's detailed information of costs and sales has been destroyed because of a computer malfunction. The following data has, however, been gleaned from various sources:

Sales volume (units)	10,000	12,000
Costs (£):		
direct materials	30,000	36,000
direct labour	28,000	33,000
overheads	20,500	24,100

Selling price per unit at all volumes of output is £12.30

Calculate:
(i) the cost of an additional 2,000 units of output;
(ii) the variable costs of 10,000 units of output;
(iii) the fixed element — if any — of each component cost;
(iv) the break-even point. *(10 marks)*

(University of London Examinations and Assessment Council: GCE A-Level)

Chapter 28

Pricing Policy

28.1 Introduction

One thing is clear – that in the long term the revenues of a firm must exceed its costs or else the firm will go out of business. If it was a company it would have to be liquidated. If it was a firm run by a sole trader he might conceivably become bankrupt. On the other hand, firms may find that in the short term costs sometimes exceed revenues; in other words the firm makes a net loss. Many firms do make losses from time to time without being forced out of business.

This being so, the way in which the prices are determined of the goods sold by the firm is of paramount importance. You may well expect that there are some definite rules which will be observed by a firm when it fixes its prices, and that these rules are followed by all businesses. Your expectations would, however, be quite wrong.

With pricing, each firm has certain features which may not apply to other firms, and this will affect its pricing policy. For instance, taking a simple illustration, let us look at the price of sugar sold by three different businesses dealing in groceries. The first business (A) is a grocer's shop in a village, it is the only grocer's shop, and the next shop at which the villagers can buy sugar is thirty miles away. The second shop (B) is also a grocer's shop in a town where there are plenty of other shops selling sugar. The last business (C) is a very large supermarket in a city, in a street where there are other large supermarkets. For a bag of sugar you might have to pay, at (A) 90p, (B) 80p, (C) 60p. The sugar may well be of exactly the same quality and be manufactured by the same company. Firm (A) buys in small quantities; consequently it pays a higher price than (B) or (C) for its sugar, but it knows that none of its customers want to go thirty miles for sugar. The owner does not want to lose self-respect by overcharging anyway, so he settles for 90p. He always reflects that if he charged more, his customers might well buy sugar in large quantities when they went to the market town to shop. Firm (B) makes hardly any profit at all out of its sugar sales; it fears that if its regular customers were to go elsewhere for their sugar they might well decide to buy other things as well, so that not only would (B) lose its sugar sales but also a great deal of its other sales. Supermarket (C) sells sugar at a loss – it does this quite deliberately to tempt in customers who come to buy cheap sugar, and then buy other items on which the supermarket makes reasonable profits.

If there can be such differences in the selling price of a bag of sugar when sold by three firms, none of whom had in fact produced the sugar, then how much more complex is the position where firms manufacture goods and then have to fix prices. This is where a study of economics helps one to get this in better perspective. Along with other economic factors, the elasticity of demand must be considered as well as whether or not the firm has a monopoly. Economics will give you a framework for your thinking but it is not the purpose of this book to be an economics text. Still you can well see that really the thinking behind pricing relies on economic analysis. We will content ourselves with accepting that this is so, and will merely look at how accounting portrays it.

28.2 Full Cost Pricing

Although there may be no clearly defined rules on pricing, it can at least be said that views of pricing can be traced to one of two attitudes. These are:

1 Ascertain the cost of the product and then add something to that for profit, the sum being the selling price. This is usually known as **full-cost pricing**.
2 Ascertain the price at which similar products are selling, and then attempt to keep costs below that level so as to make a profit.

Many of the problems connected with full-cost pricing are those concerned with absorption costing and marginal costing. In absorption costing the whole of the fixed costs were allocated to products, whereas in marginal costing the 'contribution' was found out of which fixed costs would have to come leaving the profit as the difference. The information shown in Exhibit 28.1 has been drawn up on a full-cost basis, using the following philosophy.

A considerable number of firms use the full-cost basis, very probably because it is easy to apply. This is of itself not meant as a criticism – after all the accounting that is used should be the simplest method of achieving the desired ends. There is certainly no virtue at all in using complicated methods when simple ones would be sufficient. Complicated methods mean that the accounting system costs more to operate, and if the benefits are no greater than those derived from the simple system, then the accounting system should be scrapped and replaced by the simple system. Using methods just because they are simple can, however, be harmful if they give the wrong data, when a more complex system might give the right data. The simple system of full-cost pricing is to find the cost of direct materials and direct labour and then add relevant amounts to represent overheads and profit. The selling price is calculated in a manner similar to the following:

	£
Cost of direct materials and direct labour	10
Add Variable manufacturing overhead	5
Add Share of fixed manufacturing overhead	1
	16
Add Percentage (say 50 per cent in this case) for selling, administration and finance costs	8
	24
Add Percentage for profit (in this case say 25 per cent)	6
	30

The 50 per cent for selling, administration and finance costs is probably based on the figures for the previous year, where, as a total for the year, these figures would have approximated to 50 per cent of the total of direct materials + direct labour + variable manufacturing overhead + fixed manufacturing overhead (i.e. in this case this would have amounted to £16 for one unit). Therefore, taking 50 per cent as an addition is really saying that the basic situation is similar to the previous year.

Remember that this was an example; full-cost pricing is not always done in exactly the same manner, but the example just shown is a typical one. As we have seen already in an earlier chapter the allocation of fixed costs is very arbitrary, yet here the selling price is based upon figures produced as a direct consequence of such arbitrary allocation.

28.3 Example of Full-cost Pricing

We can now look at Exhibit 28.1 where three firms are making identical products, and for the purpose of illustration we will assume that the variable and fixed costs for each firm are the same. Different accountants use different methods of allocating fixed overhead between products, even though in each case the allocation may seem to be quite rational. There is usually no one 'right' way of allocating fixed overhead; instead there are 'possible' ways. In this exhibit each of the three firms manufactures two products, and because of the different ways in which they have allocated fixed overhead they have come up with different selling prices for their products.

Exhibit 28.1

	Blue Ltd Products A	Blue Ltd Products B	Green Ltd Products A	Green Ltd Products B	Red Ltd Products A	Red Ltd Products B
	£	£	£	£	£	£
Direct labour and materials	10	12	10	12	10	12
Variable overhead	16	10	16	10	16	10
Marginal cost	26	22	26	22	26	22
Fixed overhead	6	26	22	10	14	18
Full cost	32	48	48	32	40	40
Add Profit: 12.5 per cent of full cost	4	6	6	4	5	5
	36	54	54	36	45	45

In real life, once the selling prices have been calculated the market prices of similar goods are looked at, and the price fixed on the basis of competition, etc. In this case the price might well be adjusted to £45 for both products A and B. In this case, by a coincidence – after all, the allocation of fixed overhead has been done on an arbitrary basis – Red Ltd has managed to get its selling prices calculated to exactly the average market price.

Suppose that the firms had really placed their faith in their selling price calculations but now realised they would have to fix selling prices at £45. Blue might think that as the full cost of product B was £48 then it would lose £3 for every unit sold of product B. Green Ltd might, on the other hand, think that as the full cost of product A is £48 it would lose £3 on every unit sold of product A. Blue Ltd might decide to cease production of B, and Green Ltd decide to cease production of A.

If the plans had been for each firm to sell 100 of each of products A and B, then the plans have now altered to Blue Ltd to produce and sell 100 of A only, Green Ltd to sell 100 of B only, and Red Ltd to sell both 100 of A and 100 of B. The summarised profit and loss accounts will now be as shown in Exhibit 28.2.

Exhibit 28.2

	Blue Ltd £	Green Ltd £	Red Ltd £
Sales: 100 of A × £45	4,500		4,500
100 of B × £45		4,500	4,500
Total Revenue	4,500	4,500	9,000
Less Costs: Direct labour and materials			
Product A 100 × £10	1,000		1,000
Product B 100 × £12		1,200	1,200
Variable overhead:			
Product A 100 × £16	1,600		1,600
Product B 100 × £10		1,000	1,000
Fixed overhead: does not change			
Because of cessation of production in			
Blue Ltd and Green Ltd (see text)	3,200	3,200	3,200
Total costs	5,800	5,400	8,000
Net profit			1,000
Net loss	1,300	900	

Exhibit 28.2 shows that Blue Ltd and Green Ltd would incur losses if they ceased production of product B and product A respectively. Yet if they had not ceased production they would both have made profits of £1,000 as Red Ltd has done. After all they are similar firms with exactly the same costs – the only difference was the way they allocated fixed costs. The fixed costs in each firm totalled £3,200. Blue allocated this between products as A £6; B £26. Green allocated it A £22; B £10. Red allocated it A £14; B £18. With 100 units of each product this amounted to an allocation of £3,200 for each firm. Fixed overhead does not change just because of ceasing production of one type of product. The factory rent and rates will remain the same, so will the typists' salaries and other fixed costs.

The question, therefore, arises as to which figure is relevant in deciding whether to continue the manufacture of a certain product or to cease production. The answer to this is that the marginal cost figure is the one that is relevant. If this is less than the selling price, then the difference will be the contribution towards fixed overhead, thus reducing the burden of the fixed overhead on the other products. This can be shown as:

	Product A £	Product B £
Selling price	45	45
Marginal cost	26	22
Contribution towards fixed overhead and profit	£19	£23

28.4 Using Marginal Costs

Just let us test this out with another firm in Exhibit 28.3 which has the following cost and selling information. The firm would sell 100 of each product it manufactured. Total fixed overhead is £4,800 – allocated A £5 (100), B £7 (100), C £11 (100), D £15 (100), E £10 (100), i.e. £4,800 total.

Exhibit 28.3

Violet Ltd Products	A	B	C	D	E
Cost: (per unit)	£	£	£	£	£
Direct labour and materials	8	9	16	25	11
Variable overhead	7	8	10	13	14
Marginal cost	15	17	26	38	25
Fixed overhead	5	7	11	15	10
Full cost	20	24	37	53	35
Selling price per unit	30	21	31	80	20

On the full-cost basis only A and D would seem to be profitable. Should therefore, production of B, C and E be discontinued? According to what has been said production should cease only when the selling price is less than marginal cost. In Exhibit 28.4 we will see if following our own advice brings about the greatest profit. We will also see at the same time what would have happened if production was not cut at all.

Exhibit 28.4

	(1) Following full-cost pricing, cease producing B, C and E	(2) Using marginal costing, cease producing E only	(3) Ignore costing altogether and produce all items
	£	£	£
Sales: A 100 × £30	3,000	3,000	3,000
B 100 × £21		2,100	2,100
C 100 × £31		3,100	3,100
D 100 × £80	8,000	8,000	8,000
E 100 × £20			2,000
Total revenue	11,000	16,200	18,200
Less Costs:			
Direct labour and materials:			
100 × cost per product	(£33) 3,300	(£58) 5,800	(£69) 6,900
Variable cost: 100 × cost per product	(£20) 2,000	(£38) 3,800	(£52) 5,200
Fixed overhead (does not change)	4,800	4,800	4,800
Total costs	10,100	14,400	16,900
Net profit	£900	£1,800	£1,300

The £s figures in brackets show the cost of each product, e.g. in (1) the Direct labour and Materials are A £8 + D £25 = £33.

As you can see, in Exhibit 28.4 it would be just as well if we followed our own advice. This would give a profit of £1,800 compared with £900 using the full-cost method or

£1,300 if we disregarded costing altogether. Sometimes the full-cost method will give far better results than ignoring costing altogether, but this case shows that in fact the wrong kind of costing can be even worse than having no costing at all! The marginal costing approach will, however, give the better answer in this sort of situation.

There is, however, a danger in thinking that if the marginal cost of each product is less than the selling price then activities will be profitable. This is certainly not so, and full consideration must be given to the fact that the total contributions from all the products should exceed the fixed costs, otherwise the firm will incur an overall loss. Different volumes of activity will affect this. Let us look in Exhibit 28.5 with a two-product firm making products A and B given different volumes of activity. Product A has a marginal cost of £10 and a selling price of £14. Product B has a marginal cost of £6 and a selling price of £8. Fixed costs are £1,400.

Exhibit 28.5

	Profit, or loss, at different volumes of activity							
	A	B	A	B	A	B	A	B
Units sold	100	100	200	200	300	300	400	400
	£	£	£	£	£	£	£	£
Contribution (Selling price *less* Marginal cost) A £4 per unit, B £2 per unit	400	200	800	400	1,200	600	1,600	800
Total contributions		600		1,200		1,800		2,400
Fixed overhead		1,400		1,400		1,400		1,400
Net loss		£800		£200				
Net profit						£400		£1,000

Here the selling price always exceeds marginal cost, but if activity is low the firm will incur a loss. This is shown where activity is only 100 or 200 units of each product.

The main lessons to be learned about selling prices are that:

(*a*) Selling prices should exceed marginal costs.
(*b*) In the long term the total contributions at given volumes must exceed the fixed costs of the firm.

28.5 Maximisation of Total Contribution

It should be stressed that it is the maximisation of the total contribution from a product that is important. In this the volumes of activity cannot be disregarded. Suppose for instance that a firm could only manufacture two products in future, whereas to date it had manufactured three. It may be that per unit the contribution may well have been (A) £10, (B) £8 and (C) £6. If a decision was made on this basis only then (C) would be discontinued. However, if the volumes were (A) 20, (B) 15 and (C) 30, then the total contributions would be (A) 20 × £10 = £200: (B) 15 × £8 = £120: (C) 30 × £6 = £180. As (B) has the lowest *total* contribution it should be (B) that is discontinued, not (C).

REVIEW QUESTIONS

Advice:

Obviously this chapter is really concerned with the concepts of marginal costing with reference to fixing selling prices. One has to bear in mind two aspects:

(i) a product should make a positive contribution (unless there is some overriding matter which makes the product a kind of loss-leader), and
(ii) the volume of sales should be sufficient so that in the long term (it may be different in the short term) the fixed overheads are more than covered by the total of all the contributions.

28.1 Glasses Ltd make four different products, Q, R, S and T. They have ascertained the cost of direct materials and direct labour and the variable overhead for each unit of product. An attempt is made to allocate the other costs in a logical manner. When this is done 10 per cent is added for profit. The cost of direct labour and materials per unit is Q £14; R £28; S £60; T £32. Variable overheads per unit are Q £4; R £8; S £13; T £12. Fixed overhead of £1,900 is allocated per unit as Q £2; R £4; S £7; T £6.

You are required:

(a) Calculate the prices at which the units would be sold by Glasses Ltd if the full-cost system of pricing was adhered to.
(b) What would you advise the company to do if, because of market competition, prices had to be fixed at Q £33; R £39; S £70; T £49?
(c) Assuming production of 100 units of each item per accounting period, what would be the net profit (i) if your advice given in your answer to (b) was followed, (ii) if the firm continued to produce all of the items?
(d) What would you advise the company to do if, because of market competition, prices had to be fixed at Q £17; R £48; S £140; T £39?
(e) Assuming production of 100 units of each item per accounting period, what would be the net profit (i) if your advice given in your answer to (d) was followed, (ii) if the firm continued to produce all of the items?

28.2X Bottles Ltd makes six different products, F, G, H, I, J and K. An analysis of costs ascertains the following:

Per unit	F	G	H	I	J	K
	£	£	£	£	£	£
Direct labour and direct materials	15	17	38	49	62	114
Variable cost	6	11	10	21	22	23

Fixed costs of £11,400 are allocated per unit as F £4; G £7; H £7; I £10; J £16 and K £13. Using full-cost pricing 20 per cent is to be added per unit for profit.

You are required to:

(a) Calculate the prices that would be charged by Bottles Ltd if the full-cost pricing system was adhered to.
(b) What advice would you give the company if a survey of the market showed that the prices charged could be F £26; G £26; H £66; I £75; J £80; K £220?
(c) Assuming production of 200 units per period of each unit manufactured what would be the profit of the firm, (i) if your advice in (b) was followed, (ii) if the firm continued to produce all of the items?

(d) Suppose that in fact the market survey had revealed instead that the prices charged could be F £30; G £33; H £75; I £66; J £145 and K £130, then what would your advice have been to the company?

(e) Assuming that production of each item manufactured was 200 units per month, then what would have been the profit (i) if your advice in (d) had been followed, (ii) if the company chose to continue manufacturing all items?

28.3 Jason Ltd manufactures a product called Dufton. The normal annual output of this product is 200,000 units.

The following is a cost statement relating to the production of a Dufton:

	£	£
Materials		5.00
Wages		7.00
Factory overheads:		
Fixed	4.50	
Variable	1.00	5.50
Administration overheads:		
Fixed		2.00
Selling overheads:		
Fixed	3.50	
Variable	3.00	6.50
		26.00

The selling price of a Dufton is £36.

During the year the company received enquiries about two possible special orders each involving the production of 2,000 units. One enquiry related to the production of a Super Dufton (Ref. No. 610) and the other to a Premier Dufton (Ref. No. 620). Due to normal production commitments only one of these possible orders could be handled in the factory.

The conditions of order (Ref. No. 610) are that the variable costs will increase by 25 per cent but the selling price cannot exceed £25.00 per unit. The conditions relating to order (Ref. No. 620) are that variable costs will decrease by 25 per cent but the selling price will be £19.00 per unit.

Required:

(a) A computation of the break-even point of normal trading in terms of:
    (i)   sales revenue;
    (ii) units produced;
    (iii) percentage of normal capacity (assume all units sold).   *(11 marks)*

(b) What profit would be earned in normal trading if:
    (i)   the selling price was increased to £40 per unit and output restricted to 160,000 units;
    (ii) the selling price was reduced to £28 per unit and output increased to 260,000 units?
    (8 marks)

(c) Advise the board as to which of the two special orders should be accepted. Computations must be shown and a reason given for the choice made.   *(6 marks)*
(*Associated Examining Board: GCE A-Level*)

28.4X

(a) What are the differences between marginal cost pricing and full-cost pricing?

(b) How far is it true to state that marginal cost pricing is a short-term strategy?

(c) A.S. Teriod Ltd makes five different products – Ceres, Eros, Hermes, Icarus and Vesta. The various costs per unit of the products are respectively: direct labour, £14, £8, £22, £18 and £26; direct materials, £8, £10, £13, £12 and £17; variable overheads, £11, £9, £16, £15 and £19.

The fixed expenses for the month of February 19X1 are estimated at £8,200, and this has been allocated to the units produced as Ceres £17, Eros £13, Hermes £19, Icarus £15 and Vesta £18. The company adds 20 per cent on to the total cost of each product by way of profit.

(i) Calculate the prices based upon full-cost pricing.

(ii) Advise the company on which products to produce, if competition forces the prices to: Ceres £59, Eros £25, Hermes £80, Icarus £44 and Vesta £92.

(iii) Assuming that output for the month amounts to 100 units of each model: that fixed costs remain the same irrespective of output and that unused capacity cannot be used for other products: calculate the profit or loss if the company continued to produce the whole range at the new prices; AND if the company followed your advice in (ii) above.

(*University of London: GCE A-Level*)

28.5 UZ Limited, a local bus operator, is considering adjusting its fare structure. Summer fares are to be increased by 10 per cent. This increase is expected to result in a reduction of no more than 5 per cent in the number of passenger-miles. Winter fares are to be reduced by 20 per cent to increase the number of passenger-miles by at least 10 per cent.

The company's management accounts provide the following information:

UZ Limited
Profit Statement

	Tourist season (seven months) £	Winter months (five months) £	Annual totals £
Fare income	490,000	200,000	690,000
Operating costs			
Variable	210,000	100,000	310,000
Fixed	70,000	50,000	120,000
Administration	70,000	50,000	120,000
Interest charges	35,000	25,000	60,000
	385,000	225,000	610,000
Profit (loss)	105,000	(25,000)	80,000

Required:

(a) A statement showing the revised profit (loss) if the fare structure is adjusted.   *(10 marks)*

(b) Comments on whether or not the changes to fares should be implemented.   *(2 marks)*

(c) An explanation of why it is worth while for the company to operate buses during the winter months when it is incurring losses.   *(6 marks)*

(*Welsh Joint Education Committee: GCE A-Level*)

28.6X Simons Limited is a small manufacturing company currently making three different types of chair. Each chair is made from the same raw materials by the same labour force.

The managing director presents to you the following details of revenue and cost per unit for the year ended 30 April 19X0:

Type of Chair	Standard	De Luxe	Super
Number of chairs made and sold in the past year	5,000	2,000	3,000
	Per unit	Per unit	Per unit
	£	£	£
Selling price	100	120	150
Raw material	16	20	26
Operating labour	16	20	28
Manufacturing overheads:			
Variable	4	7	9
Fixed	8	10	14

Manufacturing fixed overheads are apportioned to the three products in proportion to prime costs (i.e. materials and operating labour). Selling costs are fixed at £160,000. All units produced can be sold as soon as they are made and no stocks are kept.

The directors have been considering their plans for the year ending 30 April 19X1.

The directors intend to introduce a new design of chair to be called the 'Executive'. Raw materials will cost £40 per unit. Operating labour costs £4 per hour throughout the factory and it will take 9 hours to manufacture one 'Executive' chair. Because of labour shortages in the region only 59,300 hours of operating labour will be available to the entire company in the coming year. Variable manufacturing overhead will amount to £9 per unit for the 'Executive' chair.

In the coming year the price of the 'Super' chair will be raised to £170. The price of the 'Standard' and 'De Luxe' chairs will not be increased. It is not thought that the unit sales of each of the three existing chair models can be increased. The fixed selling costs of the company will be increased to £175,000 but other costs will not change.

Required:

(a) Prepare a statement to show the contribution made by each product during the year ended 30 April 19X0 and calculate the company's total profit for the year.

(b) Calculate the selling price of the new 'Executive' chair if the company wishes to make a contribution per 'Executive' chair of £165.

(c) The directors decide to go ahead and introduce the 'Executive' chair. Prepare a budget for the year ended 30 April 19X1 to produce the maximum profit on the basis that market research indicates that 2,500 'Executive' chairs can be made and sold.

(Reproduced by permission of the University of Cambridge Local Examinations Syndicate)

28.7 Jugs Ltd make five different products – A, B, C, D and E. These have been costed per unit as:
Direct materials and direct labour: A £16; B £19; C £38; D £44; E £23.
Variable overhead: A £11; B £17; C £23; D £14; E £9.
Fixed overhead totalling £3,600 per period is allocated per unit, on a basis of a production of 100 units of each item per period, as A £3; B £4; C £9; D £12; E £8.
When the total cost is found, 10 per cent is added for profit.

You are required to:

(a) Ascertain the selling prices of each item if the full-cost pricing system is used.

(b) Owing to competition and the general state of the market, if prices had to be fixed at A £32; B £49; C £56; D £66; E £48; what would be your advice to the directors of Jugs Ltd?

(c) Assuming production of 100 units per item what would be the net profit or loss (i) if your advice under (b) was adhered to by the company, (ii) if the company continued to produce all the items?

(d) Suppose instead that the state of the market was different, and that the prices had to be fixed at A £24; B £38; C £68; D £64; E £29; what would be your advice to the directors?

(e) Assuming production of 100 units per item, what would be the net profit or loss (i) if your advice under (d) was adhered to by the company, (ii) if the company continued to produce all the items?

28.8X Crook plc is a company which produces four different plastic moulded products for the building industry. Central to the production process is a high-pressure moulding machine. The machine is highly capital-intensive with a limited capacity and therefore the factory's production capacity cannot increase in the short term.

The machine is operated by a team of four and the direct labour costs of the operation are £20 per hour. The machine's hours of operation are limited to 2,500 per year.

Budgeted details for the year ending 31 August 19X7 are:

	Products			
	Tubing	Piping	Guttering	Facing panels
Annual demand (units)	600	600	600	600
Units details:	£	£	£	£
Selling price	125	116	87	180
Variable costs:				
Material	40	40	30	50
Labour	30	30	20	40
Overheads	25	25	22	56

The budgeted fixed overhead for the period is £30,000.

(a) Rank the products in the order in which they should be produced so as to maximise the budgeted profit. *(10 marks)*

(b) Using the ranking that you have calculated in (a), prepare the budgeted profit statement for the year ending 31 August 19X7. *(11 marks)*

(c) Explain any concerns that you may have about Crook plc using the best product mix calculated in (a) above. *(4 marks)*

(University of London Examinations and Assessment Council: GCE A-Level)

Appendix I

Examination Techniques

A large number of students do not think clearly about how they are going to tackle their GCE A-Level examinations. They will revise all the necessary stuff, and will then throw away a large number of marks because of poor examination technique. As you have progressed to A Levels you obviously cannot be completely devoid of such technique, but you can certainly improve it by reading and absorbing what is written in this appendix.

A lot of what follows was written in *Business Accounting 1*. We are going to repeat some of that here for the benefit of those who have not read that book, and to remind the others exactly what they should be doing in an examination.

Most of the main deficiencies noted by examiners have not changed at all over the past 50 years. We do hope that we can get you to tackle the examinations in the right way.

Commencing the Examination

First, take a few long deep breaths to settle your nerves, and then read the examination paper. Pay special attention to how many questions you have to answer from each section, and exactly what each question requires you to do. After this you should then select the questions to be attempted.

Students Do Not Read the Questions Properly

A large number of students do not answer the questions as set by the examiner, because they have not read the question properly. They answer what they think the examiner wants, not what he is asking for.

Let me take a simple example. Suppose the examiner sets the following question: 'Describe the use of accounting ratios in assessing the performance of businesses.'

A lot of students will immediately start to describe how to calculate various accounting ratios. Marks which will be obtained – nil. The question asked for the *use* of accounting ratios, not *how to calculate* them.

Many other students will have concentrated on the word *use*. They will then write their answer based on comparing this year's accounting ratios in a business with those of last year. They may well even mention trend ratios which will earn them some extra marks. If they keep their discussion to comparing ratios in a business in the year with other years, however, they cannot get top marks, no matter how well they have written their answers.

Why not? Well, they picked up the word 'use', but from then on they stopped reading properly. The question does not in any way limit itself to the ratios of one business only. First of all you can compare the performance of a business with its own performance in the past. Secondly, you may be able to compare one business with another business of a similar kind. In addition, if you miss out mentioning inter-firm comparisons you will lose marks.

Therefore, (*a*) *read* the question carefully, (*b*) *underline* the *key* words to get to the meaning of the questions, (*c*) *think carefully* about how widespread your answer should be.

On the other hand, there is no point in widening the question more than is needed. It is for the *use* of *accounting* ratios, *not* the use of *all types* of ratios. Besides accounting ratios there are marketing ratios – e.g. size of share of market, how long it takes to supply orders, ratios of defective goods etc. The question does not ask for all of these. If you give them, you will not get any extra marks.

Poor Time Management

Using time well to gain the highest possible marks is essential. Examiners constantly report that examinees are very poor in this aspect of tackling an examination. How then can you avoid the usual pitfalls.

First of all read the *rubric* carefully. These are the instructions at the top of the paper, e.g. 'Attempt four questions only: the three questions in Section A and one from Section B. Begin each answer on a separate page.'

You would be surprised to know that a lot of students would try to answer more than one question from Section B. If you tackle two questions from Section B you will get marks for only one of your answers. No examiner will mark both and then give you marks for your highest marked answer. They will mark the first of the optional questions answered and ignore the next unnecessary answer.

Secondly, don't annoy the examiner by not starting your answer on a separate page. It is your job to make the examiner's work as easy as possible. Examiners are only human, and it would not be surprising if their annoyance did not affect the marking of your paper.

You really must attempt each and every question to fulfil the examination requirements. If you have to answer five questions then you must not tackle only four questions.

Students often feel that they would be better off by handing in the complete answers to only four questions, instead of five incomplete answers. In accounting examinations this is not true. Why is this so?

1   Examiners use positive marking in accounting examinations. If you have done 80 per cent of an answer worth 20 marks in total, and you have got it absolutely correct, then you get $80\% \times 20 = 16$ marks.
2   The first marks in a question are the easiest to obtain. Thus it is easier to get the first 10 marks out of 20 than it is to get the second lot of marks to get full marks. By ensuring that you get the easiest marks on every question it therefore makes your task easier.

To ensure that you tackle (not necessarily finish) each question you should mark the number of minutes to be allowed by *yourself* for each question. Thus a 20-mark question, in a 100-mark examination should be given 20 per cent of the time, i.e. 3 hours × 20% = 36 minutes. When 36 minutes have gone by, *stop answering the question* unless it is the last question to be attempted, and go on to the next question.

If you don't know the answer, or part of an answer, you should guess. You don't lose marks for guessing, and if you guess correctly you get the marks. Intuition will often give the correct answer. Very often if you don't guess on part of a computational question you will be unable to go on to the remainder of the question which you can answer.

Workings

You may wonder why we have put this under a separate heading. We cannot emphasise enough how important it is that you should:

(*a*) submit all your workings, and

(*b*) ensure that the workings are set out so that the examiner can follow them.

A very high percentage of candidates in an examination are near the pass mark, within either a few percentage points above it or below it. You should know that from your study of natural curves in statistics. If you are one of these candidates, and, as we have said, there are a lot of them, handing in workings which can be understood by the examiner will often ensure you a pass mark. Conversely, no workings, or completely unintelligible workings may well ensure your failing the examination.

Tackle the Easiest Questions First

Never start off your examination by tackling a difficult question. You have got to be able to settle down properly, and not let your nerves get out of control. Starting off on the easiest question is the best way to enable you to get off to a good start. Much more about this was written in *Business Accounting 1*.

State your Assumptions

It does happen that sometimes a question can contain ambiguities. Examination bodies try to prevent it happening, but it does occur occasionally. The questions do (unfortunately) sometimes contain errors.

In both of these cases you must point out the ambiguity/error. You should then make an assumption, based on what you thought the examiner meant, and carry on with your answer. You must, however, state what your assumption is. Try to make your assumption as sensible as possible. The examiner will then mark your answer accordingly. If you make a ridiculous assumption, it is unlikely that he will give you any marks for that part of your answer. Don't be sarcastic in your comments or complain about inefficiency, there are other times and places for that.

Computational Questions versus Essay Questions

Provided you know what you are doing, it is easier to gain higher marks on computational questions than on essay questions. Therefore if you have a choice, and you can manage the computational question, then that is the one to tackle.

There are quite a few reasons for this which are all tied up with knowing how examiners set and mark the examination scripts, and using some psychological know-how to work out the best strategy. We do not propose to elaborate on this in greater detail, but can tell you that after over 60 years between us in accountancy education we feel quite happy to give you this advice.

Answering Written Questions

The problem

Unlike computational-type answers, you will not know whether your written answers are up to the mark until you receive your examination result. Likewise, written questions lack the certainty and precision of accounting problems and it is often difficult to fathom out exactly what the examiners require of you. For this reason sound examination technique is absolutely essential together with precise knowledge of relevant law and regulations.

There are several major aspects to success in written papers. These are:

- *plan* your answer
- answer the question *as set*
- pay attention to good *layout*, and
- explain in clear and simple terms what you are doing.

Remember you can only be marked on what you write down. You have no opportunity to explain some ambiguity or other and if what you write is unclear you will *not* get the benefit of the doubt.

Plan

First read the question and jot down the key *verb*, i.e. your instructions; this may be to discuss, explain, advise, set out, list, draft an audit programme, write a letter etc.

If the question requires a discussion or an explanation it should be written in proper paragraph form. Each paragraph should be self-contained and explain the point it makes. Sentences should be short and to the point. The ideal length for a paragraph is 3 sentences with 4 as a maximum. Over 4 and you are probably making more than one point and should have gone into 2 paragraphs.

Plan how many points you are going to make and what the answer is. This is essential as otherwise your answer will 'drift' as you struggle to come to some conclusion. The plan should consist of arrows connecting points to each other so that the answer will flow and be logical. The plan need not be too extensive; it is silly to waste time on a 'mini-answer'. It should consist of the *headings* you are going to use.

Answer the Question Set

Think while you are writing out your answer to make sure you are answering the question *as set*. Keep on reading the instructions and make sure you are following them. Use the question to help you to get the answer and, while this should be tackled at the planning stage, it is always possible that inspiration will strike while you are writing out your answer. In which case, jot the point down on your plan, otherwise you might forget it and that can cause frustration. What you say should be relevant but if you are in doubt about the relevance but sure about the accuracy – give it to him! You cannot lose and it may be one of the key points he was looking for.

Layout

Whenever examiners meet to discuss results, or write down their commentary on students' performance they all agree on the importance of good layout; yet students generally tends to take no notice. The range of marks between good papers and poor papers tends to be quite small. Anything you can do to put the examiner on your side will pay off in those few extra marks.

The main areas for good layout are:

1 *Tabulate* in numbered points, unless you are writing an essay-type question (as explained above).
2 Leave at least a clear line between each point or paragraph.
3 Use headings whenever possible to indicate what major point or series of points you

are about to make. Make it easy for the examiner to read your work and follow what you are doing. A solid mass of material is difficult to read, provides no respite for the eye and shows a lack of discipline.

4   Take care with your *language*. Be objective and avoid the use of the words 'I' or 'we' at too frequent intervals. Be direct and concise, say what you mean, do not use pompous terminology and use technical words in their correct meaning.

Short sentences are far more effective and punchy than long ones. An accounting programme or evaluation of an internal control system could well start with a series of *verbs*. Good ones are: test, examine, inspect, calculate, reconcile, compare, summarise, inquire, investigate. These key words will help you to make answers to these types of questions much more direct and to the point. If you start with them you are bound to avoid falling into the trap of being long-winded, or of padding-out your answer. You only have a limited time and everything you write down must earn you marks.

5   Remember that there may be clues in the exam paper that will help you answer a question — you may, for example, find a Balance Sheet presented as part of a question, while another question asks that you prepare a Balance Sheet.

Key points

Do try to find a couple of key points to each question. These are points which you feel are vital to answer the question. You may well be right and, anyway, jotting them down after you have read the question carefully can help to give your answer much needed direction.

Practice

You will need to practise the above routine. Written answers do need more practice than computational ones. Have a go at the question. Write out the answer as you would in the examination. Compare with the suggested answers.

Write out at the foot of your answer *what you left out* and *what you got wrong*.

Learn from the answers, and from the work you do, so that when you see a similar question you will produce a better answer.

Time pressure

You will experience a lot of time pressure as you progress with written questions. Do not worry; this is a good sign.

In the examination, spread your time sensibly. Start with the questions you like the look of most and, if you have to go slightly over time, do so. End with the question you think you cannot answer, but do give yourself time to have a reasonable go at it.

If a written question is included in a computational paper do not go over the time on it but do spend the allocated time. **Examiners pay great attention to the written parts of computational papers,** so do not skimp this part.

All this sounds formidable and, of course, it is. It requires skill and application and, above all, confidence. Practice makes perfect and once the skill is acquired then, like riding a bicycle, it will not be forgotten. Take pride in your work and be critical of your own efforts, but do not imagine your answers will have to be perfect to pass the examination. Suggested answers tend to be too long because tutors are afraid to reveal any signs of weakness or ignorance.

Go for the main points and make them well. That is the secret of success.

Appendix II

Answers to Review Questions

2.1

(a) The term 'contribution' is the amount remaining after the cost of the goods sold, plus all other variable expenses, have been deducted from the sales figures. No fixed expenses are therefore taken into account.

(b)

	Bexville Shop		Amstead Shop	
Sales		30		55
Less Cost of goods sold	15		23	
Other variable expenses	12	27	16	39
Contribution		3		16

(c) In percentage terms relative to sales:

	H.O.%	Bexville %	Amstead %
Gross profit %	60	50	58.2
Less Variable expenses	10	40	29.1
	50	10	29.1
Fixed expenses*	26.7	23.3	7.3
Net profit/loss	23.3%	(13.3)%	21.8%

* The Head Office expenses originally allocated to the branches have been charged back to the Head Office.

There is no great disparity in the gross profit percentage profits between the various parts of the business. However, Bexville in particular has extremely high variable expenses and fixed expenses as well.

It would appear that Amstead has made an extremely good start for a new branch. One does expect 'teething problems' in a new shop, but Amstead seems to have got through a difficult period extremely well.

However, Bexville has got off to a particularly bad start. Not only is the gross profit percentage less than the others, but the variable and fixed expenses are relatively much higher. An investigation of the reasons for these factors is urgently needed. It may be considered that the business be given rather longer to prove itself, as it has operated only for one year and it is not unusual for the first year to suffer in various ways.

(d) A retail branch shop should possibly be closed:
  (i) If there seems to be a negative contribution which will continue.
  (ii) Where it appears that in the long term a far better return can be obtained from the finance tied up in the branch by closing the branch and investing the money elsewhere.
  (iii) Allied to the above, the following detailed points, which cover everything, may be relevant:
  ● Sales unlikely to increase
  ● Population falling in the area
  ● Severe competition in the area which we are unlikely to be able to beat

- Change in consumer habits, e.g. out-of-town shopping compared with high street shopping
- Need for whole firm to rationalise.

2.3

(a)

Spencer Reddaway

Revenue Accounts for the year ended 30 June 19X1

	Branch A		Branch B	
Sales		800,000		1,200,000
Opening stock	40,000		65,000	
*1 Goods from Head Office (net)	606,000		997,000	
	646,000		1,062,000	
*2 *Less* closing stock	70,000	576,000	140,000	922,000
Gross profit		224,000		278,000
*3 Stock loss re-imbursed				
by manager				13,400
				291,400
Variable expenses	70,000		80,000	
Fixed expenses	60,000		60,000	
Managers' commission	8,000		12,000	
Allocation of Head				
Office expenses	95,000		95,000	
Provision for bad debts	12,000		18,000	
		245,000		265,000
Net profit/(loss)		(21,000)		26,400

Notes:

*1 Net after returns to Head Office

*2 Closing stocks adjusted by stock damaged, etc.
   A 3,000; B 1,900

*3 Branch A had no stock losses; it made more than 25 per cent profit on sales ($33\frac{1}{3}$ per cent on cost).

   Branch B has lost stock. Opening stock 65,000 + goods 997,000 – closing stock (unadjusted) 141,900 = unadjusted cost of goods sold 920,100. This should result in gross profit $33\frac{1}{3}$ per cent on cost = 306,700 = sales of 1,226,800. Sales were only 1,200,000, therefore stock loss is 26,800. Manager to be charged 50 per cent of this loss 13,400.

(b) Report to include (in brief)

1 Gross profit ratios A $\dfrac{224,000}{800,000}$ = 28%; B $\dfrac{278,000}{1,200,000}$ = 23.2%

   compared to 25% expected

2 Contributions made by branches to cover Head Office expenditure and profits:

	A		B	
Gross profit		224,000		291,400
Less Expenses wholly				
belonging to branch				
Variable	70,000		80,000	
Fixed expenses	60,000		60,000	
Commission	8,000		12,000	
Provision for				
bad debts	12,000	150,000	18,000	170,000
Contributions		74,000		121,400

Both branches make positive contributions to cover Head Office overheads and profits. There is no point in closing either of them unless the alternative use to which the finance released by the closure is put will bring about a greater contribution.

The calculation for branch A of a net loss per the normal profit and loss account is brought about because of the method of allocating Head Office overheads.

3   Investigation should be made as to why branch B should have managed only 23.2 per cent gross profit instead of the 25 per cent expected.

(c) (In brief)
     (i)   Much cash will be received later than if tight control used.
     (ii) Leads to more bad debts and interest costs on extra capital needed.

2.5
(a)

A Telford, R Stevenson and J Napier trading as 'Pine Products'
Trading and Profit and Loss Account for the year to 30 April 19X8

Sales (230 + 120 + 140)000s		490,000
Less Cost of goods sold		
Opening stock (31 + 16 + 19)000s	66,000	
Purchases (371 + 30)000s	401,000	
	467,000	
Less Closing stock*	91,950	375,050
Gross profit		114,950
Less Expenses		
General expenses (10,500 + 4,500 + 5,300)	20,300	
Fixed administration expenses	12,500	
Variable costs (18,900 + 8,400 + 12,200)	39,500	72,300
Net profit		42,650
Note:		
Stock per draft accounts (38,000 + 17,500 + 14,000)		69,500
Add Goods in transit		
From H.O. (12,000 + 10,000)	22,000	
From Stratnorth (16,500 – 15,000)	1,500	23,500
		93,000
Less Net losses (1,500 + 290 – 740)*		1,050
		91,950

*Assumed that closing stock figures per draft accounts need adjusting. Also that the 1,500 loss at Stratnorth has nothing to do with the (unstated) stock in transit to Pilingdown. Assumed also that stock in transit is not already included in stock figures in draft accounts.

(b)   *Appropriation Account for the year ended 30 April 19X8*

Net profit				42,650
Less Salaries:	Telford	4,500		
	Stevenson	5,000		
	Napier	3,000	12,500	
Interest on capital:	Telford	1,200		
	Stevenson	960		
	Napier	1,440	3,600	16,100
				26,550
Balance of profits:	Telford ⅓		8,850	
	Stevenson ⅓		8,850	
	Napier ⅓		8,850	26,550

(c)	Option A:	Extra gross profit (50%)		9,000
	Less	Extra variable costs	3,400	
		Extra general expenses	3,000	6,400
	Extra profit/reduced loss			2,600
	Option B:	Extra gross profit		7,000
		Saving in fixed administration costs		3,000
				10,000
	Less	Extra variable costs	700	
		Extra general expenses	400	1,100
	Extra profit			8,900

Option A offers us an extra 2,600 towards profits. We do not know how much extra capital will have to be invested in Pilingdown to do this.

The costs of closing down Pilingdown are not known, other than redundancy costs.

Option B gives us an extra annual profit of 8,900, less redundancy costs to be charged in one year only of 5,500.

Option B therefore looks more preferable, but much more information is needed about all the other implications, including non-financial ones.

3.1

(i) Does not possess the cash funds necessary.
(ii) Unable to borrow from the bank at a lower rate of interest than hire purchase interest.
(iii) Can use cash funds more profitably elsewhere.
(iv) Ignorance. Does not realise the high 'true' rate of hire purchase interest.

3.3 No set answer. One possibility now shown. Machine bought for £10,000.

	Before purchase		After hire purchase (A)		After cash purchase (B)	
Fixed assets						
Machinery		20,000	30,000			30,000
Less Owing on h.p.		–	10,000	20,000		–
Current assets						
Stock	8,000		8,000		8,000	
Debtors	2,000		2,000		2,000	
Bank	10,000		10,000		–	
	20,000		20,000		10,000	
Less Current						
liabilities	10,000	10,000	10,000	10,000	10,000	–
		30,000		30,000		30,000
Capital		30,000		30,000		30,000
		30,000		30,000		30,000

Option A shows working capital retained at 10,000. Current ratio is 2:1 and acid test ratio is 1.2 : 1.

Option B shows working capital at nil. Current ratio has fallen to 1 : 1. Acid test ratio has fallen to dangerous figure of 0.2 : 1.

4.1

Bank

Application	20,000		
Allotment (30,000 less excess applications 5,000)	25,000		
First call (119,200 × 0.25)	29,800		
Second call (119,200 × 0.375)	44,700		
D. Regan (800 × 0.9)	720	Balance c/d	120,220
	120,220		120,220

D. Regan

Ordinary share capital	800	Bank	720
		Forfeited shares	80
	800		800

Application and Allotment

Ordinary share capital	45,000	Bank	20,000
		Bank	25,000
	45,000		45,000

Ordinary Share Capital

Forfeited shares	800	Application and allotment	45,000
		First call	30,000
Balance c/d	120,000	Second call	45,000
		D. Regan	800
	120,800		120,800

First Call

Ordinary share capital	30,000	Bank	29,800
		Forfeited shares	200
	30,000		30,000

Second Call

Ordinary share capital	45,000	Bank	44,700
		Forfeited shares	300
	45,000		45,000

Forfeited Shares

First call	200	Ordinary share capital	800
Second call	300		
D. Regan	80		
Transfer to share premium	220		
	800		800

Share Premium

Balance c/d	220	Forfeited shares	220

Balance Sheet

Bank	120,220
	120,220
Ordinary share capital	120,000
Share premium	220
	120,220

4.3

(a)

Application and Allotment

19X2			19X2		
Jul 10	Bank: Refund of application money (W3)	55,000	Jun 30	Bank: Applications for rights issue (W1)	495,000
Jul 31	Ordinary share capital (rights)	495,000	Jun 30	Bank: Applications for public issue (W2)	165,000
Jul 31	Share premium (on rights issue)	445,500	Jul 31	Bank: Allotment money of rights issue (W4)	445,500
Jul 31	Ordinary share capital (public)	100,000	Jul 31	Bank: Allotment money of public issue (W5)	137,000
Jul 31	Share premium (on rights issue)	150,000	Jul 31	Allotment monies owing (W6) c/d	3,000
		1,245,500			1,245,500
Aug 1	Balance b/d	3,000			

Workings:

(W1) Total shares 240,000 + 90,000 = 330,000
  Taken up 90% = 297,000
  5 for 3 held = 297,000 × ⅗ = 495,000
  Application monies 495,000 × £1 = 495,000

(W2) Public issue. Applications 90,000 + 60,000 × £1.10 = 165,000

(W3) Refunds 90,000 – 40,000 = 50,000 × 1.10 = 55,000

(W4) 495,000 shares × 90p = 445,500

(W5) 100,000 × £1.40= 140,000 less unpaid 3,000 = 137,000

(W6) The examiner could have been more specific. It is assumed that the shares have been allotted in full and that the company allows this to be owing. In theory shares would not be allotted until allotment money was paid. However, £3,000 owing ÷ by £1.40 per share does not work out to be an exact number of shares, i.e. it is 2,142.85 shares on which allotment is owed.

Ordinary Share Capital

19X2			19X2		
Jul 31	Balance c/d	915,000	Jun 1	Balance b/d	240,000
			Jun 30	Capital redemption reserve	80,000
			Jul 31	Application and allotment	495,000
			Jul 31	Application and allotment	100,000
		915,000			915,000
			Aug 1	Balance c/d	915,000

(b)

Initial number of shares held	900
Add Rights issue 900 × ⅗	1,500
Add Bonus issue	300
Add Public issue	500
New shareholding	3,200

(c) Advantages:
  (i) Not normally refundable in the short term, e.g. as compared with a bank overdraft.
  (ii) Dividends only payable if profits are made.

  Disadvantages:
  (i) Share issues can be expensive to administer (not rights issues).
  (ii) May give control to different parties than at present.

Alternative ways of funding:
(i)   Preference shares.
(ii) Debentures.
(iii) Bank loan.

4.5

(a)   Alternative 1

Issue becomes: Ordinary share capital	2,500,000
Share premium	2,500,000
Dividend payable 20% × 2,500,000 =	500,000

Revenue account extracts:
  Profit and Loss Account for year to . . .

	(main section)
Depreciation	450,000
	(appropriation section)
Ordinary dividend	500,000

Alternative 2
  Profit and Loss Account for year to . . .

	(main section)
Interest on credit agreement	250,000
Bank interest	300,000
Depreciation	450,000

(b)   Balance Sheet extracts:

	Alternative 1		Alternative 2	
Fixed assets	3,000,000		3,000,000	
Less Depreciation	450,000	2,550,000	450,000	2,550,000
Ordinary share capital	2,500,000			
Share premium	2,500,000			
Owing on credit agreement			2,250,000	
Bank overdraft			1,500,000	

(c)   Alternative 1
(i)   Is the issue price of shares sufficient so as not to water down value of old shares?
(ii) If the dividend remains the same what is the point of taking on extra risks?

Alternative 2
Extra costs over the first 4 years will be:

Interest on credit agreement	1,000,000
Bank interest (300,000 + 100,000)	400,000
	1,400,000

That compares with extra cost per alternative 1
of 4 years' dividends × 500,000 =   2,000,000
plus perpetual dividends thereafter.
  Alternative 2 will leave greater profits for the benefit of the old shareholders.

4.7 No. of ordinary shares £2,600,000 ÷ 25p = 10,400,000
Present market capitalisation 10,400,000 × 60p = £6,240,000

1 *Rights issue at par*
This would raise capitalisation (total market value) to

£6,240,000 + £5,000,000	=	£11,240,000
Now 10,400,000 + (5,000,000 × 4)	=	30,400,000 shares
New market value per share	=	37p approx.

Advantages
(i) Gives benefit of obtaining extra shares to existing shareholders.
(ii) As dividends depend on profits, a recession or similar would not have heavy fixed charges such as debenture interest.
(iii) Shareholders can sell 'rights' if they want to.
(iv) It should raise the amount required.

Disadvantages
(i) Rights issues are usually pitched below (new) market price to make them attractive to buy, but this figure is too low.
(ii) Existing shareholders who are short of funds may be annoyed by not getting all the advantages.

2 *Rights issue at premium of 20p per share*

Extra shares £5,000,000 ÷ 45p	=	11,111,111
New total shares 10,400,000 + 11,111,111	=	21,511,111
New market value per share	=	51.6p approx.

Advantages:
(i) Raises funds needed.
(ii) Pitched slightly below (new) market value which is generally accepted as correct.
(iii) Same as (ii) and (iii) in 1 above.

Disadvantages:
Same as (ii) in 1 above.

3 *Bonus issue of ordinary shares*
Advantages: none
Disadvantages:
Bonus issue does not result in cash received, and is therefore useless.

4 *Issue of 8% preference shares of £1 each at par*

Advantages:
Would raise the amount required if the percentage return was reasonable in current conditions.
Disadvantages:
Means heavy burden of preference dividends before ordinary shareholders get anything.

5 *6% Loan Stock at par*
Advantages:
Same as in 4.
Disadvantages:
Gearing becomes very high. Heavy burden of fixed charges.

5.1

(i)

	Dr	Cr
(A1) Bank	5,000	
(A2) Ordinary share applicants		5,000
Cash received from applicants		

	Dr	Cr
(B1) Ordinary share applicants	5,000	
(B2) Ordinary share capital		5,000
Ordinary shares allotted		

	Dr	Cr
(C1) Preference share capital	5,000	
(C2) Preference share redemption		5,000
Shares to be redeemed		

	Dr	Cr
(D1) Preference share redemption	5,000	
(D2) Bank		5,000
Payment made to redeem shares		

	Balances before	Effect Dr	Cr	Balances after
Net assets (except bank)	20,000			20,000
Bank	13,000	(A1) 5,000	(D2) 5,000	13,000
	33,000			33,000
Preference share capital	5,000	(C1) 5,000		
Preference share redemption	–	(D1) 5,000	(C2) 5,000	–
Ordinary share capital	15,000		(B2) 5,000	20,000
Ordinary share applicants	–	(B1) 5,000	(A2) 5,000	–
Share premium	2,000			2,000
	22,000			22,000
Profit and loss	11,000			11,000
	33,000			33,000

(ii)

	Dr	Cr
(A1) Preference share capital	5,000	
(A2) Preference share redemption		5,000
Shares to be redeemed		

	Dr	Cr
(B1) Preference share redemption	5,000	
(B2) Bank		5,000
Cash paid on redemption		

	Dr	Cr
(C1) Profit and loss appropriation	5,000	
(C2) Capital redemption reserve		5,000
Transfer per Companies Act		

	Balances before	Effect Dr	Cr	Balances after
Net assets (except bank)	20,000			20,000
Bank	13,000		(B2) 5,000	8,000
	33,000			28,000
Preference share capital	5,000	(A1) 5,000		–
Preference share redemption	–	(B1) 5,000	(A2) 5,000	–
Ordinary share capital	15,000			15,000
Capital redemption reserve	–		(C2) 5,000	5,000
Share premium	2,000			2,000
	22,000			22,000
Profit and loss	11,000	(C1) 5,000		6,000
	33,000			28,000

(iii)

		Dr	Cr
(A1)	Bank	1,500	
	(A2) Ordinary share applicants		1,500
Cash received from applicants			

(B1)	Ordinary share applicants	1,500	
	(B2) Ordinary share capital		1,500
Ordinary shares allotted			

(C1)	Profit and loss appropriation	3,500	
	(C2) Capital redemption reserve		3,500
Part of redemption not covered by new issue, to comply with Companies Act.			

(D1)	Preference share capital	5,000	
	(D2) Preference share redemption		5,000
Shares to be redeemed.			

(E1)	Preference share redemption	5,000	
	(E2) Bank		5,000
Payment made for redemption			

	Balances before	Effect Dr	Cr	Balances after
Net assets (except bank)	20,000			20,000
Bank	13,000	(A1) 1,500	(E2) 5,000	9,500
	33,000			29,500
Preference share capital	5,000	(D1) 5,000		–
Preference share redemption	–	(E1) 5,000	(D2) 5,000	–
Ordinary share capital	15,000		(B2) 1,500	16,500
Ordinary share applicants	–	(B1) 1,500	(A2) 1,500	–
Capital redemption reserve	–		(C2) 3,500	3,500
Share premium	2,000			2,000
	22,000			22,000
Profit and loss	11,000	(C1) 3,500		7,500
	33,000			29,500

(iv)

	Dr	Cr
(A1) Preference share capital	5,000	
(A2) Preference share redemption		5,000
Shares to be redeemed		

	Dr	Cr
(B1) Profit and loss appropriation	1,250	
(B2) Preference share redemption		1,250
Premium on redemption of shares not previously issued at premium		

	Dr	Cr
(C1) Profit and loss appropriation	5,000	
(C2) Capital redemption reserve		5,000
Transfer because shares redeemed out of distributable profits		

	Dr	Cr
(D1) Preference share redemption	6,250	
(D2) Bank		6,250
Payment on redemption		

	Balances before	Effect Dr	Cr	Balances after
Net assets (except bank)	20,000			20,000
Bank	13,000		(D2) 6,250	6,750
	33,000			26,750
Preference share capital	5,000	(A1) 5,000		–
Preference share redemption	–	(D1) 6,250	(A2) 5,000	–
			(B2) 1,250	
Ordinary share capital	15,000			15,000
Capital redemption reserve	–		(C2) 5,000	5,000
Share premium	2,000			2,000
	22,000			22,000
		(C1) 5,000		
Profit and loss	11,000	(B1) 1,250		4,750
	33,000			26,750

(v)

	Dr	Cr
(A1) Bank	7,000	
(A2) Ordinary share applicants		7,000
Cash received from applicants		

	Dr	Cr
(B1) Ordinary share applicants	7,000	
(B2) Ordinary share capital		7,000
Ordinary shares allotted		

	Dr	Cr
(C1) Preference share capital	5,000	
(C2) Preference share redemption		5,000
Shares being redeemed		

	Dr	Cr
(D1) Share premium account	1,500	
(D2) Preference share redemption		1,500
Amount of share premium account used for redemption		

(E1)	Profit and loss appropriation		500		
	(E2) Preference share redemption			500	

Excess of premium payable over amount of share premium
account usable for the purpose

(F1)	Preference share redemption		7,000		
	(F2) Bank			7,000	

Amount payable on redemption

	Balances before	Effect Dr	Cr	Balances after
Net assets (except bank)	20,000			20,000
Bank	13,000	(A1) 7,000	(F2) 7,000	13,000
	33,000			33,000
Preference share capital	5,000	(C1) 5,000		–
Preference share redemption	–	(F1) 7,000	(C2) 5,000	–
			(D2) 1,500	
			(E2) 500	
Ordinary share capital	15,000		(B2) 7,000	22,000
Ordinary share applicants	–	(B1) 7,000	(A2) 7,000	–
Share premium account	2,000	(D1) 1,500		500
	22,000			22,500
Profit and loss	11,000	(E1) 500		10,500
	33,000			33,000

5.3

(a) See text Sections 4.11, 4.12 and 4.13. Apply to facts shown.

(b)

The Journal	Dr	Cr
6% Debentures	5,000,000	
Debenture redemption account		5,000,000
Transfer of nominal value of		
debentures to be redeemed		
Debenture redemption account	4,750,000	
Bank		4,750,000
Amount paid for redemption		
Debenture redemption account	250,000	
Debenture redemption reserve		250,000
Profit on redemption transferred		
Profit and loss appropriation	5,000,000	
Debenture redemption reserve		5,000,000
Nominal value of debentures redeemed transferred		
to debenture redemption reserve as per company's policy		

6.1

Duke Ltd
Balance Sheets (after takeover)

	(i)	(ii)	(iii)
Goodwill	9,000	11,000	10,000
Machinery	15,000	15,000	15,000
Fixtures	28,000	28,000	28,000
Motor vehicles	9,500	9,500	9,500
Stock	14,000	14,000	14,000
Debtors	1,500	1,500	1,500
Bank	3,000	25,000	25,000
	80,000	104,000	103,000

	(i)	(ii)	(iii)
Share capital	50,000	70,000	55,000
Share premium		4,000	1,000
Profit and loss	30,000	30,000	30,000
Debentures			17,000
	80,000	104,000	103,000

6.2 (a)

The Journal

	Dr	Cr
Realisation account	45,800	
Plant		26,000
Fixtures		4,600
Stock		9,000
Debtors		6,200
Assets taken over by Nashville		
Creditors	1,200	
Bank		1,200
Paid off creditors		
Creditors (9,000 – 1,200)	7,800	
Realisation		7,800
Creditors taken over		
Nashville Ltd	41,000	
Realisation		41,000
Sale price of assets		
Realisation	3,000	
Capital		3,000
Profit on realisation		
Capital	41,000	
Nashville Ltd		
Debentures		6,000
Preference shares		10,000
Ordinary shares: 20,000 shares at premium 25%		25,000
Settlement from Nashville Ltd which closes the books		

(b)
Nashville Ltd
Balance Sheet as at 1 January 19X2

Goodwill	11,400
Plant and machinery	17,000
Fixtures and fittings	5,000
Stock	9,000
Debtors	6,200
	48,600
11% Preference shares	10,000
Ordinary shares	20,000
Share premium	5,000
8% Debentures	6,000
Trade creditors	7,600
	48,600

(c) The difference between the agreed valuations of identifiable assets and the purchase price is treated as goodwill, i.e. £11,400.

When revenue reserves have been built up the goodwill will be written off to reserves.

6.4 (a)

Capital: Arthur

Vehicle taken over	1,500	Balance b/f	13,000
Unity Ltd: shares	20,000	Current account transferred	6,000
Cash to settle	15,200	Realisation: profit share	17,700
	36,700		36,700

Capital: Barbara

Unity Ltd: shares	20,000	Balance b/f	12,000
Cash to settle	7,620	Current account transferred	5,000
		Realisation: profit share	10,620
	27,620		27,620

Capital: Carl

Current account transferred	2,000	Balance b/f	10,000
Unity Ltd: shares	20,000	Realisation: profit share	7,080
		Cash paid in to settle	4,920
	22,000		22,000

Current Account: Arthur

Transfer to Capital	6,000	Balance b/f	6,000

Current Account: Barbara

Transfer to Capital	5,000	Balance b/f	5,000

Current Account: Carl

Balance b/f	2,000	Transfer to Capital	2,000

Workings:

Opening Balance Sheet

Capitals:	A	13,000		Goodwill	2,000
	B	12,000		Other assets	
	C	10,000	35,000	(balance)	42,000
Current:	A	6,000			
	B	5,000			
	C	(2,000)	9,000		
			44,000		44,000

Sale price to Unity Ltd: Other assets		42,000	
Goodwill		38,000	80,000
Less Vehicle not taken			2,100
Sale price			77,900
Original value 44,000 − 2,100			41,900
Profit on sale to Unity			36,000
Less Loss on vehicle 2,100 − 1,500			600
Net profit on realisation			35,400

Profit shared A $\frac{5}{10}$ 17,700: B $\frac{3}{10}$ 10,620: C $\frac{2}{10}$ 7,080

(*b*)

Unity Ltd
Balance Sheet as at 1 January 19X0

Goodwill	38,000
Other assets	39,900
	77,900
Ordinary share capital	60,000
Directors loans*	17,900
	77,900

*The net figure of 17,900 needed by the company to pay cash for the balance has come either from the partners making loans to the company or from a bank overdraft.

(*c*) (i) Against reserves (when there are any)
(ii) Against profit and loss account over term of its useful economic life.

6.6 (*a*)

Magnum Ltd
Balance Sheet as at 1 January 19X0

Fixed assets			
Intangible assets			
Goodwill (W1)		15,000	
Tangible assets			
Freehold land and buildings	60,000		
Plant and machinery	29,000	89,000	
Investments (W2)		70,000	174,000
Current assets			
Stock		7,000	
Debtors		11,000	
		18,000	
Less Creditors		12,000	
Net current assets			6,000
			180,000
Ordinary shares £0.50: Authorised			150,000
Issued (W3)			112,500
Share premium (W)			67,500
			180,000
Workings:			
(W1) Goodwill: Jones – price			110,000
Assets 60,000 + 29,000 + 7,000 +11,000 =		107,000	
Less Creditors		12,000	95,000
			15,000

(W2) Shares in Micro valued at 50,000 × 1.40 = 70,000

(W3) Shares 50p at premium 30p in payment
For Jones: price 110,000 ÷ 80p = 137,500 shares
For Micro: price 70,000 ÷ 80p = 87,500 shares
Nominal value shares = (137,500 + 87,500) × 50p = 112,500

(W4) Share premium
(137,500+ 87,500) × 30p = 67,500

(b)

Capital: John Jones

Bank taken over		3,000	Balance b/f	56,000
Shares from Magnum [*2]		63,200	⅗ profit on realisation [*1]	10,200
		66,200		66,200

Capital: Mary Jones

Shares from Magnum [*2]		46,800	Balance b/f	40,000
			⅖ profit on realisation [*1]	6,800
		46,800		46,800

[*1] Profit on realisation:

Sale price		110,000
Assets at balance sheet values except bank	105,000	
Less Creditors	12,000	93,000
		17,000
Profit apportioned: John ⅗	10,200	
Mary ⅖	6,800	17,000

[*2] Shares from Magnum:

John: 79,000 shares worth 80p each =	63,200
Mary: 58,500 shares worth 80p each =	46,800
	110,000

(c) (i) Cost concept does not take inflation into account.
(ii) It is the market value that is important, not the balance sheet value.

6.7 (a)

Mater
Net assets as at 30 September 19X0

Capital 1 April 19X0	80,000
Add net profit for 6 months ½ × 18,000	9,000
	89,000
Less Drawings for 6 months, 6 × 800	4,800
Capital 30 September 19X0 (i.e. net assets)	84,200

Pater
Net assets as at 30 September 19X0

Capital 1 July 19X0	50,000
Add net profit for 3 months, 3/9 × 9,900	3,300
	53,300
Less Drawings for 3 months, 3 × 600	1,800
	51,500

Note: Goodwill is not brought into account until 1 October 19X0.

(b)

Family Ltd
Profit and Loss Account for the six months to 31 March 19X1

Profit ($\frac{6}{12} \times 18{,}000 + \frac{6}{9} \times 9{,}900$) (after depreciation 7,500)		15,600
Less Directors' remuneration (6,000 + 4,500)		10,500
		5,100
Less Appropriations:		
Formation expenses written off	200	
Goodwill written off	1,500	1,700
Unappropriated profits carried forward		3,400

(c)

Family Ltd
Balance Sheet as at 31 March 19X1

Goodwill *less* written off (12,000 – 1,500)		10,500
Fixed assets at cost (W1)	87,000	
Less Depreciation	7,500	79,500
		90,000
Current assets (67,400 + 40,600 + 800)	108,800	
Less Current liabilities (33,500 + 12,100)	45,600	63,200
		153,200
Share capital		1,000
Profit and loss account		3,400
Directors' loan accounts (W2)		148,800
		153,200

(W1)	*Mater*			*Pater*	
Cost	90,000			60,000	
Depreciation to					
31 Mar 19X0	27,000	63,000	to 30 June 19X0	30,000	30,000
Less Further depreciation					
$\frac{6}{12} \times 9{,}000$		4,500	$\frac{3}{9} \times 4{,}500$		1,500
		58,500			28,500

87,000

(W2)	*Mater: Loan account*			
Drawings	4,800	Goodwill	8,000
Paid to bank	500	Net assets taken over	84,200
Balance c/d	92,900	Directors' remuneration	6,000
	98,200		98,200

	Pater: Loan account			
Drawings	3,600	Goodwill	4,000
Paid to bank	500	Net assets taken over	51,500
Balance c/d	55,900	Directors' remuneration	4,500
	60,000		60,000

7.1   Seeds Ltd

Available for dividends

General reserve		40,000
Foreign exchange reserve		5,000
Profit and loss		45,000
		90,000
Less retained in profit and loss by company policy		25,000
Available		65,000
Less 10% preference dividend	5,000	
30% ordinary dividend	60,000	65,000

Answer: 30 per cent ordinary dividend

Plant Ltd

Available for dividends

General reserve		70,000
Fixed assets replacement reserve		20,000
Profit and loss		63,000
		153,000
Less Retained in profit and loss by company policy		40,000
Available		113,000
Less 10% preference dividend	8,000	
35% ordinary dividend	105,000	113,000

Answer: 35 per cent ordinary dividend

7.3

(a)   **Grimble Ltd**

Profit and Loss Appropriation Account for year to 31 December 19X0

Net profit for the year (W1)		262,175
Add Retained profits brought forward		188,300
		450,475
Less Taxation on profits		60,000
		390,475
Less Appropriations		
9% Preference dividends	5,040	
Ordinary dividend *	56,000	61,040
Unappropriated profits carried to next year		329,435
(W1) Net profit per question	265,500	
Less ½ year's debenture interest	3,325	262,175

* Assumed that ordinary shares have nominal value of £1 each

(b)   *(Revised) Trial Balance as at 31 December 19X0*

	Dr	Cr
9% Preference share capital		56,000
Ordinary share capital (W2)		420,000
7% Debentures		95,000
Capital redemption reserve (W3)		7,000
Profit and loss		329,435
Taxation owing		60,000
Debenture interest	3,325	
Preference dividend (½ year)	2,520	
Ordinary dividend	56,000	

(W2) 280,000 + bonus 140,000 = 420,000

(W3) 147,000 − used for bonus shares 140,000 = 7,000

7.3 (continued)

Note: Fixed assets will have risen by £20,000 (Dr) and the revaluation reserve will have risen by £20,000 (Cr).

7.5 (*a*)

Expansion plc

Balance Sheet extracts

Paid-up share capital	
100,000 preference shares at £1	100,000
1,300,000 ordinary shares at 50p (W1)	650,000
Reserves	
Share premium (W2)	465,000
Capital redemption reserve (75,000 – bonus)	25,000
Revaluation reserve	100,000
General reserve	200,000
Asset replacement reserve	50,000
Profit and loss account	75,000
	1,665,000
Also in balance sheet	
Allotment monies owing (W3)	383,750

(W1)	Original 500,000 × 50p	250,000
	Bonus issue 100,000 × 50p	50,000
	Rights issue 600,000 × 50p	300,000
	Additional shares 50,000 + 50,000 = 100,000 × 50p	50,000
		650,000
(W2)	Original	100,000
	Rights issue 600,000 × 40p	240,000
	Additional issue 100,000 × 1.25	125,000
		465,000
(W3)	Allotment monies owing	
	On rights issue 600,000 × 40p =	240,000
	On additional 100,000 × 1.50 =	150,000
		390,000
	Less Applications overpaid by public 25,000 × 25p	6,250
		383,750

Note: normally shares would not be allotted until allotment money was received. The examiner indicates otherwise.

(*b*)

Banks

Rights issue: applications (600,000 × 10p)	60,000
Applications: additional shares (125,000 × 25p)	31,250
Rights issue: allotment (600,000 × 80p)	480,000
Additional shares: allotment (100,000 × 1.50) – (25,000 × 25p)	143,750

N.B. It is assumed that the bank account should include allotment monies.

(*c*) *See* text Section 4.2

7.7 (a)

T. Torrents Ltd
(Corrected) Balance Sheet as at 30 April 19X0

Fixed assets

Freehold land and buildings at valuation			70,000
Plant and machinery at cost (W1)		35,000	
Less Depreciation to date		9,600	25,400
Motor vehicles at cost		16,000	
Less Depreciation to date		9,600	6,400
			101,800

Current assets

Stock (W4)		27,000	
Trade debtors and amounts prepaid	14,000		
Less Provision for bad debts (W3)	340	13,660	
Bank (W2)		1,800	
		42,460	

Amounts falling due within one year

Trade creditors and accrued charges	9,800		
Proposed dividend	6,500	16,300	26,160
			127,960

Amounts falling due after more than one year

8% Debentures (40,000 – 6,000)			34,000
			93,960

Represented by:
Capital and reserves

Ordinary shares (60,000 + 5,000)	65,000
Share premium (W6)	5,800
Asset revaluation reserve	14,000
Retained earnings (W5)	9,160
	93,960

(b) *See* text Section 5.2

Workings

(W1)

	Cost	Depreciation
Machinery 30 April 19X0	47,000	14,100
Sale (at book values)	12,000	4,500
	35,000	9,600

Sale at net book value 12,000 – 4,500 =	7,500
Sold for	5,000
Loss to profit and loss	2,500

Purchases to be increased by 5,000 (sale price in goods)

(W2)

Bank	7,000
Less debentures bought	5,200
	1,800

Profit on redemption transferred to share premium account

(W3) Debtors 14,000 – prepaid 400 = 13,600
Provision = 13,600 × 2½% = 340

(W4) Stock 29,000 – belonging to customer 2,000 = 27,000

(W5)	Retained earnings		25,500
	Less Dividend	6,500	
	Less Loss on machine (W1)	2,500	
	Less Bad debts provision (W3)	340	
	Less Stock (W4)	2,000	
	Less Goods for machine (+ purchases)	5,000	16,340
	Revised figure		9,160
(W6)	Share premium		10,000
	Add Profit on debentures redeemed		800
			10,800
	Less Bonus shares		5,000
			5,800

8.1 (*a*) Whilst land is not always depreciated per SSAP 12 there are exceptions, and this is one, so depreciation is appropriate.

(*b*) This is a non-adjusting event per SSAP 17. The previous year's accounts need no adjustment. However, a note to them is appropriate if the amount is material.

(*c*) Per SSAP 18 prudence takes over. As a contingent loss of £10 million is almost certain, we should accrue this loss in last year's accounts.

(*d*) SSAP 22 would not allow this as it has not been purchased.

(*e*) Not allowed per SSAP 22. £20 million should instead be credited to a capital reserve.

(*f*) Not allowed per SSAP 9. The stock should be at lower of cost or net realisable value.

(*g*) SSAP 3 insists on its disclosure.

(*h*) It would be possible to publish one of the working capital type, but it would have to be in addition to a cash flow statement, not instead of it. *See* FRS 3.

8.3 (i) If a reduced level of activity affects the rate of depreciation in this ratio, then the treatment given is permissible.

(ii) Freehold property should be depreciated (*see* SSAP 9). Therefore, unless the valuation is to be altered, depreciation of £8,000 should be charged.

(iii) Capital reserves under company law cannot be used for payment of cash dividends. Therefore transfer to profit and loss is not allowed. Reduce net profit by £18,000.

(iv) Loan stock interest is an expense, not an appropriation. It should therefore be charged in the main profit and loss account, not in the appropriation account.

Adjustments to profit before taxation for year ended 31 May 19X2		
Original calculation		40,000
Less Depreciation on freehold property (ii)	8,000	
Less Share premium (iii)	18,000	
Less Loan stock interest (iv)	15,000	41,000
Net loss		(1,000)

8.5 (*a*) For details consult your first year's textbook.

(*b*)(i) Consistency concept. One method of depreciation has been used for several years. To change would be inconsistent and make comparisons difficult.

(ii) Accrual concept. This is because expenditure occurs in one period but includes benefit also in the following period as well.

(iii) Materiality concept. Bad debts of £20,000 (when compared with £3,000 per year) are significant. They should be brought into account and must be disclosed.

(*c*)(i) Depreciation for 19X1 on straight-line basis (15,000 + 11,000)	26,000
Depreciation for 19X1 on reducing balance basis	
(99,000 + 110,000) × 20%	41,800
Reduction in net profit	15,800

(ii)   *Revised profit for Paula Rowe Ltd for year ended 31 March 19X1*
      Original gross profit   50,000
      Less Expenses (40,000 – 7,500 c/f)   32,500
      Corrected net profit   17,500

(iii)   **Rendell Stott Ltd**

Summarised Profit and Loss Account for year ended 30 April 19X2

Gross profit		80,000
Less: Administrative expenses (W1)	32,350	
Selling and distribution expenses (W2)	12,000	
Financial charges (W3)	4,200	
Bad debts	20,000	68,550
Net profit		11,450

Workings
(W1) 2,000+1,050+19,000+8,000+1,400+900	=	32,350
(W2) 1,500+4,600+3,400+2,500	=	12,000
(W3) 2,500+1,700	=	4,200

9.1 (i) (for internal use)   **Rogers plc**

Trading and Profit and Loss Account for the year ended 31 December 19X2

Sales		288,000	
Less Returns inwards		11,500	276,500
Less Cost of sales:			
Stock 1 January 19X2		57,500	
Add Purchases	164,000		
Less Returns outwards	2,000	162,000	
Carriage inwards		1,300	
		220,800	
Less Stock 31 December 19X2		64,000	156,800
Gross profit			119,700
Distribution costs:			
Salaries and wages	2,800		
Rent and rates	3,750		
General distribution expenses	4,860		
Motor expenses	3,600		
Depreciation: Motors	6,500		
Equipment	700	22,210	
Administrative expenses:			
Salaries and wages	5,600		
Rent and rates	2,500		
General administrative expenses	3,320		
Motor expenses	3,600		
Auditors' remuneration	500		
Discounts allowed	3,940		
Bad debts	570		
Depreciation: Motors	3,500		
Equipment	1,100	24,630	46,840
			72,860

Other operating income: Royalties receivable		1,800
		74,660
Income from participating interests	660	
Interest on bank deposit	770	1,430
		76,090
Interest payable: Debenture interest		2,400
Profit on ordinary activities before taxation		73,690
Tax on profit on ordinary activities		30,700
Profit on ordinary activities after taxation		42,990
Retained profits from last year		15,300
		58,290
Transfer to general reserve	8,000	
Proposed ordinary dividend	30,000	38,000
Retained profits carried forward to next year		20,290

(ii) (published accounts)   **Rogers plc**

Profit and Loss Account for the year ended 31 December 19X2

Turnover		276,500
Cost of sales		156,800
Gross profit		119,700
Distribution costs	22,210	
Administrative expenses	24,630	46,840
		72,860
Other operating income		1,800
		74,660
Income from participating interests	660	
Other interest receivable	770	1,430
		76,090
Interest payable		2,400
Profit on ordinary activities before taxation		73,690
Tax on profit on ordinary activities		30,700
Profit on ordinary activities after taxation		42,990
Retained profits from last year		15,300
		58,290
Transfer to general reserve	8,000	
Proposed ordinary dividend	30,000	38,000
Retained profits carried forward to next year		20,290

Notes to accounts on debenture interest and auditors' remuneration.

9.2

(i)

(for internal use)

Federal plc

Trading and Profit and Loss Account for the year ended 31 December 19X4

Sales		849,000	
Less Returns inwards		5,800	843,200
Less Cost of sales:			
Stock 1 January 19X4		64,500	
Add Purchases	510,600		
Less Returns outwards	3,300	507,300	
Carriage inwards		4,900	
		576,700	
Less Stock 31 December 19X4		82,800	
Cost of goods sold		493,900	
Wages		11,350	
Depreciation of plant and machinery		1,500	
			506,750
Gross profit			336,450
Distribution costs:			
Salaries and wages	29,110		
Rent and rates	20,000		
Motor expenses	10,400		
General distribution expenses	8,220		
Haulage costs	2,070		
Depreciation: Motors	15,000		
Plant and machinery	8,000	92,800	
Administrative expenses:			
Salaries and wages	20,920		
Rent and rates	5,000		
Motor expenses	5,200		
General administrative expenses	2,190		
Bad debts	840		
Discounts allowed	5,780		
Auditors' remuneration	2,000		
Directors' remuneration	5,000		
Depreciation: Motors	7,000		
Plant and machinery	5,000		
	58,930		
Less Discounts received	6,800	52,130	144,930
			191,520
Income from participating interests		3,500	
Interest from Government Securities		1,600	5,100
			196,620
Amount written off investment in related companies		14,000	
Debenture interest		3,800	17,800
Profit on ordinary activities before taxation			178,820
Tax on profit on ordinary activities			74,000
Profit on ordinary activities after taxation			104,820
Retained profits from last year			37,470
			142,290
Transfer to debenture redemption reserve		20,000	
Proposed ordinary dividend		50,000	70,000
Retained profits carried forward to next year			72,290

(ii) (published accounts)

Federal plc

Profit and Loss Account for the year ended 31 December 19X4

Turnover		843,200
Cost of sales		506,750
Gross profit		336,450
Distribution costs	92,800	
Administrative expenses	52,130	144,930
		191,520
Income from participating interests	3,500	
Other interest receivable	1,600	5,100
		196,620
Amounts written off investments	14,000	
Interest payable	3,800	17,800
Profit on ordinary activities before taxation		178,820
Tax on profit on ordinary activities		74,000
Profit on ordinary activities after taxation		104,820
Retained profits from last year		37,470
		142,290
Transfer to reserves	20,000	
Proposed ordinary dividend	50,000	70,000
Retained profits carried forward to next year		72,290

9.5 (a)

Wilkinson Ltd

Year ended 31 December 19X0

Gross profit as calculated		97,000
Add 3 reduction in purchases (W1)		3,500
		100,500
Less 4 reduction in sales (W2)		29,525
Gross profit as revised		70,975
(W1) Returns + VAT =	4,025	
Less VAT 15/115 × 4,025	525	
To be deducted from purchases	3,500	
(W2) Original sales figure		199,525
Less returns + VAT		4,025
		195,500
Less VAT 15/115 × 195,500		25,500
New sales figure		170,000
i.e. reduction of 199,525 − 170,000 =		29,525
Net profit on ordinary activities as calculated		25,000
Add overprovision tax in previous year (1)		2,000
		27,000
Less:		
Extra depreciation (W3)	500	
Overstatement in gross profit (W4)	26,025	26,525
Net profit as revised		475

(W3)   Value 100,800 ÷ 48 years = 2,100 per year
2,100 − 1,600 previously = 500

(W4)   97,000 − 70,975 = 26,025

10.1

Owen Ltd

Balance Sheet as at 31 December 19X1

Called-up share capital not paid			150
Fixed assets			
Intangible assets			
Development costs	3,070		
Goodwill	21,000	24,070	
Tangible assets			
Land and buildings	32,000		
Plant and machinery	7,100	39,100	
Investments			
Shares in undertakings in which the company has a participating interest		35,750	98,920
Current assets			
Stock			
Raw materials and consumables	3,470		
Finished goods and goods for resale	18,590	22,060	
Debtors			
Trade debtors	17,400		
Amounts owed by undertakings in which the company has a participating interest	3,000		
Prepayments	1,250	21,650	
		43,710	
Creditors: amounts falling due within one year			
Debentures	6,000		
Bank overdrafts	4,370		
Trade creditors	12,410		
Bills of exchange payable	1,600	24,380	
Net current assets			19,330
Total assets less Current liabilities			118,400
Creditors: amounts falling due after one year			
Debentures	4,000		
Bills of exchange payable	2,000		6,000
			112,400
Capital and reserves			
Called-up share capital			75,000
Share premium account			20,000
Other reserves:			
Capital redemption reserve	5,000		
General reserve	4,000		9,000
Profit and loss account			8,400
			112,400

Notes:

(i)	Called-up share capital consists of:		£
	50,000 £1 ordinary shares		50,000
	50,000 preference shares of 50p each		25,000
			75,000
ii)	Land and buildings:	£	
	Cost		48,000
	Depreciation to 31 December 19X0	12,000	
	Depreciation for year to 31 December 19X1	4,000	16,000
			32,000
(iii)	Plant and machinery:		
	Cost		12,500
	Depreciation to 31 December 19X0	3,600	
	Depreciation for year to 31 December 19X1	1,800	5,400
			7,100

10.2

Belle Works plc

Balance Sheet as at 30 September 19X4

Fixed assets
Intangible assets
Concessions, patents, licences, trade marks
  and similar rights and assets   1,500
Goodwill   17,500   19,000

Tangible assets
Land and buildings   72,500
Plant and machinery   19,400   91,900   110,900

Current assets
Stock
Raw materials and consumables   14,320
Work-in-progress   5,640
Finished goods and goods for resale   13,290   33,250

Debtors
Trade debtors   11,260
Other debtors   1,050
Prepayments and accrued income   505   12,815
                                                                  46,065

Creditors: amounts falling due within one year
Debenture loans   6,000
Bank loans and overdrafts   3,893
Trade creditors   11,340
Bills of exchange payable   4,000
Other creditors including taxation
  and social security   14,675   39,908
Net current assets   6,157
Total assets less Current liabilities   117,057

Creditors: amounts falling due after more than one year
Debenture loans   12,000
Trade creditors   1,260   13,260

Provisions for liabilities and charges
Pensions and similar obligations   1,860
Taxation, including deferred taxation   640   2,500   15,760
                                                                             101,297

Capital and reserves
Called-up share capital   70,000
Share premium account   5,000
Revaluation reserve   10,500

Other reserves
General reserve   6,000
Foreign exchange reserve   3,500   9,500
Profit and loss account   6,297
                                                                             101,297

Notes appended to the accounts on the details of tangible assets and depreciation, also exact details of items lumped under group descriptions.

11.1 *See* text Section 11.6

11.2 *See* text Section 11.8

11.3 *See* text Section 11.4

11.4 *See* text Section 11.9

12.1 *See* text Section 12.1

12.2 *See* text Section 12.2

12.3 *See* text Section 12.6

12.4 (i)

G Ltd and subsidiary H Ltd

Balance Sheet as at 31 December 19X9

Fixed assets (52,000 + 18,000)		70,000
Goodwill (28,000 – 15,000 – 10,000)		3,000
Current assets (45,000 + 11,000 – 800)	55,200	
Less Current liabilities (15,000 + 4,000 – 800)	18,200	37,000
		110,000
Financed by		
Share capital		75,000
Reserves		35,000
		110,000

(ii)

G Ltd and subsidiary H Ltd

Balance Sheet as at 31 December 19X9

Fixed assets (52,000 + 18,000)		70,000
Goodwill 28,000 – 80% × (15,000 + 10,000)		8,000
Current assets (as (i))	55,200	
Less Current liabilities (as (i))	18,200	37,000
		115,000
Financed by		
Share capital		75,000
Reserves		35,000
Minority interest		
20% Share capital of H	3,000	
20% Reserves of H	2,000	5,000
		115,000

(iii)

G Ltd and subsidiary H Ltd
Balance Sheet as at 31 December 19X9

Fixed assets (52,000 + 18,000)		70,000
Goodwill (28,000 − 60% × (15,000 +10,000))		13,000
Current assets (as (i))	55,200	
Less Current liabilities (as (i))	18,200	37,000
		120,000
Financed by		
Share capital		75,000
Reserves		35,000
Minority interest		
40% Share Capital of H	6,000	
40% Reserves of H	4,000	10,000
		120,000

13.1 *See* text Section 13.6

13.2 *See* text Section 13.6

Difficulties lie in trying to give these measures a value in money that would get universal acceptance. How can you place a money value on living conditions, for example?

13.3 *See* text Section 13.7

13.4 Basically there are many things which could be done to improve the various parts of 'social well-being'.

(i) Benefits cost a lot of money in the short-term, and
(ii) Beneficial effects are felt only in the long term.
     Examples are better education and housing.

13.5 *See* text Section 13.10

14.1

(i) Accounting rate of return

	F	G	H
$\dfrac{\text{Average yearly profit}}{\text{Average investment}}$	$\dfrac{1,667}{10,000} = 16.67\%$	$\dfrac{1,400}{10,000} = 14\%$	$\dfrac{1,500}{10,000} = 15\%$

(ii) F = 2.29 years: G 3.8 years: H 2.6 years

(iii)

	F	G	H
0.926	× 10,000 = 9,260	× 6,000 = 5,556	× 8,000 = 7,408
0.857	× 8,000 = 6,856	× 5,000 = 4,285	× 9,000 = 7,713
0.794	× 7,000 = 5,558	× 5,000 = 3,970	× 5,000 = 3,970
0.735		× 5,000 = 3,675	× 4,000 = 2,940
0.681		× 6,000 = 4,086	
Total PV	21,674	21,572	22,031
Less Investment	20,000	20,000	20,000
NPV	1,674	1,572	2,031

(iv) Internal rate of return

Take 14% to give negative net present value

	F	G	H
0.877	× 10,000 = 8,770	× 6,000 = 5,262	× 8,000 = 7,016
0.769	× 8,000 = 6,152	× 5,000 = 3,845	× 9,000 = 6,921
0.675	× 7,000 = 4,725	× 5,000 = 3,375	× 5,000 = 3,375
0.592		× 5,000 = 2,960	× 4,000 = 2,368
0.519		× 6,000 = 3,114	
	19,647	18,556	19,680
Less Investment	20,000	20,000	20,000
	(353)	(1,444)	(320)

Also use NPVs given 8% rate shown in (iii)

$$F \quad 8\% + \left(6\% \times \frac{1,674}{1,674 + 353}\right) = 12.96\%$$

$$G \quad 8\% + \left(6\% \times \frac{1,572}{1,572 + 1,444}\right) = 11.13\%$$

$$H \quad 8\% + \left(6\% \times \frac{2,031}{2,031 + 320}\right) = 13.18\%$$

14.3

A   *Payback period:*

		A		B
Capital cost		45,000		53,000
Net cash inflow				
Sales		80,000		100,000
Less Cost of sales	40,000		50,000	
Admin. exps	15,000	55,000*	10,000	60,000*
Net cash inflows		25,000		40,000

Payback period $\dfrac{45,000}{25,000}$ = 1.8 years $\dfrac{53,000}{40,000}$ = 1.325 years

*Note: Depreciation is *not* a cash outflow and should be ignored.

Net Present value:

Year		A		B
1	0.893 × 25,000	22,325	× 40,000	35,720
2	0.797 × 25,000	19,925	× 40,000	31,880
3	0.712 × 25,000	17,800	× 40,000	28,480
4	0.636 × 25,000	15,900	× 40,000	25,440
5	0.567 × 25,000	14,175	× 37,000*	20,979
6	0.507 × 25,000	12,675		
7	0.452 × 25,000	11,300		
8	0.404 × 20,000*	8,080		
		122,180		142,499
Less Original investment		45,000		53,000
		77,180		89,499

*Net after receipt of money for scrap.

B   Would recommend B. Lower payback period and greater NPV. Also figures too far into the future, as in A, are less reliable.

C   *See* text Section 14.12.

D   Sunk costs, therefore do not concern the future and are not brought into these calculations.

14.5

	Workings Gross		Present value
Investment in Gudshotti			
50% transfer fee now	450,000		450,000
Plus in 1 year's time	150,000	× 0.877	131,550
Plus in 2 years' time	150,000	× 0.769	115,350
Plus in 3 years' time	150,000	× 0.675	101,250
Signing-on fee now	200,000		200,000
Contract: in 1 year	50,000	× 0.877	43,850
in 2 years	50,000	× 0.769	38,450
in 3 years	50,000	× 0.675	33,750
in 4 years	50,000	× 0.592	29,600
	1,300,000		1,143,800

Net cash inflows per year:
If player bought:

Spectators 33,000 × £3 × 30		2,970,000
Sponsorship		50,000
		3,020,000

Less Costs which alter:

Promotional activities	240,000	
Other players' earnings		
(6,000 × 50) + 20%	360,000	600,000
Income before fixed expenses		2,420,000

Player not bought:

Spectators 30,000 × £2.50 × 30	2,250,000

Less Costs:

Players' earnings	
6,000 × 50	300,000
Income before fixed expenses	1,950,000

Therefore extra income per year = 2,420,000 – 1,950,000 = 470,000

(a) Payback period

$$\frac{\text{Gross investment}}{\text{Extra net inflow}} = \frac{1,300,000}{470,000} = 2.77 \text{ years approx.}$$

(b) Present value of cash inflows

Year 1	470,000	× 0.877	=	412,190
Year 2	470,000	× 0.769	=	361,430
Year 3	470,000	× 0.675	=	317,250
Year 4	470,000	× 0.592	=	278,240
				1,369,110
Less Investment (*see Workings*)				1,143,800
Net present value				225,310

(c) Internal rate of return
   Investment
   (*See Workings* at start of answer)
      Taking interest rate of 30%

Transfer fee				450,000
in 1 year	150,000	× 0.769		115,350
in 2 years	150,000	× 0.592		88,800
in 3 years	150,000	× 0.455		68,250
Signing-on fee				200,000
Contract				
in 1 year	50,000	× 0.769		38,450
in 2 years	50,000	× 0.592		29,600
in 3 years	50,000	× 0.455		22,750
in 4 years	50,000	× 0.350		17,500
				1,030,700

Net income				
Year 1	470,000	× 0.769		361,430
Year 2	470,000	× 0.592		278,240
Year 3	470,000	× 0.455		213,850
Year 4	470,000	× 0.350		164,500
				1,018,020

   Net present value is negative
      i.e. 1,018,020 – 1,030,700   =   12,680
   Internal rate of return (*see* formula in text Section 14.8).

$$14\% + \left(16\% \times \frac{225,310}{225,310 + 12,680} \right) = 31.15\% \text{ approx.}$$

(d) Yes, if no better alternative is available. Meets payback criteria and gives positive NPV at cost of capital rate. Although only asked for two other points:

(i)   Have we got sufficient liquid funds to pay 450,000 + 200,000 immediately?
(ii) Effect upon morale of other players to see one player rewarded excessively.
(iii) Can we insure Gudshotti against injury?

Note: We have shown the workings in full. You could have taken various short-cuts to the same answer.

14.7
(a) *See* text Section 4.13.

(b) *See* text Section 4.12.

(c) (i)

	Ajax			Borg		
	Capital		Net cost	Capital		Net cost
Ordinary 16%	700		112.0	300		48
Preference 14%	200		28.0	200		28
Debentures 12%	100	12.0		500	60	
– Tax relief 40%		4.8	7.2		24	36
	1,000		147.2	1,000		112

Weighted average cost of capital:

Ajax $\dfrac{147.2}{1,000} \times 100 = 14.72\%$

Borg $\dfrac{112}{1,000} \times 100 = 11.2\%$

(ii) Ajax has much more ordinary capital at higher percentage dividends. Borg has debentures which are at a lower rate and also has tax relief on them.

(d) (i) First calculate the Internal Rate of Return (IRR) which really represents the cost of investing in this project.

Discount rates		12%			16%	
Year 1	55,000 × 0.893	=	49,115	× 0.862	=	47,140
Year 2	60,000 × 0.797	=	47,820	× 0.743	=	44,580
Year 3	145,000 × 0.712	=	103,240	× 0.641	=	92,945
Year 4	170,000 × 0.636	=	108,120	× 0.552	=	93,840
			308,295			278,505
Less Investment			300,000			300,000
			8,295			(21,495)

$$\text{IRR} = 12\% + \left(4\% \times \frac{8,295}{8,295 + 21,495}\right) = 13.11\% \text{ approx.}$$

(ii) Borg to invest as the return exceeds the cost of capital at present of 11.2%. Ajax not to invest as the return from investment is lower than the cost of capital.

14.8

(a) Weighted average cost of capital

Ordinary shares	1,000 × 14%			=	140
Preference shares	400 × 11%			=	44
Debentures	600 × 10%	=	60		
less tax relief 30%			18		42
Total cost					226

$$\text{Average cost} = \frac{226}{\text{Total capital}} \times 100 = 11.3\%$$

rounded off to 11%

(b) Using 11% discount   *Scheme 1*   *Scheme 2*

Year 1	$14{,}000 \times 0.901$	=	12,614	$14{,}000 \times 0.901$	=	12,614
Year 2	$10{,}000 \times 0.812$	=	8,120	$18{,}000 \times 0.812$	=	14,616
Year 3	$19{,}000 \times 0.731$	=	13,889	$27{,}000 \times 0.731$	=	19,737
Year 4	$24{,}000 \times 0.659$	=	15,816	$31{,}000 \times 0.659$	=	20,429
			50,439			67,396
Less Investment			50,000			70,000
Net present value			439			(2,604)

(c) Accept Scheme 1. Gives positive NPV.
Reject Scheme 2. Gives negative NPV.

(d)   *Scheme 1*   *Scheme 2*

PV as (b)		50,439		67,396
Year 5	$23{,}000 \times 0.594$	13,662	$32{,}000 \times 0.594$	19,008
		64,101		86,404
Less Investment		50,000		70,000
Net present value		14,101		16,404

Would now choose Scheme 2 as net present value is highest.

15.1

(a) (i) Gross profit as % of sales $\dfrac{20{,}000}{80{,}000} \times \dfrac{100}{1} = 25\%$ $\dfrac{24{,}000}{120{,}000} \times \dfrac{100}{1} = 20\%$

(ii) Net profit as % of sales $\dfrac{10{,}000}{80{,}000} \times \dfrac{100}{1} = 12.5\%$ $\dfrac{15{,}000}{120{,}000} \times \dfrac{100}{1} = 12.5\%$

(iii) Expenses as % of sales $\dfrac{10{,}000}{80{,}000} \times \dfrac{100}{1} = 12.5\%$ $\dfrac{9{,}000}{120{,}000} \times \dfrac{100}{1} = 7.5\%$

(iv) Stockturn $\dfrac{60{,}000}{(25{,}000 + 15{,}000) \div 2} = 3 \text{ times}$ $\dfrac{96{,}000}{(22{,}500 + 17{,}500) \div 2} = 4.8 \text{ times}$

(v) Rate of return $\dfrac{10{,}000}{(38{,}000 + 42{,}000) \div 2} \times \dfrac{100}{1} = 25\%$ $\dfrac{15{,}000}{(36{,}000 + 44{,}000) \div 2} \times \dfrac{100}{1} = 37.5\%$

(vi) Current ratio $\dfrac{45{,}000}{5{,}000} = 9$ $\dfrac{40{,}000}{10{,}000} = 4$

(vii) Acid test ratio $\dfrac{30{,}000}{5{,}000} = 6$ $\dfrac{22{,}500}{10{,}000} = 2.25$

(viii) Debtor/sales ratio $\dfrac{25{,}000}{80{,}000} \times 12 = 3.75 \text{ months}$ $\dfrac{20{,}000}{120{,}000} \times 12 = 2 \text{ months}$

(ix) Creditor/purchases ratio $\dfrac{5{,}000}{50{,}000} \times 12 = 1.2 \text{ months}$ $\dfrac{10{,}000}{91{,}000} \times 12 = 1.3 \text{ months}$ approx.

(b) Business B is the most profitable, both in terms of actual net profits £15,000 compared to £10,000, but also in terms of capital employed, B has managed to achieve a return of £37.50 for every £100 invested, i.e. 37.5%. A has managed a lower return of 25%. Reasons – possibly only – as not until you know more about the business could you give a definite answer.

    (i) Possibly managed to sell far more merchandise because of lower prices, i.e. took only 20% margin as compared with A's 25% margin.

(ii) Maybe more efficient use of mechanised means in the business. Note he has more equipment, and perhaps as a consequence kept other expenses down to 6,000 as compared with A's 9,000.

(iii) Did not have as much stock lying idle. Turned over stock 4.8 times in the year as compared with 3 for A.

(iv) A's current ratio of 9 far greater than normally needed. B kept it down to 4. A therefore had too much money lying idle and not doing anything.

(v) Following on from (iv) the Acid Test ratio for A is also higher than necessary.

(vi) Part of the reasons for (iv) and (v) is that A waited (on average) 3.75 months to be paid by his customers. B managed to collect them on a 2 months' average. Money represented by debts is money lying idle.

(vii) A also paid his creditors more quickly than did B, but not by much.

Put all these factors together, and it is obvious that B is running his business far more efficiently, and is more profitable as a consequence.

15.4

(a) Report in outline:

(i) Profitability

This has fallen dramatically over the last 5 years.

ROCE for 19X1 is $\dfrac{10}{500 + 100 + 350 + 50 + 20} \times \dfrac{100}{1} = 1\%$ approx.

Return on total assets is $\dfrac{10}{1,000 + 320} \times \dfrac{100}{1} = 0.8\%$ approx.

Return on total assets after revaluation is $\dfrac{10}{2,800 + 320} \times \dfrac{100}{1} = 0.3\%$ approx.

This shows such a low return that it is probable that the company will have to discontinue trading. The profits are not enough to pay dividends or provide for growth.

(ii) Liquidity

Working capital 320 – stock no value 70 = 250

Working capital ratio $\dfrac{250}{300} = 0.83$ approx.

Acid test 250 – stock 90 = $\dfrac{160}{300} = 0.53$ approx.

Both working capital and liquidity per acid test are inadequate.

Would have to investigate whether or not part of land and buildings could be sold to recover liquidity position.

Note: We are not given any indication as to why trading profits have fallen. Needs investigating before one can say much more.

(b) First ask why Positive invested in Minus in the first place:

Was it   (i)   for ROCE
             (ii)   for takeover eventually
             (iii)   for asset stripping purposes?

Why invest more? (i)   thought it could be managed more profitably
                   (ii)   sell freehold land and buildings at a profit
                   (iii)   gain access to other markets.

Depending on motive could buy other 75% of capital not yet owned for 1,500,000 × 30p = 450,000 (remember these are 25p shares).

Net assets (at revalued figures) worth 2,000,000 + 800,000 + 320,000 − 70,000 = 3,050,000 *less* current liabilities 300,000 and preference shares 100,000 = 2,650,000.

This gives value per share of $\frac{2,650,000}{2,000,000}$ shares = £1.325 per share

Even if only the sale or use of buildings or land are the motive, shares are recommended for purchase.

(c) To buy extra shares
   (i)   Own cash resources. Cash balances not known.
   (ii) Exchanging shares in Positive for those in Minus.
   (iii) Combination (i) and (ii).
   (iv) Issue of shares or debentures to raise cash.
   (v)   Bank loans.

(d)

Positive plc
Balance Sheet as at 1 January 19X1

		000s
Fixed assets		2,100
Investment in subsidiary (W1)		396
Current assets (1360 – shares 156)	1,204	
Less Current liabilities	300	904
		3,400
Financed by		
Issued share capital		1,500
Share premium account		750
General reserve		350
Retained earnings		600
		3,200
11% Debentures		200
		3,400
Working		
(W1) Shares held 500,000 at cost	240	
Extra shares 520,000 × 30p	156	
	396	

15.5   Brief points only. The answer should be in report style.

A   Advantages
   (i)   Interest of 5,000 per year (tax position not known).
   (ii) Financially safe investment.
   (iii) Can realise easily enough.

   Disadvantages
   (i)   Interest rates may fall.
   (ii) No protection against inflation.

B   Advantages
   (i)   Chance to improve business and make more profits.
   (ii) Possibly better return than with other forms of investment.

Disadvantages
(i) Have to cease present occupation with loss of money earned there unless a manager is hired. Should really bring in a deduction of the relevant amount for this to calculate super-profits.
(ii) Takes whole of cash. How about extra cash needed for financing business?
(iii) Risk element.
(iv) Unlimited liability.

C Advantages
(i) Partial security in that limited liability available.
(ii) Outlay of 50,000 for 53,000 net assets.
(iii) Chance to improve profitability.

Disadvantages
(i) Risk element normal in business.
(ii) Preference dividend 1,000 per year reduce net profit to 6,000.
(iii) Heavy fixed charges 1,600 loan stock interest and 1,000 preference dividend have prior claims each year.

D Advantages
(i) Limited liability
(ii) No heavy prior charges such as loan interest and preference dividends.

Disadvantages
(i) Normal ones of being minority shareholder (see text Section 14.6).
(ii) Return only 6.4% even if all profits are paid as dividends.

Further information
(i) Would like to have seen several years' accounts for each organisation.
(ii) Would like to know more about future prospects and plans for each organisation.
(iii) For B, to calculate super profits, would like to know present earnings of Janet James.

15.8

(a) *Trading and Profit and Loss Accounts for the year ended 31 December 19X9*

		X			Y
Sales		480,000			762,500[1]
Less Cost of goods sold		400,000	(+10,000)	610,000
Gross profit		80,000			152,500
Less Admin. expenses (−10,000)	40,000		(−2,500)	57,500
Selling expenses	15,000	55,000		35,000	92,500
Net profit		25,000			60,000

[1] Assumed 25 per cent mark-up despite wrong stock valuation.

(b)

Profitability:	X	Y
Gross profit %	20%	25%

$$\text{Net profit \%} \qquad \frac{25}{480} \times \frac{100}{1} = 5.2\% \qquad\qquad \frac{60}{762.5} \times \frac{100}{1} = 7.87\%$$

$$\text{Stockturn} \qquad \frac{400,000}{40,000} = 10 \text{ times} \qquad\qquad \frac{610,000}{45,000^{*2}} = 13.6 \text{ times}$$

[2] Adjusted to take into account inaccurate valuation.

Return on Capital Employed (ROCE) (previous owners)

$$\frac{25,000}{200,000} \times \frac{100}{1} = 12.5\% \qquad \frac{60,000}{350,000} \times \frac{100}{1} = 17.14\%$$

Based on purchase price of business the ROCE for Adrian Frampton would be:

X	Y
$\frac{25,000}{190,000} \times \frac{100}{1} = 13.15\%$	$\frac{60,000}{400,000} \times \frac{100}{1} = 15\%$

All ratios are favourable for Y. If gross profit ratios remained the same in future together with other expenses then Y business is best value.

However:
(i) Can gross profit ratios of X be improved as compared to those of Y?
(ii) Can stockturn be improved?

If so, then X could be cheapest business to buy as it gives a better ROCE.

(c) (i) Need to know current assets and current liabilities in detail.
    (ii) Are these similar businesses?
         Type of business.
         Areas in which situated.
         Competition.
         Prefer several years' accounts to gauge trends.
         Quality of staff and whether they would continue.

15.10
(a) Ratios:
Working capital 52,000/48,000 = 1.08:1

Acid test 7,000 + 11,000/48,000 = 0.375: 1

Gearing: $\frac{100,000}{100,000 + 400,000} \times \frac{100}{1} = 20\%$

The working capital of 52,000 – 48,000 = 4,000 is totally inadequate. As a ratio this is 1.08:1.
The acid test ratio reveals that the company is unable to pay its current liabilities on time. This could result in its being forced into liquidation.
The company is low geared. It is highly unlikely that there will be funds available in two years' time to redeem the debentures.

(b) The company has been treading a very dangerous path. Whilst the profits per share have been falling regularly, from 0.9p in 19X7 to 0.6p in 19X0 at the same time the dividends have been rising from 0.2p in 19X7 to 0.5p in 19X0.
It is possible that the directors have authorised the payment of dividends when there have been inadequate cash resources to fund them. This may have been done to keep the share prices up artificially, low dividends would push them down to lower values.

(c) (i)   What arrangements are being made to repay the debentures in two years' time?
    (ii) Why have higher dividends been paid than justified?
    (iii) What is the current value of freehold land and buildings?

16.1 *See* text Sections 16.1 and 16.2.

16.2 *See* text Sections 16.1 and 16.2.

16.3 *See* text Section 16.2.

16.4 *See* text Section 16.3.

16.5 *See* text Section 16.4.

16.6 *See* text Section 16.7.

17.1 (i) *f, h.* (ii) *m.* (iii) *a, c, e, g, j,* 4/5ths of *n.t.v.* ¾ of *w, x.* (iv) *b, d, i,* ⅕th of *n, p, q,* part of ¼ of *w.* (v) *l, r, s, z,* part of ¼ of *w.* (vi) *o, k, v, y.*

17.3

Raw materials consumed (120,000 + 400,000 − 160,000)		360,000
Haulage costs		4,000
Direct labour 70% × 220,000		154,000
Royalties		1,600
(*a*) **Prime cost**		519,600
Factory overhead		
Factory indirect labour	66,000	
Other factory indirect expenses	58,000	
Travelling expenses	100	
Depreciation: Factory machinery	38,000	
Firms canteen expenses	4,000	
		166,100
(*b*) **Production cost**		685,700
Administration expenses		
Salaries	72,000	
Travelling expenses	200	
Firm's canteen expenses	2,000	
Depreciation: Acctg. & office machinery	2,000	
Cars of admin. staff	1,600	
Other administrative expenses	42,000	
		119,800
Selling and distribution expenses		
Salaries	8,000	
Commission	1,400	
Travelling expenses	2,900	
Depreciation: Equipment	300	
Salesmen's cars	3,800	
Other selling expenses	65,000	
Carriage costs on sales	7,800	
		89,200
Finance costs		
Interest on loans and overdrafts		3,800
(*c*) **Total cost**		898,500

18.1

(a) Answers to be drafted by students in proper memo form.
   Introduction:

Marginal cost is:	Direct labour	3.00
	Direct materials	3.50
	Variable expenses	2.25
		8.75

As selling price £9.00 exceeds marginal cost £8.75 we should accept (but see below)*

Proof	*Without new order*	*With new order*
Direct labour	6,000	6,300
Direct materials	7,000	7,350
Factory indirect expenses		
Variable	4,500	4,725
Fixed	500	500
Administration expenses	1,200	1,200
Selling and distribution expenses	600	600
Finance expenses	200	200
	20,000	20,875
Sales	22,000	
Sales 22,000 + 900		22,900
Profit	2,000	2,025

*Depends on how other things affected besides simple accounting calculation.

(b) For extra order:

Marginal costs per unit (*see* (a))	8.75
Depreciation £300 p.a. ÷ 150	2.00
Running costs £600 p.a. ÷ 150	4.00
Marginal costs per unit	14.75

As £14.75 is greater than selling price £10 do NOT accept.

18.3

Year 1	(A) Magellan Ltd (Marginal)		(B) Frobisher Ltd (Absorption)	
Sales £29 × 900		26,100		26,100
Less Variable costs				
Direct labour £3 × 1,200	3,600		3,600	
Direct materials £5 × 1,200	6,000		6,000	
Variable overheads £2 × 1,200	2,400		2,400	
Total variable cost	12,000		12,000	
Less in (A) Valuation closing stock				
$\frac{300}{1,200}$ × £12,000	3,000			
Less in (B) Valuation closing stock				
$\frac{300}{1,200}$ × £21,000			5,250	
	9,000		6,750	
Fixed overhead	9,000		9,000	
Total costs		18,000		15,750
Gross profit		8,100		10,350

		(A)		(B)
Year 2				
Sales £29 × 1,200		34,800		34,800
Less Variable costs				
Direct labour £3 × 1,300	3,900		3,900	
Direct materials £5 × 1,300	6,500		6,500	
Variable overheads £2 × 1,300	2,600		2,600	
Total variable cost	13,000		13,000	
Add in (A) Opening stock b/fwd	3,000			
Add in (B) Opening stock b/fwd			5,250	
	16,000		18,250	
Less in (A) Valuation closing stock				
$\frac{400}{1,300} \times 13,000$	4,000			
Less in (B) Valuation closing stock				
$\frac{400}{1,300} \times £22,000$			6,769	
	12,000		11,481	
Fixed overhead	9,000		9,000	
Total costs		21,000		20,481
Gross profit		13,800		14,319

		(A)		(B)
Year 3				
Sales £29 × 1,100		31,900		31,900
Less Variable costs				
Direct labour £3 × 1,250	3,750		3,750	
Direct materials £5 × 1,250	6,250		6,250	
Variable overheads £2 × 1,250	2,500		2,500	
Total variable cost	12,500		12,500	
Add in (A) Opening stock b/fwd	4,000			
Add in (B) Opening stock b/fwd			6,769	
	16,500		19,269	
Less in (A) Valuation closing stock				
$\frac{550}{1,250} \times £12,500$	5,500			
Less in (B) Valuation closing stock				
$\frac{550}{1,250} \times £21,500$			9,460	
	11,000		9,000	
Fixed overhead	9,000		9,000	
Total costs		20,000		18,809
Gross profit		11,900		13,091

18.5

(a) Subject to points raised in (c) the extra production should be taken on, as this results in greater profits amounting to £1,562,000. Proof is as follows:

Extra revenue 60,000 × £150		9,000,000
Less Extra costs		
Direct materials (W1)	3,141,600	
Direct labour 60,000 × 18.70 × 120% =	1,346,400	
Variable overhead 60,000 × 7.50	450,000	
Fixed costs	2,500,000	7,438,000
Extra profit		1,562,000
(W1) 60,000 × 74.80		4,488,000
Less saving 10% on extra materials	448,800	
saving 10% on materials		
used on day shift		
10% × 120,000 × 74.80	897,600	1,346,400
		3,141,600

(b) Break-even point to justify night shift

Sale price per unit		150.00
Less Costs per unit		
Material	74.80	
Direct labour 18.70 + 20%	22.44	
Variable overhead	7.50	104.74
Contribution per unit		45.26

Total fixed costs $\dfrac{2,500,000}{45.26}$

= Break-even at 55,236 units.

Note: No 10% reduction on materials because demand less than extra 60,000 units.

(c) (i)   Would firm be able to maintain selling price of £187 on first 120,000 units per year?
(ii) Would it have been more profitable to subcontract extra units needed?
(iii) Could we diversify into a more profitable alternative product?
(iv) Could extra day facilities have been more profitable?

18.7 (a)

Arncliffe Ltd
Revenue Statement for the year ended ...

	Crowns		Kings		Total	
Sales		60,000		25,000		85,000
Direct costs: Raw materials	8,000		2,000		10,000	
Labour	20,000		10,000		30,000	
Machine running costs	12,000	40,000	3,000	15,000	15,000	55,000
Contribution		20,000		10,000		30,000
Rate of contribution to sales		33.3%		40%		35.3%

(b) Best product mix for next year:
   Crowns manufactured per hour = 20,000/8,000 = 2.5 per hour
   Kings manufactured per hour = 10,000/2,000 = 5 per hour
Kings gives best contribution rate, so produce Kings up to maximum requirements.

	Crowns		Kings	
	Units	Hours	Units	Hours
Minimum required	6,000 ÷ 2.5	2,400	6,000 ÷ 5	1,200
Produce up to maximum				
of 36,000 Kings			30,000 ÷ 5	6,000
		2,400		7,200

Still (10,000 – 7,200 – 2,400)
= 400 hours left, so
now produce Crown 1,000 ÷ 25

		400		
		2,800		7,200

Best mix is therefore: Crowns   (6,000 + 1,000) = 7,000

Kings   (6,000 + 30,000) = 36,000

Sales therefore	7,000 × £3	21,000	36,000 × £2.5 =	90,000

Contributions:	Crowns (33.3%)		7,000	
	Kings (40%)		36,000	43,000
Floorspace costs			15,000	
Insurances			600	15,600
Profit				27,400

(c) Product mix with extra machine

As maximum requirements for Kings have already been met in (b), all new output will be of Crowns.

	Crowns	Kings
Sales (as before) in £s	21,000	90,000
Extra (10,000 hours × 2.5) = 25,000 × £3 =	75,000	
	96,000	90,000
Contributions: Crowns (33.3%)	32,000	
Kings (40%)	36,000	68,000
Hire of extra machine	20,000	
Floorspace costs	15,000	
Insurance	600	35,600
		32,400

(d) Briefly:
  (i)   Market demand maintained.
  (ii) Flexibility of return of extra machine if demand falls.
  (iii) To see if wholesaler will guarantee minimum orders.
  (iv) Are there outlets possible other than wholesaler?
  (v)   Selling price to wholesaler.

18.9 (a)

Paul Wagtail

Manufacturing Trading and Profit and Loss Account
for the year ended 30 April 19X9

	Marginal method		Absorption method	
Purchases of raw materials (125,000 – 2,100)		122,900		122,900
Carriage of raw materials		1,500		1,500
		124,400		124,400
Less Stock raw materials		8,900		8,900
Cost of raw materials consumed		115,500		115,500
Production wages		105,270		105,270
Prime cost		220,770		220,770
Factory overhead expenses:				
Factory power	12,430		12,430	
Factory supervisors' wages	29,600		29,600	
Factory repairs	19,360		19,360	
Factory insurance (40%)	1,920		1,920	
Factory heating and lighting (40%)	1,440		1,440	
Depreciation of plant	17,600	82,350	17,600	82,350
		303,120		303,120
Less Work-in-progress (W1)		11,038		15,156
Production cost of goods completed c/d		292,082		287,964
Sales		464,360		464,360
Production cost b/d	292,082		287,964	
Less Stock finished goods (W2)	18,447	273,635	18,187	269,777
Gross profit		190,725		194,583
Less Expenses:				
Administration expenses	46,700		46,700	
Distribution expenses	25,400		25,400	
Selling expenses	23,800		23,800	
Insurance (60%)	2,880		2,880	
Heating and lighting (60%)	2,160		2,160	
Depreciation: delivery vehicles	35,200	136,140	35,200	136,140
Net profit		54,585		58,443

Workings

(W1) 625 × 80% = 500 equivalent making total 9,500 + 500 = 10,000

$$\text{Valuations:} \quad \text{Marginal} \quad \frac{500}{10,000} \times 220,770 = 11,038$$

$$\text{Absorption} \quad \frac{500}{10,000} \times 303,120 = 15,156$$

$$\text{(W2)} \quad \text{Marginal} \quad \frac{600}{9,500} \times 292,082 = 18,447$$

$$\text{Absorption} \quad \frac{600}{9,500} \times 287,964 = 18,187$$

(b) *See* text.

19.1

	Production Departments				Service Departments		
	A	B	C	D	K	L	M
Indirect labour	4,000	6,000	8,000	2,000	1,500	3,000	4,100
Other expenses	2,700	3,100	3,600	1,500	4,500	2,000	2,000
	6,700	9,100	11,600	3,500	6,000	5,000	6,100
Apportionment of costs:							
Dept K	1,500	1,800	1,200	600	(6,000)		900
Dept L	3,000		1,500	500		(5,000)	
							7,000
Dept M		2,100	3,500	1,400			(7,000)
	11,200	13,000	17,800	6,000	–	–	–

(*a*) Overhead rates per direct labour hour

Department A $\dfrac{£11,200}{2,000} = £5.6$

Department C $\dfrac{£17,800}{4,450} = £4.0$

(*b*) Overhead rates per machine hour

Department B $\dfrac{£13,000}{2,600} = £5.0$

Department D $\dfrac{£6,000}{2,400} = £2.5$

19.2

Job Cost Sheet Job 351 Dept. A

Direct materials		190
Direct labour	56 × £2.1	117.6
Factory overhead	56 × £5.6	313.6
		621.2

Job Cost Sheet Job 352 Dept. B

Direct materials		1,199
Direct labour	178 × £1.7	302.6
Factory overhead	176 × £5.0	880
		2,381.6

Job Cost Sheet Job 353 Dept. C

Direct materials		500
Direct labour	130 × £2.4	312
Factory overhead	130 × £4.0	520
		1,332

Job Cost Sheet Job 354 Dept. D

Direct materials		666
Direct labour	90 × £2.3	207
Direct overhead	64 × £2.5	160
		1,033

Job Cost Sheet Job 355 Depts. C and B

Dept C	Direct materials		560
	Direct labour	160 × £2.4	384
	Factory overhead	160 × £4.0	640
Dept B	Direct materials		68
	Direct labour	30 × £1.7	51
	Factory overhead	20 × £5.0	100
			1,803

19.5

(a) *See* text Section 19.5

(b) (i)

	Materials		Labour		Overhead	
Finished items	4,000		4,000		4,000	
Work-in-progress (600)	540	(90%)	450	(75%)	330	(55%)
Total units	4,540		4,450		4,330	

(ii) Cost per complete unit

Material   £8,172 ÷ 4,540 = 1.80
Labour   £7,120 ÷ 4,450 = 1.60
Overhead £5,196 ÷ 4,330 = 1.20   £4.60

(iii) Value of work-in-progress

Material   540 × 1.80   = 972
Labour   450 × 1.60   = 720
Overhead 330 × 1.20   = 396   £2,088

19.7

(a) Allotment: where overheads traced directly to units.
Apportionment: where overheads not directly traceable and have to be apportioned between units.
Absorption rates: the total amount of overheads calculated as being charged to each unit.

(b) Because the figures belong to the future and therefore cannot be known precisely.

(c) (i) and (ii). Note that parts (i) and (ii) illustrate two different methods in use. The method in (iii) is not in the text.

Continuous apportionment (repeated distribution)

Line		Production departments			Service departments	
	A	B		C	X	Y
1 Allocation per analysis	14,000	12,000		8,000	4,000	3,000
2 Allocation of X(4,000) (35%)	1,400 (30%)	1,200 (20%)		800	(4,000) (15%)	600
3 Allocation of Y(3,600) (30%)	1,080 (40%)	1,440 (25%)		900	(5%) 180	3,600 (3,600)
4 Allocation of X (180) (35%)	63 (30%)	54 (20%)		36	(180) (15%)	27
5 Allocation of Y (27) (30%)	8 (40%)	12* (25%)		7	(5%) 0	(27)
	16,551	14,706		9,743	(= total 41,000)	

*Rounded off

Explanation:

Steps: (1) Allocate X overheads to others by % shown.
 (2) Allocate Y overheads to others by % shown.
 Keep repeating (1) and (2) until the figures left under X and Y are insignificant.

(c) (iii) Elimination method.

Line		Production departments			Service departments	
	A	B		C	X	Y
1 Allocation per analysis	14,000	12,000		8,000	4,000	3,000
2 Allocate service (35%) dept X	1,400 (30%)	1,200 (20%)		800	(4,000) (15%)	600
					–	
3 Allocate service dept Y (30/95)	1,137 (40/95)	1,516 (25/95)		947		(3,600)
	16,537	14,716		9,747 (total 41,000)		–

Explanation:

Steps: (1) Allocate service department overheads which does largest proportion of work for other departments, i.e. department X.

(2) Allocate next service department per (1), in this case is only Y.

(3) When doing (2) nothing is charged to service departments already allocated, i.e. in this case X.

(4) Note that since (3) happens the ratios in the next allocation change. As X 5% of Y is not returned then A gets 30/95 of Y, not 30% and so on.

(iv) The answer will depend on whichever approach is adopted. No one can categorically state which method is the most accurate; there is no 'ideal' method.

19.9 (*a*) and (*b*) *See* text.

(*c*) (i)   *Batch No. 23*

Raw materials 300 × 1.60	480
Direct labour 4.20 × 20 hours	84
Setting up of machine	21
Overheads 3.60 × 20 hours	72
Total cost	657

Cost per unit 657 ÷ 30 = £2.19

(ii)   *Batch No. 23*

Raw materials 300 × 1.60	480.00	
Less Received for scrap 20 × 0.86	17.20	462.80
Direct labour: Normal 20 × 4.20	84.00	
Rectification 9 × 4.20	37.80	121.80
Setting up: Normal	21.00	
Rectification	18.00	39.00
Overheads: Running time 3.60 × 20	72.00	
Rectification 3.60 × 9	32.40	104.40
		728.00

Per usable unit £728 ÷ 280 = 2.60

(iii)

Loss because of extra costs 728 − 657 =	71.00
Loss because of faulty products 657 × 20/300	43.80
	114.80

20.1

(*a*)

Opening stock	120
Add Production	?
Less Sales	630
	150

By arithmetical deduction the figure of production is 660 units. Divide by 12 to give production figures of 55 per month. This has been tested to ensure that stock never becomes a negative figure.

(b) Starting with above figures

	Jan	Feb	Mar	Apr	May	Jun	Jul	Aug	Sep	Oct	Nov	Dec
Opening stock	120	105	70	65	80	105	140	175	200	195	180	145
Add Production	55	55	55	55	55	55	55	55	55	55	55	55
	175	160	125	120	135	160	195	230	255	250	235	200
Less Sales	70	90	60	40	30	20	20	30	60	70	90	50
Closing stock	105	70	65	80	105	140	175	200	195	180	145	150

Lowest figure of closing stock is March 65. If stock is not to fall below 110 units then an extra (110 − 65) 45 units will have to be produced in January, making January's production:

$$55 + 45 = \quad \underline{\underline{100}} \text{ units}$$

20.2

Opening stock	50
Add Production	?
Less Sales	650
Closing stock	120

By deduction the year's production will be 720 units.

Compared with the first half year, the second half will show greater production of 20 × 6 = 120 units. Production first half therefore $\dfrac{720 - 120}{2} = 300$ units

(a)	Production: January to June	50 units per month	=	300
(b)	Production: July to December	70 units per month	=	420
				720

21.1

(a)

B. Ukridge

Cash Budget	May	Jun	Jul	Aug	Sept	Oct
Balance b/fwd	5	5,305	4,305	1,305		
Overdraft b/fwd					6,695	9,695
Receipts from debtors	400	4,000	8,000	12,000	9,000	5,000
Capital	5,000					
	5,405	9,305	12,305	13,305	2,305	(4,695)
Payments	100	5,000	11,000	20,000	12,000	7,000
Balance c/fwd	5,305	4,305	1,305			
Overdraft c/fwd				6,695	9,695	11,695

(b) There are the possibilities of delaying payments to creditors, delaying purchases or somehow of getting debtors to pay up more quickly. Apart from these it is possible that a credit factoring firm could help in 'buying' the amounts of debtors from Ukridge.

   If none of these are possible, only a really fantastic product could warrant interest at 100 per cent per annum. This could be the case, although there are many people whose optimism about their products exceeds the true profitability.

21.3

(a)

	Cash Budget		
Receipts	Jul	Aug	Sep
Cash sales (W1)	9,600	4,800	7,200
Credit sales (W2)	17,640	14,112	7,056
	27,240	18,912	14,256
Payments			
Purchases	3,600	5,400	8,100
Direct labour	1,600	2,400	3,600
Direct production expenses	4,800	2,400	3,600
Variable selling expenses	4,000	3,200	1,600
Fixed expenses	1,820	1,820	1,820
	15,820	15,220	18,720
Balance start of month	+3,900	+15,320	+19,012
Balance at end of month	+15,320	+19,012	+14,548

(W1) July	800 × 40% × £30	=	9,600
August	400 × 40% × £30	=	4,800
September	600 × 40% × £30	=	7,200

(W2) July	1000 × 60% × £30	=	18,000 – 2% = 17,640
August	800 × 60% × £30	=	14,400 – 2% = 14,112
September	400 × 60% × £30	=	7,200 – 2% = 7,056

(b) (i) Can forecast when and if money needs to be borrowed.
(ii) Can forecast when surplus funds are available so that they can be invested elsewhere.
(iii) To use as basis when dealing with supplier as to creditworthiness, or bank for borrowing powers.

21.5

Receipts	Jul	Aug	Sept	Oct
Sales this month 20%		9,000	9,000	9,000
Sales last month 70%			31,500	31,500
Sales 2 months ago 10%				4,500
Other receipts from debtors	40,000	32,000	4,000	
	40,000	41,000	44,500	45,000
Payments				
Wages	2,000	2,000	2,000	2,000
Bank loan and interest	242	242	242	242
Drawings	500	500	500	500
Purchases	34,000	38,250	38,250	45,750
PAYE tax	500	500	500	500
Rent	1,250			1,250
Rates				2,250
Value added tax	5,000			3,950
Motor van		8,150		
	43,492	49,642	41,492	56,442
Current account balances				
Start of month	5,000	1,508	(7,134)	(4,126)
End of month	1,508	(7,134)	(4,126)	(15,568)

21.6

(a) In brief:

Current ratio of 210,000 : 150,000 = 1.4 : 1

Acid test ratio not known. Very dangerous situation because if bank manager asks for repayment of overdraft it is unlikely it can be repaid in the short term.

Profits get ploughed back into the company in all sorts of ways, e.g. extra fixed assets, more stock. It has no direct connection with the balance at the bank. (Use cash flow funds statements as an illustration.)

(b) *Cash Budget*

Receipts	Apr	May	Jun	Jul
Cash sales	40,000	40,000	40,000	40,000
Credit sales	65,000	70,000	70,000	70,000
	105,000	110,000	110,000	110,000
Payments				
Purchases	60,000	58,000	61,000	55,000
Selling and administration	5,700	6,600	6,600	6,600
Administration charges	10,000	10,000	10,000	13,500
Final dividend 19X9/X0		7,500		
Interim dividend 19X0/X1				4,000
	75,700	82,100	77,600	79,100
Balance overdraft start of month	(150,000)	(120,700)	(92,800)	(60,400)
Balance overdraft end of month	(120,700)	(92,800)	(60,400)	(29,500)

(c) Would seem to be proceeding satisfactorily to eliminate overdraft.

Could be further reduced by:
(i)   Issuing new shares
(ii) Getting debtors to pay more quickly
(iii) Delaying payment of creditors
(iv) Selling off fixed assets
(v)   Issuing debentures.

22.1

Cash Budget	Jan	Feb	Mar	Apr	May	Jun
Opening balance	25,000	+890				
Opening overdraft			-370	-600	-740	-600
Received (*see* schedule)	400	600	1,750	2,200	2,900	3,550
	25,400	1,490	1,380	1,600	2,160	2,950
Payments (*see* schedule)	24,510	1,860	1,980	2,340	2,760	3,460
Closing balance	+890					
Closing overdraft		-370	-600	-740	-600	-510

Cash Receipts Schedule	Jan	Feb	Mar	Apr	May	Jun
Cash sales	400	600	800	1,000	1,300	1,400
Credit sales	–	–	800	1,200	1,600	2,000
Rent received			150			150
	400	600	1,750	2,200	2,900	3,550

Cash Payments Schedule	Jan	Feb	Mar	Apr	May	June
Drawings	250	250	250	250	250	250
Premises	20,000					
Shop fixtures	3,000					
Motor van	1,000					
Salaries of assistants	260	260	260	260	260	260
Payments to creditors		1,200	1,320	1,680	2,100	2,800
Other expenses		150	150	150	150	150
	24,510	1,860	1,980	2,340	2,760	3,460

D. Smith

Forecast Trading and Profit and Loss Accounts for the 6 months ended 30 June 19X4

Sales			16,500
Less Cost of goods sold			
Purchases		11,410	
Less Closing stock (130 × £7)		910	10,500
Gross profit			6,000
Add Rent received			300
			6,300
Less Expenses			
Assistants' salaries		1,560	
Other expenses		900	
Depreciation: Shop fixtures		150	
Motor van		100	2,710
Net profit			3,590

Balance Sheet as at 30 June 19X4

Fixed assets	Cost	Depn	Net
Premises	20,000	–	20,000
Shop fixtures	3,000	150	2,850
Motor van	1,000	100	900
	24,000	250	23,750
Current assets			
Stock-in-trade		910	
Debtors		5,400	
Less Current liabilities		6,310	
Creditors	2,310		
Other expenses owing	150		
Bank overdraft	510	2,970	
Net current assets			3,340
			27,090
Financed by			
Capital			
Cash introduced			25,000
Add Net profit			3,590
			28,590
Less Drawings			1,500
			27,090

22.3

N. Morris

Cash Budget	Jul	Aug	Sep	Oct	Nov	Dec
Balance b/fwd	1,200		250			
Overdraft b/fwd		260		160	540	420
Receipts	4,000	6,400	5,800	8,000	6,000	9,500*
	5,200	6,140	6,050	7,840	5,460	9,080
Payments (see schedule)	5,460	5,890	6,210	8,380	5,880	5,410
Balance c/fwd	–	250				3,670
Overdraft c/fwd	260		160	540	420	

*Includes £2,500 legacy

Payments Schedule

	Jul		Aug
Raw materials 320 (Jul) × £4	1,280	350 (Aug) × £4	1,400
300 (Jun) × £1	300	320 (Jul) × £1	320
Direct labour 320 × £8	2,560	350 × £8	2,800
Variable 300 × £1 + 320 × £1	620	350 × £1 + 320 × £1	670
Fixed expenses	400		400
Drawings	300		300
	5,460		5,890

	Sep		Oct
Raw materials 370 (Sep) × £4	1,480	380 (Oct) × £4	1,520
350 (Aug) × £1	350	370 (Sep) × £1	370
Direct labour 370 × £8	2,960	380 × £8	3,040
Variable 370 × £1 + 350 × £1	720	380 × £1 + 370 × £1	750
Fixed expenses	400		400
Drawings	300		300
Machinery	–		2,000
	6,210		8,380

	Nov		Dec
Raw materials 340 (Nov) × £4	1,360	310 (Dec) × £4	1,240
380 (Oct) × £1	380	340 (Nov) × £1	340
Direct labour 340 × £8	2,720	310 × £8	2,480
Variable 340 × £1 + 380 × £1	720	310 × £1 + 340 × £1	650
Fixed expenses	400		400
Drawings	300		300
	5,880		5,410

22.5

(*a*)

Issa Ltd

Trading and Profit and Loss Account for the year ended 31 December 19X1

	£000s	£000s
Sales		900.0
Less Cost of goods sold		
Opening stock	80.0	
Purchases (difference)	570.0	
	650.0	
Less Closing stock	65.0	585.0
Gross profit		315.0
Less Expenses		
Administration expenses	63.6	
Selling and distribution expenses (54 + 15)	69.0	
Financial charges	20.8	
Provision for doubtful debts	2.5	
Depreciation	60.0	215.9
Net profit		99.1
Profit on sale of land and buildings		150.0
Retained earnings from last yea		350.0
		599.1
Less Appropriations		
Bonus share issue	50.0	
Preference share dividends	9.0	
Ordinary dividend	7.5	66.5
Retained earnings carried to next year		532.6

(*b*)

Balance Sheet as at 31 December 19X1

	£000s	£000s	£000s
Fixed assets at cost (750 – 50)		700.0	
Less Depreciation to date		204.0	496.0
Investment in Yates Ltd at cost			100.0
Current assets			
Stock		65.0	
Trade debtors	100.0		
Less Provision	7.5	92.5	
Bank		350.1	
		507.6	
Less Current liabilities			
Trade creditors	56.0		
Expense creditors	15.0	71.0	436.6
			1,032.6
Financed by			
Ordinary share capital (200 + 100)			300.0
Share premium (150 – 50)			100.0
9% Preference shares			100.0
Retained earnings			532.6
			1,032.6

(c) Advantages:
  (i) Business can establish desired profit in advance. It can then take necessary action to try to achieve it.
    Desired ROCE can be set as target.
    Also helps in forecasting dividends/planning for taxation purposes/organising necessary finance/for use with financial backers.
  (ii) Manage working capital to ensure its sufficiency when needed.
    Managing cash balances to seek overdrafts/loans from bank when needed. Ensure creditors paid on time to gain discounts. Invest surpluses as and when they may occur.

22.7

A (*a*) *Debtor budget*

	Jul	Aug	Sep	Oct
Balances from last month	52,250	52,250	49,500	51,750
Add Credit sales	24,750	24,750	27,000	33,000
	77,000	77,000	76,500	84,750
Less Paid by debtors	24,750	27,500	24,750	24,750
Balances at end of month	52,250	49,500	51,750	60,000

Note: Sales are Jul 900, Aug 900, Sep 900, Oct 1,100. October is taken to be June figure + 10%.

(*b*) *Raw material budget* (in kgs)

	Jul	Aug	Sep	Oct
Stock from last month	1,800	1,800	1,800	2,200
Add purchases	1,800	1,800	2,200	2,200
	3,600	3,600	4,000	4,400
Less Used	1,800	1,800	1,800	2,200
Stock at end of month	1,800	1,800	2,200	2,200

B See text Section 15.8

$$EOQ = \sqrt{\frac{2 \times 12,000 \times £10}{£6}} = 200 \text{ units}$$

  (i) Based on estimates which obviously can vary a lot from actual.
  (ii) Consumption may be uneven at times, EOQ assumes even usage.
  (iii) Such things as strikes, catastrophes, etc. can render it useless.

22.8 A

Workings:
  1 Raw materials 294,400 ÷ 64,000 = 4.6 per unit
  2 Direct labour 236,800 ÷ 64,000 = 3.7 per unit
  3 Power 38,400 ÷ 64,000 = 0.60 per unit
  4 Repairs are 51,200 − 25%(12,800) = 38,400 fixed. Variable 12,800 ÷ 64,000 = 0.20
  5 Indirect wages 64,000 − 15%(9,600) = 54,400 fixed.
    Variable 9,600 ÷ 64,000 = 0.15

Bedford Ltd
Flexible Budget at varying levels of production

Level of Production	60%	70%	75%	90%	85%	Actual	Variance
Units	48,000	56,000	60,000	72,000	68,000	68,000	+ (−)

Variable costs £						
Raw materials	220,800	257,600	276,000	331,200	312,800	310,750	2,050
Direct labour	177,600	207,200	222,000	266,400	251,600	249,100	2,500
Power	28,800	33,600	36,000	43,200	40,800	39,800	1,000
Repairs and maintenance	9,600	11,200	12,000	14,400	13,600	14,650	(1,050)
Indirect wages	7,200	8,400	9,000	10,800	10,200	10,850	(650)
	444,000	518,000	555,000	666,000	629,000	625,150	3,850

Fixed costs						
Repairs and maintenance	38,400	38,400	38,400	38,400	38,400	38,400	–
Insurance	1,300	1,300	1,300	1,300	1,300	1,350	(50)
Heating/lighting	1,250	1,250	1,250	1,250	1,250	1,200	50
Indirect wages	54,400	54,400	54,400	54,400	54,400	54,400	–
	95,350	95,350	95,350	95,350	95,350	95,350	–

| Total costs | 539,350 | 613,350 | 650,350 | 761,350 | 724,350 | 720,500 | 3,850 |

Briefly: generally efficient as most variances are favourable. Comment in detail on each variance.

B *See* text.

23.1 A

Contract Account

Materials purchased	765,000	Materials transfers out	8,000
Materials transfers in	23,000	Architects' certificates (W2)	1,830,000
Direct labour	448,000	Stock of materials c/d	38,000
Direct labour accrued	19,500	Value of plant c/d	80,000
Indirect labour	63,000	Work not certified c/d	86,000
Indirect labour accrued	2,400		
Plant delivered	120,000		
Hire charges	57,000		
Hire charges owing	3,200		
Head Office charges	48,000		
	1,549,100		
Profit to profit and loss account (W1)	279,310		
Reserve (part of apparent profit not yet recognised) c/d	213,590		
	2,042,000		2,042,000

Workings:

(W1)

Apparent profit $2,042,000 - 1,549,100 = 492,900$

To recognise $492,900 \times \frac{2}{3} \times \dfrac{\text{Cash received}}{\text{Work certified}}$

$= 492,900 \times \frac{2}{3} \times \dfrac{1,555,500}{1,830,000} = 279,310$

Reserve is $492,900 - 279,310 = 213,590$

(W2)

Architects' certificates $- 1,555,000 \times \dfrac{100}{85} = 1,830,000$

B   See text.

C   The multinational company should:

- (i) As far as possible offer the chance of redundancy for those voluntarily wishing to retire from the company, rather than force it on unwilling employees.
- (ii) See if alternative jobs can be offered elsewhere in the multinational.
- (iii) Explain to the workforce why the move is necessary.
- (iv) Have staff from the job centre explain about any alternative jobs or occupations.
- (v) Give the redundant people advice about new skills training.
- (vi) Have them given financial advice about investing redundancy monies, etc.
- (vii) Advice re possible claims from the DSS.
- (viii) Try to ensure fairness and not victimise certain employees.

23.3

(a) Note that the question asks for *cost* accounts NOT contract accounts.

Cost accounts for year ended 31 October 19X9
Plymouth Contract (£000)

Balance b/f		Plant transferred	13
Work completed	240	Materials on site c/f	12
Materials on site	18	Plant on site c/f	55
Plant at WDV	90	Cost of work completed	462
Materials	60		
Wages	75		
Subcontractors	10		
Salaries	18		
Plant received	6		
Head Office costs	25		
	542		542

Torquay Contract (£000)

Balance b/f		Materials on site c/f	28
Work completed	80	Plant on site c/f	80
Materials on site	6	Cost of work completed	466
Plant at WDV	25		
Materials	130		
Wages	105		
Subcontractors	46		
Salaries	32		
Plant received	115		
Head Office costs	35		
	574		574

Truro Contract (£000)

Materials	80	Materials on site c/f	35
Wages	30	Plant on site c/f	52
Salaries	8	Cost of work completed	118
Plant at WDV	77		
Head Office costs	10		
	205		205

(b)

Plymouth: Total contract price			600
Less Costs to date		462	
Future costs		60	522
Total expected profit			78

If the anticipated costs, including contingencies, are adequate the full proportion of profits to date may be taken. Prudence should be the keynote, but this contract is almost complete.

$$\text{Profit} = \frac{\text{Work certified}}{\text{Contract price}} \times \text{Total profit}$$

$$= \frac{500,000}{600,000} \times 78 = 65,000$$

Torquay: As the contract is only about 50 per cent complete, prudence must take over. Work certified – cost to date = 450 – 466 = loss to date £16,000. Prudence dictates that all the loss, £16,000, should be taken into account.

Truro: As the contract is in its early stages prudence must take over. The formula is:
Apparent profit $\times \frac{2}{3}$ = 125,000 – 118,000 = 7,000 $\times \frac{2}{3}$ = 4,667

24.1

(A) *Standard cost per unit*

	X		Y		Z	
Material 1			1.8		2.4	
Material 2	0.6		2.1			
Material 3	3.0		2.5		1.5	
Material 4	0.4	4.0		6.4	0.9	4.8
Labour: Dept A	4.0		2.4		4.8	
Dept B	3.0	7.0	1.8	4.2	3.6	8.4
Production cost		11.0		10.6		13.2
Overheads						
Production (1.8 per hour)		9.0		5.4		10.8
		20.0		16.0		24.0
Administration (50%)		10.0		8.0		12.0
Selling		5.0		4.0		6.0
Standard cost		35.0		28.0		42.0
Profit (⅐ of standard cost)		5.0		4.0		6.0
Standard selling price		40.0		32.0		48.0

(b) *Sales budget in units*

	X	Y	Z
Budgeted at standard price	800,000	1,280,000	2,400,000
Unit selling price	40.0	32.0	48.0
Sales budget in units	20,000	40,000	50,000

(c) *Production budget in units*

	X	Y	Z
Needed for sales	20,000	40,000	50,000
For stock purposes	5,000	10,000	10,000
To produce	25,000	50,000	60,000

(d) *Direct materials purchases budget*

Materials	1	2	3	4
Product X ⎫	–	100,000	300,000	480,000
Product Y ⎬ kgs	900,000	700,000	500,000	
Product Z ⎭	1,440,000		360,000	1,080,000
	2,340,000	800,000	1,160,000	1,560,000
Cost in £	£234,000	£120,000	£290,000	£78,000

25.1

(i)   Net variance:

	Actual cost per unit 37 × £18	666
	Standard cost per unit 34 × £20	680
	Net variance (favourable)	£14

Made up of:

	Favourable price variance £2 × 34	68
	Adverse usage variance 3 × £18	54
	Net variance (favourable)	£14

(ii)   Net variance:

	Actual cost per unit 46 × £19	874
	Standard cost per unit 50 × £17	850
	Net variance (adverse)	£24

Made up of:

	Favourable usage variance 4 × £17	68
	Adverse price variance 46 × £2	92
	Net variance (adverse)	£24

(iii)   Total variance:

	Actual cost per unit 18 × £14	252
	Standard cost per unit 15 × £12	180
	Variance (adverse)	£72

Made up of:

	Adverse price variance 15 × £2 (+ £6 common)	36
	Adverse usage variance 3 × £12	36
	Total variance (adverse)	£72

(iv)   Total variance:

	Actual cost per unit 27 × £37	999
	Standard cost per unit 29 × £40	1,160
	Total variance (favourable)	£161

Made up of:

	Favourable price variance 27 × £3	81
	Favourable usage variance 2 × £37 (+ £6 common)	80
		£161

(v)   Total variance:

	Actual cost per unit 154 × £8	1,232
	Standard cost per unit 145 × £7	1,015
	Total variance (adverse)	£ 217

Made up of:

	Adverse price variance 145 × £1 (+ £9 common)	154
	Adverse usage variance 9 × £7	63
		£ 217

(vi)	Total variance: Actual cost per unit 9,850 × £22		216,700
	Standard cost per unit 10,000 × £25		250,000
	Total variance (favourable)		£ 33,300
	Made up of: Favourable price variance £3 × 9,850		29,550
	Favourable usage variance 150 × £22 (+ £450 common)		3,750
			£ 33,300

25.3

(i)	Actual cost per unit	218 × £2.1	457.8
	Standard cost per unit	220 × £2.1	462
	Favourable labour efficiency variance		£4.2

(ii)	Actual cost per unit	115 × £1.9	218.5
	Standard cost per unit	115 × £1.7	195.5
	Adverse wage rate variance		£23.0

(iii)	Actual cost per unit	240 × £1.8	432
	Standard cost per unit	200 × £1.8	360
	Adverse labour efficiency variance		£72

(iv)	Actual cost per unit	104 × £2.0	208
	Standard cost per unit	120 × £2.0	240
	Favourable labour efficiency variance		£32

(v)	Actual cost per unit	68 × £1.5	102
	Standard cost per unit	68 × £1.8	122.4
	Favourable wage rate variance		£20.4

(vi)	Actual cost per unit	34 × £1.7	57.8
	Standard cost per unit	30 × £1.7	51
	Adverse labour efficiency variance		£ 6.8

(vii)	Actual cost per unit	77 × £1.6	123.2
	Standard cost per unit	70 × £1.6	112
	Adverse labour efficiency variance		£ 11.2

(viii)	Actual cost per unit	100 × £2.0	200
	Standard cost per unit	100 × £1.9	190
	Adverse wage rate variance		£10

25.5

(a) *See* text

(b)	Standard hours produced in March	
	Dishwashers 150 × 10	1,500
	Washing machines 100 × 12	1,200
	Refrigerators 90 × 14	1,260
	Total standard hours	3,960

(c)	(i)	Standard hours × standard hourly rate		
		3,960 × £4	15,840	
		Actual wages	18,450	
		Total direct labour variance	2,610	(Adverse)

(ii) Standard pay 4,100 × £4   16,400
      Actual pay   18,450
      Direct labour rate variance   2,050   (Adverse)

(iii) Direct labour efficiency variance
      Standard hours – actual hours × standard rate
      3,960 – 4,100 × £4 = 560 (Adverse)

(d) Labour rate variance:
   1   Higher grade labour used than necessary.
   2   Job running behind time so extra people brought in to help.

Direct labour efficiency variance:
   1   Using unsuitable machinery.
   2   Workers slowing up work so as to get overtime rates paid.

25.7

(a)

Profit Statement for the month of July 19X1

	Budgeted		Actual	
Sales		1,000,000		1,071,200
Less Manufacturing costs				
Direct materials	200,000		201,285	
Direct labour	313,625		337,500	
Variable overheads	141,400		143,000	
Fixed overheads	75,000	730,025	71,000	752,785
Gross profit		269,975		318,415
Less: Variable sales o/h	64,400		69,500	
Administration costs	150,000	214,400	148,650	218,150
		55,575		100,265

(b) (i)   Material price variance =
        (Standard price – actual price per unit) × quantity purchased
        = 10.00 – 10.65 = 0.65 × 18,900 = 12,285 Adverse
        Material usage =
        (Standard quantity – actual quantity used) × standard price
        = (20,000 – 18,900) × 10 = 11,000 Favourable

Summary:	Material price variance	12,285	(A)
	Material usage variance	11,000	(F)
	Material cost variance	1,285	(A)

(ii) Labour rate variance =
        (Standard rate per hour – actual wage rate) × actual hours worked
        = (6.50 – 6.75) × 50,000 = 12,500 (A)
        Labour efficiency variance =
        (Standard labour hours – actual hours) × standard rate per hour
        = (48,250 – 50,000) × 6.50 = 11,375 (A)

Summary:	Labour rate variance	12,500	(A)
	Labour efficiency variance	11,375	(A)
	Labour cost variance	23,875	(A)

(c) In each case find out why the variance has occurred. Then it must be established whether the variances were outside the control of anyone in the firm or whether they were caused by the actions, or lack of action, by people in our organisation. Any necessary corrective action can then be taken.

26.1

(a)
Actual overhead	5,840
Overhead applied to production × £6	6,000
Favourable budget (or spending) variance	£ 160

(b)
Actual overhead	21,230
Overhead applied to production 5,000 × £4	20,000
Adverse budget (or spending) variance	£ 1,230

(c)
Actual fixed overhead	11,770
Budgeted fixed overhead	12,000
Favourable fixed overhead spending variance	£ 230

(d)
Actual fixed overhead	41,390
Budgeted fixed overhead	40,000
Adverse fixed overhead spending variance	£ 1,390

(e)
Actual hours × standard rate (7,940 × £3)	23,820
Budgeted hours × standard rate (8,000 × £3)	24,000
Favourable efficiency variance	£ 180

(f)
Actual hours × standard rate (15,000 × £4)	60,000
Budgeted hours (4,860 × 3) × standard rate (14,580 × £4)	58,320
Adverse efficiency variance	£ 1,680

26.3

The standard variable overhead rate is:

$$\frac{£400,000}{80,000} = £5 \text{ per direct labour hour and } £10 \text{ per unit}$$

The standard fixed overhead rate is:

$$\frac{£160,000}{80,000} = £2 \text{ per direct labour hour and } £4 \text{ per unit}$$

The variances are:

Variable overhead

(i)   *Budget or spending variance*
Actual overhead	403,600
Overhead applied to production 78,500 × £5	392,500
Adverse budget (or spending) variance	£11,100

(ii) *Efficiency variance*
Actual hours × standard rate 78,500 × £5	392,500
Budgeted hours × standard rate (42,000 units which should be produced in 42,000 × 2 hours = 84,000 hours × £5	420,000
Favourable efficiency variance	£27,500

Fixed overhead

(i) *Efficiency variance*

Actual units produced × standard rate 42,000 × 2 hours per unit × £2	168,000
Actual Labour hours × standard rate 78,500 × £2	157,000
Favourable efficiency variance	£11,000

(ii) *Spending (or budget) variance*

Actual overhead	157,200
Budgeted overhead	160,000
Favourable spending variance	£2,800

(iii) *Volume variance*

Actual hours × standard rate 78,500 × £2	157,000
Budgeted hours × standard rate 80,000 × £2	160,000
Adverse volume variance	£3,000

The variances can be explained further:

Variable overhead

Actual overhead	403,600
Budgeted overhead for actual production	
42,000 units × £10	420,000
Net favourable variance (made up of favourable efficiency	
variances £27,500 *less* Adverse budget variance 11,100)	£16,400

Fixed overhead

Actual overhead	157,200
Overhead based on units of production 42,000 × £4	168,000
Net favourable variance (made up of favourable efficiency variance £11,000	
plus favourable spending variance £2,800 *less* Adverse volume variance £3,000)	£10,800

26.5

				£
Actual units sold	150,000 × Budget price	£2.50	=	375,000
	150,000 × Actual price	£2.375	=	356,250
ADVERSE PRICE VARIANCE		£0.125		18,750

					£
Actual units sold	150,000 × Budget gross profit	£1.00	=		150,000
Budgets units sold	125,000 × Budget gross profit	£1.00	=		125,000
FAVOURABLE VOLUME VARIANCE					25,000

26.7

	Actual units sold	*Budget price*	*Actual price*	*Unit price variance*	*Total price variance*
		£	£		
M	840	5	5.10	+0.10	+84
N	1,680	8	7.90	−0.10	−168
P	280	7	7.30	+0.30	+84
	2,800		Total price variance		0

	Actual units sold	Actual units in budget %	Budget sales units	Variance in units	Budget gross profit per unit £	Total variance £
M	840	700	800	−100	1.00	−100
N	1,680	1,400	1,600	−200	1.50	−300
P	280	700	800	−100	1.20	−120
	2,800	2,800	3,200	−400	Adverse volume variance	−520

	Actual units in budget %	Actual units sold	Variance in units	Budget gross profit per unit £	Total variance £
M	700	840	+140	1.00	+140
N	1,400	1,680	+280	1.50	+420
P	700	280	−420	1.20	−504
	2,800	2,800	−	Favourable mix variance	+56

Summary of Sales Variance

Price variance	0
Volume variance adverse	520
Mix variance favourable	56
Net adverse variance	464

26.9

(a) *See* text Section 25.1.

Singleton Ltd

(b)   (i) Manufacturing Account for the year ended 31 August 19X9

	Actual £	Budget £	Variance £
Raw material consumed	90,000	80,000	(10,000)
Direct labour wages	115,600	120,000	4,400
Direct expenses	6,000	5,800	(200)
Prime cost	211,600	205,800	(5,800)
Factory overhead expenses:			
Factory rent	10,000	10,000	−
Factory maintenance	6,100	6,700	600
Heating and lighting	3,900	2,900	(1,000)
Depreciation	10,500	8,900	(1,600)
Wages, maintenance labour	24,000	18,000	(6,000)
Other factory overhead	10,000	12,700	2,700
Production cost of goods completed	276,100	265,000	(11,100)

(ii) Trading Account for the year ended 31 August 19X9

	£	£
Sales		405,000
Stock of finished goods 1 Sep X8	28,900	
Production cost	276,100	
	305,000	
Less Stock of finished goods 31 Aug X9	35,000	
Cost of sales		270,000
Gross profit		135,000

(c) *See* text.

Note to Exercises on Break-Even Analysis
The general idea of the questions is to get you to draw up the schedules of costs and revenues and then to draw them carefully on graph paper. It will be a waste of time if you do not use graph paper. It illustrates that accounting data can be represented in diagram form for some users in a more effective way than just using figures. It also puts over the idea that businesses exist to make a profit, and that until sufficient volume is achieved then the business will incur losses. The impact of fixed costs on firms can be revealed quite sharply by this sort of analysis.

27.1 (*i*)

No. of units	Fixed cost	Variable cost	Total cost	Revenue	Profit	Loss
0	8,000	–	8,000	–	–	8,000
1,000	8,000	4,000	12,000	6,000		6,000
2,000	8,000	8,000	16,000	12,000		4,000
3,000	8,000	12,000	20,000	18,000		2,000
4,000	8,000	16,000	24,000	24,000	nil	nil
5,000	8,000	20,000	28,000	30,000	2,000	
6,000	8,000	24,000	32,000	36,000	4,000	
7,000	8,000	28,000	36,000	42,000	6,000	
8,000	8,000	32,000	40,000	48,000	8,000	
9,000	8,000	36,000	44,000	54,000	10,000	
10,000	8,000	40,000	48,000	60,000	12,000	

(ii) The same as Exhibit 27.2 in the textbook. As it really needs graph paper we regret that one cannot be provided in this answer section.

27.2
(*a*) (i) £24,000 (ii) £36,000 (iii) £44,000 (iv) £30,000
(*b*) (i) £18,000 (ii) £48,000 (iii) £33,000.

27.4
(i) Loss £2,000 (ii) Profit £12,000 (iii) Nil (iv) Profit £6,000 (v) Profit £9,000.

27.6
(*a*) (*i*) Break-even point = $\dfrac{\text{Total fixed costs}}{\text{Selling price per unit – Variable costs per unit}}$

For 19X1 = $\dfrac{250,000}{130-110}$ = 12,500 units
= sales of 12,500 units × £130 = £1,625,000 sales

For 19X2 = $\dfrac{275,000}{129-118.5}$ = sales of 26,190 units × £129 = £3,378,510 sales

For 19X3 = $\dfrac{275,000}{128.5-122}$ = sales of 42,308 units × £128.5 = £5,436,578 sales

(ii)

Polemic Ltd

Actual and Forecast Profit and Loss Accounts for years to 30 September (£000s)

	Actual 19X1		Forecast 19X2		Forecast 19X3	
Sales		6,500		6,708		6,810.5
Direct materials	2,500		2,860		2,915	
Direct labour	1,500		1,638		1,749	
Variable production	500		572		636	
Direct expenses	250		260		318	
Variable sales overhead	750	5,500	832	6,162	848	6,466
Contribution		1,000		546		344.5
Fixed costs						
Production	50		55		55	
Overhead	200	250	220	275	220	275
		750		271		69.5

(b) Should best be on graph paper. General idea follows:

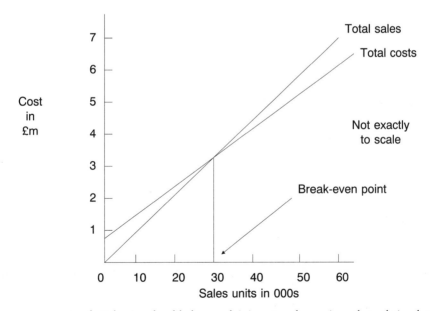

(c) The management of Polemic should be explaining to the union that their demand is unreasonable. As it is, profits have fallen dramatically and the break-even point in 19X3 will be over three times higher than in 19X1.

It is therefore almost impossible for the company to raise prices still further and maintain their level of sales. To try to do so would almost certainly mean a fall in demand and a shedding of a large part of the workforce.

(d) See text.

27.8A

Hampshire plc

Profit Statement for first and second quarters

	First quarter		Second quarter	
Sales		126,000		143,640
Materials	32,850		39,420	
Labour	18,900		22,680	
Variable factory o/h	12,600		15,120	
Variable selling costs	7,650	72,000	9,180	86,400
Contribution		54,000		57,240
Fixed costs:				
Factory overhead	21,375		21,375	
Selling and administration	16,125	37,500	16,125	37,500
Net profit		16,500		19,740

$$\text{Contribution per unit} \qquad \frac{54,000}{9,000} = 6.00 \qquad\qquad \frac{57,240}{10,800} = 5.30$$

B   Draw on graph paper. Break-even points are at:

$$\text{First quarter} \quad = \quad \frac{37,500}{14.00 - 8.00} = 6,250 \text{ units}$$

$$\text{Second quarter} = \frac{37,500}{13.30 - 8.00} = 7,075 \text{ units}$$

Margins of safety above these points.

C   Profit statements incorporating suggestions

	(i)	(ii)	(iii)	(iv)	(v)
No. of units sold	11,880	11,556	12,960	10,800	10,800
Sales (W1)	158,004	158,317	155,131	143,640	143,640
Materials	46,926	43,913	47,304	39,420	
Labour	24,948	27,734	27,216	22,680	*see* (W2)
Variable factory o/h	16,632	16,178	18,144	15,120	87,900
Variable selling o/h	10,098	9,823	11,016	11,340	
Total variable costs	98,604	97,648	103,680	88,560	87,900
Contribution	59,400	60,669	51,451	55,080	55,740
Fixed costs					
Factory	21,375	21,375	21,375	21,375	*see* (W3)
Selling, etc.	16,125	16,125	16,125	12,025	35,000
	37,500	37,500	37,500	33,400	35,000
Net profit	21,900	23,169	13,951	21,680	20,740
Redundancy					12,000

Workings

(W1)   Selling price per unit (i) 13.30 (ii) 13.70 (iii) 11.97 (iv) 13.30 (v) 13.30.

(W2)   Per accounts of second quarter in A 86,400 + extra costs 5p per component, 30,000 × 0.5p = 1,500. Total 87,900.

(W3)   Fixed costs 37,500 – saving 2,500 = 35,000. Assumed that the 20 per cent of the firm's fixed costs would still continue as they would have to be paid anyway. Question not too clear on this point.

D Briefly:

    (i) Would increase profit by 21,900 − 19,740 = 2,160. Seems to be a sensible opportunity which should be considered.

    (ii) Apparently increases profit by 23,169 − 19,740 = 3,429. No mention as to what the cost of maintaining the guarantee is likely to be. Until this is known it is impossible to come to a conclusion.

    (iii) Fall in profit of 19,740 − 13,951 = 5,789. Should not be considered.

    (iv) Increases profit by 21,680 − 19,740 = 1,940. Have to renegotiate terms of employment with sales staff. Worth considering.

    (v) Firm

        (*a*) If we stop making components how can we be certain that suppliers will not later raise prices?

        (*b*) Would we have to keep larger stocks of components in case of breakdown of supply?

        (*c*) Possible that newly established firm has got its prices wrong and will be unable to maintain at this price for long.

        (*d*) Effect on morale of other employees. Local community: write generally about effects of unemployment and knock-on effects.

E *See* text Section 27.4

27.10

(*a*)

Magwitch Ltd
Summarised Profit and Loss Account for the year to 31 May 19X1

Sales volume: units	20,000
	£
Sales £1.50 + 10% = 1.65 per unit	33,000
Variable costs (20–10) 0.50 + 10% = 55p per unit	11,000
Contribution	22,000
Fixed costs 0.50 + 10% = 55p per unit	11,000
Profit	11,000

(*b*)

Compeyson plc
Balance sheet as at 31 May 19X1

Fixed assets (40 + 160)		200
Current assets (65 + 340 − 24 *see* W2)	381	
Short-term liabilities (26 +110)	136	245
		445
Share capital (200 + 60 *see* W2)		260
Share premium (60 × 0.80)		48
Reserves (190 − 53)		137
		445

Workings

(W1)	Purchase price 12 × 11 =		132
	Net assets taken over	71	
	+revalued property	8	79
	Goodwill written off to reserves		53

(W2) Method of payment of purchase price
      Shares 40 × 3/2 = 60 × 1.80   108
      Cash (balance)   24   132

(c) Shares 6,000 × 3/2 = 9,000 shares
     Cash 6,000/40,000 × 24,000 = £3,600

28.1

(a)

	Q	R	S	T
Direct labour and materials	14	28	60	32
Variable overheads	4	8	13	12
Fixed overhead	2	4	7	6
Total cost per unit	20	40	80	50
Add Profit 10 per cent	2	4	8	5
Selling price	22	44	88	55

(b) Discontinue S. All other items are above marginal cost.

(c)

	(i) Followed our advice	(ii) Produced all items
Sales Q 100 × £33	3,300	3,300
R 100 × £39	3,900	3,900
S 100 × £7	–	7,000
T 100 × £49	4,900	4,900
	12,100	19,100
Less Costs		
Direct labour and materials		
(i) 14 + 28 + 32 × 100	7,400	
(ii) 14 + 28 + 60 + 32 × 100		13,400
Variable overhead		
(i) 4 + 8 + 12 × 100	2,400	
(ii) 4 + 8 + 13 + 12 × 100		3,700
Fixed overhead	1,900	1,900
	11,700	19,000
Net profit	400	100

Note: The net profit or loss could have been worked out using contributions per items e.g. (i) Contributions per unit (i.e. Selling price less Marginal cost).

Q	33 – (14 + 4) =		15		
R	39 – (28 + 8) =		3		
R	49 – (32 + 12) =		5	23 × 100 of each =	2,300
	Less Fixed costs				1,900
	Net profit (same as using method shown)				400

In (ii) the contribution from S would be a negative one.

(d) Discontinue Q and T. All other items are above marginal cost.

(e)

		(i) *Followed our* *advice*	(ii) *Produced* *all items*
Sales	Q 100 × £17	–	1,700
	R 100 × £48	4,800	4,800
	S 100 × £140	14,000	14,000
	T 100 × £39	–	3,900
		18,800	24,400

Less Costs			
Direct labour and materials			
(i) 28 + 60 × 100		8,800	
(ii) 14 + 28 + 60 + 32 × 100			13,400
Variable costs			
(i) 8 + 13 × 100		2,100	
(ii) 4 + 8 + 13 + 12 × 100			3,700
Fixed overhead		1,900	1,900
		12,800	19,000
Net profit		6,000	5,400

28.3

(a) (i)   Sales revenue: Breakeven $= \dfrac{\text{Total fixed costs}}{\text{Selling price per unit} - \text{Variable costs per unit}}$

$$= \frac{200,000 \times (4.50 + 2.00 + 3.50)}{36.00 - 5.00 - 7.00 - 1.00 - 3.00} = \frac{2,000,000}{20}$$

= 100,000 units × 36 = £3,600,000

(ii)   Units produced, as (i) 100,000 units
(iii)   100,000/200,000 = 50%

(b)

Profit Statement

	(i)160,000 units £000		(ii) 260,000 units £000	
Sales		6,400		7,280
Variable costs (£16 per unit)	2,560		4,160	
Fixed costs (£10 × 200,000)	2,000	4,560	2,000	6,160
Net profit		1,840		1,120

(c)

Profitability: 2,000 units

	Ref 610 £000	Ref 620 £000
Sales	50	38
Variable costs 610 (16 + 25%)	40	
Variable costs 620 (16 − 25%)		24
Contribution	10	14

The order for Premier Dufton 620 should be accepted as it gives the greatest contribution.

Revised profit/loss	Tourist	Winter	Total
Fare income (W1)	512,050	176,000	688,050
Operating costs			
Variable	199,500	110,000	309,500
Fixed	70,000	50,000	120,000
Administration	70,000	50,000	120,000
Interest charges	35,000	25,000	60,000
	374,500	235,000	609,500
Profit/(loss)	137,550	(59,000)	78,550

Workings (W1) (490,000 + 10%) × 95% = 512,050 (200,000 × 80%) + 10% = 176,000.

(b) The proposed changes would result in a net overall drop of £1,450 in profits. This would not be a wise move, unless it was more or less forced by conditions as yet unknown.

If possible, it would have been better to bring in new tourist fares and leave winter fares as they were.

(c) Winter operations, on revised figures as per (a) above, offer a positive contribution towards overheads, i.e.

Fare income	176,000
Less Variable costs	110,000
Contribution	66,000

To close in the winter would therefore lose the contribution towards overheads and would lower total annual profits. Therefore do not cease winter operations.

No information given about whether or not fixed operating costs, administration and interest charges would be affected by closure. This could alter the advice.

28.7
(a)

	A	B	C	D	E
Direct labour and materials	16	19	38	44	23
Variable overhead	11	17	23	14	9
Fixed overhead	3	4	9	12	8
	30	40	70	70	40
Profit 10%	3	4	7	7	4
Selling Price	33	44	77	77	44

(b) Discontinue C

(c)

			(i) Followed our advice	(ii) Produced all items
Sales	A	100 × £32	3,200	3,200
	B	100 × £49	4,900	4,900
	C	100 × £56	–	5,600
	D	100 × £66	6,600	6,600
	E	100 × £48	4,800	4,800
			19,500	25,100

Less Costs:

Direct labour materials

(i)	$(16 + 19 + 44 + 23) \times 100$	10,200	
(ii)	$(16 + 19 + 38 + 44 + 23) \times 100$		14,000

Variable costs

(i)	$(11 + 17 + 14 + 9) \times 100$	5,100	
(ii)	$(11 + 17 + 23 + 14 + 9) \times 100$		7,400

Fixed Costs	3,600	3,600
	18,900	25,000
Net profit	600	100
Net loss	–	–

(d) Discontinue A and E

(e)

			(i) *Followed our advice*	(ii) *Produced all items*
Sales	A	$100 \times £24$	–	2,400
	B	$100 \times £38$	3,800	3,800
	C	$100 \times £68$	6,800	6,800
	D	$100 \times £64$	6,400	6,400
	E	$100 \times £29$	–	2,900
			17,000	22,300

Less Costs:

Direct labour and materials

(i)	$(19 + 38 + 44) \times 100$	10,100	
(ii)	$(16 + 19 + 38 + 44 + 23) \times 100$		14,000

Variable costs

(i)	$(17 + 23 + 14) \times 100$	5,400	
(ii)	$(11 + 17 + 23 + 14 + 9) \times 100$		7,400

Fixed costs	3,600	3,600
	19,100	25,000
Net profit	–	–
Net loss	2,100	2,700

It is assumed that the firm is to continue operating though it will make a loss in this period.

Index